The Making of Anthropology in East and Southeast Asia

Asian Anthropologies
General Editors:
Shinji Yamashita, The University of Tokyo,
and
J.S. Eades, Ritsumeikan Asia Pacific University

Globalization in Southeast Asia: Local, National and Transnational Perspectives
Edited by Shinji Yamashita and J.S. Eades

Bali and Beyond: Explorations in the Anthropology of Tourism
Shinji Yamashita

The Making of Anthropology in East and Southeast Asia
Edited by Shinji Yamashita, Joseph Bosco, and J.S. Eades

Contents

First published in 2004 by

Berghahn Books
www.berghahnbooks.com

Library of Congress Cataloging-in-Publication Data

The making of anthropology in East and Southeast Asia
/ Edited by Shinji Yamashita, Joseph Bosco, and J.S. Eades
p. cm. -- (Asian anthropologies)
Includes bibliographical references and index.
ISBN 1-57181-258-X (alk. paper: cloth) -- ISBN 1-57181-259-8 (alk. paper: pbk.)
1. Ethnology--Asia, Southeastern--Research. 2. Ethnology--Asia, Southeastern, History.
3. Ethnology--East Asia--Research. 4.Ethnology--East Asia--History. 5. East Asia--
Social Life and customs. 6. Asia, Southeastern--Social life and customs. I. Yamashita,
Shinji. II. Bosco, Joseph, 1957- III. Eades, J.S. (Jeremy Seymour), 1945- IV. Series.

GN635. S58M33 2004
306' 0959--dc22   2004050332

British Library Cataloguing in Publication Data
A catalogue record for this book is available from the British Library.

Printed in the United States on acid-free paper

The Making of Anthropology
in East and Southeast Asia

Edited by

Shinji YAMASHITA
Joseph BOSCO
J.S. EADES

Berghahn Books
New York • Oxford

List of Contributors

David ASKEW is Associate Professor (Legal Studies), Ritsumeikan Asia Pacific University, Beppu, Japan. He also teaches at Monash University, Melbourne, Australia.

Joseph BOSCO is Associate Professor of Anthropology, Chinese University of Hong Kong.

Sidney C.H. CHEUNG is Associate Professor of Anthropology, Chinese University of Hong Kong.

J.S. EADES is Professor of Asia Pacific Studies and Director of the Media Resource Center, Ritsumeikan Asia Pacific University, Beppu, Japan, and Senior Honorary Research Fellow, University of Kent, Canterbury UK.

Kwang-ok KIM is Professor of Anthropology, Seoul National University, Korea.

Takami KUWAYAMA is Professor of Cultural Anthropology, University of Hokkaido, Sapporo, Japan.

Xin LIU is Associate Professor of Anthropology and Chair of the Center for Chinese Studies, University of California at Berkeley.

Alicia P. MAGOS is Professor of the Social Sciences Division of the University of the Philippines Visayas in Miagao, Iloilo, the Philippines.

Gordon MATTHEWS is Associate Professor of Anthropology, Chinese University of Hong Kong.

A.B. SHAMSUL is Professor of Social Anthropology and Director of the Institute of the Malay World & Civilization (ATMA), and the Institute of Occidental Studies (IKON) at Universiti Kebangsaan Malaysia (UKM), Bangi, Malaysia.

TAN Chee-Beng is Professor and Chair of the Anthropology Department, Chinese University of Hong Kong.

David Y.H. WU was Professor and Chair of the Anthropology Department, Chinese University of Hong Kong.

Shinji YAMASHITA is Professor of Cultural Anthropology, The University of Tokyo.

ZHUANG Kongshao is Director, Institute of Anthropology, Renmin University of China, Beijing.

Preface

The idea for this book originated at the Fourteenth International Congress of Anthropological Sciences held at The College of William and Mary, Williamsburg, Virginia, in July 1998. The conference included two panels with clearly related themes: "The Making of Anthropology in Asia: The Past, the Present and the Future," organized by Shinji Yamashita and Takeo Funabiki, with contributions by Shinji Yamashita, A.B. Shamsul, Xin Liu, and Takami Kuwayama; and "Indigenization of Anthropology in East and Southeast Asia," organized by Joseph Bosco, and including contributions by Joseph Bosco, Sidney Cheung, David Wu, and Tan Chee-beng. In the wake of the conference, the present structure of the book gradually crystallized. Additional contributions were invited to provide better regional coverage, including the papers by Zhuang Kong-shao, Kwang-ok Kim, and Alicia Magos. The final papers to be added were the co-authored first chapter and David Askew's paper on early Japanese anthropology, a welcome addition given the lack of material on this subject available in English. The original group of authors have updated their papers in the light of more recent material, as will be seen from the bibliographies, and most of the final drafts included here date from the first half of 2004. The jobs of final editing, indexing, and typesetting fell to Jerry Eades.

The editors would like to thank first and foremost Marion Berghahn for her continued commitment to the cause of anthropology in Asia, despite the lengthy gestation period of this particular volume. Jerry Eades would like to thank Saee Haldule and Radoslawa Jankowska of APU for their help with checking and formatting the bibliographies at various stages of completion, Neil MacNeil for his technical expertise and help in getting the files to the publisher, Carla Eades for the use of the cover photograph, and Maria R. Reyes of the Berghahn New York office for seeing the final version through the press. In addition to his own chapter, David Askew provided considerable help with the final editing and correction, as well as his expertise with the Japanese language sources

In the text, Japanese, Korean, and Chinese names have generally been written in the conventional order for these countries, with family names first, the major exception being writers publishing in English, where the Western order has been preferred. As for the names of contributors in the Table of Contents, chapter headings, and page headers, we have used the forms the authors themselves prefer when publishing in English. While Japanese authors generally adopt the Western order, practice among Chinese scholars varies, and this is reflected here. In each case we have marked the family name in small capitals, so there should be no confusion as to their identity in relation to their other work. As a result, there are inevitably minor inconsistencies, as when Kwang-ok Kim cites his own name together with other Korean authors using the Korean order, but we hope that readers can bear with these.

For the transliteration of Japanese words, we have generally followed the familiar Hepburn system, the major difference being the use of circumflexes rather than macrons to denote long vowels for ease of typesetting, in line with earlier books in this series. Long vowels have not been marked for place names that are familiar in English, such as Tokyo (Tôkyô), Kyoto (Kyôto), Honshu (Honshû), or for words that have been absorbed into English, such as Shinto (Shintô).

Transliterating Chinese is always a problem where the PRC and Taiwan are discussed in the same volume because of the differences between the *pinyin* and Wade-Giles systems. Here we follow the authors' own usage for their names, but use *pinyin* in transliterating titles of books and articles. Where authors' names are well-known both in Wade-Giles and *pinyin* forms, e.g. Fei Hsiao-tung or Xiaotong, the variants have been noted in brackets as necessary. For transliteration of Korean titles and hyphenation of Korean names, we have relied on the usage supplied by Professor Kwang-ok Kim.

In the titles of works in Japanese, Chinese and Korean, the first letter and proper nouns have been capitalized, following the *Chicago Manual of Style*. For works in English, titles of books and journals have been capitalized and italicized, while titles of articles remain in lower case except for proper nouns and are enclosed in quotation marks. Translations of foreign titles in bibliographies are enclosed in square brackets. In some cases, books and articles in Asian languages have "official" titles in English which are sometimes paraphrases rather than direct translations, so that in some instances titles and translations may not exactly match. In the case of the Japanese title of the much-cited *Japanese Journal of Ethnology*, where the transliteration varies over time, we have used a single form, *Minzokugaku-kenkyû,* throughout the book.

Shinji Yamashita, Joseph Bosco, Jerry Eades
July 2004.

Chapter 1

Asian Anthropologies: Foreign, Native, and Indigenous

Shinji YAMASHITA, *Joseph* BOSCO, *and J.S.* EADES

This book is about socio-cultural anthropology in East and Southeast Asia, its development, its distinctive characteristics, and its relation to anthropology in the rest of the world. We examine how anthropology is affected by the location of fieldwork, writing, and teaching, by its different histories in different countries, and by the identities of the researchers, whether local or foreign. We examine the national and international intellectual climates within which anthropology is practiced, and the significance of these differences for the development of a universalistic, global, or transcultural anthropology in the twenty-first century.[1]

The concern with the history of anthropology thus defined and its indigenization is not new, but since the early 1990s, there has been an explosion of interest in the subject within East and Southeast Asia.[2] Part of the reason for this activity can be traced back to Western anthropology's increasing reflexivity in relation to its own history, methods, and theories, but there are also other causes. They include the rapid growth in the number of anthropologists in Asia within the expansion of higher education as a whole, and their attempts to make the discipline relevant to local issues such as problems of ethnic identity. There is also the flow of students and scholars between Asia and the traditional centers of research in North America and Europe, the increasing awareness of differences in national anthropological traditions, and a growing concern among scholars based outside America and Europe about the rise of a "world-system" of anthropology in which the means of publication and evaluation lie mainly in the hands of the major universities and publishing houses in the West.[3]

In Western accounts, the development of socio-cultural anthropology is often presented in terms of the intersecting biographies of a small number of leading scholars linked to major departments in North America and Europe. In

1

America, the list extends from Franz Boas, via figures such as Margaret Mead and Ruth Benedict, to Clifford Geertz and the rest of the postwar generation. In the United Kingdom, it extends from Malinowski and his pupils, of whom the main figures in relation to Asia were Fei Xiaotong (Hsiao-tung), who completed his first monograph on China in the 1930s (Fei 1939); Edmund Leach, whose research in Burma was interrupted by the war (Leach 1954); and Raymond Firth, who carried out research in Malaya following his earlier work in the Pacific (Firth 1946). There were also the groups of Dutch and French scholars carrying out work in their colonial empires, in the Dutch East Indies (now Indonesia), and in French Indochina (now Vietnam, Laos, and Cambodia). What is left out of many of these accounts is the activity taking place among Asian scholars, with the exception of those like Fei whose work became part of the Western canon. It also leaves out all those scholars engaged in forms of research and writing closely related to modern anthropology, but who lacked the legitimacy which training in the core Western departments bestowed. In the case of Japan, it ignores completely the fact that a major school of anthropology had developed in the late nineteenth century, paralleling and in some cases even preceding the developments taking place in the West. This school was in part a result of Japan's encounter with Western scholars during the Meiji period (1868-1912), but was also a response to Japanese nationalism and colonialism, as the chapters by Askew and Yamashita in this volume show.

The aims of this introduction, therefore, are two-fold. The first is to give a brief historical sketch of some of the main strands of development in Asian anthropology, many of which are unfamiliar to scholars in the West. The second is to examine some of the main issues in the relationship between anthropology in Asia and the rest of the world, such as the problem of Western dominance, the uses of theory, the process of indigenization, languages of publication, the audiences to which anthropology is addressed, and the possible contribution of anthropology in Asia to the development of the discipline world-wide.

Anthropology in Japan

As mentioned above, Japan has a history of anthropology going back to the latter half of the nineteenth century, and it also has the largest number of anthropologists in Asia. The Japanese Society of Cultural Anthropology (*Nihon Bunkajinruigakkai*, formerly the Japanese Society of Ethnology or *Nihon Minzokugakkai*) is one of the largest anthropological associations in the world, numbering around 2,000 members at present. Japan is thus the largest center for anthropological research in Asia. What, then, are the characteristics of Japanese anthropology in terms of its history and its structural position in the world as a whole?

2

Origins and development

As Askew and Yamashita note in their papers in this volume, the origins of Japanese anthropology date back to 1884, when a group of young scholars formed a group called *Jinruigaku no Tomo* (Friends of Anthropology) (Terada 1981: 7). This was founded as a response to the theories of Edward Morse, a professor in the biology department at Tokyo Imperial University (now the University of Tokyo) who had carried out some archeological excavations on an ancient shell-mound. From the evidence of the bones he found there, he suggested that cannibalism had once been practiced in central Japan. The members of the group felt that the origins of the Japanese should be investigated by the Japanese themselves rather than outsiders (Shimizu 1998: 115; 1999: 126), so the formation of the group was partly inspired by Japanese nationalism. After two years, the workshop evolved into a society called *Tokyo Jinruigakkai* (Anthropological Society of Tokyo), later known as *Nihon Jinruigakkai* (usually translated in English as the "Anthropological Society of Nippon"). The leading figure in the group, Tsuboi Shôgorô, later studied for three years in London, and became the first professor of anthropology at the University of Tokyo in 1892. He remained active in the debate on the origins of the Japanese in the early years of the twentieth century until his death in 1913.

The annexation of Taiwan in 1895 marked the start of the Japanese colonial empire, and as this expanded, ethnographers followed in the wake of the military and the administrators, much as they did in the empires of the West. The materials they collected remain some of the most important early sources of information on these societies. One of the most remarkable figures was Torii Ryûzô, Tsuboi's successor as professor of anthropology at Tokyo Imperial University, who traveled extensively throughout the entire region from Mongolia to Southeast Asia, as described in the chapters by Askew and Yamashita. He not only collected extensive written data, but also built up an early photographic archive of the region, a total of over 1,800 prints (Suenari 1995: 3).

In 1913, the year of Tsuboi's death, Torii published a paper based on his extensive fieldwork, proposing the establishment of a discipline he called *Tôyô jinshugaku* or *Tôyô minzokugaku* ("Oriental ethnology"). This was similar to the "Japanese Orientalism" advocated by the historian Shiratori Kurakichi (see Tanaka 1993; Kang 1996; and Yamashita in this volume). Torii advocated the study of the Orient by Oriental scholars because they were assumed to be in a better position than Western scholars to study these regions (Torii 1975: 482-83). Because of his extensive field research abroad, Torii was much more concerned with cultures outside Japan's national boundaries than Tsuboi had been. His article marked a new stage in the history of Japanese anthropology, one in which Japan began to observe others, and not merely be observed (Shimizu 1998: 116). In this new stage, the object of study shifted from the origins of the Japanese people and Japanese culture to Japan's "colonial Others" in Asia. Interest in ethnological research continued to develop with further Japanese colonial expansion, into Micronesia in 1919, Manchuria in 1933, and Southeast Asia in 1941.

The *Nihon Minzokugakkai*, or Japanese Society of Ethnology, was formed during the same period, in 1934. The Orientalist historian Shiratori Kurakichi mentioned above was the first president. Interestingly its establishment was stimulated by the First International Congress of Anthropological and Ethnological Sciences held in London that same year. The rationale was stated as follows:

> Ethnology in Japan has a history of several decades. However, we have not yet reached an international standard [of research] ... Ethnological studies in Japan have been concerned with native culture and ancient cultural survivals in Japan under the name of *minzokugaku* [here meaning folklore studies]. But we should develop the discipline through comparisons with other cultures, using the results of the development of the discipline in the West to consider cultural origins and diffusion. In particular, through participation in the First International Congress of Anthropological and Ethnological Sciences held at London this summer, we have realized that we should promote ethnological research in Japan. This is the reason why we are reorganizing the former *Minzokugakkai* [i.e. Society for Folklore Studies] into the *Nihon Minzokugakkai* [i.e. the Japanese Society of Ethnology]. (Minzokugaku Shinkôkai 1984: 4, translation by Yamashita)

This statement is interesting because it shows the growing cleavage in Japanese anthropology, between scholars whose primary concern was the origins of Japanese society and culture, and scholars who were interested in the kind of comparative anthropology then developing in the West. The two groups were about to part company institutionally as well as intellectually. In 1935, the influential Japanese folklorist, Yanagita Kunio, founded an association called *Minkandenshô no Kai* (Group for Research into Popular Traditions). Yanagita was an influential figure in Japanese literature for over half a century (Oguma 2002: chapter 12). He had a dual career as a diplomat and writer, and his book based on Tohoku folk tales, *Tôno Monogatari* (Tales of Tôno, Yanagita 1975 [1909]) was one of the key texts in Japanese folklore studies (Yamashita 2003: chapter 9). The group he founded later evolved into an association also romanized as *Nihon Minzokugakkai* though using different characters (meaning "Folklore Society of Japan"). As the result, scholars specializing in Japanese folklore and ethnological studies (or *Volkskunde* in German) became separated from those interested in comparative ethnology

4

(Völkerkunde in German). These two traditions have continued side by side until the present, but as Cheung shows in his chapter in this volume, the balance has continued to shift in favor of a comparative socio-cultural anthropological approach over the years. A defining event in relation to this was the Eighth Congress of the International Union of Anthropological and Ethnological Sciences (IUAES), held in Japan in 1968. This trend was symbolized most recently in the decision of the Japanese Society of Ethnology to change its name to the Japanese Society of Cultural Anthropology, from the Spring of 2004.

From the annexation of Taiwan in 1895 onwards, ethnologists had been used by the Japanese colonial government, and they also became involved in the war effort after 1941 (cf. Shimizu and Bremen 2003). A number of ethnographic research institutes were set up, some of which had colonial origins. These included the *Tôyô Bunka Kenkyûsho* (Institute of Oriental Studies) at the University of Tokyo, which still exists, plus departments of ethnology in the Japanese imperial universities in Seoul and Taipei. Other shorter-lived ethnographic research institutes were established during the Pacific War: the *Minzoku Kenkyûsho* (Institute of Ethnic Research) in Tokyo (1943-45) and the *Seihoku Kenkyûsho* (Northwestern Research Institute) in Mongolia (1944-45). Both of these were closed at the end of the war, but their longer-term significance was that some of the leading figures in anthropology in postwar Japan such as Mabuchi Tôichi and Umesao Tadao carried out their first research in such institutions.

After the war Japan lost its colonies, and the interests of Japanese ethnology were once again confined to Japan. Fieldwork became mainly confined to groups such as the Ainu of Hokkaido (also discussed in Cheung's paper in the volume) and the Okinawans. But during the Korean War, the Japanese economy began a long period of high-speed economic growth which lasted for over twenty years. By 1964, the year of the Tokyo Olympic Games, restrictions on overseas travel and foreign exchange for Japanese were finally removed, and Japanese scholars once again began to focus more on "other cultures" outside Japan and less on Japanese culture itself.

Several things can be noted from this brief history. First, Japanese anthropology started with a search for the origins of the Japanese and their culture in response to the theories of foreign researchers. From the outset, it was a nationalistic project, as was also true of some other anthropologies in Asia. Second, unlike other Asian countries, Japan itself became a colonial power in Asia and the Pacific, and Japanese anthropology reflected this colonial experience. Its history was more similar to that of Western anthropology than other Asian anthropologies, even if Japanese anthropologists did tend to see their colonial Others through the lens of what Yamashita describes in his chapter in this volume as "Japanese Orientalism." As in early British and American anthropology, the dividing line between amateur and professional

5

anthropologists was often rather vague, as shown in the chapters by Askew and Yamashita. Yamashita's paper focuses on research in the Nan'yô or Japanese "South Seas" (Micronesia and Palau). Interest in this region continued after the war, and one of the major preoccupations remained the light that these societies could cast on the cultural origins of Japan itself.

Third, the regional concerns of Japanese anthropology have varied historically, along with the power and influence in Japan. In his examination of the articles in *Minzokugaku-kenkyû* (Japanese Journal of Ethnology) from 1935 to 1995, Sekimoto Teruo has noted a centrifugal tendency in Japanese research over the years (Sekimoto 1996: 138-39). In each historical period, Japanese anthropologists have generally been more interested in regions peripheral to Japan than in Japan itself. Cheung's chapter makes a similar point: by the 1960s, Japanese anthropologists were diversifying rapidly, both geographically (away from the traditional fields of research of the Ainu, Okinawa, Taiwan, North China, Korea, and Japan), and also theoretically, bringing their interests more in line with those of anthropology in the West. This trend eventually resulted in the long debate over the name of the Japanese Society of Ethnology during the 1990s which Cheung describes, and which has only been resolved very recently.

However, these areas of research now have little connection with Japan's wider economic interests: Japanese anthropologists have generally been more interested in Africa and Latin America than they have in the United States, where Japanese economic interests are vital (Shimizu 1998: 121).

Finally, it should also be noted that, despite the large numbers of anthropologists in Japan and the immense volume of work they publish, it is still surprising how little of this work is known in the West.

Japanese anthropology in the anthropological world-system

This brings us to the consideration of Japan's position in what Kuwayama, in his chapter in this volume and elsewhere, has called the "academic world-system" (see e.g. Kuwayama 1997; 2000; 2004). In his analysis, he draws on models of the capitalist world-system developed by Frank, Wallerstein, and others. The "core" of this system consists of the United States, Britain, and France, which define what kinds of anthropological knowledge carry the highest prestige (see also Gerholm and Hannerz 1982), together with the language in which anthropologists must write if they wish to be taken seriously. In this model, Asian anthropologies are generally classified as "peripheral," though Japanese anthropology is "semi-peripheral," historically intermediate in influence between the rest of Asia and the West. The course of the subsequent debate is described in detail by Kuwayama in his chapter in this volume.

Here the point can be made that anthropology has now become so international that it is becoming increasingly difficult to see where the "center" really is. The most powerful anthropology departments in the United States have many teachers and students from "peripheral" areas, just as Asian universities have many scholars from the West. The division is made even fuzzier by the rise of the new information technology, and the ease of information flow, so that center and periphery are now intermingled in very complex ways.

Anthropological production and language

Perhaps the most critical structural problem for Japanese anthropology in the anthropological world-system is the problem of language. Japanese anthropologists are generally very knowledgeable about the main trends in Western anthropology, as shown in the bibliographies of articles in the *Minzokugaku-kenkyû* and other leading journals. Graduate students are required to read works in English or other European languages. However, Japanese scholars mainly write in Japanese, which makes access difficult for non-Japanese readers. In this respect, Japanese cultural anthropology, unlike the Japanese economy, imports too much and exports too little.

One result of the "balance of payments" problem is that it is difficult for theoretical ideas from Japan to be adopted more widely. Unlike France, which has always been a major source of theoretical ideas for the Anglophone world, the ideas of Japan's theoretically more adventurous anthropologists have had little impact outside Japan. Indeed, Mathews's chapter in this volume goes as far as arguing that Japan has become an "intellectual colony" of the West. Japanese anthropologists "sometimes seem to reduce Japanese anthropology to being a matter of collecting data to confirm Western theory." Like Kuwayama, he argues that the problem arises from power relations in the academic world-system, with Japanese anthropology remaining constantly in the shadow of Western hegemony.

Eades (2000) has discussed some of the other institutional factors that might explain this reluctance to write in English, and argues that major differences between the career structures of anthropologists and the publishing industries in the West and Japan may be partly to blame. In the West, and especially America, there is immense pressure on the most prestigious journals and publishers from academics wanting to publish with them. The lengthy peer review system and subsequent revisions mean long delays in publication, often of the order two to three years. Books from major academic presses can also take years to produce. Even though peer review is assumed to safeguard and guarantee quality, the long lead-time in publication means that in situations of rapid social change much of the empirical material is dated before it is published. A final point is that publishing in the West requires mastery of complex theoretical vocabularies and writing styles that are constantly changing, and these are extremely difficult for non-native speakers to acquire and keep up with.

Japanese academics, in contrast, publish much of their work in university in-house journals, where delays are a matter of weeks or months rather than years. Japanese book publishers are much more efficient than those in the West, and titles are frequently published within six months. Books published in Japanese in Japan generally sell more copies than books published in the West. It is therefore not surprising that few Japanese academics attempt to publish their work through conventional Western channels. Most publish quickly in Japanese and then move rapidly on to the next piece of research. Japanese anthropologists often focus more on empirical data and less on theory than researchers in the West. Historically speaking, it is not the Japanese system which is out of line with the rest of the world, but rather the West, where pressures of competition have led to rapid changes in the publishing system since World War II. Paradoxically, it is the Western system that has become the role model for scholars elsewhere, because of the power and prestige it has managed to accumulate.

Theory and its audiences

However, there is a related question: to what extent is it worth translating anthropological work written in one language into others? Work may be translated for two basic reasons, either because it contains interesting data, or because it contains interesting theoretical insights. Generally it seems to be agreed that one of the hallmarks of Japanese research is the richness of the data presented. However, this does not mean that theory is not highly valued in Japan: it clearly is. The works of leading Western theoreticians appear in Japanese translations very quickly, and many Japanese academics adopt as a career-building strategy exegesis and interpretation of a particular theorist for local audiences. However, it makes little sense to translate this work into other languages in which many similar works of interpretation already exist. Mathews in his chapter makes a related point, noting that some theoretical issues that are still current in Japan are of little interest to scholars in the West, such as the search for the origins of Japanese traditions.

It can be argued that all academic anthropologists feel a need to address two different kinds of audience: the global community of scholars, and the local societies in which they live. Because of the sheer size of the American anthropology profession and the fact that its members write in English, scholars based in America can often assume that the global community of anthropologists and their local audience are one and the same. For Japanese anthropologists, the distance between these two poles is much greater. Addressing the global community raises the problems of writing and publishing in English discussed above. Addressing the local audience can be done in Japanese, which is much easier. These factors tend to reinforce the belief among many

Japanese researchers that their main responsibility is to communicate with their local audience, which is Japanese. The end result is a distinctive school of domestic anthropology with its own preoccupations, such as the origins of Japanese culture and identity, and its own canon of literature for citation.

Minorities in Japan

A final area to be explored in relation to the anthropology of Japan is that of minorities. It is often said that Japan is a "homogeneous society," but historically speaking, as Oguma (2002) has pointed out, Japanese images of themselves have been much more complex. He argues that from the late nineteenth century to the Japanese colonial period, Japanese leaders and intellectuals generally saw Japan as a mixed nation. From time immemorial, the Japanese had successfully assimilated a variety of peoples from outside Japan, from both Northeast and Southeast Asia. The corollary of this belief was that the Japanese advance into Asia was "a return to the Japanese homeland," and that the assimilation of the peoples there should be easy due to existing ties of kinship (Oguma 2002: 321). After 1945, with the collapse of the empire and the reduction in the number of non-Japanese in Japan, an alternative myth of ethnic homogeneity took over. Not surprisingly, this myth has encountered increasing criticism over the years, and there has been a growing body of research both by Japanese scholars and outsiders on minorities in Japan, including permanently resident Koreans (Ryang 1996; Fukuoka 2000), the people of Okinawa (Hook and Siddle 2001; Allen 2002), and the Ainu of Hokkaido (Siddle 1996; Fitzhugh and Dubreuil 1999; Walker 2001).

Cheung's chapter in this volume reveals some of the political complexities of carrying out this research, especially for scholars, Japanese or foreign, wishing to publish the results in Japanese. The Ainu share much in common with other minority aboriginal ethnic groups of the Pacific Rim. They were the original inhabitants not only of Hokkaido, but also Sakhalin and the Kurile Islands, and probably of parts of northern Honshu. Now they form a small minority in Hokkaido alone. As a result of Japanese conquest and assimilationist policies, they lost control of their land, and found much of their culture, their language, and their traditional modes of subsistence officially suppressed. These measures, coupled with intermarriage, meant that little of their original culture survived, apart from arts and performances that could be salvaged as the basis of a tourist industry. Their culture was only officially recognized by the Japanese government in 1997. Thus when Cheung submitted a paper on images of the Ainu to a major Japanese-language anthropology journal in 1995, relations between the Ainu, the anthropology establishment, and the state were still highly sensitive.

A final issue raised by Cheung's chapter is that of the definition of anthropological insiders and outsiders. Japanese anthropology has internationalized to the point where we have a continuum of roles. Japanese anthropologists who write mainly in Japanese for local audiences, Japanese anthropologists who write in both Japanese and foreign languages for different audiences, (e.g. Yamashita, Kuwayama), Japanese scholars based in the West who write mainly in English (e.g. Emiko Ohnuki-Tierney, Takie Sugiyama Lebra, Lisa Yoneyama), foreigners based or trained in Japan who can write in Japanese (e.g. Cheung and the Chinese anthropologists based in Japan mentioned in the next section), foreigners based in Japan writing mainly in English (e.g. Eades), and so on. The number of categories can be multiplied if we consider whether or not these scholars are writing about Japan or elsewhere, or if we take into account scholars of Japanese heritage with other nationalities. Clearly the question of who are the "native" or "indigenous" anthropologists, as opposed to "outsider" or "foreign" anthropologists, is become increasingly complex in relation to Japan, and a similar situation is developing in relation to China.

Anthropology in China

As Ishikawa Yoshihiro has recently argued, the early development of Chinese anthropology also had links with Japan, as ideas of race and evolution made their way in from Europe via Japanese translations at the end of the nineteenth century (Ishikawa 2003). Among those most interested in the new ideas were intellectuals opposed to Manchu rule, who found Torii's classification of the Manchu as a Tungus people from Siberia useful as a stick with which to beat the Qing regime. An alternative strategy was to hypothesize that the Han themselves were different because they had originated from elsewhere, as suggested by the eccentric French historian, Terrien de Lacoupérie, who proposed that Chinese civilization could be traced back to ancient Mesopotamia. His ideas also seem to have arrived via Japan and enjoyed a brief vogue among Chinese intellectuals as well (Ishikawa 2003: 22). More significantly, as Liu notes in this volume, the ideas of Spencer, Morgan, and Engels were also becoming known in China via Japan (cf. Guldin 1994: 24). These ideas were also popular among revolutionary students who saw in evolutionary theory a justification for regime change (Guldin 1994: 25). By the early 1920s, some scholars were attempting to apply these theories to the evolution of Chinese society. Institutional structures were also being established, such as the Academia Sinica in Nanjing (Guldin 1994: 31-32). In the interwar years, until the onset of the war with Japan, increasing numbers of Chinese were going abroad for training, including Fei Xiaotong and Lin Yaohua, and distinguished foreign scholars were starting to come to China. The list of monographs on China written by Chinese scholars in English was also starting to grow.

The end of the Pacific War in 1945 left Chinese anthropology little time to recover before the onset of civil war, the removal of the Guomindang regime to

Taiwan, and the communist victory in 1949. There followed a long period of very mixed fortunes for the social sciences. In mainland China, sociology was closed down as a discipline until after the death of Mao (Wong 1979), while ethnology was reorganized around a new Central Institute for Nationalities (CIN), the task of which was to identify, research, and help formulate national policy towards China's minorities (Guldin 1994: 101). Major surveys of language and social history were carried out, starting in the late 1950s. However the political campaigns that swept across the country, starting with the Great Leap Forward, caused increasing disruption, and from 1966-71 the work of the CIN was halted. Attacks against leading ethnologists such as Lin and Fei escalated, and most of their fieldnotes and books disappeared (Guldin 1994: 193). Accounts by foreign scholars during the period before 1978 were also few and far between, exceptions being the studies by Hinton (1966; 1983) and the Crooks (1959; 1966), authors from outside anthropology with special access because of their own pro-regime credentials.[4]

Many of the postwar generation of Western specialists on China had taken to working in Taiwan and Hong Kong during the years of chaos on the mainland. On the positive side, the closure of the mainland led to an extraordinary concentration of research in Hong Kong and Taiwan, much of it of a very high quality. The precursor in Hong Kong was Maurice Freedman, whose book, *Lineage Organization in Southeastern China* (1958) proved highly influential. This was followed by a major series of studies of the New Territories of Hong Kong, by Baker (1968), Potter (1968), James Watson (1975) and Rubie Watson (1985), making this one of the most intensively researched areas in the world. However, even within this area there were striking differences between villages, and minor variations in the environment could have dramatic effects on development patterns and social structure. Another substitute for fieldwork in mainland China itself was to gather data from Chinese who had emigrated to Hong Kong, and this formed the basis of several other studies (e.g. Parish and Whyte 1978; Whyte and Parish 1984; Chan et al. 1984; and Oi 1989).

The other alternative to research on the mainland was to go to Taiwan. As Bosco shows in his chapter in this volume, much of the research on Taiwan during the colonial period had been Japanese research on the aboriginal population (cf. Eades 2003). Chinese researchers carried on the tradition of aboriginal research after the separation of Taiwan from the mainland, at a time when much of the work on the Han Chinese was categorized as "sociology." However, Taiwan also saw an influx of Western "anthropologists" studying the Han Chinese, including Gallin (1966), Pasternak (1983), Cohen (1976), Ahern (1973), A. Wolf and Huang (1980), and M. Wolf (1972). Meanwhile, Japanese scholars led by Mabuchi were starting to return to Taiwan to resume their own work there (cf. Suenari 1995; 1998).

The situation for anthropologists on the mainland gradually improved with the end of the Cultural Revolution. Fei emerged from years of persecution to become one of China's most influential establishment academics, and travel to China by Western scholars became more common. At first many of these visits were short, but gradually longer-term fieldwork became possible, resulting in a fine series of monographs, which documented the upheavals of the revolutionary period and the early years of economic reform (e.g. Endicott 1988; S. Huang 1989; Siu 1989; Potter and Potter 1990; Judd 1994). Senior scholars in the major American departments such as Arthur Wolf, Myron Cohen, and James Watson who had previously carried out research in Hong Kong and Taiwan had students who increasingly chose to do their fieldwork on the mainland.

Since the late 1980s, the research interests of younger Western scholars in China have diversified to include an increasing number of projects relating to urban and cultural studies (e.g. Jankoviak; 1993; Bruun 1993; Davis et al. 1997; Davis 2000; Tang and Parish 2000; Dutton 1998; Barmé 1999), as well as ethnic identity among the minorities (e.g. Gladney 1991; Rudelson 1997; Hanson 1999; Schein 2000). There have also been an increasing number of studies by mainland Chinese scholars educated in the West after the Cultural Revolution who returned to China for their fieldwork (Yan 1996; Jing 1996; Liu 2000). To these must be added several major studies by mainland Chinese scholars based in Japan, such as Nie (1992) and Han (2000). These bodies of work are particularly interesting in the comparison they offer between the different effects of American and Japanese training on Chinese scholars of very similar background. In general, the Western-trained scholars tend to produce work on rather focused topics heavily influenced by recent theory, whereas the Japanese-trained scholars produce classic all-round village studies exceptionally rich in historical and empirical data, in the tradition of Fei's early work from the 1930s.[5] As with the research on Japan, the internationalization of research on China has resulted in a complex body of work in Chinese, Japanese and English, written by a variety of Chinese and foreign scholars variously based in mainland China, Hong Kong, Taiwan, Japan, and further afield.

Two other chapters on China in this volume, by Zhuang and Wu, represent other facets of recent Chinese anthropology. Zhuang's paper is an interesting case study of a scholar using anthropology critically in order to achieve practical reforms. He uses the anthropology of education as the starting point for a critique of traditional and contemporary Chinese education. He begins with an outline of the main characteristics of Confucian education, highlights the political elements inherent in it, and suggests that many Confucian traits have survived in the modern Chinese system. Passive students, rote learning, a one-way flow of information, an emphasis on examinations, and constraints on free discussion in class clearly place constraints on creativity and require reform. Much of what he describes fits well with other analyses of higher education throughout East Asia in the past few years and the current processes of reform underway in a number of countries there (cf. Goodman 2001).

Finally, Zhuang provides fascinating information on the teaching of anthropology in Chinese universities, including the changes in the curriculum that have taken place since the 1980s.

Wu's paper focuses on a very different subject, that of traditional dance, which in China provides not only a focus for expressions of local and ethnic identity, but also an important element in a burgeoning tourist industry. As he notes, indigenous and foreign anthropologists may well experience and interpret these dances in very different ways. The dances themselves can be seen both as genuine attempts to preserve and stage traditional forms in ways that are meaningful to modern audiences, and as classic examples of reinvented tradition. Wu himself is well aware of the reinvented nature of the spectacle, and he also examines the role of the state in the process. After the revolution, dance teachers could impose their own meanings on what they taught, but ultimately they could not challenge the interpretations of the state. Even into the 1990s, despite the growth of the capitalist market and opportunities for performers to "moonlight" and accept other work in the free economy, the state still continued to attempt to control performers and maintain what it saw as acceptable standards. But now, as Wu wistfully comments, the market has done its worst: "Today, almost anything can be staged as long as it makes profit for the performers and organizers."

The Meaning of "Indigenous"

What Wu's paper also highlights is the importance of the position of anthropologists in relation to their subjects and in the interpretations they make of what they observe. His own position is ambiguous, as someone who is Taiwanese but was born in mainland China, raised in Taiwan, educated in Australia, and long resident in Hong Kong and Hawaii. He was therefore able to act as both "insider" and "outsider" in relation to his mainland subjects. As we have seen in the cases of both Japanese and Chinese anthropology, there is increasing complexity in the notions of indigenous/foreign, insider/outsider, and subject/object. One of the most important themes underlying the papers in this volume is to examine critically notions of "native" or "indigenous" anthropology, and how useful they are for an understanding of the development of anthropology in East and Southeast Asia.

Indigenous as homegrown research

According to Webster's dictionary, the term "indigenous" in ordinary usage means, "having originated in and being produced, growing, living, or occurring naturally in a particular region or environment." Anthropology cannot be said to have originated in Asia, but it is certainly being produced in Asia, where it has certain characteristics that make it different from anthropology elsewhere. Thus, the term "indigenization" is now sometimes used to mean the rise of anthropology in places that were previously only studied by foreign anthropologists. This actually excludes the United States and Europe where local anthropology has generally been carried out by local people rather than foreigners.

Indigenous as local research

Sometimes "indigenous" is also used to refer to local rather than overseas research. In local research, fieldworkers and informants share a common culture. For example, indigenous anthropology in Taiwan often refers to research by Taiwan anthropologists about Taiwanese society. As has often been noted, a common culture between fieldworker and informants allows symbols and allusions to be more readily grasped (Aguilar 1981). Despite the danger that familiarity can be deceptive (Greenhouse 1985), the likelihood that linguistic competence of the anthropologist will be much higher allows for a deeper exploration of meaning (Ohnuki-Tierney 1984).[6]

The definition of indigenous anthropology as studying one's own culture over-generalizes, however, by ignoring intra-cultural differences (Narayan 1993). Taking the case of Chinese anthropologists, if an anthropologist from Beijing were to conduct research in Hong Kong, this might now be considered "indigenous" anthropology when seen from a national perspective. However, because of the differences in language and lifestyle, it could be argued that this is comparable to a British anthropologist carrying out research in Italy or Spain, i.e. within the European Union. A northern Chinese researcher in Hong Kong may well experience a degree of culture shock, an experience made more complex by the tension between the assumption of Chinese cultural unity and the discovery of great cultural difference. At the same time, a certain commonality in background is undeniable, and the interplay of difference and commonality can be used to see things in a new light.

A range of commonality and difference thus in fact exists between "native" or "indigenous" researchers and the societies they research. This range can be described as a scale, but is in fact more complex since it includes physical appearance, ethnicity, language, class, gender, age, and other separate factors. Hu Tai-li (1984) has described her experience as an anthropologist of mainlander parentage studying a Taiwanese village where she was a daughter-in-law. She had to learn a new field language (Minnanhua and Mandarin are mutually unintelligible, even though they share a common writing system), and found that life in a rural village was quite different from what she was accustomed to in the city. A number of scholars have noted that particular commonalities and differences need to be considered, since class, gender, age, ethnicity, and other factors will affect the research experience (Aguilar 1981). Within this range of commonality and difference, there are some projects we would recognize as "native" or "indigenous" anthropology, in which anthropologists study people who speak the same (or nearly the same) language as they themselves grew up with, with whom they can blend in physically and behaviorally, and who share the same cultural background. In addition, some scholars of local ancestry but born and educated abroad may be viewed as "native" by the local people, even if they themselves do not feel that they are (see e.g. Hamabata 1990).

It is often assumed by anthropologists in the West that their colleagues in East and Southeast Asian countries overwhelmingly study their own societies, but the case studies in this book show that this is something of an oversimplification. It is true that in many countries, including China, the Philippines, and Taiwan, most research has been local and students are primarily interested in their own societies. For instance, at the Chinese University of Hong Kong, courses are taught on Chinese society and culture, on Chinese "minorities," and Hong Kong culture, but not on the other major regions studied by anthropologists such as Africa, South Asia, Europe, Latin America, or the Middle East.[7] In most of the countries represented in this volume, government funding agencies are primarily interested in the contribution that anthropology can make to nation-building and development. Neither these agencies nor the students are particularly interested in exotic comparisons or distant peoples, given that funds for overseas research and travel, together with economic ties with other areas of the world, are restricted. The major exception is Japan, as described above, even though the Japanese government was certainly interested in the contribution anthropologists could make to nation-building in the early years of Japanese anthropology. For other countries, a link between research and political, economic and business interests is often essential for funding, despite academic pretensions of scientific disinterestedness. Anthropology – indeed most social science research – is funded primarily by states that have economic development and nation-building agendas, so most research and teaching has focused on people within the national borders. Thus, the inward looking nature of much Asian anthropology is in large part the result of funding priorities which make distant research unjustifiable. When national priorities change, so does the pattern of research. In Taiwan, interest in the anthropology of Southeast Asia has recently grown, coinciding with the island's foreign investment in that region. Research on Taiwan's aboriginal communities has also taken a new turn, given the aborigines' historical and cultural links with Southeast Asia and the Pacific, and Taiwan's own search for an identity distinct from that of the mainland.

Indigenous as locally published research

Local anthropology can be divided into two types by where a work is published; some writers make a distinction between "native" and "indigenous"

15

anthropology, and this may be useful in some instances. "Native" anthropologists are defined as those that share a common language and cultural background with their informants, often having grown up in the same society, but they write in a foreign language and act as cultural translators for a foreign audiences. By this definition, Fei's *Peasant Life in China* (1939) was a work of "native" anthropology since he came from China and did research in his home area, but wrote in English.

In contrast, "indigenous" anthropology can be defined as written by local anthropologists for local readers. Indigenous anthropologists share a common culture with their informants, and write in their common language. Since they are usually based in their home countries, they usually teach students with whom they share a common culture about themselves and their countrymen, rather than about foreign peoples.

Using this distinction, anthropological works can be divided along two dimensions: similarity between fieldworker (author) and informants, and similarity between intended audience and informants, yielding a four-fold table (see Figure 1). The distinction between native anthropologists and indigenous anthropologists hinges on whether the audience is the same as the informants. Both native and indigenous anthropologists write about the culture they were raised in, but native anthropologists write for foreign audiences (e.g. Fei 1939; Befu 1971) while indigenous anthropologists write for domestic audiences (e.g. Chuang 1977; Myerhoff 1979). In indigenous anthropology, informants, fieldworker, and audience all speak the same language.

Native and indigenous anthropology can be contrasted with the two other cells in the table. In "regular/exotic" anthropology, which is the dominant model in North America, the anthropologist goes to a foreign place, using a foreign language to interview informants, and writes in English, which is a foreign language to the informants. Examples include M. Wolf (1960) and Bestor (1989). This has long been regarded as the norm in anthropology in the United States, United Kingdom, France (Rogers 2001: 490) and Japan.

In rare cases, the anthropologists do fieldwork in places that are foreign and different for them, and then publish in the language of the informants. Here the fieldworkers and informants have cultural differences, but the culture of the audience and the informants is the same (or at least overlaps). One example is the research published in English by Korean-born Choong-Soon Kim (1977) on race relations in the southern United States. Because such scholars sometimes feel their audience does not treat them seriously (see e.g. Kim 1990; Hsu 1973), we label them here "foreign experts/Cassandras." The closest example in this book is that of Cheung who describes his experience writing on the Ainu for a Japanese audience on the Ainu, which was viewed as politically sensitive.

The distinction between native and indigenous anthropology is not hard and fast, since some native scholars also publish articles and books in their native language, and thus participate in the academic dialogue "back home," as is the case with the Australian-based Japanese sociologist, Yoshio Sugimoto (e.g., Sugimoto 1993, 1997) and Kuwayama in this volume. Furthermore, in some instances, because of the prestige they have as academics overseas, native anthropologists often have substantial influence in the anthropological community of their country of origin, even if they do not publish very often in their native language. An interesting case here is that of Harumi Befu (who was actually born in America, but who spent much of his youth in Japan, returning to America after World War II). Thus, making a clear distinction between "native" and "indigenous" anthropology is often problematic.

Nevertheless, the advantage of this distinction between native and indigenous anthropology is that it focuses on the intended audience in addition to the characteristics of the researcher. In both cases the anthropologist claims a special authority based on cultural commonality with the people studied, but the distinction recognizes that the writer will make different assumptions depending on the intended audience. Audiences of "outsiders" need more background, while "natives" will find descriptions of the obvious to be of little scientific merit.

Anthony Giddens is purported to have said that sociology is stating what we know but are not aware of. Anthropologists studying exotic societies, on the other hand, have traditionally written about things that their audience did not know about. Now that travel, news media, and documentaries mean that fewer societies seem exotic, anthropology has had to adapt. Part of this change is the growth of an anthropology that is indigenous, in the sense described here, with local anthropologists writing in the language of their informants.

Intentional indigenization

The term "indigenization" in some cases refers to the purposeful adaptation of anthropology to local conditions, resulting in a viewpoint different from that of mainstream anthropology. Some anthropologists call for indigenous theories to replace imported theories, and for the voices and views of the local people to be given priority. Often the result is research questions which are very different from those in the United States and Western Europe. Sometimes this localism is based on a rejection of a universal science of human culture, but in many cases the argument is that indigenous theories are of superior scientific value and/or practical use to the local society. An additional motivation in some countries (e.g. China) is to make anthropology politically acceptable by claiming that it is indigenous and not "Western." Furthermore, many Asian scholars feel that their contributions have not been sufficiently recognized by Western scholars, while Western scholars make reputations merely reporting what is common knowledge, and treat local schol-

Figure 1: Difference and sameness among audience,
fieldworker, and informants.

Fieldworker and Informants
Same

INDIGENOUS	NATIVE
Chuang Ying-Chang *Lin Yi Pu* B. Myerhoff *Number our Days*	Hsiao-tung Fei *Peasant Life in China* Harumi Befu *Japan*
FOREIGN EXPERTS/ CASSANDRAS	REGULAR/EXOTIC
Choong-Soon Kim *An Asian Anthropologist* *in the South*	M. Wolf *The House of Lim* T.Bestor *Neighborhood Tokyo*

Audience
and
Informants
Same

Audience
and
Informants
Different

Fieldworker and Informants
Different

ars as assistants rather than intellectual partners.[8] Thus, indigenization as a purposeful movement is in response to the perceived hubris of Western anthropologists who see themselves as defining the field and imposing their own practices as the rules of the game.

There are, of course, national traditions in anthropology, but they are not always purposely created. Sometimes they are simply side effects of the developmental process in social science. Present-day Japanese anthropologists do not seek to consciously indigenize anthropology, even though, like Kuwayama in this volume, they may see it as a Western-dominated "world-system." But a large body of writing in Japanese inevitably creates a Japanese tradition of scholarship, within which scholars research and write, making reference primarily to previous work in Japanese, often written by members of their intended audience, rather than to work written in English. The same is true to a lesser extent of work in French, German, and Spanish. But some early Japanese anthropologists, as we have seen, did operate with a nationalist agenda, in making a case for the development of an "Oriental" ethnology or history, distinct from that in the West. Memories of the equation between anthropology and colonialism still linger in many parts of the world, with the result that Western anthropology is still linked in the minds of some scholars with colonial, neocolonial, or postcolonial hegemony, and denounced accordingly.

18

The clearest example in this volume is the chapter by Magos. She argues that it has long been recognized that "Western concepts, theories, and methods are inappropriate to the Asian setting" and that a "change in the anthropologist's role and perspective might require a set of theories based on non-Western precepts and assumptions." Colonial education "imposed ... concepts, ideas, beliefs, and practices which were alien to the natives," and the process of indigenization is presented as a struggle against this outside hegemony by particular groups of local scholars. As her chapter makes clear, the development of anthropology in the Philippines has to be seen within the context of the turbulent history of the country, in which Spanish, American and Japanese colonialism were followed by years of political instability and dictatorship. It is also clear from her paper just how complex the notion of "indigenization" is in the context of the Philippines. At one level it expresses the aspirations of the peoples of the Philippines for freedom from domination from outside. At another level, it also expresses the struggle among the ethnic minorities in the Philippines, including the Muslims in the south and aboriginal groups, for their own ethnic identities to be recognized (cf. Tokoro 2003; Shimizu 2003). Readers may disagree with parts of Magos' argument, or find the shifts in the use of the word "indigenization" to describe these different contexts unsettling, but the editors of this book decided that it was important to include this chapter as an example of the kind of challenge to a universal anthropology that is common in many of parts of Asia, as in other parts of the postcolonial world. There are also similarities between the cases of the Philippines and Korea, as discussed by Kim in his chapter in this volume, in that Korean anthropologists have also been struggling to liberate themselves from a colonial legacy, in this case Japanese.

National, ethnic, and indigenous

Other types of cleavage and conflict underlie the two chapters in this volume on Malaysia. Shamsul is also interested in the links between colonialism and anthropology, given that colonial knowledge "subsequently came to be accepted as the basis of the history and the territorial and social organization of the postcolonial state." Postcolonial nations are still officially seen as consisting of the various ethnic groups documented by colonial anthropology, though anthropologists are also seen as useful specialists in mediating the relations between these groups. Like Zhuang, Shamsul discusses the politics of the curriculum in anthropology departments, and comments that anthropology graduates are considered employable partly because of their supposed expertise in multi-ethnic situations. However, he is loathe to use the word "indigenization" in the Malaysian context, preferring to see the development of the discipline in Malaysia as a process of "Malaysianization" after the crisis of 1969, with a shift from the old emphasis on "Malay studies" to one on the multi-ethnic pluralism of the Malaysian state. "Indigenous" in the Malaysian context has become a word associated with just one of the local ethnic groups, the Malays. Tan also discusses contemporary Malaysian anthropology, and the influence on it of the ethnic diversity within the country, including aboriginal groups (the Orang Asli), the Chinese, and the minorities in East Malaysia. Like the country itself, anthropologists are recruited from a variety of ethnic groups, giving them very different viewpoints. This makes the dichotomy between "foreign" and "indigenous" researchers largely meaningless, as the most important divisions lie within the country, not between Malaysia and the outside world.

Beyond Indigenization?

When "indigenization" is viewed as the adaptation of anthropology to suit local settings, it is inherently particularistic. From this viewpoint, instead of anthropology being seen as a universal science, it is seen as primarily a Western construct that needs to be tailored and modified to make it useful in Asia and elsewhere. If the proposition that anthropology always needs to be indigenized to be valid were to be taken to its logical conclusion, the discipline would be divided into a host of mutually incompatible national projects with no grand aspirations in common. Though nationalistic pride will continue to drive some anthropologists to argue for the creation of new forms of "indigenous" anthropology, the more difficult challenge in the discipline is to reconcile the universalistic goals of anthropology as a science with the particularistic problems and viewpoints of the local, and to use local viewpoints to inform and improve the universal enterprise. Among anthropologists in China, there seems to be a consensus that anthropology needs to be indigenized (*bentuhua*), yet at the same time, the same scholars argue for increased exchange to learn from the West (see for examples the papers in Rong and Xu 1998).

The analysis of the uses of the terms "native" and "indigenous" anthropology above suggests that it may be useful in some contexts to limit the term "native anthropology" to mean research conducted by a native of the culture, and "indigenous" research to refer to research and publication by native anthropologists in their own languages. However, the case studies of the "indigenization" of anthropology in East and Southeast Asia in this book show that there is no universal process of indigenization, and that the only utility the term may have comes in highlighting local differences. The key issues affecting native and indigenous anthropology are issues that affect anthropology everywhere: audience and context.

Audience

One of the major weaknesses of the universalistic models of anthropology as a science is the lack of recognition that writing must address an audience. An audience has certain assumptions upon which writing must build, or which it must seek to undermine. In general, these assumptions are simply the ethnocentric understandings of the readers' own cultures. What strikes anthropologists as worth studying is usually that which seems odd from their common sense point of view. Even though anthropologists should ideally study questions that emerge from received theory, in practice, many of our questions originate from our own times and social contexts. Postmodernist critics have noted that politics and emotions, and not just theory, mediate knowledge. The chapters in this book suggest that the culture of the audience forms a kind of hidden substructure on which we build our theory. Whether we notice and accept theories and interpretations is based, in part, on how well they fit with our received common sense. In our areas of specialization, we can hope to transcend culture-bound perspectives to some degree, using cross-cultural anthropological theory, but because we address a culturally based audience and do not write in a universal language (even English is not universal), the reception of all writing is affected by the culture of the intended audience.

One experience that leads scholars in China to feel that indigenization is necessary is the odd sense of seeing their own cultural practices described in Western categories. Despite the deserved praise received in the West by books such as Yan's *The Flow of Gifts* (1996) and Jing's *The Temple of Memories* (1996), some scholars in China have dismissed the books as "written for foreigners" because they describe things (*guanxi* and social memory) that "everybody in China knows" and because they "do not address the real problems of China." Undoubtedly, the books would have been written differently had they been written first in Chinese. The intended audience matters. This is the basic reason why the monographs written by the Chinese scholars based in Japan address rather different issues to those written by Chinese scholars based in the West, despite the similar Chinese origins of the two groups.

The chapters in this volume show that much indigenous anthropology is motivated by a desire to record a vanishing past. As in the West, this nostalgia for the past is in part a critique of capitalism and materialism and the rationalization of society. In addition, however, it is driven by controversies over national identities and by attempts at nation-building. Many of the authors point to nation-building as one of the primary purposes of anthropology. The position of anthropology is often similar to that of history, ethnomusicology, and other disciplines. The resulting research is much like Western folklore: empirical, atheoretical, and oriented towards collecting and classification. These characteristics, which are often cited by outsiders as limitations of indigenous research, can be understood as due to the audiences of their work and the context of the research funding – and not due to the nature of the fieldworker.

Context

It has been said that "foreign anthropologists are less affected than local ethnographers by the political and social world of their research" (Kapferer 1990: 299). From our discussion above, it is clear that the key differences arise from the audiences for which the anthropologists write. Indigenous anthropologists write in the same language as their informants, so will have their work scrutinized by their informants. Ethnographers are increasingly concerned about the ethical and legal issues that arise when informants read their published work (see e.g. Allen 1997). The freedom previously enjoyed by foreign anthropologists was entirely premised on the assumption that the subjects would not read the ethnographies, but as Tan points out in his chapter, this can no longer be assumed. Given that this assumption of separation is increasingly untenable in our increasingly globalized world, all anthropologists are affected by the political and social world in which they do research.[9] Here again the distinction between indigenous and foreign anthropology fades as one realizes that the primary issue is that of the audience which reads the ethnography, and as one realizes the degree to which the world is interconnected. Anthropologists are increasingly being confronted with individuals claiming to be "natives," and therefore to have more authority than anthropologists regardless of data (their experience being the only necessary datum).

Each chapter of this book shows how various aspects of context have strongly affected what is studied as part of anthropology. Tan in this volume notes that he had to abandon his hope of doing fieldwork in northern Thailand because doing so would make him unemployable back home in Malaysia. Magos describes the localism that led young scholars to want to do fieldwork in the Philippines. In developing countries, economic development and topics related to nation-building are more likely to receive government funding, leading scholars to specialize in these areas. Thus, the job market and the national political context both strongly affect the nature of indigenization. This should not come as a surprise; Joan Vincent (1990) has ably demonstrated the influence of national agendas on political anthropology in the United States and the United Kingdom, and there has been much commentary since the early 1990s on the way in which the area studies approach in the United States was a response to the Cold War.[10]

Though it probably should not have been a surprise, one thing we have discovered in editing this book is how widely the nature of the process of indigenization, the adaptation of anthropology to local conditions, varies from country to country. In the Philippines, as Magos' chapter makes clear, the word "indigenous" operates at different levels, both national (minorities versus the majority) and international (Filipinos versus outsiders). In Malaysia, for historical reasons, the term "indigenous," has come to mean "Malay" and hence the study of Malay society in contrast to Chinese, Indian, or British society (Cheah 1996). Thus, both Malaysian authors in this book (Shamsul and Tan) hesitate to use the term "indigenous" in their chapters. The Malaysian case highlights the political and nationalistic usage of the concept of indigenous. Given the many variables along which one can be an "insider" or "outsider," and the obvious nationalistic and ethnic manipulation of the term "indigenous," it perhaps behooves us, as anthropologists, to view "indigenous anthropology" with caution and even skepticism. All the chapters in this book show how the local context and history have affected local anthropological theory, concepts, and fieldwork. But their writers also note the importance of an international dialogue among scholars, not only between Asia and the United States and Europe, but also among scholars in Asia.

Conclusion: Asian and Global Anthropology

Focusing on one country at a time, as the chapters of this book do, risks obscuring the connections between countries, overlooking both the students that go overseas for degrees and postdoctoral research and the visitors and fieldworkers that come and influence local scholars. Yet many of the chapters focus on connections, and the reader is left in no doubt as to the importance of travel and contact with foreign anthropologists. The world economic system is the most prominent influence: Filipino scholars have ties with the United States, scholars in Taiwan and Korea have contacts with the United States and Japan, and Malaysian scholars have ties with the United Kingdom and Australia. So far, however, there has been very limited communication between anthropologists from different Asian countries. As Kuwayama notes, quoting Gerholm and Hannerz (1982: 7), residents of the peripheral islands within the anthropological world map always look to the mainland center, but they know little about each other. Japan has the largest anthropology industry in the region, and Japanese anthropologists have always been most deeply concerned with Asia, but Japan has failed to develop as the major regional hub in the discipline, partly because of the language factor discussed above, and partly as a legacy of its imperial and colonial past. This is well illustrated in the chapter on Korea in this volume by Kim. In recent years, a number of scholars have been anxious to create links within the region, through meetings, exchanges, and joint research and publication.[11] Given this trend, there are several interesting possibilities for future cooperation between Asian anthropologists.

The first issue to be confronted is the historically ambiguous position of Japanese anthropology in relation to Japanese colonialism and imperialism. During the colonial period, Japanese anthropology practiced its own kind of Orientalism, in which the people of Asia were seen as "*dojin*" or "indigenous peoples" (cf. Kawamura 1993). They were also ranked as "progressive" or "backward" instead of being treated equally. This historical period could be examined not only by Japanese but also by other Asian scholars as a joint project on the history of colonialism and anthropology in Asia.

A second issue is that of the differences and tensions between anthropology as practiced in Japan and elsewhere in the region, following on from Mathews' discussion of Japan and the United States. For example, Japanese anthropologists have historically been less concerned with the anthropology of development than anthropologists elsewhere in Asia. This raises the question of the reasons for these differences in emphasis between Asian anthropologies, and in what ways they can learn from each other.

Third, given that anthropology in each Asian country has its own national characteristics, how can the discipline deal with common problems such as development, environment, migration, or ethnic conflict in the postcolonial world? In order to answer these questions, one solution might be to set up an Asian network for anthropological studies which can hold regional meetings, rather like the European Association of Social Anthropologists established in the late 1980s. This would also enable Asian anthropologists to develop their own distinctive projects rather than simply depending on the West for ideas. However, even though there are national and regional differences in anthropology, we still see anthropology as a unified global enterprise. We are not advocating the development of "Asian" anthropology as opposed to "Western" anthropology. What is required is interaction between Western and Asian anthropologies that can enrich the discipline world-wide. An interactive anthropology is global, because it is neither national nor international but transcends both, allowing anthropologists to work with anyone on the globe "and to appreciate the worldwide processes within which and on which they work" (Albrow 1990: 7). Anthropology is a cultural product. If culture travels, as James Clifford (1992) puts it, anthropology travels, too. Through traveling the world, anthropology can be enriched and transformed by adjusting it to the local situation. The anthropology of the twenty-first century will be constructed on the basis of the "glocal," namely the interaction of global and local relations (Robertson 1995), in the same way as other major forms of cultural production in the world are constructed, and in the process it could radically change the map of the anthropological world-system.

Notes.

1   Unless otherwise stated, the term "anthropology" is used throughout the book to refer to American-style cultural anthropology or European style social anthropology, rather than the broader "four field" anthropology practiced in the United States, which also includes archeology, linguistics, and bio-medical or physical anthropology. Generally socio-cultural anthropology is by far the largest of the four fields. There are national differences in terminology within Asia. In Japan, the meaning of the term *jinruigaku* is as wide as that of "anthropology" in America. The term for "cultural anthropology" is *bunkajinruigaku*, though the older term *minzokugaku* ("ethnology") is also often used. As in some European countries, there is also a strong tradition of folklore studies (also pronounced *minzokugaku* in Japanese, though written with different characters). Terms using similar characters are also found in mainland China, though "anthropology" (*renleixue*) is not as widely used as the term "ethnlogy" (*minzuxue*). This usually refers to research on national minorities which in the past used Marxist-Leninist evolutionary theory, a model adopted from the former Soviet Union. "Sociology" is used for work on the Han Chinese. A number of former colonial countries in East Asia follow the British tradition, in which social anthropology is often taught alongside sociology, whereas in Japan and the United States the two disciplines are more distinct. At the level of graduate research in Asia, differences between sociology, American-style cultural anthropology, and European-style social anthropology are often elided as scholars focus on similar social issues using similar bodies of theory. In this book we regard contemporary socio-cultural anthropology as a fairly homogeneous discipline which uses an internationally accepted body of theory and research methods, while the various research traditions from which it arose are now in practice inextricably intertwined.

2   On indigenization, see the edited volumes resulting from conferences organized by the Wenner Gren Foundation at Burg Wartenstein (Fahim 1982; Messerschmidt 1981) and the Association of Social Anthropologists in the United Kingdom (Jackson 1987). For earlier work on Asia, see Befu and Kreiner (1992) on national traditions of Japanese studies, and Chiao (1985), and Yang and Wen (1982) for research on the sinicization of the social sciences. Since the early 1990s, Eades and Yamashita have organized a series of panels at the Annual Meetings of the American Anthropology Association, focusing on the history and current state of anthropology in Japan. One of these resulted in a volume on Japanese research on China, edited by Suenari, Eades, and Daniels (1995). In 1996, a number of articles on the history of anthropology in Taiwan were published (see Li 1996, Chang 1996, and the special forum in the *Bulletin of the*

Institute of Ethnology, no. 80). A conference entitled "Forty Years of Anthropology in Taiwan" was held in March 1997 at the Institute of Ethnology of the Academia Sinica in Taipei. (The Chinese title is actually slightly different from the official English title: *Renleixue zai Taiwan de fazhan* literally means "The Development of Anthropology in Taiwan."). In May 1997, Jan van Bremen convened an international workshop in Leiden on the indigenization of Asian anthropology (Bremen 1997). The same year also saw the publication of a book edited by Yamashita, Kadir Din and Eades on the anthropology of tourism, consisting mainly of papers by Asia scholars (Yamashita, Kadir Din, and Eades 1997). In China, two volumes have focused on the localization and indigenization of anthropology, edited by Rong Shixing and Xu Jieshun (1998) and Xu Jieshun (2000), and many major conferences in China now include papers on this issue. The Fourteenth International Congress of Anthropological and Ethnological Sciences held in Williamsburg, Virginia, in July 1998 included two panels which formed the starting point for this book: "The Making of Anthropology in Asia: The Past, The Present, and the Future" organized by Shinji Yamashita and Takeo Funabiki, and "Indigenization of Anthropology in East and Southeast Asia," organized by Joseph Bosco. In the same year, the Japanese Society of Ethnology published the first issue of a new English-language journal, *Japanese Review of Cultural Anthropology*, designed to make the results of research by Japanese scholars more readily available to scholars elsewhere. More recently, the Department of Anthropology at the Chinese University of Hong Kong has launched its own English-language journal, *Asian Anthropology*, and the Institute of Ethnology of the Academia Sinica in Taipei has launched the new bilingual *Taiwan Journal of Anthropology*. There is also the Berghahn series of which this volume is part. This is only a partial list: other references can be found in the chapters throughout this book. Not only are there a growing number of Asian anthropologists studying their own and other societies, but they are also increasingly interested in publicizing this research internationally.

3   See the chapter by Kuwayama in this volume. A session of the 2000 Japan Anthropology Workshop (JAWS) conference was also devoted to this theme, and the papers were published in Asquith (2000).

4   Hinton went to China as an agriculturalist. For many years after his first volume, *Fangshen*, was published (Hinton 1966), he was prevented from returning to China, due to the American government's seizure of his passport and by the onset of the Cultural Revolution (Hinton 1983: xiii-xiv). He later retired to Mongolia. The Crooks stayed on in China as translators, but David Crook was incarcerated for much of the Cultural Revolution, and was only released in 1973. He died aged 90 in 2000 (Davin 2000).

5   In the case of Nie, this is not a coincidence. She was Fei's student at Beijing

University before moving to Japan, and she discusses the influence of Fei on her fieldwork in the introduction in the book based on her Tokyo Ph.D. thesis (Nie 1992).

6 Note that this excludes the study of minorities in one's own society, such as the study of Native Americans in the United States and of minority nationalities in China. This type of study, which has often been seen as part of a colonial agenda (Asad 1973), takes advantage of proximity, government funding, and the fact that informants are often bilingual. Anthropologists from the dominant society generally do not claim to share the culture of their informants, even though there may in fact be many commonalities because of education and popular culture.

7 While is not unusual for universities in the United States and United Kingdom to focus their research on a small number of ethnographic regions, they still usually claim to teach anthropology as a global subject, drawing on material from all over the world. In Asia outside Japan, however, the focus is usually firmly on the home region.

8 In the worst case, as noted by Whyte (1984: 211), the project was designed overseas, and it only used local scholars as informants and to collect data; the local scholars got a stipend but no credit in publications which came out in English.

9 The discussion in *Anthropology Newsletter*, October 1999, p. 4, in relation to the work of Gilbert Herdt, illustrates this issue well.

10 Ironically, as this volume goes to press, there is another discussion starting in America of the status of area studies programs in the wake of the 9/11 attacks on New York and Washington in 2001. Some area studies scholars now see themselves as under attack from neo-conservatives as "subversive," and "anti-American" because they are seen as supporting and representing the interests of the peoples they study.

11 For instance, in Japan, a symposium entitled "Cultural anthropology and Asia: The past, the present and the future" was organized in 1995 at the annual meeting of the Japanese Society of Ethnology at Osaka. The aim was to discuss the state of cultural anthropology in Asia and the possibility of cooperation in future. Anthropologists from China, Korea, Japan, Taiwan, the Philippines, Indonesia, and Malaysia participated, and the Turkish anthropologist, Nur Yalman of Harvard University, gave the keynote speech. There have also been research exchange programs at institutions such as the National Museum of Ethnology at Osaka and joint research projects with financial support from the Japanese Ministry of Education, Culture, Sports, Science, and Technology, the Japan Society for the Promotion of Science, the Japan Foundation, the Toyota Foundation, and others. An Asia Center was specially established by the Japan Foundation in 1995 in order to promote mutual understanding of Asian peoples and their cultures.

References

Aguilar, John L. 1981. "Inside research: An ethnography of a debate," pp. 15-26 in *Anthropologists at Home in North America: Methods and Issues in the Study of One's Own Society*, ed. Donald A. Messerschmidt. Cambridge: Cambridge University Press.

Ahern, Emily. 1973. *The Cult of the Dead in a Chinese Village*. Stanford: Stanford University Press.

Albrow, Martin. 1990. "Introduction," pp. 3-13 in *Globalization, Knowledge and Society: Readings from International Sociology*, eds. Martin Albrow and Elizabeth King. London: Sage Publications.

Allen, Matthew. 2002. *Identity and Resistance in Okinawa*. Lanham, Md.: Rowman & Littlefield.

Allen, Charlotte. 1997. "Spies like us: When sociologists deceive their subjects," *Lingua Franca* (November): 31-39.

Asad, Talal, ed. 1973. *Anthropology and the Colonial Encounter.* London: Ithaca Press.

Asquith, Pamela, ed. 2000. *Japan Scholarship in International Academic Discourse*. Beppu, Japan: Ritsumeikan Asia Pacific University, Research Center for Asia Pacific Studies. (*Ritsumeikan Journal of Asia Pacific Studies*, vol. 6).

Baker, Hugh D.R. 1968. *A Chinese Lineage Village: Sheung Shui.* Stanford: Stanford University Press.

Barmé, Geremie R. 1999. *In the Red: On Contemporary Chinese Culture*. New York: Columbia University Press.

Befu, Harumi. 1971. *Japan: An Anthropological Introduction*. San Francisco: Chandler.

Befu, Harumi, and Josef Kreiner, eds. 1992. *Otherness of Japan: Historical and Cultural Influences on Japanese Studies in Ten Countries*. Munich: Iudicium.

Bestor, Theodore. 1989. *Neighborhood Tokyo*. Stanford: Stanford University Press.

Bremen, Jan van. 1997. "Prompters who do not appear on the stage: Japanese anthropology and Japanese studies in American and European Anthropology," *Japan Anthropology Workshop Newsletter* 26/27: 57-65.

Bruun, Ole. 1993. *Business and Bureaucracy in a Chinese City*. Berkeley: Institute of East Asian Studies.

Chan, Anita, Richard Madsen, and Jonathan Unger. 1984. *Chen Village: The Recent History of a Peasant Community in Mao's China.* Berkeley: University of California Press.

Chang Hsun. 1996. "Guangfu hou Taiwan renleixue Hanren Zhongjiao zhi huigu" [A review of anthropological studies of Han Chinese religion in Taiwan, 1945-1995], *Bulletin of the Institute of Ethnology, Academia Sinica*

81: 163-215.

Cheah, Boon Kheng. 1996. "Writing indigenous history in Malaysia: A survey on approaches and problems," *Crossroads: An Interdisciplinary Journal of Southeast Asian Studies* 10 (2): 33-81.

Chiao Chien, senior ed. 1985. *Xiandaihua yu Zhongguo wenhua yantaohui lunwen huibian* [Proceedings of the Conference on Modernization and Chinese Culture], eds. Rance P.L. Lee, Ambrose Y.C. King, Lau Siu-kai and Kuan Hsin-chi. Hong Kong: Faculty of Social Science and Institute of Social Studies, The Chinese University of Hong Kong.

Chuang Ying-chang. 1977. *Lin Yi Pu: Yige Taiwan shizhen de shehui jingji fazhan shi* [Lin Yi Pu: The social and economic history of a Chinese township in Taiwan]. Nankang: Institute of Ethnology, Academia Sinica.

Clifford, James. 1992. "Traveling Cultures," in *Cultural Studies*, eds. L. Grossberg, C. Nelson and P. Treichler. New York and London: Routledge.

Cohen, Myron. 1976. *House United, House Divided: The Chinese Family in Taiwan.* New York: Columbia University Press.

Crook, Isabel and David Crook. 1959. *Revolution in a Chinese Village: Ten Mile Inn.* London: Routledge.

Crook, Isabel and David Crook. 1966. *The First Ten Years of Yangyi Commune.* London: Routledge.

Davin, Delia. 2000. "David Crook" (Obituary), *The Guardian*, March 18.

Davis, Deborah S. ed. 2000. *The Consumer Revolution in Urban China.* Berkeley: University of California Press.

Davis, Deborah S., R. Krauss, B. Norton, and E. Perry eds. 1997. *Urban Spaces in Contemporary China.* Cambridge: Cambridge University Press.

Dutton, Michael. 1998. *Streetlife China.* Cambridge: Cambridge University Press.

Eades, J.S. 2000. "'Why don't they write in English?' Academic modes of production and academic discourses in Japan and the West," *Ritsumeikan Journal of Asia Pacific Studies*, 6: 58-77.

Eades, J.S. 2003. "Ethnographies of the vanishing? Global images and local realities among the Aborigines of Taiwan, 1600-2000," pp. 226-52 in *Globalization in Southeast Asia: Local, National and Transnational Perspectives,* eds. Shinji. Yamashita and J.S. Eades. Oxford and New York: Berghahn Books.

Endicott 1988. *Red Earth: Revolution in a Sichuan Village.* London: I.B. Tauris.

Fahim, Hussein, ed. 1982. *Indigenous Anthropology in Non-Western Countries. Proceedings of a Burg Wartenstein Symposium.* Durham, N.C.: Carolina Academic Press.

Fei, Hsiao-tung [Fei Xiaotong]. 1939. *Peasant Life in China.* London: Kegan Paul, Trench, Teubner & Co.

Firth, Raymond. 1946. *Malay Fishermen: Their Peasant Economy.* London:

Kegan Paul, Trench, Teubner & Co.

Fitzhugh, W.W. and C.O. Dubreuil, eds. 1999. *Ainu: Spirit of a Northern People.* Seattle: University of Washington Press.

Freedman, Maurice. 1958. *Lineage Organization in Southeastern China.* London: Athlone Press.

Fukuoka, Yasunori. 2000. *Lives of Young Koreans in Japan.* Melbourne: Trans Pacific Press.

Gallin, Bernard. 1966. *Hsin Hsing, Taiwan: A Chinese Village in Change.* Berkeley: University of California Press.

Gerholm, Thomas and Ulf Hannerz. 1982. "Introduction: The shaping of national anthropologies," *Ethnos* 47: 6-33.

Gladney, Dru C. 1991. *Muslim Chinese: Ethnic Nationalism in the People's Republic.* Cambridge, Mass.: Harvard Council on East Asian Studies.

Goodman, Roger. 2001. "The state of higher education in East Asia: Higher education in East Asia and the state," *Ritsumeikan Journal of Asia Pacific Studies*, 8: 1-29.

Greenhouse, Carol. 1985. "Anthropology at home: Whose home?" *Human Organization* 44 (3): 261-64.

Guldin, Gregory Eliyu. 1994 *The Saga of Anthropology in China: From Malinowski to Moscow to Mao.* Armonk, NY: M.E. Sharpe.

Hamabata, Matthews M. 1990. *Crested Kimono: Power and Love in the Japanese Business Family.* Ithaca: Cornell University Press.

Han, Min. 2000. *Social Change and Continuity in a Village in Northern Anhui, China: A Response to Revolution and Reform.* Osaka, Japan: National Museum of Ethnology (Senri Ethnological Studies, 58).

Hanson, Mette H. 1999. *Lessons in Being Chinese: Minority Education and Ethnic Identity in Southwest China.* Seattle: Washington University Press.

Hinton, William. 1966. *Fanshen: A Documentary of Revolution in a Chinese Village.* New York: Monthly Review Press.

Hinton, William. 1983. *Shenfan: The Continuing Revolution in a Chinese Village.* New York. Random House.

Hook, G.D. and R. Siddel, eds. 2001. *Japan and Okinawa: Structure and Subjectivity.* London: Routledge.

Hsu, Francis L.K. 1973. "Prejudice and its intellectual effects in American anthropology: An ethnographic report," *American Anthropologist* 75 (1): 1-19.

Hu, Tai-li. 1984. *My Mother-in-Law's Village: Rural Industrialization and Change in Taiwan.* Taipei: Academia Sinica Institute of Ethnology (Monograph Series B, no. 13.)

Huang, Shu-min. 1989. *The Spiral Road: Change in a Chinese Village through the Eyes of a Communist Party Leader.* Boulder, Colo.: Westview.

Ishikawa, Yoshihiro 2003. "Anti-Manchu racism and the rise of anthropology in early 20th century China," *Sino-Japanese Studies* 15: 7-26.

Jackson, Anthony, ed. 1987. *Anthropology at Home*. London: Tavistock.

Jankowiak, William R. 1993. *Sex, Death, and Hierarchy in a Chinese City.* New York: Columbia University Press.

Jing, Jun. 1996. *The Temple of Memories: History, Power and Morality in a Chinese Village*. Stanford: Stanford University Press.

Judd, Ellen R. 1994 *Gender and Power in Rural North China*. Stanford: Stanford University Press.

Kang Sang Jung. 1996. *Orientarizumu no kanata e* [Beyond Orientalism], Tokyo: Iwanami Shoten.

Kapferer, Bruce. 1990. "From the periphery to the centre: Ethnography and the critique of ethnography in Sri Lanka," pp. 280-302 in *Localizing Strategies: Regional Traditions of Ethnographic Writing*, ed. Richard Fardon. Edinburgh and Washington D.C.: Scottish Academic Press and Smithsonian Institution Press.

Kawamura Minato. 1993. "Taishû Orientarizumu to Ajia ninshiki" [Popular Orientalism and Japanese perceptions of Asia], pp. 107-36 in *Iwanami kôza kindai Nihon to shokuminchi* [Iwanami series on modern Japan and its colonies], vol. 7. Tokyo: Iwanami Shoten.

Kim, Choong S. 1977. *An Asian Anthropologist in the South: Field Experiences with Blacks, Indians, and Whites*. Knoxville, Tenn.: University of Tennessee Press.

Kim, Choong S. 1990. "The role of the non-Western anthropologist reconsidered: Illusion versus reality," *Current Anthropology* 31 (2): 196-201.

Kuwayama Takami. 1997. "Genchi no jinruigakusha: Naigai no Nihon kenkyû o chûshin ni [Native anthropologists: With special reference to Japanese studies inside and outside Japan], *Minzokugaku-kenkyû* [Japanese Journal of Ethnology], 61 (4): 517-42.

Kuwayama, Takami. 2000. "Native anthropologists: With special reference to Japanese studies inside and outside Japan," *Ritsumeikan Journal of Asia Pacific Studies*, 6: 7-33.

Kuwayama, Takami. 2004. *Native Anthropology*. Melbourne: Trans Pacific Press.

Leach, Edmund. 1954. *Political Systems of Highland Burma: A Study of Kachin Social Structure*. London: G. Bell & Sons.

Li Yi-yuan. 1996. "Taida kaogu renleixuexi yu Zhongguo renleixue de fazhan," [Department of Anthropology and Archaeology and the development of anthropological research in Taiwan], *Guoli Taiwandaxue kaogu renleixue kan* 51: 1-5.

Liu, Xin. 2000. *In One's Own Shadow: An Ethnographic Account of the Condition of Post-Reform Rural China*. Berkeley: University of California Press.

Messerschmidt, Donald A., ed. 1981. *Anthropologists at Home in North America: Methods and Issues in the Study of One's Own Society*. Cam-

31

bridge: Cambridge University Press.

Minzokugaku Shinkôkai. 1984. *Zaidanhojin minzokugaku shinkôkai gojunen no ayumi: Nihonminzoku gakuhudan ryakushi* [Fifty Years of the Shibusawa Foundation for Ethnological Studies]. Tokyo: Minzokugaku Shinkôkai.

Myerhoff, Barbara. 1979. *Number Our Days*. New York: Dutton.

Narayan, Kirin. 1993. "How native is a 'native' anthropologist?" *American Anthropologist* 93 (4): 671-86.

Nie Lili. 1992. *Ryû Hô* [Liu Village]. Tokyo: Tokyo Daigaku Shuppankai.

Oguma, Eiji. 2002. *A Genealogy of "Japanese" Self-Images*. Melbourne: Trans Pacific Press.

Ohnuki-Tierney, Emiko. 1984. "'Native' Anthropologists," *American Ethnologist* 11: 584-86.

Oi, Jean. 1989. *State and Peasant in Contemporary China: The Political Economy of Village Government*. Berkeley: University of California Press.

Parish, William and Martin King Whyte. 1978. *Village and Family in Contemporary China*. Chicago: Chicago University Press.

Pasternak, Burton. 1983. *Guests in the Dragon: Social Demography of a Chinese District, 1895-1946*. New York: Columbia University Press.

Potter, Jack M. 1968. *Capitalism and the Chinese Peasant*. Berkeley: University of California Press.

Potter, Sulamith Heins, and Jack M. Potter. 1990. *China's Peasants: The Anthropology of a Revolution*. Cambridge: Cambridge University Press.

Robertson, Roland. 1995. "Glocalization: Time-space and homogeneity/heterogeneity," pp. 25-44 in *Global Modernities,* eds. M. Featherstone, Scott Lash, and Roland Robertson, London: Sage Publications.

Rogers, Susan C. 2001. "Anthropology in France," *Annual Review of Anthropology*, 30: 481-504.

Rong Shixing and Xu Jieshun, eds. 1998. *Renleixue bentuhua zai Zhongguo* [Nativization of anthropology in China]. Nanning: Guangxi Nationalities Publisher.

Rudelson, Justin J. 1997. *Oasis Identities: Uyghur Nationalism along China's Silk Road*. New York: Columbia University Press.

Ryang, Sonia. 1996. *North Koreans in Japan*. Boulder, Colo.: Westview Press.

Schein, Louisa. 2000. *Minority Rules: The Miao and the Feminine in China's Cultural Politics*. Durham, N.C.: Duke University Press.

Sekimoto Teruo. 1995. "Nihon no jinruigaku to Nihon shigaku" [Anthropology in Japan and Japanese historiography], pp. 123-47 in *Iwanami kôza Nihon tsûshi. Bekkan 1* [Iwanami Complete History of Japan. Supplementary vol.1], eds. Asao Naohiro et al. Tokyo: Iwanami Shoten.

Shimizu Akitoshi. 1998. "Nihon no jinruigaku" [Anthropology in Japan], pp. 111-133 in *Bunkajinruigaku no susume* [Invitation to cultural anthropology], ed. Funabiki Takeo. Tokyo: Chikuma Shobô.

Shimizu, Akitoshi. 1999. "Colonialism and the development of modern anthropology in Japan," pp. 115-171 in *Anthropology and Colonialism in Asia and Oceania*, eds. Jan van Bremen and Akitoshi Shimizu. Richmond, Surrey: Curzon.

Shimizu, Akitoshi and Jan van Bremen, eds. 2003. *Wartime Japanese Anthropology in Asia and the Pacific.* Osaka: National Museum of Ethnology (Senri Ethnological Studies, 65).

Shimizu, Hiromu. 2003. "Diaspora and ethnic awakening: The formation of cultural consciousness among the Ayta of Mt. Pinatubo after the eruption of 1991," pp. 179-201 in *Globalization in Southeast Asia: Local, National and Transnational Perspectives,* eds. Shinji Yamashita and J.S. Eades. Oxford and New York: Berghahn Books.

Siddle, R. 1996. *Race, Resistance and the Ainu of Japan.* London: Routledge.

Siu, Helen F. 1989. *Agents and Victims in South China: Accomplices in Rural Revolution.* New Haven: Yale University Press.

Suenari, Michio. 1995. "Chinese anthropology in Japan: A view from inside," pp. 1-16 in *Perspectives on Chinese Society: Anthropological Views from Japan*, eds. Michio Suenari, J.S. Eades and Christian Daniels. Canterbury: University of Kent, Centre for Social Anthropology and Computing.

Suenari, Michio. 1998. "Exodus from Shangri-La? Anthropological studies in Japan of the Aborigines of Taiwan after 1945." *Japanese Review of Cultural Anthropology*, 1: 33-66.

Suenari, Michio, J.S. Eades and Christian Daniels, eds. 1995. *Perspectives on Chinese Society: Anthropological Views from Japan.* Canterbury: University of Kent, Centre for Social Anthropology and Computing.

Sugimoto Yoshio. 1993. *Nihonjin o yameru hôhô* [How to stop being Japanese]. Tokyo: Chikuma Shobô.

Sugimoto, Yoshio. 1997. *Introduction to Japanese Society.* Cambridge: Cambridge University Press.

Tanaka, Stefan. 1993. *Japan's Orient: Reading Pasts into History*. Berkeley: University of California Press.

Tang, W. and W.L. Parish. 2000. *Chinese Urban Life Under Reform.* Cambridge: Cambridge University Press.

Terada Kazuo. 1981. *Nihon no jinruigaku* [Anthropology in Japan]. Tokyo: Kadokawa Shoten.

Tokoro, Ikuya. 2003. "Transformation of shamanic rituals among the Sama of Tabawan Island, Sulu Archipelago, Southern Philippines," pp. 175-78 in *Globalization in Southeast Asia: Local, National and Transnational Perspectives,* ed. Shinji Yamashita and J.S. Eades. Oxford and New York: Berghahn Books.

Torii Ryûzô. 1975. *Torii Ryûzô zenshû* [The complete works of Torii Ryûzô] Vol.1. Tokyo: Asahi Shinbunsha.

Vincent, Joan. 1990. *Anthropology and Politics: Visions, Traditions, and*

Trends. Tuscon, Ariz.: University of Arizona Press.

Walker, Brett L. 2001. *The Conquest of Ainu Lands.* Berkeley: University of California Press.

Watson, James. 1975. *Emigration and the Chinese Lineage.* Berkeley: University of California Press.

Watson, R. 1985. *Inequality among Brothers: Class and Kinship in South China.* Cambridge: Cambridge University Press.

Whyte, Martin King and William Parish 1984. *Urban Life in Contemporary China.* Chicago: Chicago University Press.

Whyte, William F. 1984. *Learning from the Field: A Guide from Experience.* Beverly Hills, Calif.: Sage.

Wolf, Arthur and Chie-shan Huang. 1980. *Lineage and Adoption in China, 1845-1945.* Stanford: Stanford University Press.

Wolf, Margery. 1960. *The House of Lim: A Study of A Chinese Farm Family.* Englewood Cliffs, N.J.: Prentice-Hall.

Wolf, Margery. 1972. *Women and the Family in Rural Taiwan.* Stanford: Stanford University Press.

Wong, Siu-lun. 1979. *Sociology and Socialism in Contemporary China.* London: Routledge & Kegan Paul.

Xu Jieshun, ed. 2000. *Bentuhua: renleixue de da qushi.* [Nativization: The great trend of anthropology]. Nanning: Guangxi Nationalities Publisher.

Yamashita, Shinji. 2003. *Bali and Beyond: Explorations in the Anthropology of Tourism.* Oxford and New York: Berghahn.

Yamashita, Shinji, Kadir Din and J.S. Eades, eds. 1997. *Tourism and Cultural Development in East Asia and Oceania.* Bangi, Malaysia. UKM Press.

Yan, Yunxiang. 1996. *The Flow of Gifts: Reciprocity and Social Networks in a Chinese Village.* Stanford: Stanford University Press.

Yanagita Kunio. 1975 [1909]. *Tôno monogatari* [Tales of Tôno]. Tokyo: Kadokawa Shoten.

Yang Kuo-shu and Wen Chung-I, eds. 1982. *Shehui ji xingwei kexue yanjiu de Zhongguohua* [The Sinicization of social and behavioral science research in China]. Nankang, Taipei: Institute of Ethnology, Academia Sinica (Monograph Series B, no. 10).

Chapter 2

The "World-System" of Anthropology: Japan and Asia in the Global Community of Anthropologists[1]

Takami K*UWAYAMA*

Introduction

"Native" or "indigenous" anthropology is a major issue today, as anthropology has come to be practiced worldwide, including in countries that were formerly objects of research. As the offspring of a western science with "colonial roots," anthropologists used to observe and write about people in distant lands without considering how the people who had been described would respond to their representations. The distant, "exotic" Others were merely objects of thought, and their voice was seldom heard in the civilized world where knowledge about them was produced. Since the end of World War II, however, many former colonies have gained political independence, and anthropologists are no longer able to keep a comfortable distance from the people they study as they did in the past. Indeed, they are now in a position of being observed by the "exotic" Others, who possess enough power and resources to contest their authority. The anthropologists' gaze has been returned. At the center of the current debate on "native" anthropology, then, is the question of whether or not reciprocity is possible between the describer and the described as scholarly partners.

The relationship between the two is particularly difficult and complex when the described are literate and have a "native" (henceforth used without quotation marks) tradition of scholarship that may be evoked to challenge the describer's authority. In my earlier work written in Japanese (Kuwayama 1997a), I examined this problem by noting the power inequality between the describer and the described, or more generally, the dimension of power in cultural representation. Briefly, I argued that native discourse has been underestimated because anthropology constitutes a "world-system," in which the United States, Great Britain, and France are positioned at the "center" or core. Their hegemonic power has relegated other countries, especially those with non-Western intellectual traditions, to the "periphery" or margin of the system. The relationship between the center and the periphery is not always one of domination and subjugation, but the inequality of power involved has made it difficult to engage in dialogue on an equal basis. (For readers who cannot read Japanese, my article is summarized in the Appendix to this chapter.)

In what follows, I expand on this argument and examine the "politics" regarding the production, dissemination, and consumption of knowledge about other cultures on a global scale. In the first section, I discuss the concept of "world-system" by responding to the critiques made by Jan van Bremen (Bremen 1997) and others, who read my article in the original and raised important questions. They were instrumental in making my thesis known outside Japan.[2] While the focus of the first section is the relationship between the center and the periphery in the "world-system," that of the second section is the relationship between peripheries in Asia. The main purpose of this paper is to raise awareness of the imbalance of power in anthropological practice and of various problems that result from it, rather than offering concrete solutions.

The Center and the Periphery in the "World-System" of Anthropology

Before getting down to specifics, I must acknowledge my debt to the late Swedish anthropologist Tomas Gerholm, whose work inspired me in developing my ideas. In his article "Sweden: Central ethnology, peripheral anthropology," Gerholm (1995: 159) wrote, "Both ethnology and anthropology have enough practitioners internationally for us to be able to speak of a world-system of ethnology and a world-system of anthropology. These world-systems of academic disciplines, just like any world-system, have their centers and their peripheries." In another article, which was coauthored with Ulf Hannerz, Gerholm further stated:

> It seems that the map of the discipline shows a prosperous mainland of British, American and French anthropologies, and outside it an archipelago of large and small islands – some of them connected to the mainland by sturdy bridges or frequent ferry traffic, others rather isolated. On the mainland, people can go through their professional lives more or less unaware of what happens on the islands. The reverse seems not so often to be the case. If international anthropology to a great extent equals American + British + French anthropology, in other words, then these national anthropologies need hardly take external influences into account to more than a very limited degree. (Gerholm and Hannerz 1982: 6. Quoted in Gerholm 1995: 159-60)

Below, I first take up the critiques of the notion of the "world-system" of anthropology, especially those made by van Bremen. His main criticism concerns the monolith and static image of the "world-system." As he wrote, "The problem in Kuwayama's analysis [and that of Gerholm and Hannerz as quoted above] is the excessive weight given to center-periphery relations and positions and the static view taken of them" (Bremen 1997: 62). He also stated, "More disturbing is Kuwayama's suggestion that there is an inherent discord between peripheral native and dominant center anthropologists" (ibid.). Gordon Mathews, an American who teaches in Hong Kong, made a similar point. He commented that, instead of a single center and a single periphery, there are a few centers and multiple peripheries, and that most anthropologists, regardless of their nationality, feel more or less marginalized relative to a small number of heroes at the dominant centers (personal communication). Van Bremen and Mathews were probably not alone in pointing out the need to reconsider the binarism posited in the "world-system." Obviously, this binarism parallels oppositions like the West/the Rest, colonizer/colonized, and us/them.

To clarify my position, I will focus on three issues here. First, my original thesis implied, though did not make explicit, the plurality of the center and of the periphery. To begin with the former, I maintained, following Gerholm and Hannerz, that the center of the "world-system" of anthropology is located in *three* countries – the United States, Great Britain, and France. Besides the fact that these constitute three centers rather than one, it is important to note the differences between them. Since it is obvious that France belongs to a tradition different from that of the United States and Great Britain, I compare the United States and Great Britain. In Japanese studies, the British are generally more interested in collaborating with Japanese and other European scholars than are Americans. For example, Joy Hendry (1998: 2) noted that a major strength of her edited volume, *Interpreting Japanese Society* (2nd edition), lies in the collaboration between Japanese and European scholars. She compared this feature with the "rather closed American literature" (ibid.) on Japan. Also, Harumi Befu (1992: 28) remarked that scholarly communication is naturally more intensive within the same linguistic community than between different communities, but that the Europeans "tend to be much more aware of scholarship in the United States than Americans scholars are aware of European scholarship on Japan." These comments in no way blame Americans for being "parochial." They suggest, however, that with the largest anthropological organization in the world, the United States is by far the most powerful of the three core countries. Because of their dominant position, Americans may ignore foreign scholarship without seriously risking their careers.

Second, regarding the plurality of the periphery in the "world-system," it should be noted that Japan is not the only marginalized country. On the contrary, many small European countries, to say nothing of the majority of non-Western countries, are in a similar situation to Japan. Unfortunately, the internal diversity of Europe has all too often been overlooked because of the all-inclusive word "the West." It is important to remember that "the West" is a relational concept that has meaning only in comparison with, or in opposition to, other categories such as "the East." In a way similar to the relativist conception of culture, it dramatizes the differences between the West and the non-West, while minimizing the differences within the West. In other words, the notion of "the West" homogenizes the Euro-American Self as it constructs an Other called "the East" or "the Orient." The homogenized "West" has made it difficult to see the different, sometimes competing, traditions of anthropology in Europe and the United States. Significantly, the critique by Gerholm and Hannerz of the "world-system" came from the periphery within the dominant West. The complexity of Asia will be examined later.

Finally, marginalization within the center is different from marginalization on the periphery. This point is critical to an understanding of the "world-system." In American anthropology, the study of Japan has been pushed toward the periphery for a variety of reasons, and Japan specialists have long suffered a sense of alienation. (For that matter, we might even complain about the marginal status of anthropology as a discipline throughout the world!) Yet their marginalization has taken place within the most powerful center of the world's anthropologies. And their objections, as well as their demand for more respect, take place in the context of competition for access to power that is hardly available to those on the periphery. Thus, even if successful, their contestation will merely replicate the existing power structure of the "world-system" and may even strengthen the dominance of the center over the periphery. Indeed, it may end up in an increase in the power, small as it is at the center but not negligible *vis-à-vis* the periphery, which American specialists of Japan already have over their native counterparts in the international community. By contrast, the objection to marginalization voiced by peripheral scholars has seldom reached the center, but it does have the potential to change the power structure itself. In this regard, "resistance" on the periphery is "transformative" and "counterhegemonic" (cf. Dirks, Eley, and Ortner 1994: 18-19).[3]

Another line of criticism of the "world-system" concerns my view of Japan as peripheral. Van Bremen (Bremen 1997) argued strongly that Japanese anthropology is not as marginal as is commonly thought. To support his view, he cited three Japanese anthropologists who (in his opinion) had influenced their Western colleagues, especially in the study of Southeast Asia: Mabuchi Tôichi (1910-1988), Nakane Chie (b. 1926), and Tanabe Shigeharu (b. 1943). According to van Bremen, when Rodney Needham formulated his theory of "dual sovereignty," he drew on Mabuchi's 1964 work, "Spiritual Predominance of the Sister." Van Bremen also contended that this article, along with another paper by Mabuchi, inspired Claude Lévi-Strauss when he wrote Chapter 11 of *The View from Afar* (where Mabuchi is mentioned only once in passing). In addition, van Bremen remarked that Tanabe's book *Ecology and*

Practical Technology (1994) has been internationally acclaimed as a major achievement in the study of Thai society. As for Nakane, she is a major figure in structural functionalism, and is widely known as the author of *Garo and Khasi* (1967) and *Japanese Society* (1970). Therefore, van Bremen (1997: 60) maintained, "Japanese anthropology is not so marginal, certainly in Asia, where over the past century it has been a veritable presence." He then pointed to "the need to be more precise and inclusive in one's statements about the place of Japanese anthropology in the world" (ibid.).

This criticism is pertinent, and Japan may better be called "semi-peripheral" than peripheral. In terms of numbers, Japanese anthropology is neither negligible nor powerless, given a membership of around 2,000 academics in the Japanese Society of Cultural Anthropology. Also, in terms of research and teaching, Japan has had some influence over its Asian neighbors, especially China and Korea, from which many students have come to study ethnology or anthropology since the days of Japan's colonial rule. These facts show that while Japan is peripheral to the center, it is central within the periphery, so that it should be defined as "semi-peripheral." While this definition has the advantage of reflecting the Asian reality more accurately, it is like calling the Japanese "honorable whites" in apartheid because of their economic power. As such, it has the disadvantage of overlooking the inequalities that do exist between Japan and the core Western countries, thus concealing the power dimension of the "world-system" of anthropology.

Perhaps the most difficult problem that faces anthropologists working on the periphery is the use of a non-native language, especially one that is completely different from their own, such as English for the Japanese. This difficulty does not simply relate to language fluency or lack thereof; rather, it relates to the social construction of language, and more importantly, to inequalities in the power of different languages in relation to the dominant forms of discourse (cf. Asad 1986: 156-60). As long as the dominant anthropological discourse is constructed using the languages of the core countries (i.e., English and to a lesser extent French), knowledge that is considered "authentic" and "legitimate" is more easily obtained and produced in those languages than in others. Conversely, knowledge more easily amenable to peripheral languages, including Japanese, tends to be devalued and considered a lesser asset *unless* it is successfully related to the dominant discourse. Thus, "local knowledge," to use the celebrated phrase of Clifford Geertz, may be appreciated only when it is rendered intelligible to the center.

Herein lies a major source of discontent among peripheral/native scholars. On the one hand, they must conform to the dominant discourse at the center in order to be recognized. It inevitably influences, if not determines, the choice of the language and style in which to present their arguments, as well as of the theories and methods they use. The power imbalance between the center and the periphery is such that only those who are familiar with the major academic traditions at the center (usually those people who have studied there) can manage to meet these demands. This structure produces a result that is desired on neither side of the system – Anglo-Americanization of peripheral/native anthropologists with a slight French flavor. It explains why these scholars seem lacking in originality: they feel compelled to develop and express their ideas according to the Anglo-American (and also French) pattern in order to reach the international community beyond their own. However, whatever originality they may have tends to be lessened or lost in the very process of Anglo-Americanization. Thus, anthropologists outside the core countries are caught in a "Catch 22" situation.

Discourses constructed in different languages and drawing on different intellectual traditions have merits of their own. It is unlikely that anthropologists who practice cultural relativism in "the field" when doing fieldwork miss this point. However, their respect for difference is frequently lost upon their departure for home. What we see instead is a judgment of foreign discourses, and even the act of ranking them, according to home standards. A case in point is the review process for major journals in the core Western countries. As Pamela Asquith (1998: 19) has shown, taking the example of Japanese primatology, submissions from peripheral scholars tend to be ranked low because the authors are not familiar enough with the central discourse to make their arguments impressive. Even when their papers are accepted for publication, editors often ask them to make changes, in style or content or both, in order to render their ideas intelligible to the readers.[4] This practice poses a great dilemma for peripheral/native scholars because conformity to the center may be derided as imitative, whereas nonconformity will likely result in dismissals of their work for being incomprehensible. The late Edwin Reischauer (1988: 200) captured this dilemma when he wrote, "The Japanese are often accused of being intellectually not very creative ... When thinkers have drawn more heavily from native Japanese inspiration, as in the case of the philosopher Nishida Kitaro in the first half of the twentieth century, who was strongly influenced by Zen concepts, the rest of the world has not been much impressed."

This dilemma bears a close parallel to Third World novels. The literary critic Masao Miyoshi observed in his book *Off Center* that texts written by Third World writers produce an acute sense of difference and even discomfort in First World readers. To domesticate or neutralize the exoticism of the texts, the First World will try to tame them according to its own pattern. If the texts turn out to be intransigent, however, they will be dismissed as inferior products. As Miyoshi (1991: 9) wrote:

> Every experience of reading a marginal text is at least potentially upsetting. When a Third World text is read in the First World, the sense of unfamiliarity is often marked, and the reader's discomfort is proportion-

ately acute. To restore the accustomed equilibrium, the reader either domesticates or neutralizes the exoticism of the text. The strategy of domestication is to exaggerate the familiar aspects of the text and thereby disperse its discreteness in the hegemonic sphere of First World literature ... Third World texts will be tamed, with the hegemony of the First World conferring the needed authority. Should a particular sample happen to be intransigent, it can always be rejected as an inferior product. The principle of canonicity never fails. The experience of reading a foreign text is nearly always transformed into an act of self-reaffirmation.

The view that Japanese anthropology is not marginal should be examined in this context. The three scholars cited earlier as examples of Japan's international influence – Mabuchi, Nakane, and Tanabe – have been acclaimed, not just because they are excellent, but because they wrote in English. A more crucial factor, though, is their familiarity with European and American anthropologies, which has enabled them to think and write in terms familiar to the people who have the power to determine their value in the international market (Kuwayama 1997c). Many other brilliant anthropologists in Japan have remained unknown abroad because they lack the qualities that have brought the international recognition to their more fortunate colleagues.

This is not to say, of course, that all scholarly work is of equal value. On the contrary, there are both good and bad writings in any academic community, whether central or peripheral. Poor-quality scholarship that does not even deserve domestic attention is not an issue. The problem arises, however, when there is *a consistent pattern of neglect* regardless of the quality of research. When this neglect is justified by the assumption that only the West is able to produce knowledge that is worth dissemination – and here I am putting aside the differences within the West that have been discussed – we may say that it is ideologically motivated. By "ideology" I mean a discourse that serves to "establish and sustain relations of domination" (Thompson 1990: 56). As such, ideology legitimizes the power of a dominant group or groups, which in our context refer to those situated at the center of the "world-system."[5]

In a different context, Henrietta Moore (1996) asked, "Who are the producers of knowledge?" Moore contended that although anthropologists acknowledge non-Western peoples as producers of knowledge about cosmological theories and medical cures, for example, they have seldom considered non-Western knowledge useful outside the local context. As Moore contended, this failure to recognize different Others as producers of knowledge that may provide alternatives to existing Western theories, is, ironically, also to be observed among deconstructivists or postmodernists who insist on the partial and local nature of all theories. Moore (1996: 3) could have been speaking for myself when she remarked,

41

Anthropologists from the developing world, for example, may produce theoretically innovative work, but if they claim that it draws on theoretical traditions outside mainstream western social science, they are likely to find that it will be denigrated as partial and/or localized. If they are critical of western social science, they may find that they are sidelined. Western social science consistently repositions itself as the originary point of comparative and generalizing theory.

Akhil Gupta and James Ferguson (1997: 27) made a strikingly similar observation:

In most standard accounts of the history of anthropological theory, the canonical narrative examines the relationship between national traditions of anthropology only in the United States, Britain, and France. Other national traditions are marginalized by the workings of geopolitical hegemony, experienced as a naturalized common sense of academic "center" and "periphery." Anthropologists working at the "center" learn quickly that they can ignore what is done in peripheral sites at little or no professional cost, while any peripheral anthropologist who similarly ignores the "center" puts his or her professional competence at issue.

I must hasten to add that the works of Moore (1996) and Gupta and Ferguson (1997) came to my attention after my article on native anthropologists (Kuwayama 1997a) was published. I make this trifle observation lest I be accused of plagiarism. This fact, while the reverse would hardly apply, attests to the power difference between the center (Great Britain and the United States) and the periphery (Japan) that Moore and Gupta and Ferguson have problematized.[6]

There are certainly problems in dividing the world into center and periphery and conceptualizing their relationship as one of binary opposition in which there is little interaction. We must remember that there is always an exchange between them, whether academic or personal, and no individual, however powerful, is completely free from an external influence. A dualistic model, including my conception of the "world-system," has the weakness of overlooking this complex, fluid reality. Also, we should note that the link between scholars at the center and those on the periphery is often stronger than that between central or peripheral scholars with each other. As Immanuel Wallerstein (1979: 102) pointed out, elites in central and peripheral countries tend to form a symbiotic relationship.[7] Generally, however, from the standpoint of the periphery, the interaction just mentioned has been initiated, if not imposed, by the powerful center, and reflects the will of people situated at the center, whether made explicit or not. It is, therefore, very important to not lose sight of the power inequalities and of the concomitant relations of domination in the intellectual community of the world.[8]

Relations on the Periphery in the "World-System": The Asian Case

I now turn from center-periphery relations in the "world-system" to the relations among peripheries in Asia. The first point we must make about Asia is that "there is no Asian in Asia" (Kuwayama 1994). "Asia" or "the Orient" is a concept that only has meaning in relation to "non-Asia" or "the Occident." Its internal diversity makes it difficult to lump together all the countries located in the region and to label them as "Asian" as if there were some sort of unity among them. The same is true, as we have already discussed, with "the West" and also with such categories as "Hispanic" (Oboler 1995). However, the complexity of Asia far surpasses that of any other region of the world, especially in terms of language and religion. If we take the example of East Asia, the most meaningful distinction is whether one is Chinese or Korean or Japanese. Any sense of solidarity that Asians may have as a group will emerge only when they are pitted against or compared with Americans, for example. It is important to remember the complex multiplicity of Asia because in the United States, and to a lesser extent in Europe, there is a "generalized Asian stereotype" (Johnson 1988: 8) that erases the vast differences between Asian countries.[9]

To illustrate this point, I briefly compare Japan with a few of its Asian neighbors. Japan is one of the few non-Western countries in the world in which almost all academic instruction is given in the national language from elementary to graduate schools. Obviously, this fact derives from Japan's modern history as an independent nation that escaped colonization by Western Europe and the United States. There is no denying the Western influence on Japan in every aspect of life, but it remains that, with so many translations of Western scholarship available in Japanese, intellectual activities *could* be conducted without using dominant European languages such as English. Thus, Japanese anthropologists, or for that matter scholars in any other field, can think and write in Japanese and continue to pursue their careers. Moreover, anthropology, which specializes in the study of other cultures, is a thriving field in Japan, where the slogans of "internationalization," or more recently, "globalization" are on the lips of the country's leaders. The large domestic market for anthropological books, both at the professional and nonprofessional levels, has even made some anthropologists (e.g., Umesao Tadao, Nakane Chie, and Yamaguchi Masao) national figures.

All this points to the fortunate situation in which Japanese anthropologists find themselves. There is, however, an opposite side to the picture: what is fortunate inside Japan is a misfortune outside it. Because the Japanese can easily find an outlet for their writings domestically, they do not feel the need to write and publish in the dominant languages of the world, even though Japanese academics know very well that, as long as their publications remain in Japanese, the rest of the world will not comment on them. The only exception may be books on Korea, which, according to Ito Abito (1996: 8-9), are

43

often subjected to the scrutiny of Koreans who suspect an Orientalist bias on the part of their former colonizers. It is only natural then that Japanese discussion tends to be self-contained and for "domestic consumption" only. The same may be said of Americans, but as already mentioned, their dominant position in the "world-system" means that what is domestic is also international.

The Japanese situation contrasts with that in Southeast Asia, where, despite its ethnic diversity, elites constitute a unified world through the use of a common language – English (Nakane 1987: 159). This linguistic unity, as well as a limited degree of intellectual unity that arises from it, has its roots in the unfortunate experience of colonization by the Western powers. Its positive side should not be overlooked, however. At international conferences, for example, Southeast Asian intellectuals are far more confident and eloquent than the Japanese, not simply because they speak better English, but because their Western-style intellectual training has made it possible for them to argue in ways that appeal to the Western-dominated world academic community. Perhaps one of the positive legacies of Western colonialism is that it has educated a class of local elites who know how to "talk back" to their colonizers using the colonizers' language.

I suspect that the "peculiar intimacy" between the colonizer and the colonized to which I have just alluded has contributed to the prominence of India and its adjacent countries in the world's anthropology. Although India was colonized by the British, the British were, unlike the Japanese, victors in World War II, and many of the leading figures in postwar India were educated at prestigious universities in Great Britain. Speaking English with an educated British accent is in fact a distinct marker of social prestige. From this background have emerged personal networks of intellectuals between the two countries (regions), which go beyond the simple binarism of the colonizer/ruler and the colonized/ruled. In particular, the familiarity of Indians with discourse at the center of the "world-system" on the one hand and their colonial experience on the other has enabled them to theorize their "otherness" – the Indian Self as the Other to European Others – by using the language of the colonizers. ("Language" should be understood here not merely as a medium of communication, but rather as a totality that expresses the "world view" of the people who use it). Referring to Homi Bhabha's exposition of "hybridity," Chen (1998: 23) wrote, "Although the colonizer looks down on [the colonized], the latter can still use the colonizer's language to insert denied knowledge and traditions into the dominant discursive space, and in turn, the colonizer's unfamiliarity with this whole set of cultural codes puts the colonizer in crisis, and hence undoes his authority." It would not be a mistake to say then that although colonization by the Western powers has been an unfortunate experience, it has nevertheless worked in some positive ways, as is shown in the prominence of Indian scholars in postcolonial studies. Japanese intellectuals, too, have had a similar colonial experience since the middle of the nineteenth century, but Japan's fortunate past as a politically independent nation (except for a short period after World War II) has ironically worked against them in making themselves understood by the outside world.

Not only was Japan independent, but it also had its own colonies in Asia. Indeed Japan's colonial past, which has no parallel outside Western Europe and the United States, has left deep scars in East and Southeast Asia. Like European anthropology, Japanese ethnology/anthropology was a product of colonialism, but its reputation was damaged more strongly than its Western counterparts because of the harshness of Japanese colonial rule.[10] Even today, I have heard that there are some Korean scholars who refuse to use data the Japanese collected during the colonial period, however academically valuable, because of the hard feelings that still remain against the Japanese (see Kim's paper in this volume). Parenthetically, in Korea and China, there is a division, if not a conflict, between Western-trained, Japanese-trained, and home-trained anthropologists.

This cursory review makes it clear that not only is the Asian intellectual community diverse, but that there is also not much substance in the notion of a unified "Asian anthropology." (Note that this term is used here in the singular as distinguished from "Asian anthropologies" in the plural.) At least, it is something in the making, not a reality yet, which reflects the growing awareness among Asian scholars that it is time to make a social science of their own that is free from Eurocentrism.[11] There is, however, one thing that unites Asian anthropologists. This is the fact that all of them belong to the periphery in the "world-system" as discussed in the previous section. The complex relations between anthropologies in Asia may only be understood by considering their peripheral status *vis-à-vis* the center.

As Gerholm and Hannerz pointed out, the relationship between the center and the periphery in the "world-system" may be likened to that between the mainland and remote islands. People on the mainland can go through their life more or less unaware of what happens on the islands, but island people can only live in relation to the mainland. Because of the overwhelming importance of the mainland, the island people have been eager to form ties with it, but have paid only inadequate attention to the relationships *among* themselves. Thus, to borrow the metaphor of Gerholm and Hannerz, there is frequent "ferry traffic" between the mainland and the islands, but the latter have been isolated from each other.

The mutual ignorance and indifference among Asian anthropologists may be explained from this point of view. Not only do they not know each other well, but only a few of them have made serious efforts to improve the situation. Unfortunately, the intellectual distance between Asian countries is far greater than that between Asia and Europe or America. Geographic proximity does not always bring about intellectual exchange. To give an example, very few Japanese anthropologists are familiar with scholarship in Korea, Japan's closest neighbor. Since 1968, the Korean Society for Cultural Anthropology has been publishing a journal called *Han'guk munwha illyuhak* [Korean Cultural Anthropology]. One volume I happened to see (i.e., Volume 26, 1994) contains a special thematic section on food. In this appears an article entitled "Some foods are good to think with: *Kimchi* and the essence of national identity," which was written by Han Kyung-koo. Using Emiko Ohnuki-Tierney's widely read book *Rice as Self* (1993), Han showed how the Koreans' favorite food *kimchi* (pickles made of Chinese cabbage with hot red pepper) was invented and appropriated as Korea's national symbol in the process of building a modern nation-state.[12] Han's article is of particular interest to the Japanese in two respects. First, *kimchi* became popular in Japan from the mid-1980s, and it is today a familiar item in the Japanese diet. This fact illustrates a sea change that has occurred in the two countries' relationships, for until recently *kimchi* was a symbol of the Japanese contempt for Koreans. The question of what *kimchi* signifies within and across nations is scholarly interesting. Second, Ohnuki-Tierney is one of the few internationally known anthropologists who was born and educated in Japan. In Han's work, we can see a starting point for an intellectual dialogue between Korea and Japan on the one hand and, via Ohnuki-Tierney, between the United States and the Far East on the other. Such a dialogue has the potential of overcoming the double barrier between mainland and islands on the one hand, and among islands, on the other.

Carol Gluck's (1995: 36) observation about Japanese historiography applies neatly to anthropologies in Asia. As she points out, Japanese historians have long been engaged in a conceptual exchange with Western historians. Although the "balance of trade" has always been in favor of the West due to the one-way traffic of translations, there has still been a sustained and active intellectual exchange between the two regions. This fact has brought about surprising similarities between Western and Japanese historiographies. By contrast, Gluck says, the trade between Japan and the rest of Asia has been virtually nonexistent. The need to establish or reestablish commonality in Asia has been recognized, but much of the task still remains to be done.

Regarding the relations of domination involved in the "world-system," Asian anthropologists, and for that matter those in any other peripheral region, should be cautious of the danger of cultural nationalism. As the political scientist Hans Kohn (1995 [1944]) pointed out during World War II, developing countries in modern times have often been trapped in a cultural nationalism that stresses their distinctiveness and even spiritual superiority over rivals that are materially more powerful. A look at prewar Germany and Japan shows how destructive the consequences of cultural nationalism can be. In particular, Japan's search for spiritual autonomy and political independence

46

from the West (e.g., the idea of the "family state" centered on Emperor worship) brought about what may be called an "anachronistic fantasy." This point is very important to remember because culture and politics are inseparably related, as Ernest Gellner (1983) and Nishikawa Nagao (1992) among others have shown. The quest for cultural (including academic) autonomy may easily be politicized. If the problems of European and American anthropologies come from their colonial past, the problems of Asian anthropologies stem from nationalism or nationalization of culture.

The aforementioned attempt to create an "Asian social science" free from Eurocentrism is understandable, given the subordinate role Asia has been forced to play in modern history. However, if this attempt, out of national (regional) pride, refuses to see the power inequalities that undoubtedly exist between Asia and Euro-America, it will merely result in a utopian struggle. And if the refusal to see the reality of power leads to the wishful thinking that an Asian science can be created without drawing on the intellectual legacy of the West, it will be self-defeating. For there is no modern, indigenous system of thought that has not been influenced in one way or another by Western science. A quintessential example is that of Yanagita Kunio, the founder of Japanese folklore studies, who is commonly thought to have drawn on Japan's native tradition. He in fact was an avid reader of books written by European ethnologists.[13] In the academic "world-system," the periphery is enmeshed with and dependent upon the center in much the same way as the countryside is connected with urban centers in the modern state. Denying this relationship dogmatically or attempting to subvert it without a sufficient basis of power may have the effect of satisfying temporarily the heightened sense of national (regional) pride, but in the long run it may merely damage one's intellectual potential.

A more practical and fruitful approach is, in my mind, to accept the core countries' achievement as the common heritage of all anthropologists throughout the world. Just because E. E. Evans-Pritchard, for instance, was British and his bust is displayed at the University of Oxford does not mean that he belongs exclusively to the British; rather, he left us a legacy on which to build better theories for a better understanding of human beings. It certainly injures the pride of Asians that their intellectual ancestors have not been regarded as highly as Evans-Pritchard, even if they were of his caliber, but origin is not the most important thing. After all, great ideas transcend ethnic and national boundaries and refuse to be identified with a particular group or nation.

This is not to say, of course, that anthropologists of the center can be complacent about their past achievements. They should, first of all, become aware of their privileged position and understand that the plight of peripheral anthropologists is not solely their responsibility, but often comes from the unwillingness of the people at the center to listen to the voices from the margin.

Conclusion

In this chapter, I have delivered two different messages to two different audiences. My message to the anthropologists of the center, in the United States, Great Britain, and France, is a plea to realize, first, that their overwhelming power has created relations of domination and subordination in anthropological practice; and, second, that because of their dominant position they have suppressed the voices from the margin, if not intentionally. To peripheral anthropologists in Asia and other regions, my message is about the danger of becoming nationalistic or even chauvinistic and of dogmatically rejecting everything Western (i.e., the central discourse) in the desire to be intellectually independent.

With the globalization of anthropology, the anthropological self – that which observes and describes other cultures – has diversified. Anthropology is no longer the monopoly of a few major countries in the West. It is practiced today in many other countries in many other regions, including Asia, which used to be objects of anthropological inquiry. Under these circumstances, we have no Anthropology with a capital A. Instead, we have a multiplicity of anthropologies. The attempt to create an "Asian social science" is just one example of the fundamental changes that are taking place in the "world-system."

This does not mean, however, that the gravity of power is shifting from the core Western countries to elsewhere. On the contrary, we may say that they are strengthening their hold as the main generator of the globalizing forces. As I emphasized throughout, there are *persisting* inequalities between the center and the periphery, and no analysis of anthropological practice would be complete without considering this fact. Theorizing the complex flow of knowledge that has been caused by globalization without losing sight of the power inequalities involved is called for. My approach to the "world-system" is an attempt at such theorization.

Appendix

Below is an English summary of my article mentioned in the Introduction (Kuwayama 1997a). This summary appeared at the end of the Japanese original. It gives the gist of my argument, but is not long enough to cover the details. Interested readers should refer to its extended version (Kuwayama 1997b) or a full-length article that was subsequently published (Kuwayama 2000).

Despite the recent research focus on reflexivity in fieldwork experience, little has been said about what happens when natives read what anthropologists have written about them. In particular, the relationship between Western anthropologists and native anthropologists in the non-West has been almost completely unexplored. Native anthropologists are a special kind of other whom Westerners encounter in fieldwork: they have the professional competence to engage in scholarly dialogue, but they are part of the cultural community under study. In this regard, native anthropologists may be defined as "professional Others."

In *Argonauts of the Western Pacific*, Bronislaw Malinowski argued that, since "primitives" are unable to explain their own customs and manners, they must be studied and described by professionally trained Westerners. He also contended that if natives could offer a systematic analysis of themselves, there would be no difficulty in ethnological work (Malinowski 1984 [1922]: 11-12; 396-97; 453-54). Putting aside his Orientalist outlook on the world, I question Malinowski's view in light of the controversy that often arises between Western and native anthropologists. As Japanese criticisms of Ruth Benedict's *The Chrysanthemum and the Sword* show, native anthropologists are often fierce critics of Western analyses and interpretations of their culture.

In this article, I argue that this discord is derived from the structure of anthropological knowledge, rather than from personal and emotional conflict. More specifically, I submit that native scholars' dissent is related to the marginal role assigned to them in what I call the "world-system" of anthropology. In this system, the "core" is occupied by the United States, Great Britain, and France, which have the power to determine the kinds of desired knowledge in anthropology. Put another way, they dictate the anthropological discourse with which scholars from "peripheral" countries must comply if they wish to be recognized. I further contend that in ethnographic representation, natives (those who are represented) are posited, but not spoken to, and that their exclusion is another source of discontent among native anthropologists, who are emotionally involved in matters that concern the natives. During fieldwork, natives are eagerly approached for the information they can provide ethnographers, but once fieldwork is over and the writing of research results begins, they are no longer addressed because the audience in ethnographic writing is the academic community to which the researcher belongs. The scholarly value of an ethnography is determined not by those who have been observed and described, but those in a faraway land who may feign indifference to the adverse consequences that the representation may entail. The political basis for this "predatory" relationship has been Western hegemony in the modern colonial system.

In order to strike a balance of power, a forum is necessary that would allow Western and native anthropologists to engage in fruitful dialogue on an equal basis. For this purpose, I propose that ethnographic representation be made as "open" as possible. By "open," I mean, first of all, the kind of representation that posits a diverse audience, both native and non-native, which contrasts with the "closed" representation that has assumed, as in the past, a homogeneous audience from one's own cultural community. "Open" representation will also permit "coauthorship" by the observer and the observed, as has already been experimented with in the construction of life histories, and even "plural authorship," in which ethnographic texts may be written by more than one person, with the authors taking turns writing and reading to produce an open-ended forum for dialogue in the manner of a computer conference. If this idea is unrealistic, we may, as an interim alternative, consider publishing a new journal, whether in print or on the Internet, in which native scholars comment on articles by non-native scholars, who in turn reply to the comments they have received, thereby reconceptualizing their ethnographic observations in both native and non-native contexts. Given the fact that Japan is one of the few non-Western countries in which anthropology is established as a profession, and given its rich economic resources, this type of journal is worth serious consideration. It would also help Japanese studies play a leading role in future anthropological discourse, in which native anthropology is likely to emerge as a major issue as we enter the postcolonial era.

Notes

1   An earlier version of this paper appeared as chapter 3 of my book, *Native Anthropology* (Kuwayama 2004: 48-63).
2   My article entitled "Native anthropologists: With special reference to Japanese studies inside and outside Japan," appeared in *Minzokugaku-kenkyû*, the journal for the Japanese Society of Ethnology, in 1997. Because the use of Japanese is limited internationally, I posted an English summary of this article on an Internet mailing list called EASIANTH (East Asian Anthropology). In the period of about a week, I received response from approximately 30 scholars from different parts of the world. Also, my posting triggered a lively discussion on the Internet and subsequently in print. In particular, Jan van Bremen (Leiden University, the Netherlands) read my article in the original and wrote a critique, which later appeared, along with my reply, in the newsletter of Japan Anthropology Workshop (JAWS), a British-based organization of Japanese studies (Bremen 1997; Kuwayama 1997c). Later still, Pamela Asquith (University of Alberta, Canada) contributed an article to the same newsletter, in which she discussed the politics of knowledge production by taking the example of Japanese primatology (Asquith 1998; 1999). To further examine the issues, a panel was organized under the title of "Japanese Disciplinary Perspectives and International Discourses" as part of the 12th JAWS meeting,

which was held at the National Museum of Ethnology in Osaka, 1999. In 2000, the results of this panel were published in *The Ritsumeikan Journal of Asia Pacific Studies* (volume 6), in which appeared the English version of "Native Anthropologists" (Kuwayama 2000). The English version is also included as chapter 2 of my book, *Native Anthropology* (Kuwayama 2004: 15-47).

3 As Nicholas Dirks, Geoff Eley, and Sherry Ortner (1994: 19) stated, "The difference between competing for access within an already constituted system and transforming the system itself" is familiar to "subordinate or marginalized groups as they seek to contest the power of hegemonic formations, whether these are constituted within academic disciplines, particular institutional fields, or at the level of whole societies."

4 A fuller exposition of Asquith's thesis has appeared in her recent work (Asquith 1999). For a perceptive critique of how Japanese primatology has been treated in the West, see Asquith (1996). Also, in the introduction to *Trajectories* (1998), the editor Kuan-Hsing Chen criticized the "hegemony of the English language and the controlled circulation of publications" (Chen 1998: 5). According to Chen, when the manuscripts of a book he had edited were reviewed by some Western publishers, "one of the interested publishers responded that if we got rid of the Asian names, then they would do it" (Chen 1998: xvii). This episode suggests that not only is foreign discourse at a disadvantage, but that foreign names, especially unfamiliar Asian names, are considered a sort of "stigma" in the English-language publishing industry.

5 Chapter 1 of John Thompson's *Ideology and Modern Culture* (1990) provides a most useful review of the concept of ideology from a Marxist perspective. Also useful is Terry Eagleton's (1991: 1-31) overview of the subject. As is often pointed out, one of the best known formulations of ideology in anthropology, that of Clifford Geertz who defined ideology as a "cultural system," overlooks the dimension of power and domination, which is critical to an understanding of the "world-system."

6 Furthermore, the fact that there was no reference, in either Moore or Gupta and Ferguson, to Gerholm and Hannerz (1982), is another testimony to the scant attention central anthropologists pay to the periphery. Gerholm's and Hannerz's article appeared in *Ethnos*, an English-language journal that used to be published in Sweden.

7 Wallerstein (1979: 102) has this to say about the bourgeoisie in semi-peripheral countries: "The degree to which this [semi-peripheral] indigenous bourgeoisie is structurally linked to corporations located in the core countries varies, but the percentage tends to be far larger than is true of the bourgeoisie within any core country; indeed, this is one of the defining characteristics that differentiates a contemporary core and 'non-socialist' semiperipheral country."

8 There is an interesting parallel here to postcolonial studies. Earlier theories posited irreducible binary oppositions, such as colonizer/colonized, domination/subordination, and center/margin. Recent analysis, however, has shifted from this rigid binarism to a more flexible model that accommodates "cultural exchange" and "peculiar intimacy" between the two parties. As Bill Ashcroft, Gareth Griffiths, and Helen Tiffin (1995: 86) stated, "Theorizing this complex 'intimacy' without giving away the fact of persisting and historic *inequalities* within those relations and structures [of colonialism] is perhaps *the* major focus of contemporary postcolonial theory" (italics in the original).

9 The "generalized Asian stereotype" emphasizes those characteristics, usually racial and cultural, that distinguish Asians from white Americans. Thus, the differences between "us" (white Americans) and "them" (Asians) are stressed to the neglect of the differences among "them," let alone the similarities that exist between "us" and "them" as members of the human species.

10 Even today, when more than half a century has passed since the end of World War II, the association between the Japanese word *minzokugaku* (ethnology) and Japanese imperialism has not disappeared completely, especially in Asian countries. For this and other complex reasons, it was proposed in 1995 that Japan's national association of cultural anthropologists should change its name from the Japanese Society of Ethnology to the Japanese Association of Cultural Anthropology. This proposition was turned down on several occasions after long deliberation, before finally being adopted in 2003. For the debate about the name change, see the records of the Japanese Society of Ethnology (1995a; 1995b; 1996; 1997), and Cheung's paper in this volume.

11 An outcome of this awareness was the formation of the Asia-Pacific Sociological Association in 1997. Its first annual meeting was held in Kuala Lumpur in Malaysia (Sugimoto 1997).

12 Although written in Korean, an English summary is attached to Han's article, like other articles in the volume. With the help of a Korean student, I was able to grasp the main points of Han's argument. As for Ohnuki-Tierney, she has translated her book *Rice as Self* into Japanese under the title of *Kome no jinruigaku* [The Anthropology of Rice] (Tokyo: Iwanami Shoten, 1995). In contrast to the high reputation of the English original in the United States, the latter has received only scant attention in Japan. This is just one example of the mutual indifference between American and Japanese anthropologists as discussed in my previous articles (Kuwayama 1997a; 2000). It also suggests that the language barrier alone does not explain why works acclaimed in one country are almost ignored in another and vice versa. The politics of knowledge is as important as the "poetics and politics of ethnography."

13 This is not to say that Yanagita freely borrowed European ethnologists' ideas without acknowledging them. He was an original thinker who developed a distinctive approach to the study of folklore, which was different from that of his European contemporaries in many respects. The fact remains, however, that Yanagita was familiar with the major works in European ethnology of his time and that he found it necessary to refer to them, whether positively or negatively, to establish his own tradition. With the power imbalance between the center and the periphery, it was imperative for him to begin with a critical analysis of European scholarship in order to create something new. Indeed, a careful reading of his book *Minkan denshôron* [The science of popular tradition] (Yanagita 1998 [1934]) reveals that Yanagita seldom failed to mention European scholars, most notably Charlotte Burne and James Frazer, when he discussed theoretically important ideas. His remarks, however, were usually critical and negative. Parenthetically, Yanagita had a degree of international influence. In a recent Korean textbook of folklore studies (Lee, Chang, and Lee 1991), for instance, his theories are introduced briefly.

References

Asad, Talal. 1986. "The concept of cultural translation in British social anthropology," pp. 141-164 in *Writing Culture: The Poetics and Politics of Ethnography,* James Clifford and George E. Marcus, eds. Berkeley: University of California Press.

Ashcroft, Bill, Gareth Griffiths and Helen Tiffin, eds. 1995. *The Post-Colonial Studies Reader.* London: Routledge.

Asquith, Pamela J. 1996. "Japanese science and Western hegemonies: Primatology and the limits set to questions," pp. 239-56 in *Naked Science: Anthropological Inquiry into Boundaries, Power, and Knowledge,* Laura Nader, ed. New York and London: Routledge.

Asquith, Pamela J. 1998. "The 'world-system' of anthropology from a primatological perspective: Comments on the Kuwayama-van Bremen debate," *Japan Anthropology Workshop Newsletter* 28: 16-27.

Asquith, Pamela J. 1999. "The 'world-system' of anthropology and 'professional others,'" pp. 31-49 in *Anthropological Theory in North America,* E. L. Cerroni-Long, ed. Westport, Conn.: Bergin & Garvey.

Befu, Harumi. 1992. "Introduction: Framework of analysis," pp. 15-35 in *Othernesses of Japan: Historical and Cultural Influences on Japanese Studies in Ten countries,* Harumi Befu and Joseph Kreiner, eds. Munich: Iudicium.

Bremen, Jan van. 1997. "Prompters who do not appear on the stage: Japanese anthropology and Japanese studies in American and European anthropology," *Japan Anthropology Workshop Newsletter* 26/27: 57-65.

Chen, Kuan-Hsing, ed. 1998. *Trajectories: Inter-Asia Cultural Studies.* London: Routledge.

Dirks, Nicholas B., Geoff Eley, and Sherry B. Ortner. 1994. "Introduction," pp. 3-45 in *Culture/Power/History: A Reader in Contemporary Social Theory,* Nicholas B. Dirks, Geoff Eley, and Sherry B. Ortner, eds. Princeton: Princeton University Press.

Eagleton, Terry. 1991. *Ideology: An Introduction.* London: Verso.

Gellner, Ernest. 1983. *Nations and Nationalism.* London: Blackwell.

Gerholm, Tomas. 1995. "Sweden: Central ethnology, peripheral anthropology," pp. 159-170 in *Fieldwork and Footnotes: Studies in the History of European Anthropology,* Hans F. Vermeulen and Arturo Alvarez Roldán, eds. London: Routledge.

Gerholm, Tomas, and Ulf Hannerz. 1982. "Introduction: The shaping of national anthropologies," *Ethnos* 47 (I-II): 5-35.

Gluck, Carol. 1995. "Sengo shigaku no metahisutori" [A meta-history of postwar historiography], pp. 3-43 in *Iwanami kôza Nihon tsûshi. Bekkan 1* [Iwanami Complete History of Japan. Supplementary vol.1], eds. Asao Naohiro et al. Tokyo: Iwanami Shoten.

Gupta, Akhil, and James Ferguson. 1997. "Discipline and practice: 'The field' as site, method, and location in anthropology," pp. 1-46 in *Anthropological Locations: Boundaries and Grounds of a Field Science,* Akhil Gupta and James Ferguson, eds. Berkeley: University of California Press.

Han Kyung-koo. 1994. "Otton eumsikeun saengkak hagie jota: Kimchiwa Han'guk minjokseong eu jeongsu" [Some food is good to think with: *Kimchi* and the essence of Korean national identity], *Han'guk munwha illyuhak* [Korean Cultural Anthropology] 26: 51-68.

Hendry, Joy. 1998. "Introduction: The contributions of social anthropology to Japanese studies," pp. 1-12 in *Interpreting Japanese Society: Anthropological Approaches* (2nd edition). Joy Hendry, ed. London: Routledge.

Ito Abito. 1996. *Kankoku* [Korea]. Tokyo: Kawade Shobô Shinsha.

Japanese Society of Ethnology. 1995a. *Gakkai meishô henkô teian kanren shiryô* [Material relating to the proposal for changing the name of the society.] Tokyo: Japanese Society of Ethnology.

Japanese Society of Ethnology. 1995b. *Fôramu* [Forum]. Tokyo: Japanese Society of Ethnology.

Japanese Society of Ethnology. 1996. *Fôramu* [Forum]. Tokyo: Japanese Society of Ethnology.

Japanese Society of Ethnology. 1997. *Gakkai meishô mondai nado kentô iinkai hôkoku* [A report by the investigative committee on the name change of the Society and other matters]. Tokyo: Japanese Society of Ethnology.

Johnson, Sheila K. 1988. *The Japanese through American Eyes.* Tokyo: Kodansha International.

Kohn, Hans. 1994 [1944]. "Western and eastern nationalisms," pp. 162-65 in

Nationalism, John Hutchinson and Anthony D. Smith, eds. Oxford: Oxford University Press.

Kuwayama, Takami. 1994. "Japan's place in the global community: Is Japan eastern or western?" *Virginia Geographer* 26: 1-10.

Kuwayama Takami. 1997a. "Genchi no jinruigakusha: Naigai no Nihon kenkyû o chûshin ni" [Native anthropologists: With special reference to Japanese studies inside and outside Japan], *Minzokugaku-kenkyû* (Japanese Journal of Ethnology), 61(4): 517-42.

Kuwayama,Takami. 1997b. "Native anthropologists: With special reference to Japanese studies inside and outside Japan," *Japan Anthropology Workshop Newsletter* 26/27: 52-56.

Kuwayama, Takami. 1997c. "Response to Jan van Bremen,"*Japan Anthropology Workshop Newsletter* 26/27: 66-69.

Kuwayama, Takami. 2000. "Native anthropologists: With special reference to Japanese studies inside and outside Japan," *Ritsumeikan Journal of Asia Pacific Studies,* 6: 7-33.

Kuwayama, Takami. 2004. *Native Anthropology.* Melbourne: Trans Pacific Press.

Lee Sa-Hyun, Chang Su-Kun, and Lee Kwang-Kyu. 1991. *An Introduction to Korean Folklore Studies: A New Edition.* Seoul: Il Cho Kak. (In Korean.)

Malinowski, Bronislaw. 1984 [1922]. *Argonauts of the Western Pacific.* Prospect Heights, Ill.: Waveland Press.

Miyoshi, Masao. 1991. *Off Center: Power and Culture Relations between Japan and the United States.* Cambridge, Mass.: Harvard University Press.

Moore, Henrietta L. 1996. "The changing nature of anthropological knowledge: An introduction," pp. 1-15 in *The Future of Anthropological Knowledge,* Henrietta L. Moore, ed. London: Routledge.

Nakane, Chie. 1967. *Garo and Khasi: A Comparative Study in Matrilineal Systems.* Paris and The Hague: Mouton.

Nakane, Chie. 1970. *Japanese Society.* London; Weidenfeld & Nicolson.

Nakane, Chie. 1987. *Shakai jinruigaku* [Social anthropology]. Tokyo: University of Tokyo Press.

Nishikawa Nagao. 1992. *Kokkyô no koekata* [Beyond national boundaries]. Tokyo: Chikuma Shobô.

Oboler, Suzanne. 1995. *Ethnic Labels, Latino Lives: Identity and the Politics of (Re)presentation in the United States.* Minneapolis, Minn.: University of Minnesota Press.

Ohnuki-Tierney, Emiko. 1993. *Rice as Self: Japanese Identities through Time.* Princeton: Princeton University Press.

Reischauer, Edwin O. 1988. *The Japanese Today: Change and Continuity.* Cambridge, Mass.: Harvard University Press.

Sugimoto Yoshio. 1997. "Ajia taiheiyô shakai gakkai tanjô" [The birth of the Asia-Pacific Sociological Association], *Asahi Shinbun* (evening edition).

October 29: 7.

Tanabe, Shigeharu. 1994. *Ecology and Practical Technology: Peasant Farming Systems in Thailand.* Bangkok: White Lotus.

Thompson, John B. 1990. *Ideology and Modern Culture: Critical Social Theory in the Era of Mass Communication.* Stanford: Stanford University Press.

Wallerstein, Immanuel. 1979. *The Capitalist World-Economy.* Cambridge: Cambridge University Press.

Yanagita Kunio. 1998 [1934]. "Minkan denshôron" [The science of folk tradition], pp. 3-194 in *Yanagita Kunio zenshû 8* [The complete works of Kunio Yanagita, Vol 8]. Tokyo: Chikuma Shobô.

Chapter 3

Debating the "Japanese" Race in Meiji Japan:

Towards a History of Early Japanese Anthropology[1]

David ASKEW

Introduction

In 1908, the medical doctor and amateur archaeologist, Neil Gordon Munro (1863-1942), published a work entitled *Prehistoric Japan* (Munro 1911 [1908]). Munro was a ship's doctor who landed on the shores of Yokohama in 1892 and in effect remained in Japan for the rest of his life, during which he also pursued his interests in archaeology, the Ainu, and the origins of the Japanese.[2] In his book, he argued that the Ainu were the original inhabitants of Japan: they had once populated the main islands of the archipelago, but had been pushed northwards by the arrival of the "alien Yamato" (Munro 1911 [1908]: 661). He also mentioned a third people, the Koro-pok-guru (which he romanized as Koropok-guru), whose existence had been proposed by Tsuboi Shôgorô (1863-1913), one of the founding fathers of Japanese anthropology. However, Munro was skeptical. "Neither in Honshu, nor in any other part of Japan, have the bones of a [Neolithic] race distinctly alien to the Ainu been unearthed from the shell-mounds [of Japan]," he stated, determining the Koro-pok-guru to be the product of "myth" (Munro 1911 [1908]: 670, 85). However, Munro was far less skeptical about other peoples. Indeed, he suggested that the "alien Yamato" should be viewed as a *mixed nation*, "a mixture of several distinct stocks," the product of a blend of "Negrito, Mongolian, Palasiatic and Caucasian features" (Munro 1911 [1908]: 676). Like many early anthropologists of the period, Munro assumed that *race* determined *class*, and that the modern history of the Western conquest of the non-West could be viewed through the prism of race and projected back onto the past.[3]

The leaders, if we may judge from the Caucasian and often Semitic physiognomy seen in the aristocratic type of Japanese, were partly of Caucasic [sic], perhaps Iranian, origin. Some support of this proposition is found in the *Haniwa*, which not seldom exhibit features inclined to the Caucasian ... type ... These were the warriors, the conquerors of Japan, and afterwards the aristocracy, modified to some extent by mingling with a Mongoloid rank and file and by a considerable addition of Ainu, that is to say, of Palasiatic (proto-Caucasian?), blood. (Munro 1911 [1908]: 679)

In other words, the domination of the twentieth century world by "the Caucasian ... type" was not merely a modern phenomenon, but universal in terms of both time and geography. The white ruling class and darker proletariat observed in Ireland by Beddoe was also discovered in Japan. S. B. Kemish (1860: 138), for example, noted that members of the Japanese ruling class boasted "complexions as fair and cheeks as ruddy as those of Europeans," while "vagabonds on the highways ... have a skin of a colour between copper and brown earthy hue."[4]

At almost the exact same time as Munro's heavy tome was launched on an unsuspecting public, James Murdoch (1856-1921), another Scotsman, published the first volume of his *A History of Japan*, entitled *From the Origins to the Arrival of the Portuguese in 1542 A.D.*[5] Here, Murdoch stated that the literature seemed to agree "that the earliest inhabitants of these islands [of Japan] were the Ainu – or the Yemishi [Emishi], as they are called in the oldest Japanese annals." The Ainu indigenes had been challenged for and deprived of their land by (Chinese) migrants who arrived via the Korean peninsula and settled in and around "Idzumo." Murdoch also argued for a prehistoric melting pot. Just as England had its Angles, Saxons, and Jutes, ancient Japan too could boast of a number of tribes. In addition to the migrants from the continent, others arrived from the south, and were "known at first as Kumaso and later as Hayato" (Murdoch 1996 [1910]: 47, 48, 50).[6] Like Munro, Murdoch claimed that the early Japanese nation was a product of miscegenation. Indeed, according to legend, this mix of blood was seen in "the first earthly generation of the Imperial line." Like Munro, he also described how this new, masculine and aggressive people had conquered Japan. "The combination of this branch of the [southern] Kumaso and the [continental or northern] Idzumo men proved irresistible; they pushed their conquests eastward along both shores of the Inland Sea, and ultimately established a strong central State in Yamato, at the expense of the aboriginal Ainu" (Murdoch 1996 [1910]: 51).

Thus the narratives of both Munro and Murdoch were based on the assumption of an ancient melting pot that produced the Japanese "race" or nation (*minzoku*), and on a hypothetical (pre)history of displacement, whereby an earlier indigenous people was vanquished by later migrants.[7] The work of both authors reflected a debate in Japan, in which some looked to the north and others to the south in an attempt to determine where the original Japanese came from.

This chapter will examine the debate on the Japanese race in Meiji Japan that produced these common assumptions by the start of the twentieth century. In addition to discussing the social construction of racial ideologies in Meiji Japan, I will attempt to provide an outline of the early anthropological debate on the Japanese race, focusing in particular on the work of the Westerners who introduced the methodologies and language of anthropology and related sciences such as archaeology to Japan.[8] First, however, in order to contextualize this debate, I discuss Japanese anthropology and the impact of the Japanese empire.

Colonialism and Orientalism: Anthropologists in Japan and Japanese Anthropologists

Residents of the large metropolitan areas of the Great Japanese Empire consumed the products of that empire, and basked in the increased prestige they gained from it. One important aspect (or object of consumption) of the empire that lent itself to an enhancement of Japanese prestige was the existence within expanding imperial borders of *non-Japanese Japanese*, or internal Others. Indeed, in addition to the economic, political, and military aspects of Japanese imperialism, there was also a cultural dimension, in which empire, colonialism, and interaction with the colonized Other became significant constitutive elements in the construction of a modern Japanese national identity. An examination of the works of the first Japanese anthropologists demonstrates that the racial self-identity of the Japanese was constantly negotiated and renegotiated through interaction with Japan's major Others. This took place on and through Japan's expanding frontier, a space that was more than a geographical border demarcating the boundaries of the Great Japanese Empire at any particular time. Rather, as recent research in other areas and times has demonstrated, the frontier was a flexible and ambiguous place of interaction between the peoples of the empire, a space where the Japanese Self negotiated its identity through interaction with the subordinate and alien Other.[9] Anthropologists, among others, used this ambivalent space to forge a national identity. The Japanese defined themselves by and through the definition of the peoples of their empire, coupled with an awareness of the peoples of the West lurking in the background.[10] As I argue in this chapter, this was an endeavor in which the earliest Japanese anthropologists frequently followed in the footsteps of earlier Western writers, such as, for instance, John Batchelor (1854-1944), and his work on the Ainu.[11]

The establishment of the Japanese empire was a process in which the subordinate and colonized Other was defined and classified, racialized and hierarchized, and in which the identity of the dominant, colonizing Self was forged in relation to, and in contrast with, various Others. As Japan expanded, these Others came to include the *hisabetsu burakumin* (the Japanese "untouchables," a political and economic underclass frequently depicted as an alien ethnic group), the Ainu, the peoples of Okinawa and Taiwan, and the Koreans, together with the various peoples of Japan's colonies and the Japanese puppet-state of Manchukuo (Manchuria). The imperial ideology of the Japanese race shifted dramatically over the course of the history of the empire. As the empire grew, the late Meiji, Taishô, and early Shôwa periods saw a change whereby the Japanese, who had initially seen themselves as an inferior race in relation to the West, became more and more willing to view themselves as superior, not only in comparison with the colonized Others, but even with the West.

The importance of the frontier to anthropology and in defining the Self is exemplified in the life of the major prewar Japanese anthropologist, Torii Ryûzô (1870-1953). Indeed, the expanding frontiers of the Japanese empire provided the major sites of his fieldwork. Born in Tokushima in 1870, he joined the Tokyo Anthropological Society in 1886, and began to correspond with Tsuboi. In 1895, he surveyed the Liaodong Peninsula, making the first of many overseas trips in the wake of the Japanese military (the Sino-Japanese War of 1894-95 had finished just months before). In 1896, 1897, and 1898 he traveled to Taiwan, ceded to Japan in 1895, stopping off in Okinawa in 1896, and visiting Chishima (the Kurile Islands) in 1899. In 1900, he returned to Taiwan. In 1902-03, he visited southwestern China to study the Miao, and in 1904 he returned to Okinawa. In the following year, 1905, Japan emerged victorious in the Russo-Japanese War of 1904-05, and Torii made his second trip to Manchuria after his appointment as Lecturer at Tokyo Imperial University. From 1906 to 1908 he concentrated on Mongolia, but returned to Manchuria in 1909. In 1910 and 1911, he traveled to Korea, annexed by Japan in 1910, and also visited Karafuto (Sakhalin) in 1911. In 1912, he went to Korea and Manchuria. From 1913 to 1916, he traveled four times to Korea. He visited Siberia in 1919 and Sakhalin and Siberia in 1921. He returned to China in 1926, and Manchuria in 1927. In 1928, he went to Siberia and Manchuria again, then Mongolia once more in 1930. Torii traveled frequently to Manchuria between 1931 and 1935, in the immediate aftermath of the 1931 Manchurian Incident. In 1937, he went to South America – the one and only time he moved beyond the broadly defined frontier of the Great Japanese Empire – but was back in China in 1938 following the outbreak of the Sino-Japanese War of 1937-45. He accepted a position at Yanjing (Yenching) University in 1939, remaining in China until 1951, when he returned to Japan.[12]

This brief outline of a full and vigorous life indicates, to a certain extent at least, the way in which anthropology and empire were linked, and it maps the process of negotiation and renegotiation with Japan's Others. Japanese imperialism involved relationships between geographic neighbors, and Torii's field-work can be interpreted as an attempt to unearth the racial origins of the Japanese. Given the geographical proximity and cultural affinity between Japan and its colonized Others, it is hardly surprising that the politics of difference were not mapped in terms of color onto the body in imperial Japan, but in terms of culture, politics, and economy. Conceptualizing difference was a process that differed from the Western invention of the white-black dichotomy (although it did borrow from the Victorian passion for the concept of civilization). As a result, one characteristic of Japanese anthropology was that it was a lot closer to *Volkskunde* – the study of the internal and/or close Others within the state – than was anthropology as generally understood in the West.[13]

A second major characteristic was that, as Shimizu (1999: 160-61) notes, unlike anthropology in the West, a central focus of prewar Japanese anthropological inquiry was the "Japanese" people and culture. This interest in Self as opposed to Other was part of the search for identity. Japanese self-identity, together with its constitutive elements, was a product of modernity, an ambiguous and evolving ideology of power, which replaced pre-modern local identities centered on the "*han*" or feudal domain. It emerged together with a modern, centralized Japanese nation-state that defined itself as an empire from its very birth, and the various assimilationist policies that this nation-state entailed. One of the catalysts in this process was the impact of the West and the deeply felt anxieties it triggered. There was a growing realization that the world's peoples and cultures were ranked in a hierarchy, and that Westerners were interested in Japan's place in this hierarchy.[14] As Shimizu (1998: 115) notes, "anthropology in Japan began from the shocking realization that the Japanese were the objects of Western observation" (this is true of the anthropology of Japanese academics, but not of that of Western writers). The search for a national identity within the context of the impact of the West had a crucial influence on the nature and character of Japanese anthropology. At the same time, the peoples of the Great Japanese Empire served as an important foil in the forging of national identity.

The imperialist or colonial period of modern Japanese history saw the birth and growth not only of modern Japanese academic anthropology but also (albeit slightly later) of ethnology and archaeology, during a time when Japan was subjected both to the Orientalizing gaze of the West and to cultural imperialism on an unprecedented scale. It would be an exaggeration to say that anthropology in Japan was born from colonialism and/or Orientalism, but it certainly developed within the context of both, following roughly the three stages identified by Stocking (1989: 208-09) – and subsequently criticized as the "mythistory of anthropology" by van Bremen and Shimizu (1999: 3). Here, the amateur ethnographer was followed by the armchair anthropologist, who was followed in turn by the academically trained professional. In Meiji Japan, the first two groups consisted of a mixture of Westerners and Japanese, while the third consisted solely of Japanese. In other words, as Western amateurs were replaced by an institutionalized and increasingly professional group of Japanese anthropologists, the Western gaze to which Japan had been subjected was replaced by a Japanese gaze, first upon the Japanese themselves, and then upon the peoples and cultures of neighboring countries. In terms of anthropology, as in much else, Japan was a colonized colonizer; an object of the Orientalist gaze that later objectified its own Others.

Another way of looking at the general history of anthropology is to focus on paradigms. In his "Paradigmatic traditions in the history of anthropology," Stocking summarizes a number of paradigms, including the "biblical," "developmental," and "polygenetic" schools of thought. The biblical tradition included a number of key concepts, such as a three-branched genealogical tree in conceptualizing human beings – the three branches founded by the sons of Noah, with Japheth in Europe, Sem in Asia, and Ham in Africa – and the notion of the Tower of Babel. The evolutionist or developmental tradition emphasized not a degeneration of knowledge as mankind moved further and further away from direct knowledge of God, but rather a progressive learning process. Finally, the polygenetic tradition viewed not only culture and ethnos as distinct within the framework of a universal anthropos, but claimed that anthropos was not a universal concept, and that "races" were truly different (Stocking 1992: 347-49). All three paradigms were seen in Japanese anthropology, although some substituted the Kiki myths that emerged from *Kojiki* and *Nihon Shoki* for the Bible.

The Debate in Japan

Yet another framework within which Japanese anthropology can be examined is provided by Kiyono Kenji (1885-1955). Kiyono (1944) divided prewar Japanese anthropological discourses into a Meiji period Koro-pok-guru theory, a Taishô period Ainu theory, and a Shôwa period Japanese Proper theory. This rough generalization provides a starting line from which the early anthropological debate in Japan can be analyzed.

One element in the early debate was a strong nationalistic reaction to the West. Indeed, the rivalry with, and antagonism to, Western predecessors is clear from even a cursory reading of the literature. Thus, for instance, Shirai Mitsutarô (1863-1932) welcomed the establishment of the Tokyo Anthropological Society in 1886 as a means of regaining Japanese control over the discourse on Japan. Tsuboi removed Morse's collection of archaeological findings from the Ômori shell-mound from Tokyo Imperial University (Edward Sylvester Morse [1838-1925] will be discussed below). Torii played down Morse's role as the founder of Japanese anthropology in favor of Tsuboi

(Shirai 1886: 4; Oguma 2002: 13; Torii 1975 [1927]: 450-61; Shimizu 1999: 163, note 12).

The first major debate to take place within the context of the process of the institutionalization and professionalization of Japanese anthropology, coupled with Japanese antagonism to Western authors, concerned the prehistoric people(s) of Stone Age Japan. The two main positions among Japanese scholars were represented, on the one hand, by Tsuboi, who claimed that the true indigenes were a pre-Ainu people, the Koro-pok-guru; and, on the other hand, by Koganei Yoshikiyo (1858-1944), a friend of Tsuboi and the father of Japanese physical anthropology, who thought that the Stone Age inhabitants of Japan were the Ainu.[15] These positions were later supplemented by Torii, who not only agreed that the indigenous people of Japan were the Ainu, but also argued that a second Stone Age people, the "Japanese Proper," existed as well. This second people was a hybrid nation that emerged from a melting pot of peoples from Northeast Asia, Indochina and Indonesia (Torii 1975 [1918]; Askew 2003). Shimizu (1999: 125) claims that this controversy continued among leading anthropologists of the day "for more than two decades," effectively ending when Tsuboi died in 1913. This is correct, but his view that "no foreign scholars participated in it" is not.[16] In fact, as this chapter will demonstrate, not only did a similar debate take place among "foreign scholars," but this not infrequently *preceded* the discussion by the Japanese.

It has been argued that imperial Japan was dominated by a belief in the ethnic homogeneity of the Japanese nation. Michael Weiner (1997: 1), for instance, writes that "The modality of nationalism which emerged in the context of post-restoration [i.e. post-1868] Japan was one which idealized cultural and 'racial' homogeneity as the foundation of the nation-state." This chapter will demonstrate that the discourse on "race" or ethnicity in imperial Japan was in fact much more complicated than this might suggest. The dominant narratives advocated first by amateur Western anthropologists, and later developed by amateur and professional Japanese anthropologists, were ones that focused on heterogeneity – narratives that came to be known as the "mixed nation theory" (*kongô minzokuron*).[17] It is however true, especially from the second half of the Meiji period, that many of these narratives argued that racial mixing had taken place so long ago that the "Japanese" were to all intents and purposes a single homogeneous race. However, they also acknowledged that many modern "Japanese" were in fact members of minority ethnic groups. Indeed, the fundamental logic of territorial expansionism and imperialism almost by definition implied ethnic pluralism or heterogeneity.

As Weiner notes, during the last decades of the nineteenth century in particular, "attempts to establish the criteria for what constituted 'Japaneseness' occupied the energy and resources of statesmen, bureaucrats and unofficial publicists alike" (Weiner 1997: 4; cf. Weiner 1994: 15). Of necessity, the discourse focused on the Other in defining Self, and Weiner (1994: 6) claims that the discourse on Self was to a large extent based on a racial categorization, an imperial construct that reflected and responded to changes in the environment from which it emerged.[18]

The discourse on national identity was developed in many academic fields, including anthropology. Indeed, as noted above, early anthropology in Japan was dominated by a discussion about the earliest inhabitants of the Japanese archipelago and the prehistoric culture of Japan, and was thus deeply interested in the question of the racial origins of the Japanese (Terada 1975: 5). The anthropological discourse on the origins of the Japanese race and nation in the prewar Great Japanese Empire can be divided into three different narratives: the first claimed that one nation or "race" had replaced or displaced another; the second claimed that two or more nations had coexisted and mixed their blood; while the third focused on the role of evolution. The early Western authors developed the first two narratives, and these will be examined here.[19]

It hardly needs be said that the Meiji period discourse examined here was one in which several assumptions about race were widely accepted. The first was that "race" was a biological concept rather than a social construct, and that human populations could be divided into groups (races) based on specific biological characteristics that remained more or less constant across generations. The second was that these groups could be arranged in a hierarchy in which some were deemed to be inherently more intelligent and better adapted for modern life than others. Needless to say, this argument facilitated a justification of imperialism, which was sometimes seen as the "natural" rule of the inferior Other by the superior Self, although in the case of Japan, the Others were frequently depicted as inferior in terms of culture and politics rather than race.

Once the notion was established that various races existed, and that these races (or their cultures) could be classified and ranked in a hierarchy, such as the classic (and sexist) categories of savage, barbarian, and civilized man, it became possible to rewrite national histories around the theme of a racial struggle for survival and domination. The works of Munro and Murdoch discussed above encapsulate this reconstruction. In the case of Japan, as elsewhere, (pre)history was interpreted to demonstrate that a superior people or peoples had vanquished inferior foes. In this chapter, I hope to summarize the early debate on the Japanese race, focusing on the Western amateur anthropologists who were to influence the later Japanese professionals, and demonstrate that the notion of heterogeneity was widely accepted.

Edo Beginnings

Although the first reference in the Japanese literature to a prehistoric site (a shell-mound) occurs in a work compiled in approximately 713, the *Hitachi-no-kuni Fudoki* [The Hitachi-no-kuni Domain: Records of Wind and Earth], it was not until the Edo period that the prehistoric stone tools unearthed in various regions of Japan attracted much attention, and that systematic, academic theories about the Stone Age inhabitants of the archipelago began to develop (Bleed 1986: 57-76; Oguma, 2002: chapter 1; Terada 1975: 5-6).[20] These theories were based on Japanese myths and oral legends (Kiyono 1944; Ikeda 1973: 5). According to Kiyono Kenji in his work on the Japanese race that proved to be the crowning achievement of this prewar genre, *Nippon Jinshuron Hensenshi* [A History of the Evolution in Theories of the Japanese Race], there were three main schools of thought about the people responsible for the stone tools, in addition to the traditional notion that they were the work of gods or giants: the first argued that those responsible were the legendary Koro-pok-guru; the second argued that they were the ancestors of the modern Japanese; and the third, which had become dominant by the end of the Edo period, argued that they were the ancestors of the Ainu (Kiyono 1944: 9-26; cf. Ikeda 1973: 5; Kudô 1979: 19-36). As will be argued below, the Edo period debate was to influence the later Western debate about the origins of the Japanese, and so I briefly introduce it here.

Arai Hakuseki (1657-1725) argued that the stone tools were not in fact the products of the gods, as previously believed, but rather man-made artifacts, the products of the Shukushin, a Tungus people thought to have lived in the northeastern area of ancient China.[21] The events of Japanese prehistory known as the "Age of the Gods" were therefore really human events. Hakuseki also argued that the "Emishi" that appeared in ancient texts were the Ainu, and that the Ainu were a northern race which had once lived in northern Honshu but had subsequently been driven out by the early Heian period general, Sakanoue-no-Tamuramaro (758-811) (Kudô 1979: 7). Kinouchi Sekitei (1724-1808), the author of the most important work on archaeology in Edo period Japan, *Unkonshi* (1773-1801), a catalogue of his collection of rocks, fossils and artifacts, also argued that the stone-tools were man-made. However, noting that the Ainu still used stone tools, he claimed that they were responsible for the prehistoric ones as well, suggesting that the Ainu were the Shukushin.[22]

In 1781, Tô Teikan (1732-1797) published his *Shôkôhatsu* [Impulsive Remarks], in which he challenged the dates given in *Nihon Shoki*, arguing that the earliest dates had to be brought forward by about 600 years. He claimed that the "unbroken line of Emperors" had in fact been broken, and also argued that the language, names, and customs described in *Nihon Shoki* were similar to those of the Asian continent and especially the Korean peninsula. (This notion would reemerge later as *Nissen Dôsoron*, the theory that the Japanese and Koreans shared a common ancestor, and that the roots of the Imperial Family could be traced back to Korea.) Teikan thus argued that the stone tools were artificial and that a race other than the "Japanese" were responsible for the tools. He also challenged some aspects of the historical narrative as unfolded in the Kiki myths (Kudô 1979: 14).[23]

Pre-Meiji Western Theories

A number of Western writers were also active during this period. Earlier authors such as João Rodrigues (1562-1633) looked to China and Korea to explain the origins of the Japanese, while Pedro Morejon (1562-1634?), in his *Historia y Relación de lo sucedido en los Reinos de Iapon y China* (1621), claimed that some of the ancestors of the Japanese came from China, while others were Tartars who came from the north and who were related to the American Indians. Although it was sometimes argued that the Chinese, Japanese, and Tartars were descended from the twelve tribes of Israel, Morejon thought that they had probably intermarried with peoples already in East Asia (Cooper 1974: 307; 2001: 49-50; Kudô 1979: 37-39).

In his work, *The History of Japan*, Engerbert Kaempfer or Kömpfer (1651-1716) argued that there was insufficient proof that the Japanese were descended from the Chinese, and instead looked to language to provide clues about "the true origin of" the Japanese nation. Indeed, "it may be laid down as a constant rule, that in proportion to the numbers of strangers, who come to settle and live in a Country, words of the tongue spoke by them will be brought into the language of that Country."[24] However, an examination of the Japanese language demonstrated that any Japanese intercourse with neighboring peoples had been minimal. Japanese was "so entirely different from" Chinese "that there is no room left to think that these two Nations gave birth to each other." The same could be said of Korean. Moreover, the differences in religion, customs, and national character also demonstrated that Japan had *not* been settled by a people from the mainland. If the Japanese were not descended from the Chinese, Kaempfer asks, "from what parts of the world" is it possible "to trace out their original descent"? The answer was a surprising one: the Japanese were directly descended from the people of Babylon. Indeed, "the Japanese language is one of those, which Sacred Writs mention, that the all-wise Providence hath thought fit, by way of punishment and confusion, to infuse into the minds of the vain builders of the Babylonian Tower." Furthermore, Japanese was so "pure" that the Japanese must have fled directly to the archipelago, without spending much time in the various lands they would have encountered on the way (Kaempfer 1977 [1727-28]: 83, 84, 86).

Kaempfer's argument is of interest for a number of reasons. The idea that the Japanese were descended from the world described in the Bible was to be repeated in other prewar discussions of the origins of the Japanese, most notably N. McLeod (discussed below) and later Takahashi Yoshio (Oguma 2002: chapter 10; Takahashi 1884). As late as 1925, J. Ingram Bryan was arguing for an Egyptian origin! Kaempfer's position sits firmly within the biblical tradition of anthropology. His emphasis on language was to be taken up with far more sophistication by linguists. Finally, he carefully hedged his bets with regard to the racial makeup of the Japanese. On the one hand, he claimed that the Japanese language had changed so little that the various recorded migrations of peoples from the Korean peninsula and Chinese mainland "must have been very inconsiderate with regard to the bulk of the Japanese Nation" – or in other words that the Japanese were effectively homogeneous. On the other hand, he also acknowledged the existence of a minority people, an "unknown nation" within the borders of Japan – the Pygmies of "the most Northern Islands" who lived on Pygmy Island.[25] Moreover, regional differences in the appearances of the Japanese suggested "that from time to time, different and new branches were grafted into the original Tree of this Nation" (Kaempfer 1977 [1727-28]: 92, 95). In other words, the notion of both homogeneity and heterogeneity coexisted uncomfortably in Kaempfer's work.

Another figure who was to have a long-lasting impact on theories of the racial origins of the Japanese was Philipp Franz von Siebold (1796-1866). Indeed, it is often said that Siebold was the first individual to write in a scientific fashion about the origins of the Japanese.[26] In his *Nippon*, Siebold – who had been provided with access to Sekitei's collection – took the secular position that the stone tools unearthed in various parts of Japan were the products of the Ainu, an aboriginal people, and that the Ainu were later conquered by a Tartar nation. As will be discussed below, this argument was later supported by his son, Heinrich (or Henry) von Siebold (1852-1908).

Philipp von Siebold thus viewed the Ainu as the indigenes of Japan. Through an examination of the physical characteristics of the Japanese, together with an analysis of Japanese language, culture, and religion, he argued that the Japanese originated in areas such as Korea, Sakhalin, and northern China (Manchuria). According to Siebold, the Japanese were related to the Tartars, as well as to the peoples of the new world, in Peru and Colombia. The Japanese language was related to the languages of the Ainu and Koreans. Thus, in stark contrast to Kaempfer, Siebold looked to Japan's immediate region, or to geography rather than Holy Scripture, as the crucial factor to explain the origins of the Japanese. He proposed that the Ainu were the indigenes, and that there had been a later conquest by people from outside the archipelago (Kudô 1979: 43-48).

The Meiji Enlightenment

Views of the Japanese race as developed during the early Meiji period by Western authors adopted various positions. First, there was the debate about the original inhabitants of Japan, in which Morse's pre-Ainu theory was opposed by the Ainu theory as developed by both Siebolds and John Milne (1850-1913). Second, there was an early version of the "mixed nation theory" as proposed by the German, Erwin von Bälz (also spelt Baelz) (1849-1913), a medical doctor who taught at the Tokyo School of Medicine and who is further discussed below. Finally, there was the "Caucasian theory" as advocated by authors such as McLeod.

Despite the sophistication of the Edo period ethnographic discourse, it was not until the Meiji period that "anthropology" as a modern scientific discipline was established in Japan.[27] Morse's paper, "Shell mounds of Omori" (1879), is generally regarded as marking the birth of Japanese anthropology and archaeology.[28] Although he was a zoologist rather than an anthropologist or archaeologist by training, Morse was a highly intelligent man of science, who, at the age of 38, had already become a member of the National Academy of Sciences in the United States and vice-head of the American Association for the Advancement of Science (Ôta 1988: 19). He also had some experience in excavating shell-mounds in the United States. He traveled to Japan hoping to collect and study *Brachiopoda*, arriving in Yokohama on 18 June 1877, and met with immediate success. The very next day, when travelling by train to Tokyo, he realized that he had "discovered" a shell-mound, observing that the rail track had cut through a *Kjoekkenmoedding*, but that no one seemed to be aware of the importance of what had been exposed. In addition, he was quickly offered a position as Professor of Zoology at Tokyo Imperial University. Having decided to accept the offered position, Morse returned to Ômori, where his examination of the shell-mound led him to conclude that a pre-Ainu people had lived on the Japanese archipelago, a people with the skills required to make pottery and a taste for human flesh (Morse 1877; 1879). His work was followed by a flood of papers that dealt with anthropological themes by other highly educated men of letters, including individuals such as Milne, Edmund Naumann (1854-1927) and H. von Siebold (the last two may in fact have examined the shell-mound at Ômori before Morse). These early papers demonstrated an interest in themes which would have attracted Victorian gentlemen – race especially, but also skin color, intelligence, and the relative superiority or inferiority of the "Japanese race" when compared to others.[29] In reconstructing the history of Japan's buried past, these interests were projected back onto the prehistoric inhabitants of the archipelago. Morse's examination of the history of prehistoric man in the Japanese archipelago unfolded under the influence of Darwinism and played a central role in the introduction of anthropology, archaeology, and ethnology to Japan.[30]

In his "Shell mounds of Omori," Morse did not mention race, but did make the controversial claim that a prehistoric people in the archipelago had been cannibals, saying that "One of the most interesting discoveries connected with the Omori Mound is the evidence of cannibalism which it affords, this being the first indication of a race of anthropophagi in Japan" (Morse 2539 [1879]: 17). At the same time, he also published his "Traces of an early race in Japan," in which he argued from his findings at Ômori that the Stone Age inhabitants of the archipelago had possessed the ability to create pottery and were cannibalistic, neither characteristic seen in modern Ainu. Assuming that any people that had once learned to make pottery would never subsequently lose that knowledge, he concluded that the pottery-making and man-eating pre-Ainu had been replaced first by the Ainu and then the modern Japanese (Morse 1879).[31] Morse also used the Kiki myths, and in particular the story of the Jinmu Emperor, to argue that the "Japanese" had arrived from the south, and subsequently moved northwards up the archipelago, pushing the Ainu to the north. In other words, despite his sophistication, Morse viewed the Kiki myths as depictions of the past. Finally, he thought that the Ainu had originated from the north, and had moved southwards, down the archipelago.

Since Morse believed that the Ômori cannibals were not the Ainu, his understanding of the racial history of Japan can be summarized as follows. First, a pre-Ainu people, the indigenous cannibals, had existed, but had been pushed aside by the Ainu who came from the north. Second, the Ainu had in turn suffered the fate they had inflicted on the pre-Ainu, as a new people, the modern Japanese, arrived from the south and pushed the Ainu back. As will be demonstrated below, Morse's depiction of prehistoric Japan shares much in common with the Koro-pok-guru theory.

Of the various individuals involved in the debate on the racial origins of the Japanese, one of the most important was Milne, a geologist and seismologist who, like Morse, played a crucial role in the early days of anthropology, prehistory, and archaeology in Japan.[32] Milne first arrived in Japan on 8 March 1876 to take up a position at the *Kôgakuryô*, which later became the Faculty of Engineering at Tokyo Imperial University, where he taught geology and mining. (His interest in seismology was only triggered after he came to Japan and experienced his first earthquake.) The first anthropological-cum-archaeological surveys by Milne that we can date are those of the summer of 1878 in Hokkaido and Chishima. As a sign of how much work was being done in Japan at the time, it is interesting to note that Morse was also in Hokkaido in July-August of 1878 to inspect a number of sites, as was H. von Siebold from August of that year. Milne's work in Chishima was the first scientific survey of the area: the first survey by a Japanese was that of Torii in 1899 (Yoshioka 1993: 101).

Echoing Kaempfer on the Pygmies of Pygmy Island, Milne argued that a pygmy people known as the Koro-pok-guru had existed in Hokkaido (the Koro-pok-guru were mentioned in Ainu legends) during the Jômon period, and that the Ainu had lived in the main island of Honshu. After the ancestors of the modern Japanese invaded Honshu, the Ainu were pushed into Hokkaido, and the Koro-pok-guru disappeared. Again, one nation emerged victorious, with the losing nations disappearing from history. This argument was developed in a number of papers.

In his "Notes on stone implements," Milne (1880: 61) argued that the prehistoric stone implements found in Japan were left not by the pre-Ainu but by the Ainu, a people which "still inhabit Yezo" and once "probably" lived throughout Japan. They left shell-mounds behind, but "were driven back towards the north by the Japanese advancing from the south." Milne argued that his research on archaeological sites (the pit-dwellings or *tateana* houses) in Chishima and Nemuro had led him to the conclusion that the people responsible for these were not the Ainu, but another people, the pit-dwellers or Koro-pok-guru. Milne viewed these people as the ancestors of the peoples of the northern Kuriles, whom he had observed still living in pit-dwellings. This was the first time that the Koro-pok-guru were mentioned specifically in the academic discourse on the Japanese race, although Kaempfer had already alluded to them, and Matsuura Takeshirô (1819-1888) had mentioned that the "natives" *(dojin)* of Hokkaido, the Ainu, claimed that "dwarfs" were responsible for pit-dwellings (Milne 1880: 82; Kudô 1979: 30).

In his paper, "The Stone Age in Japan," Milne mentions, among others, Morse, Naumann, Siebold, and *Unkonshi*, and was obviously highly aware of the recent work being done on Japanese prehistory. Using the Kiki myths, together with place-names, language, and the faces of some of the modern Japanese, he again argued that it was probable that the Ainu had inhabited Japan, but had been pushed north by the Japanese (Milne 1881; cf. Milne 1893: 502-03). Acknowledging that Morse had argued that the Ainu were not pot-makers, and therefore could not be responsible for the shell-middens, Milne drew on his own research in Hokkaido and Chishima to dismiss this particular objection: there was some evidence that the Ainu had been, and remained, pot makers (Milne 1880: 82; 1893: 502). He was skeptical of the claim of cannibalism. "In reply to this, all I can say is that, so far, the only evidences of cannibalism are those found by Professor Morse at one heap at Omori. Although diligent search has been made by several persons interested in these enquiries ... not only in the Omori heap, but in many others, not a trace of similar evidence has yet been found" (Milne 1881: 410). Moreover, he used Japanese sources to undermine Morse's claim that the Ainu were too "mild and gentle" a people to have practiced cannibalism. In the past, they had demonstrated a "ferocious" nature, and so, if cannibalism was eventually proved, Milne thought it not unlikely that the Ainu may have been responsible (Milne 1881: 411; cf Milne 1880: 82-83). The Ainu were therefore the "predecessors" of the Japanese. They were not, however, the indigenes of Hokkaido: Milne suggested that the "Kamschadales or Alutes" or "Kurilsky" had predated the Ainu: they were a different race, and had been forced north through Chishima, and into Kamchatka as the Ainu were pushed into Hokkaido by the Japanese advance through the archipelago from the south. This was clearly linked with a Darwinian struggle for existence (Milne 1880: 87; 1882: 188; 1893: 503).

Milne also attempted to date the shell-mound at Ômori. Using a series of maps dating back several hundred years, he argued that it was possible to estimate the distance the sea had retreated, and thus possible to estimate when the shell-mound had been on the seaboard. His estimate was that this had been 1,500 to 3,000 years ago, and since "History tells us that about 2,500 years ago Jinmu Tenno [the Jinmu Emperor] came to Japan and fought against the Ainos," it was "very probable that the Omori deposit" had been produced by the Ainu.[33]

Another important figure was Heinrich von Siebold (or "Siebold the younger," as he is frequently described in the Japanese literature). His early work on archaeology, *Notes on Japanese Archaeology with Especial Reference to the Stone Age* (1879) was, as Kiyono Kenji notes, a solid work based on as much information as could be collected at the time.[34] As was the case with many of his contemporaries, Siebold accepted the narrative given in the Kiki myths as based on history. He thus claimed that "The tribes of savages with whom Jimmu Tenno [the Jinmu Emperor] met when he advanced northwards, whom his descendants had to conquer, and who were called *Ebisu*, *Kuma Osso* or *Osso* ... are none else than the Ainos." He argued that the Japanese were the product of a huge melting pot of peoples, and that there were regional differences in origins within Japan. For instance, not only did the people of southern Kyushu share much in common with the inhabitants of "Corea and Loochoo" (i.e. the Ryukyu Islands), but "history proves ... that ... Japan has [interacted] with no less than sixteen different peoples, and it cannot be doubted that these have had much effect on the race." Based on Japanese mythology, he argued that the Ainu had resided in and around the "Bay of Yedo" until at least 110 AD, and therefore that the shell-mounds unearthed there (including of course that examined by Morse) were "not older than from fifteen hundred to two thousand years" (H. von Siebold 1879: ii, 13). As Milne was to do later, Siebold cast doubt on Morse's evidence that cannibalism had been practiced, but provided himself with a way out: although the Ainu of the day were "certainly mild and peaceable," this had not always been the case – they had once been ferocious warriors (H. von Siebold 1879: 14).

Siebold used the Kiki myths, and in particular the story of the Jinmu Emperor's Eastern Expedition, to shed light on the story of prehistoric Japan. According to this story, the Japanese had moved north, up the archipelago, conquering barbarian tribes known as the Ebisu (Emishi) and Kumaso. Using ideas developed during the Edo period, Siebold argued that these barbarian tribes were in fact the Ainu. According to his reading of the Kiki myths, Prince Yamato-Takeru-no-Mikoto had fought and conquered the Ainu living around the Edo Bay in 110 AD, and therefore those responsible for the Ômori shell-mound must have existed prior to this.

The debate was a vigorous one. In his "Some recent publications on Japanese archaeology," Morse replied to the criticisms advanced by Milne and also discussed the work of Siebold (Morse 1880). Morse remained unconvinced that the Ainu were or had been pot makers. He was harshly critical of Milne's belief that the Ainu might have once practiced cannibalism because of their past "cruel modes of punishments" (Morse 1880: 659). Similar reasoning, Morse noted, might lead one to assume that the Scots had once been cannibals! Siebold was also criticized: he had copied some of his information from Morse, and faithfully reproduced a mistake in the original (Morse 1880: 661).

As mentioned above, another German active in Meiji Japan was Bälz, whose major contribution to the debate on the Japanese race was his thesis that two distinctive "types" of Japanese existed – the upper-class and the lower-class.[35] This was a more sophisticated version of the older idea of a pale Caucasian nobility and darker proletariat. According to Bälz, the Ainu were the original inhabitants of the archipelago. They were not a Mongolian people, but were "closely related to the Caucasian race," based on their physical appearance (Bälz 1907: 526). He also claimed that the modern Japanese, who only had a little Ainu blood in their veins, could be divided into a "Chôshû type" and a "Satsuma type," based on the shape of their heads. Bälz claimed that the minority Chôshû type, which predominated among the ruling class, had long heads, long, thin faces, tall and slender build, narrow eyes, straight noses, small mouths and single-edged eyelids (this description corresponds to the dolichocephalic type in the anthropology and racial studies of the day). The majority Satsuma type, which predominated among the common people, had square or round faces, short and stocky build, short, large noses, large, round eyes, and double-edged eyelids (the brachycephalic type).[36] Moreover, the Chôshû type (the north or true Mongolian type) resembled the Chinese and Korean peoples, and had come to the southwest of the archipelago from the continent and through the Korean peninsula, whereas the Satsuma type (the south Mongolian or Malayan type) resembled the Malays. Both types had mingled with the aboriginal peoples of the archipelago, and the modern Japanese were a product of a mixture between the three.

Bälz therefore argued that the Japanese nation was the product of an ethnic melting pot and that there had been two waves of migration to Japan, both via the Korean peninsula, one from the north and one from the south. Moreover, he clearly believed that the mixing of blood was incomplete, and that evidence of past intermarriage could be read from present physical appearance. The notion of a melting pot, though different from Bälz' version, was to become the dominant view of imperial Japan, as was the notion of a southern *and* a northern origin. Bälz claimed that the Japanese language belonged to the Ural-Altaic family of languages, and that an Akkadian people had moved east to Japan (this view echoed the position advocated by Kaempfer). Finally, he too argued that the arrival of the Japanese in the archipelago was reflected in the Izumo myths and the story of the descent to earth of the Japanese descendants of the Sun-Goddess.

Of the authors who argued for a Caucasian link, the most interesting work was the nonacademic *Epitome of the Ancient History of Japan* (1875) by McLeod, a writer who managed to bring together most if not all of the various theories that had been advanced during the Edo and early Meiji periods. Race played a central role in his history of ancient Japan – his work begins: "The

Empire of Japan is peopled by three distinct races." In addition to "a few" Koreans, "descendants of a Negro race," and the Japanese "untouchables" (the *hisabetsu burakumin* viewed by McLeod as an alien race, but at least some of whom he viewed as Korean), the three races were the *majority* Aino ("Aa. Inu"), a "little race, the aborigines of the south," and finally "the Jewish race"! Of the three races, the "Aa. Inu" and the Jewish-Japanese had intermarried to produce a "mixed race" (McLeod 1875: 1).[37] The Japanese thus were the product of a highly complicated process of interracial marriage, on which, fortunately, McLeod was able to shed some light.

McLeod had a unique view of Japanese history. The Tokugawa Bakufu was founded by descendants of the "Aa. Inu," whereas those who had opposed the Tokugawa, the *tozama daimyô* together with the Imperial Family – "people of Jin Mu Tenno [the Jinmu Emperor]" – were Jews. The "Aa. Inu" had once ruled Japan, including "the Little Race the descendants of Ham." This Little Race lived in the south of Japan, where McLeod had discovered them among the lower classes in Kyushu and Shikoku. A Malay people, they had "thick lips, flat noses, high cheekbones, full faces, large black eyes, low foreheads," dark complexions, and were weaker than the two other main races. The Jinmu Emperor and his Jewish warriors arrived in the south of Japan. McLeod informed his readers that in an ancient picture he had purchased, but unfortunately not reproduced in his book, "the Princes are clad in the ancient armour of Assyria and Media, and shod like the ancient Princes of Israel ... they wear the tachi or Persian sword, and some have the ancient Israelitish [*sic*] unicorn shaped spears; others have the spear formerly worn by the ancient Median infantry." These new arrivals and their wonderful weaponry proved to be too powerful for the "Aa. Inu" to oppose, and they gradually pushed north, conquering the archipelago. Unlike all other accounts of Japan, however, McLeod believed that the conquering newcomers were later vanquished, and it was not until the Meiji Restoration that they regained control of Japan. He foresaw a bright future for the Jewish rulers of Japan: "The probability is that China, Japan and Corea, will again be united under the power of the Jewish race, with the Emperor of Japan at their head" (McLeod 1875: 1-2, 5, 27, 36).

Although ancient Japanese history thus provided a wonderful, almost global, forum where the various races of the world struggled for dominance – "Truth is stranger than fiction" (McLeod 1875: 129) – McLeod also had some interesting insights into Korea. The indigenous people of Korea had originally traveled directly there "after the dispersion of Babel and are a pure Caucasian race." These indigenes were then conquered by another people, perhaps led by some of Alexander the Great's generals who, after his death, "divided his Empire amongst them, [and] penetrated with their veterans into" Korea (McLeod 1875: 21-22). Again, social hierarchy was given a biological basis and justification – one moreover that flattered the Western Self – and was projected onto the past.

Thus the notion that a number of different races existed in Japan, that there was racial intermarriage, that not only wealth and status but also race separated the ruling class and the working classes, that differences in physical appearance could be explained by racial differences, that racial ethnology could be used to explain hierarchies of power within Japan, and finally the idea of a connection with Babel, all appear in McLeod's account of ancient Japan. As I have argued here, many of these ideas were commonplace in Western discourses throughout the prewar years. Thus, for instance, Bryan (1925: 90-91) claimed "the Japanese are clearly of very mixed descent," and were "a blend of various bloods," while as late as 1941, Nag (1941: 29) wrote that the agricultural (rural) population of Japan consisted of the descendants of southern migrants, the broad-headed "Negrito" from Malaysia who had intermarried with "Indonesian or Mongolian elements," while the urban population or "conquering class" was, we may assume, a long-headed people that "was partly Caucasian and partly Mongolian" and formed "the aristocratic type."

Conclusion

Several theories of the "racial" origins of the Japanese emerge from an examination of the intellectual history of the concept of the Japanese nation as developed by the early Western writers examined here. One of the major schools of thought argued that one people had invaded the archipelago, conquering another people who were pushed out, a narrative which would have made sense to men steeped in the traditions of European imperialism and the new ideology of Darwinism. (Among his other accomplishments, Morse also introduced Darwinism to Japan.) This "interchange of races theory" *(jinshu kôtai setsu)* claimed that one nation had replaced another at least once. There are several versions, the main difference between them being the question of which groups were replaced. The Siebolds, for instance, argued that the Ainu were the indigenous people of the prehistoric archipelago, and that they were later conquered by a Tartar nation, the modern Japanese. This argument was based on the idea that two nations or races had competed for ownership of the archipelago, and that one emerged victorious. Other theorists argued that there were three nations. Morse claimed that a pre-Ainu people had existed, and that this nation was different from both the Ainu and majority Japanese. The pre-Ainu had been replaced by the Ainu, who in turn (following the Siebold view of history) had been displaced by the modern Japanese. Milne also argued that a third people had existed, the Koro-pok-guru. After the ancestors of the modern Japanese invaded Honshu, the Ainu were pushed northwards into Hokkaido, where they displaced the Koro-pok-guru. Again, one nation emerged victorious, with the losing nations either disappearing from history (in the case of the pre-Ainu and Koro-pok-guru), or finding themselves facing extinction (as was frequently assumed to be the case with the Ainu).

The other major school argued not for a zero-sum game in which one race displaced another, but claimed that two or more nations coexisted in the archipelago. This second "mixed blood" (*konketsu*) or "mixed nation" theory viewed the modern Japanese nation as having emerged from a prehistoric melting pot, a mixture between different races. Torii's Japanese Proper theory is representative of this position, but there were several versions. One argued that the process of racial intermarriage and integration was well and truly finished, so that the modern Japanese nation was effectively homogeneous. The other version, much more popular with the early Western authors, claimed that this process was still not complete, and that racial differences could thus be detected. Bälz' notion that there were two distinct types of Japanese with different geographical roots, in addition to the Ainu, and that the modern Japanese were a product of a mixture between the Ainu (similar to Europeans), mainland Asians (Koreans and Chinese), and people from the south (a Malay people), is representative of this latter school of thought.

Within the broader narrative that argued that a mixture had occurred, there was frequent disagreement about the place of origin of the various peoples who were said to have inhabited the ancient archipelago. Some argued that one people had come from the north and conquered and/or intermarried with another from the south, whereas others argued that a people from the south had conquered others from the north. There was also disagreement about which people had mixed with which. The questions of whether the Japanese were descended from the Chinese, Koreans, Malays, Tartars or Tungus, or whether they were Ural-Altaic, Caucasian, or Mongolian, remained unresolved in the prewar years. However, the view that the Japanese were the product of some kind of prehistoric melting pot did predominate in the prewar Great Japanese Empire.

Much of this early Western discourse was inherited by the first Japanese anthropologists. Although Japanese anthropology as practiced by Japanese anthropologists developed within the context and framework of imperialism, it differed from Western anthropology which, in Asad's (1998 [1973]: 103) words, was "a holistic discipline nurtured within bourgeois society, having as its object of study a variety of non-European societies which [had] come under its economic, political and intellectual domain," and which was based on a series of binary oppositions: black and white, civilized and noncivilized, superior and inferior. Japanese anthropology was based on notions of hierarchy, in which the *distance* between the Japanese Self and the almost-Japanese Other was stressed. Moreover, Western anthropology tended to link the concept of progress and development to racial preoccupations and skin color to a much greater extent than Japanese anthropology, especially in the nineteenth century. To the Westerner, savages were dark, barbarians were red or brown, the

75

semi-civilized were yellow, and the civilized were white (Stocking 2001 [1994]). For obvious reasons, this form of racialized discourse was one that nationalistic Japanese could only engage in if the Japanese were first defined as white.

At the same time, the classification of peoples, the way in which they were understood, perceived and ranked, was a process that, in Japan, took place on two levels: the classification on a global scale of the Japanese *vis-à-vis* the peoples of the West, and the classification on a regional scale of the various peoples (ethnic and other minorities) of the Japanese empire *vis-à-vis* the majority Japanese. Within the empire, Japanse perceptions created a hierarchy, and those at the top were treated differently from those at the bottom. In relation to the West, Japan managed to "write back," creatively engaging in the Western conversation about Japanese culture and race.

Colonial anthropology in prewar Japan, therefore, was not the study or invention of a simple dichotomy of Self and Other. Rather, it was the study of the closely related Other. Anthropology is sometimes viewed as a body of knowledge constructed around the descriptions of various Others encountered by the European Self in the course of European overseas expansion (Stocking 1992 [1990]: 347). Japanese imperialism differed from Western imperialisms; and it is perhaps only natural that Japanese anthropology did too. The debate about the racial origins of the Japanese during the early Meiji period was dominated by highly educated Western sojourners in Japan who had access to "modern" Western science, who had established a hegemony in the modern "scientific" discourse on Japan, and who were responsible for the first anthropological writings on the origins of the Japanese. The narratives on prehistoric Japanese quickly became highly sophisticated. As early as 1908, Munro (1911 [1908]: 669, footnote) was able to write dismissively in his *Prehistoric Japan* that Morse was "the pioneer of primitive archaeology in Japan." As younger generations of Japanese moved through the new, Westernized and "modern" education system of Meiji Japan, however, this hegemony was quickly overthrown, and Japanese scholars came to dominate the debate on the origins of the Japanese. Although these Japanese scholars developed a far more sophisticated discourse on the origins of the Japanese race than the earlier amateur Western anthropologists, in many respects the characteristics of the earlier debate remained constant. First, anthropologists retained their eclectic interests in anthropology, archaeology, prehistory, mythology (the Kiki myths), ethnology, folklore and linguistics in a fashion a Franz Boas (1858-1942) would have recognized.[38] Second, the dispute about racial origins remained a major focus of attention.

The challenge to the hegemony of Westerners interested in Japan was symbolized by the establishment in 1884 of the first Japanese anthropological association, a research group named *Jinruigaku no Tomo* (Friends of Anthropology), also called *Jinruigakkai* (Anthropological Society), and *Jinruigaku Kenkyûkai* (Anthropology Research Society). Centered on Tsuboi, a student

76

of the Faculty of Science at Tokyo Imperial University, the association heralded the birth of a Japanese scientific discourse on anthropology (Saitô 1995 [1974]: 108-15; Tsuboi 1904; Yamaguchi et al. 1998: 119). The research group was formally renamed *Jinruigakkai* when the first issue of its journal was published in February 1886. In May of the same year, it was decided to change the name to the *Tôkyô Jinruigakkai* (Tôkyô Anthropological Society), a change reflected in the next issue of the journal, published in June 1886. Thus the group's journal, *Jinruigakkai Hôkoku* (The Bulletin of the Anthropological Society) was renamed the *Tôkyô Jinruigakkai Hôkoku* in June 1886, and also for the first time started carrying an English title, *The Bulletin of the Tôkyô Anthropological Society*, on the back cover. In August 1887, the journal was again renamed, becoming the *Tôkyô Jinruigakkai Zasshi* (The Journal of the Anthropological Society of Tôkyô), and then the *Jinruigakkai Zasshi* (in English, Journal for the Anthropological Society of Nippon) in 1911, while the English name of the association itself became the "Anthropological Society of Nippon."[39] (In a move which keeps foreign academics on their toes, the English-language titles were sometimes not changed until some time after the Japanese-language ones.)

In its early stages, the association was heavily influenced by the theories of Western researchers. Thus, for example, Tsuboi in effect combined the theories of Morse and Milne, arguing that the pre-Ainu were the Koro-pok-guru (Tsuboi 1887). On the other hand, Koganei developed the Siebold theory of the Ainu as an indigenous people, arguing against Tsuboi's theory of the Koro-pok-guru. Japanese theorists also engaged in a debate between those who argued for *jinshu kôtai*, "interchange of races" or displacement, and those who argued for *konketsu*, "mixture of blood" or coexistence.

Yet another position was that there had been no displacement. Rather than agreeing that an indigenous people had lived in the archipelago during the Jômon period and had been conquered by a second nation that arrived later, this third major school of thought held that the Japanese nation had always existed in Japan, and that the differences both between the body shapes of the Jômon people and the Yayoi people, and those between modern Japanese from different regions, were the product of changes in life-style and environment. This third theory is known as the transition theory (*ikô setsu*) or continuity theory (*renzoku setsu*). Thus, for instance, Furuhata Tanemoto (1891-1975), a specialist in medical jurisprudence and a researcher into blood-types, surveyed the blood-types of both the Japanese and peoples of surrounding areas, and strongly argued that the Japanese showed a blood-type ratio that was unique. He concluded, therefore, that there had been no racial intermarriage. Hasebe Kotondo (1882-1969), a professor of medicine at Tôhoku Imperial University, and to a lesser extent Kiyono Kenji, a professor of medicine at Kyoto Imperial University, argued against the theory of displacement, based on an analysis of detailed measurements of excavated bones and the physical shape of modern Japanese. Both were to establish themselves as leaders of Japanese physical anthropology in the immediate postwar years.[40]

The complex interplay between these discourses influenced both the construction of a modern Japanese identity and the nature of Japanese colonial rule. The English-language literature has yet to focus on the three discourses and examine how they shaped Japanese narratives of Japan's colonies and their peoples. This, however, remains a story for another day.

Notes

1   A much earlier version of this chapter appeared as Askew (2002). Some sections also appeared in Askew (2003). I am deeply grateful to the editors of the *Japanese Review of Cultural Anthropology* for allowing me to utilize material from these articles. I would also like to take this opportunity to acknowledge the support and encouragement, and comments of Jerry Eades and Peter Kirby.

2   On Munro, see "N.G. Munro ryakunenpô" [A short chronology of N.G. Munro], in Munro (2002 [1962]: 245-49), together with Wilkinson (1993).

3   The leading British anthropologist John Beddoe (1826-1911), for instance, wrote in 1905 that while "the natives of the east of Ireland, the descendants of the later invaders, the upper classes, the people with English or Scottish surnames, tend to fairness," those "natives of the west, the indigenæ, the labourers and peasants, the people with Keltic [*sic*] surnames, are darker, at least in hair colour." He later stated that he regretted "the diminution of the old blond lympho-sanguine stock, which has hitherto served England well in many ways, but is apparently doomed to give way to a darker and more mobile type, largely the offspring of the proletariat" (Beddoe, 1905: 236, 237).

4   MacFarlane (1852: 141) claimed in a similar vein that "Many of the Upper classes, or members of the old families, are tall[,] exceedingly handsome in figure and countenance, and are far more like Europeans than Asiatics." See also Kemish (1860: 138) and Steinmetz (1860: 347).

5   Note that Murdoch's second volume, *During the Century of Early Foreign Intercourse (1543-1651)*, was published first.

6   A number of tribes are mentioned in the *Kojiki* (The Record of Ancient Matters, compiled in 712) and *Nihon Shoki* (The Chronicles of Japan, complied in 720), including the Emishi, Hayato, Izumo, Kumaso, and Tsuchigumo. The Meiji period writers frequently assumed that these tribes should be differentiated in terms of ethnicity – "race" in the terminology of the times – rather than culture, language or geography, but, with the exception of the Emishi, a people (mistakenly) assumed to be the Ainu, they disagreed about what race (s) they represented.

7   Although falling outside the bounds of this chapter, it is useful to note that

these common assumptions remained more or less unchanged throughout the prewar era. Thus, for instance, Kalidas Nag's *Prehistoric Japan* mentions the Ainu or proto-Ainu as indigenes, and states "The ethnic type which finally emerges as the Yamato or Japanese proper is ... a mixture of several distinct stocks" (Nag 1941: 28).

8   For an introduction to the issues dealt with here, see Ikeda (1973; 1982), Kiyono (1944), Kudô (1979), Oguma (2002), Sofue (1961), Yamaguchi et al. (1998), Yamashita in this volume, Yoshioka (1987; 1993), and finally the various papers in van Bremen and Shimizu eds. (1999), and Shimizu and van Bremen eds. (2003), especially Sekimoto (2003), Shimizu (1999), and van Bremen and Shimizu (1999). For histories of anthropology in general, see Darnell (1977), Faubion (1993), and Vermeulen and Roldán eds. (1995), in addition to Stocking's many works including Stocking (1982 [1968]).

9   See Daunton and Halpern (1999: 3) and Morgan (1999: 54). In writing the following section of this chapter, I have drawn upon Calloway (1987), Canny (1973), Daunton and Halpern eds. (1999), Gillinghan (1987), Hall (2002), Hechter (1999), White (1991), and Williamson (1996).

10   The Others of the Japanese empire also took part in this debate. Despite the inherent interest of what these Others had to say – and perhaps in particular those who were subordinate in the metropolitan centers of the empire but dominant on the peripheries, such as the Taiwanese and Korean entrepreneurs and soldiers in Japan's colonies and areas such as Manchukuo dominated by Japan – space does not permit an examination of this theme here.

11   See Batchelor (1892).

12   For details of Torii's life and fieldwork trips, see the detailed chronology contained in the supplementary volume *(bekkan)* of his Complete Works (Torii 1977: 180-222). See also Askew (2003), Sasaki (1993: 16-17), Suenari (1988: 50), and Terada (1975: 68). The large number of detailed research reports Torii wrote following his various field surveys are available in his Complete Works. See Torii (1975-77).

13   See Stocking (2001 [1982]: 287) and his discussion of how the nature of anthropology in imperial countries such as Great Britain, where the object of anthropological enquiry was "dark-skinned 'others' in the overseas empire," differed from that in many parts of the European continent, where the object was the internal peasant Other. Although it would be an exaggeration to define prewar Japanese anthropology as falling within the tradition of *Volkskunde* rather than *Völkerkunde*, it is important to note that Japan's external Others could be (and frequently were) redefined as internal Others.

14   For hierarchies of race, see Stocking (1987) and Pagden (1995).

15   For representative papers, see, for instance, Tsuboi (1887), a reply to an earlier paper by "MS" (Shirai Mitsutarô) which had rejected the notion

that the Koro-pok-guru had ever existed, and Koganei (1926 [1904]).

16 In one representative paper, for instance, the list of references cites twenty-nine authors (including the author of the paper in question), of which 15 were Japanese and 14 Western (Koganei 1926 [1904]). Not only were Western authors writing extensively on the Ainu, the subject of this particular paper by Koganei, but there was at least a degree of interaction in that Japanese authors were citing the findings of their Western competitors. Also see Munro (1908 [1911]: 69, 258, 648, 670) where he returns the compliment, citing Koganei.

17 For the dominance of this theory, see Oguma (2002).

18 This general theme is discussed at length in Oguma (2002). Also see Askew (2001). Weiner's argument that the discourse on Self was based on a *racial* categorization is to a certain extent true, but I myself believe that this discourse was based to a much larger extent on a *cultural* categorization that included as members of Self those who had adopted particular cultural attributes, notably respect for the Emperor and the ability to speak Japanese.

19 In a later paper I hope to examine the third narrative together with the complex interplay between these discourses, and to demonstrate how this interplay influenced both the construction of a modern Japanese identity and the nature of Japanese colonial rule.

20 For the *Hitachi-no-kuni Fudoki* in English, see Aoki (1997).

21 Arai Hakuseki, *Koshitsû* (Ancient History), cited in Kudô (1979: 22-23). There is a huge amount of work on Hakuseki. See for instance Saitô (1985: 5-10). In English, see Ackroyd (1982: ix-liv).

22 Kinouchi Sekitei, cited in Kudô (1979: 35-36). For Kinouchi Sekitei, also see Saitô (1985: 14-20).

23 Japanese *kokugakusha* were outraged by Teikan's position. For instance, Motoori Norinaga wrote a detailed rebuttal, *Kenkyôjin*, in which he condemned Teikan's ideas as "the words of a mad man." It is interesting to note that many of the later Western authors were to take a far less critical view of the Kiki myths than Teikan. For Tô Teikan, see Saitô (1985: 20-26; 1990: 99-115).

24 I have modernized the romanization of Kaempfer's English here and elsewhere.

25 The mythical Koro-pok-guru were also a northern pygmy people, which suggests that Kaempfer here is referring to them.

26 Hanihara (1993: 85), Yamaguchi et al. (1998: 117). Philipp Franz von Siebold's *Nippon: Archiv zur Beschreibung von Japan und dessen Neben- und Schutzlandern Jezo mit den sudlichen Kurilen, Sachalin, Korea und den Liukiu-Inseln* is readily available in Japanese translation. Also see P. von Siebold (1973).

27 For the early Meiji period, see Kiyono (1944: 27-58). For the writings of

various Westerners, see Kiyono (1944: 251-80).

28 For Morse's work as an anthropologist, see Morse (1877; 1879; 2539 [1879]; 1892; 1925). The literature on Morse is huge. See in particular Yoshioka (1987). Sofue (1961: 174) mistakenly gives Morse's name as "Stephen Morse."

29 See, for instance, St. John (1873: 248), where he speaks of the Ainu as follows. "The colour of their skin is dark; a copper colour, with an olive tint, or a dirty copper ... Their features are regular, good, and decidedly pleasing; entirely distinct from the Mongolian, having neither the high-cheeked bone nor oblique upper eyelid peculiar to that race. Many have intelligent faces." As suggested by Kemish and his notion of fair aristocrats and dark vagabonds, it was common in the racial discourse of the time to conflate physical characteristics, on the one hand, and moral disposition and behavior, on the other.

30 Morse actually corresponded with Darwin, sending him sections of his work on the Ômori shell-mound. For Darwin's reply, see Morse (1925: 440).

31 Morse was particularly interested in the pottery that emerged from the shell-mound, calling it "cord marked pottery," a term translated as Jômon. The term Jômon is still used for the earliest culture of the Japanese archipelago.

32 For Milne's work as an anthropologist, see Milne (1879; 1880; 1881; 1882; 1893). For an introduction to Milne, see Yoshioka (1993). Also see Herbert-Gustar and Nott (1980).

33 Milne (1881: 420, footnote). Also see Milne (1880: 86), where he states that the Ômori deposit "rather than being more than 2,600 years old, is probably less."

34 H. von Siebold (1879). Kiyono (1944: 262). Heinrich published in English under the name "Henry." For this Siebold, see H. von Siebold (1996).

35 For Bälz' *Das Leben eines deutschen Arztes im erwachenden Japan*, his autobiography, see Bälz (1972) and Schottlaender (1995). Also see Bälz (2001), which contains (in translation) his major papers on race, and finally Bälz (1907). Another author who argued for two types of Japanese was William Elliot Griffis (1843-1928), who claimed that there was a Yamato type (the ruling class) and a northern or Ainu type (the peasants). See Griffis (1876: chapter 2).

36 By way of comparison, see, for instance, Closson's (1879) idea of a Europe populated by a tall, blonde, superior, economically successful, progressive, active, urban, educated and mobile group (the long-headed or dolichocephalic Nordics), a shorter, darker, inferior, passive, rural group (the broad-headed or brachycephalic Alpines), and an even more inferior and thus even darker Mediterranean brachycephalic population. Within the context of Europe, the dolichocephalic Nordics are clearly Protestants, while the brachycephalic Alpines are Catholic (race determines religion!),

an aspect of the polygenetic tradition of anthropology that could not easily be applied to Japan.

37 McLeod uses the term "Aa. Inu" rather than the more common Aino or Ainu because he saw himself as a linguist. "This word is derived from the Japanese A A which means contempt, and Inu a dog ... this name was given to them by the Samurai of Jin Mu Tenno, or the Jewish race, who as shown from other sources contemptuously called all gentiles dogs" (McLeod 1875: 4).

38 Franz Boas defined anthropology in 1904 as covering "the biological history of mankind in all its varieties; linguistics applied to people without written languages; the ethnology of people without historic records, [sic] and prehistoric archaeology." See Boas (1904: 523).

39 From 1911 to 1992, the journal remained the *Jinruigakkai Zasshi* in Japanese, but in English it changed from *The Journal of the Anthropological Society of Tokyo* to the *Journal for the Anthropological Society of Nippon*, and finally, the *Journal of the Anthropological Society of Nippon*. It was renamed *Anthropological Science* in 1992. From 1998, it became two journals, an English-language *Anthropological Science*, and a Japanese-language *Anthropological Science* (Japanese Series).

40 For physical anthropology in Japan, see Nobayashi (2003).

References

Ackroyd, Joyce. 1982. "Introduction," pp. ix-liv in *Lessons from History: The Tokushi Yoron by Arai Hakuseki*. St. Lucia: University of Queensland Press.

Aoki, Michiko Y. 1997. *Records of Wind and Earth: A Translation of Fudoki with Introduction and Commentaries*. Ann Arbor, Mich.: Association of Asian Studies.

Asad, Telal. 1998 [1973]. "Two European images of non-European rule," pp. 103-18 in *Anthropology and the Colonial Encounter*, ed. Talal Asad. New York: Humanities Press.

Asad, Talal. ed. 1998 [1973]. *Anthropology and the Colonial Encounter*. New York: Humanities Press.

Askew, David. 2001. "Oguma Eiji and the construction of the modern Japanese national identity," *Social Science Japan Journal* 4 (1): 111-16.

Askew, David. 2002. "The debate on the 'Japanese' race in imperial Japan: Displacement or coexistence?" *Japanese Review of Cultural Anthropology* 3: 79-96.

Askew, David. 2003. "Empire and the anthropologist: Torii Ryûzô and early Japanese anthropology," *Japanese Review of Cultural Anthropology* 4: 133-54.

Baelz, Erwin [Erwin von Bälz]. 1932. *Awakening Japan: The Diary of a Ger-*

man Doctor. New York: Viking Press.

Bälz, Erwin von. 1907. "Prehistoric Japan," pp. 523-47 *in Annual Report [of the] Smithsonian Institution*. Washington D.C.: Smithsonian Institution.

Bälz, Erwin von. 2001. *Berutsu Nihon bunkanron* [Bälz on Japanese culture]. Tokyo: Tôkai Daigaku Shuppankai.

Batchelor, John. 1892. *The Ainu of Japan: The Religion, Superstitions, and General History of the Hairy Aborigines of Japan*. New York: Fleming H. Revell.

Beddoe, John. 1905. "Colour and race," *Journal of the Anthropological Institute of Great Britain and Ireland* 35 (July-December): 219-50.

Bleed, Peter. 1986. "Almost archaeology: Early archaeological interest in Japan," pp. 57-67 in *Windows on the Japanese Past: Studies in Archaeology and Prehistory*, eds. Richard J. Pearson et al. Ann Arbor, Mich.: The University of Michigan.

Boas, Franz. 1904. "The history of anthropology," *Science* 20 (512, 21 October): 513-24.

Bremen, Jan van, and Akitoshi Shimizu. 1999. "Anthropology in colonial context: A tale of two countries and some," pp. 1-10 in *Anthropology and Colonialism in Asia and Oceania*, eds. Jan van Bremen and Akitoshi Shimizu. Richmond, Surrey: Curzon.

Bremen, Jan van, and Akitoshi Shimizu eds. 1999. *Anthropology and Colonialism in Asia and Oceania*. Richmond, Surrey: Curzon.

Bryan, J. Ingram. 1925. "The origin of the Japanese race," *Transactions and Proceedings of the Japan Society London* 22: 90-105.

Calloway, Colin G. 1987. *Crown and Calumet: British-Indian Relations, 1783-1815*. Norman, Okla.: University of Oklahoma Press.

Canny, N. "The ideology of English colonization: From Ireland to America," *William and Mary Quarterly* 30 (4): 574-98.

Closson, Carlos C. 1897. "The hierarchy of European races," *American Journal of Sociology* 3 (3): 314-27.

Cooper, Michael. 1974. *Rodrigues the Interpreter: An Early Jesuit in Japan and China*. New York and Tokyo: Weatherhill.

Cooper, Michael, ed. 2001. *João Rodrigues's Account of Sixteenth-Century Japan*. London: The Hakluyt Society.

Darnell, Regna. 1977. "History of anthropology in historical perspective," *Annual Review of Anthropology* 6: 399-417.

Daunton, Martin, and Rick Halpern. 1999. "Introduction: British identities, indigenous peoples, and the empire," pp. 1-18 in *Empire and Others: British Encounters with Indigenous Peoples, 1600-1850*, eds. Martin Daunton and Rick Halpern. London: UCL Press.

Daunton, Martin and Rick Halpern eds. 1999. *Empire and Others: British Encounters with Indigenous Peoples, 1600-1850*. London: UCL Press.

Faubion, James D. 1993. "History in anthropology," *Annual Review of An-*

David Askew

thropology 22: 35-54.

Gillingham, John. 1987. "Images of Ireland 1170-1600: The origins of English imperialism," *History Today* 37 (February): 16-22.

Griffis, William Elliot. 1876. *The Mikado's Empire*, Book 1, *History of Japan: From 660 B.C. to 1872 A.D.* New York: Harper & Bros.

Hall, Catherine. 2002. *Civilising Subjects: Colony and Metropole in the English Imagination, 1830-1867.* Chicago: University of Chicago Press.

Hanihara Kazurô. 1993. "Nihonjin no keisei" [The formation of the Japanese], pp. 83-114 in *Iwanami kôza Nihon tsûshi* [Iwanami Complete History of Japan] vol. 1, *Nihon rettô to jinrui shakai* [The Japanese archipelago and human society], eds. Asao Naohiro et al. Tokyo: Iwanami Shoten.

Hechter, Michael. 1999. *Internal Colonialism: The Celtic Fringe in British National Development.* New Brunswick, N.J.: Transaction Publishers.

Herbert-Gustar, A. L., and P. A. Nott. 1980. *John Milne, Father of Modern Seismology.* Tenterden, Kent: Paul Norbury Publishing.

Hitchcock, Romyn. 1982. "Letters to the editor: Pre-Aino race in Japan," *Science* 20 (502, 16 September): 163-64.

Ikeda Jirô. 1973. "Kaisetsu" [Introduction], in *Ronshû Nihonbunka no kigen* [A collection of essays on the origins of Japanese culture], vol. 5, *Nihonjinshuron gengogaku* [Theories of the Japanese race and linguistics], eds. Ikeda Jirô and Ôno Susumu. Tokyo: Heibonsha.

Ikeda Jirô. 1982. *Nihonjin no kigen* [The origins of the Japanese]. Tokyo: Kôdansha Gendai Shinsho.

Kaempfer, Engerbertus. 1977 [1727-28]. *The History of Japan, Giving an Account of the Ancient and Present State and Government of that Empire, together with a Description of the Kingdom of Siam*, translated by F. G. Scheuchzer, vol. 1, reprint of the 1727-28 edition. Tokyo: Yushodo.

Kemish, S.B. 1860. *The Japanese Empire: Its Physical, Political, and Social Condition and History.* London: Partridge & Co.

Kiyono Kenji. 1944. *Nippon jinshuron hensenshi* [A history of the evolution of theories of the Japanese race]. Tokyo: Koyama Shoten.

Koganei Yoshikiyo. 1926 [1904]. "Nihon sekki jidai no jûmin" [The stone-age residents of Japan], *Tôyô Gakugei Zasshi* 259 (260): 289-362, reprinted in Koganei Yoshikiyo, *Jinruigaku kenkyü* [Anthropological research], Tokyo: Okayama Shoten.

Kudô Masaki. 1979. *Nihon jinshuron* [The debate on the Japanese race]. Tokyo: Yoshikawa Kôbunkan.

MacFarlane, Charles. 1852. *Japan: An Account, Geographical and Historical.* New York: George P. Putnam & Co.

McLeod, N. 1875. *Epitome of the Ancient History of Japan, Including a Guide Book.* Nagasaki, Japan: "Rising Sun" Office.

Milne, John. 1879. "On the Stone Age in Japan," *Report of the British Association for the Advancement of Science* (1879): 401.

Milne, John. 1880. "Notes on stone implements from Otaru and Hakodate: With a few general remarks on the prehistoric remains in Japan," *Transactions of the Asiatic Society of Japan* 8: 61-91.

Milne, John. 1881. "The Stone Age in Japan: With notes on recent geological changes which have taken place," *Journal of the Anthropological Institute of Great Britain and Ireland* 10: 389-423.

Milne, John. 1882. "Notes on the Koro-poku-guru or Pitdwellers of Yezo and the Kurile Islands," *Transactions of the Asiatic Society of Japan* 10: 187-98.

Milne, John. 1893. "Notes on a journey in Northeast Yezo and across the island," *Supplementary Papers of the Royal Geographical Society* 3: 479-516.

Morgan, Philip D. 1999. "Encounters between British and 'indigenous' peoples, c. 1500-c. 1800," pp. 42-78 in *Empire and Others: British Encounters with Indigenous Peoples, 1600-1850*, eds. Martin Daunton and Rick Halpern. London: UCL Press.

Morse, Edward S. 1877. "Traces of early man in Japan," *Nature* 17 (29 November): 89.

Morse, Edward S. 1879. "Traces of an early race in Japan," *The Popular Science Monthly* 14 (January): 257-66.

Morse, Edward S. 2539 [1879]. "Shell Mounds of Omori," *Memoirs of the Science Department, University of Tokio* 1 (1).

Morse, Edward S. 1880. "Some recent publications on Japanese archaeology," *American Naturalist* 14 (September): 656-62.

Morse, Edward S. 1892. "Letters to the editor: A pre-Aino race in Japan," *Science* 20 (501, 9 September): 148-49.

Morse, Edward S. 1925. "Shell mounds and changes in the shells composing them," *The Scientific Monthly* (October): 429-40.

Munro, Neil Gordon. 1911 [1908]. *Prehistoric Japan*. Yokohama.

Munro, N.G. 2002 [1962]. *Ainu no shinkô to sono gishiki*. Tokyo: Kokusho Kankôkai. [Translation of N.G. Munro, *Ainu Creed and Cult*. London: Routledge & Kegan Paul, 1962].

Murdoch, James. 1996 [1910]. *A History of Japan*, vol. 1, *From the Origins to the Arrival of the Portuguese in 1542 A.D.* London and New York: Routledge.

Nag, Kalidas. 1941. *Prehistoric Japan*. Tokyo: Kokusai Bunka Shinkôkai.

Nobayashi, Atsushi. 2003. "Physical anthropology in wartime Japan," pp. 143-50 in *Wartime Japanese Anthropology in Asia and the Pacific*, eds. Akitoshi Shimizu and Jan van Bremen. Osaka: National Museum of Ethnology.

Oguma, Eiji. 2002. *A Genealogy of "Japanese" Self-images*, translated by David Askew. Melbourne: Trans Pacific Press.

Ôta Yüzô. 1988. *E. S. Môsu: "Furuki Nihon" o tsutaeta shinnichi kagakusha*

[E. S. Morse – A pro-Japanese scientist on "Old Japan"]. Tokyo: Riburopôto.

Pagden, Anthony. 1995. *Lords of All the World: Ideologies of Empire in Spain, Britain and France c. 1500-c. 1800.* New Haven: Yale University Press.

St. John, H.C. 1873. "The Ainos: Aborigines of Yeso," *Journal of the Anthropological Institute of Great Britain and Ireland* 2: 248-54.

Saitô Tadashi. 1985. *Kôkogakushi no hitobito* [Figures the history of (Japanese) archaeology]. Tokyo: Daiichi Shobô.

Saitô Tadashi. 1990. *Nihon kôkogakushi no tenkai* [The development of archaeology in Japan]. Tokyo: Gakuseisha.

Saitô Tadashi. 1995 [1974]. *Nihon kôkogakushi* [The history of Japanese Archaeology]. Tokyo: Yoshikawa Kôbunkan.

Sasaki Kômei ed. 1993. *Minzokugaku no senkakusha – Torii Ryûzô no mita Ajia* [Pioneer of ethnology: Torii Ryûzô in Asia]. Suita, Osaka: Kokuritsu Minzoku Hakubutsukan [National Museum of Ethnology].

Schottlaender, Felix. 1995. *Nihon ni okeru ichi Doitsujin ishi no shôgai to gyôseki* [The life and achievements of a German medical doctor in Japan]. Tokyo: Ôzorasha.

Sekimoto Teruo. 1995. "Nihon no jinruigaku to Nihon shigaku" [Anthropology in Japan and Japanese historiography], pp. 123-47 in *Iwanami kôza Nihon tsûshi. Bekkan 1* [Iwanami Complete History of Japan. Supplementary vol.1] eds. Asao Naohiro et al. Tokyo: Iwanami Shoten.

Sekimoto, Teruo. 2003. "Selves and Others in Japanese anthropology," pp. 131-42 in *Wartime Japanese Anthropology in Asia and the Pacific*, eds. Akitoshi Shimizu and Jan van Bremen. Osaka: National Museum of Ethnology.

Shimizu Akitoshi. 1998. "Nihon no jinruigaku" [Anthropology in Japan], pp. 111-33 in *Bunkajinruigaku no susume* [An invitation to cultural anthropology], ed. Funabiki Takeo. Tokyo: Chikuma Shobô.

Shimizu, Akitoshi. 1999. "Colonialism and the development of modern anthropology in Japan," pp. 115-71 in *Anthropology and Colonialism in Asia and Oceania*, eds. Jan van Bremen and Akitoshi Shimizu. Richmond, Surrey: Curzon.

Shimizu, Akitoshi and Jan van Bremen eds. 2003. *Wartime Japanese Anthropology in Asia and the Pacific*. Osaka: National Museum of Ethnology.

Shirai Mitsutarô. 1886. "Norito" [Celebratory remarks], *Jinruigakkai Hôkoku* [The Bulletin of the Tôkyô Anthropological Society], 1 (February): 3-4.

Siebold, Henry von. 1879. *Notes on Japanese Archaeology with Especial Reference to the Stone Age.* Yokohama: C. Levy.

Siebold, Henry von. 1996. *Shô-Shiiboruto Ezo kenbunki* [Siebold the Younger on Yesso]. Tokyo: Heibonsha.

Siebold, Philipp Franz von. 1973. *Manners and Customs of the Japanese in the Nineteenth Century: From the Accounts of Dutch Residents in Japan and from the German Work of Dr. Philipp Franz von Siebold.* Rutland, Vermont and Tokyo: Charles E. Tuttle.

Sofue, Takao. 1961. "Anthropology in Japan: Historical review and modern trends," *Biennial Review of Anthropology* 2: 173-214.

Steinmetz, Andrew. 1860. *Japan and Her People.* London: Routledge, Warne, & Routledge.

Stocking, George W., Jr. 1982 [1968]. *Race, Culture, and Evolution: Essays in the History of Anthropology.* Chicago and London: University of Chicago Press.

Stocking, George W., Jr. 1987. *Victorian Anthropology.* New York: Free Press.

Stocking, George W., Jr. ed. 1988. *Bones, Bodies, Behavior: Essays on Biological Anthropology.* Madison, Wisc.: University of Wisconsin Press, c1988

Stocking, George W., Jr. 1989. "The ethnographic sensibility of the 1920s and the dualism of the anthropological tradition," pp. 208-76 in *Romantic Motives: Essays on Anthropological Sensibility,* ed. George W. Stocking Jr. Madison, Wisc.: University of Wisconsin Press, 1989.

Stocking, George W., Jr. ed. 1989. *Romantic Motives: Essays on Anthropological Sensibility.* Madison, Wisc.: University of Wisconsin Press.

Stocking, George W., Jr. 1991. *Colonial Situations: Essays on the Contextualization of Ethnographic Knowledge.* Madison, Wisc.: University of Wisconsin Press.

Stocking, George W., Jr. 1992. *The Ethnographer's Magic and Other Essays in the History of Anthropology.* Madison, Wisc.: University of Wisconsin Press.

Stocking, George W., Jr. 2001 [1982]. "The shaping of national anthropologies: A view from the center," pp. 281-302 in *Delimiting Anthropology: Occasional Essays and Reflections,* ed. George W. Stocking, Jr. Madison, Wisc.: University of Wisconsin Press.

Stocking, George W., Jr. 2001 [1994]. "The turn-of-the-century concept of race," pp. 3-23 in *Delimiting Anthropology: Occasional Essays and Reflections.* Madison, Wisc.: University of Wisconsin Press.

Stocking, George W., Jr. 2001 [1995]. "Delimiting anthropology: Historical reflections on the boundaries of a boundless discipline," pp. 303-29 in *Delimiting Anthropology: Occasional Essays and Reflections.* Madison, Wisc.: University of Wisconsin Press.

Suenari Michio. 1988. "Torii Ryûzô: Higashi Ajia jinruigaku no senkakusha" [Torii Ryûzô: A pioneer of East Asian anthropology], pp. 47-64 in *Bunkajinruigaku gunzô 3, Nihon* [Major Figures in Cultural Anthropology 3, Japan], ed. Ayabe Tsuneo. Kyoto: Academia Shuppan.

Takahashi Yoshio. 1884. *Nihon jinshu kairyôron* [On improving the Japanese race]. Tokyo: Ishikawa Hanjirô.

Terada Kazuo. 1975. *Nihon no jinruigaku* [The anthropology of Japan]. Tokyo: Shisakusha.

Thomas, Nicholas. 1994. *Colonialism's Culture: Anthropology, Travel, and Government*. Princeton: Princeton University Press.

Torii Ryûzô. 1975 [1918]. "Yûshi izen no Nihon" [Prehistoric Japan], pp. 167-453 in *Torii Ryûzô zenshû* [The complete works of Torii Ryûzô], vol. 1. Tokyo: Asahi Shinbunsha.

Torii Ryûzô. 1975 [1927]. "Nihon jinruigaku no hattatsu" [The development of Japanese anthropology], pp. 459-70 in *Torii Ryûzô zenshû* [The complete works of Torii Ryûzô], vol. 1. Tokyo: Asahi Shinbunsha.

Torii Ryûzô. 1975-77. *Torii Ryûzô zenshû* [The complete works of Torii Ryûzô], vols.1-13. Tokyo: Asahi Shinbunsha.

Torii Ryûzô. 1977. *Torii Ryûzô zenshû* [The complete works of Torii Ryûzô], *Bekkan* [Supplementary Volume]. Tokyo: Asahi Shinbunsha.

Tsuboi Shôgorô. 1887. "Korobokkuru Hokkaidô ni sumishinarubeshi" [The Koro-pok-guru once resided in Hokkaido], *Tôkyô Jinruigakkai hôkoku* 2 (12): 93-97.

Tsuboi Shôgorô. 1904. "Tôkyô jinruigakkai man-20-nen kinen enzetsu" [Speech to mark the twentieth anniversary of the Tôkyô Anthropology Society], *Tôkyô Jinruigakkai Zasshi* 20: 1-12.

Vermeulen, Hans F. and Arturo Alvarez Roldán eds. 1995. *Fieldwork and Footnotes: Studies in the History of European Anthropology*. London and New York: Routledge.

Weiner, Michael. 1994. *Race and Migration in Imperial Japan*. London and New York: Routledge.

Weiner, Michael. 1997. "The invention of identity: 'Self' and 'Other' in pre-war Japan," pp. 1-16 in *Japan's Minorities: The Illusion of Homogeneity*, ed. Michael Weiner. London and New York: Routledge.

White, Richard. 1991. *The Middle Ground: Indians, Empires, and Republics in the Great Lakes Region, 1650-1815*, Cambridge and New York: Cambridge University Press.

Wilkinson, Jane. 1993. "A Scottish doctor's vocation: Gordon Munro and the Ainu collections at the National Museums of Scotland," in *European Studies on Ainu Language and Culture*, ed. Josef Kreiner. Munich: Iudicium.

Williamson, Arthur H. 1996. "Scotts, Indians and empire: The Scottish politics of civilization 1519-1609," *Past & Present* 150 (February): 46-83.

Wolf, Eric R. 1994. "Perilous ideas: Race, culture, people," *Current Anthropology* 35 (1): 1-12.

Yamaguchi Bin et al. 1998. *Nihonjin no kigen no nazo* [Mysteries of the origin of the Japanese]. Tokyo: Nihon Bungeisha.

Yoshioka Ikuo. 1987. *Nihon jinshu ronsô no makuake – Môsu to Ômori kaizuka* [The beginning of the debate on the Japanese race: Morse and the Ômori shell-mound]. Tokyo: Kyôritsu Shuppan, 1987.

Yoshioka Ikuo. 1993. *Mirunu no Nihon jinshuron – Ainu to Koropokuguru* [Milne on the Japanese race: The Ainu and the Koro-pok-guru]. Tokyo: Yûzankaku.

Chapter 4

Constructing Selves and Others

in Japanese Anthropology:

The Case of Micronesia and Southeast Asian Studies

Shinji YAMASHITA

Introduction

It is now commonplace to relate the history of Western anthropology to colonialism, imperialism and Orientalism, however they may be defined. As Shimizu Akitoshi has noted, in this sort of discussion, dichotomies such as the West versus the non-West, the colonizer versus the colonized, the powerful versus the powerless, and the observer versus the observed are presupposed. It seems that this schema, which is based on the Western definition of anthropology, cannot allow for the possibility of colonial anthropology in Japan, since Japan belongs to the non-West, the Oriental world (Shimizu 1999: 115).

By reviewing the history of anthropology in Japan, this chapter examines the ways in which Self and Others are constructed by Japanese scholars, in order to clarify the features of Japanese anthropology. I focus particularly upon Micronesia and Southeast Asia, the region formerly called "Nan'yô,"[1] which literally means the "South Seas." This region was seen as a "backward" and "primitive" world which belonged neither to the East nor the West, the two "civilized" regions recognized by the Japanese. Nan'yô was a region of interest to anthropologists whose role in the modern intellectual division of labor was to study anything considered "primitive," "savage," "ancient," or "undeveloped." By examining the history of Japanese anthropology in relation to Nan'yô, I hope to demonstrate that Japan had its own distinctive style of colonial anthropology. In his paper, "Anthropological futures," Adam Kuper has paid special attention to the anthropologies which have developed outside the western metropolitan centers (Kuper 1994), of which Japanese anthropology is a good example. This is important for the history of world anthropology as a whole, and might lead to a redefinition of the discipline in the future, as Shimizu (ibid.) has suggested.

The Birth and Growth of Japanese Anthropology

According to Terada Kazuo (1981: 7), anthropology in Japan began 1884 with a group of young scholars who formed a discussion group called *Jinruigaku no Tomo* or "Friends of Anthropology" which later became the Anthropological Society of Nippon (see also Askew's chapter). Stimulated by the excavation in 1877 of an ancient shell-mound in Tokyo by Edward Morse, an American zoologist, they had become interested in the origins of the Japanese and Japanese culture.[2] The central figure in this group was Tsuboi Shôgorô (1863-1913). Tsuboi later spent three years studying in London, and on his return in 1892, he was appointed as the first Professor of Anthropology at the Tokyo Imperial University.

The first academic journal in Japanese anthropology, entitled *Jinruigaku Zasshi* (Anthropology Magazine) was published in 1886 – thirteen years before the first edition of the *American Anthropologist* in 1899. An association for ethnologists or socio-cultural anthropologists, the *Nihon Minzokugakkai* (Japanese Society of Ethnology), originated nearly fifty years later, in 1934. Its journal, *Minzokugaku-kenkyû* (*Japanese Journal of Ethnology*) was first published in 1935. By 1936 the Society already had 332 members (Minzokugaku Shinkôkai 1984: 6), and by 2003 the membership numbered approximately 2,000.[3]

Throughout the history of Japanese anthropology, there have been two fundamental concerns. One is a concern with the Japanese people and their culture, and the other is a concern with "other cultures," particularly in the Asian region. The first concern existed, as we have seen, at the very birth of Japanese anthropology. Early anthropologists devoted themselves to the study of the Stone Age in Japan and investigating the racial origins of the peoples of the Japanese islands, particularly the Ainu. In the early twentieth century, Tsuboi was the leading figure in the debate over the original inhabitants of Japan, and especially the origins of the Ainu people.

In the development of Japanese socio-cultural anthropology, two important figures might be mentioned: Torii Ryûzô (1870-1953) and Yanagita Kunio (1875-1962). Torii studied privately with Tsuboi,[4] but while Tsuboi was mainly concerned with Japan, Torii carried out fieldwork further afield, as Askew has noted in his chapter. Beginning in the Liaodong Peninsula in Northeastern China in 1894, he later travelled to places such as Taiwan (1896, 1897, 1898, 1900), the Chishima Islands (1899), China (1902-03), Korea (1911-1916), Eastern Siberia (1919, 1921), Manchuria (1905, 1909, 1927, 1928, 1933, 1935, 1940-41) and Mongolia (1906, 1907, 1930, 1933) (Suenari 1988: 50). This progression clearly reflected Japanese imperialist expansion into other parts of Asia: Taiwan was occupied in 1895, Korea in 1910, Micronesia in 1919, Manchuria in 1933, and Southeast Asia in 1941.

In his time, Torii became something of a national hero, as he brought back information on the exotic and unknown areas that Japan was then colonizing. This work by a non-Western anthropologist carrying out fieldwork among East Asians predated that of Bronislaw Malinowski among the Trobriands Islanders by nearly twenty years. Shimizu (1999: 132) compares Torii's work with that of the early "field anthropologists" in the West, such as Haddon and Rivers. Like the historians of the period, Torii saw "Oriental ethnology" (*Tôyô jinshugaku* or *Tôyô minzokugaku*) as a distinct discipline, the study of the Orient by Oriental scholars who were assumed to better placed to study the region than scholars from the West (Torii 1975: 482-483).

Another important figure in the early stages of the development of Japanese cultural anthropology was Yanagita Kunio. While working as a bureaucrat at the Ministry of Agriculture and Commerce, Yanagita studied Western anthropology on his own and developed a distinctive approach to the study of the Japanese and their culture, mainly in the late 1920s. He contributed to the publication of the first ethnological journal in Japan, *Minzoku* (Ethnos), in 1925, together with Oka Masao (1898-1982) who later became the leading figure in Japanese ethnology of his generation. However, the journal lasted for only three and a half years and stopped publication in 1929. Tired of both his editing and his relations with Yanagita, Oka went off to study ethnology in Vienna.

In 1929, the same year when *Minzoku* ceased publication, a new journal called *Minzokugaku* (Folklore Studies) was launched by a group called the Minzokugakkai (Society of Folklore Studies).[5] The central figures of this group was Orikuchi Shinobu, another founding ancestor of Japanese folklore studies, and other members included scholars of folklore, ethnology, rural sociology, and myth. In 1934 some members of the group were instrumental in establishing the Nihon Minzokugakkai (Japanese Society of Ethnology), under the stimulus of the First International Congress of Anthropological and Ethnological Sciences held in London the same year (Minzokugaku Shinkôkai 1984: 218).

By this time, Yanagita's research had taken a nationalistic turn, and he parted company with the ethnologists in order to establish his own school of Japanese folklore studies (Oguma 1995: 205-34). He established his own research group called initially *Mokuyôkai* (Thursday Workshop) and later *Minkandenshô no Kai* (Society for the Study of Folk Traditions). This subsequently developed into another association called *Nihon Minzokugakkai* (meaning in this case "Japanese Society of Folklore Studies"). He consciously neglected the ethnic heterogeneity of the expanding Japanese Empire at that time, and concentrated his research on the *jômin*, the common, rural, rice cultivating, "homogeneous" Japanese who made up 70 percent of the total Japanese population.

In addition to these major figures, one should also mention Shiratori Kurakichi (1865-1942), the founder of *Tôyô shigaku* ("Oriental historical science"). Shiratori was a historian specializing in China who had studied Western (i.e. German) historical science as a member of the first generation of students at Tokyo Imperial University. He believed that Asian (Japanese) researchers could achieve a much deeper understanding of Asian culture than Western researchers, and *Tôyô shigaku* was established on the basis of this belief. As Stefan Tanaka (1993) and Kang Sang Jung (1996) have discussed, this "Orientology" can be regarded as a Japanese version of Orientalism, the conceptualization of "the Orient" as being essentially different from "the West," as described by Said (1978) for the Middle East. Shiratori was also on good terms with Gotô Shinpei, the director-general of the civil administration of Taiwan who later became the first president of the Southern Manchurian Railroad Company. The areas in which this Japanese Orientalism became most evident were, needless to say, the areas controlled by Japanese imperialism: Taiwan, Korea, Manchuria, China, Micronesia, and Southeast Asia. Interestingly, it was Shiratori who became the first president of the Japanese Society of Ethnology when it was established in 1934.

Institutionally, the Department of Sociology at Seoul Imperial University in Korea (established 1926) and the Department of Anthropology/Ethnology (in Japanese, *dozoku jinshugaku*, or the study of indigenous peoples) at Taipei Imperial University in Taiwan (established 1928) also played important roles in pre-World War II ethnographic research. These departments carried out anthropological fieldwork under the colonial regime, and they trained cultural anthropologists such as Izumi Seiichi (1915-1970) and Mabuchi Tôichi (1909-1988) who were to become Japan's leading anthropologists after World War II. It can be argued that the institutionalization of anthropology began in the colonized periphery rather than the metropolitan center of Japan. It is also interesting to see that this colonial version of anthropology emphasized fieldwork and the functionalist approach, while the metropolitan anthropology based in Tokyo was usually armchair anthropology (cf. Shimizu 1999: 117).

During the further wave of Japanese colonialist expansion to Asia in 1941, the *Tôyô Bunka Kenkyûsho* (Institute of Oriental Culture) was established at the Tokyo Imperial University to promote the understanding of the cultures of Asia and the Orient. The rationale for its foundation was as follows:

> Oriental culture is different from Occidental culture owing to its people, climate and history. The study of Oriental culture must be in the hands of Oriental scholars. Of course there are Western researchers who could achieve good work in this field but they are not be compared to Oriental

scholars in understanding Oriental culture. However, it is regrettable to say that in Japan we have so far not been no sufficiently successful in the study of Oriental culture. (Tokyo Daigaku Tôyô Bunka Kenkyûsho 1991: 3)

This is exactly the same idea as that on which *Tôyô shigaku* was based. It was in this Institute that the first chair in cultural anthropology was established in a Japanese national university in 1949, after World War II.

Another institute called the *Minzoku Kenkyûsho* (Institute of Ethnic Research) was founded in Tokyo in 1943 under the Ministry of Education and Culture. Its aim was "to carry out research on ethnic matters in order to contribute to ethnic policy," because of the urgency of ethnic research "to accomplish the Great Asian War to construct Greater Asia" (Nakao 1997: 50). Oka Masao and Furuno Kiyoto (1899-1979) were among those involved. Yet another institute, the *Seihoku Kenkyûsho* (Northwestern Research Institute), was established in Mongolia in 1944. Imanishi Kinji (1902-1992), Ishida Eichirô (1903-1968) and Umesao Tadao (1920-) were involved in projects there. However, both institutes closed soon after, with the end of World War II in 1945.[6]

Developments after World War II

Japanese ethnology after World War II restarted with the organization of a workshop devoted to the origins of Japanese culture in 1948, chaired by Ishida Eiichirô. Other participants included Oka Masao, the Oriental historian Egami Namio, and the archeologist Yawata Ichirô. The group investigated the roots of Japanese culture through comparisons with the neighboring peoples of East, North and Southeast Asia and Oceania. It created something of a sensation when Egami proposed that an ancient ruling class, the *kibaminzoku* (horse-rider people), including the ancestors of the emperor and the imperial family, had come from somewhere in Korea or China to conquer the commoner Japanese. This interest in Japanese cultural history was further developed later on by Ôbayashi Taryô in his comparative study of Japanese mythology (Ôbayashi 1961).

Ishida, who had studied ethnology in Vienna following Oka's example, was very active during this period. He proved an able editor of *Minzokugaku-kenkyû*, and also contributed greatly to the establishment of a Department of Cultural Anthropology at the University of Tokyo in 1954. This was the first cultural anthropology department in a Japanese national university to offer an undergraduate course, although a course in biological anthropology had been established earlier, in 1939. Nanzan University, a private Christian university in Nagoya, had started its cultural anthropology course in 1952, and the Graduate School of Tokyo Metropolitan University set up a course in social anthropology in 1953.

Although Ishida had studied within the German tradition of historical ethnology, he introduced American style "general anthropology" into the newly established anthropology curriculum after a visit to American universities in 1952-1953 (Ishida 1970a: 122-56). The name "cultural anthropology" (*bunkajinruigaku*) rather than "ethnology" (*minzokugaku*) was adopted, not only because of American dominance after World War II, but also as a reaction against the negative image which ethnology had acquired due to its association with the ethnic policies of the Japanese Empire, in which the Minzoku Kenkyûsho had played a role (Ishida 1970b: 17).[7]

Nakane Chie wrote a review of the main trends in Japanese cultural anthropology from the 1950s to the early 1970s which was published in English (Nakane 1974). According to her, Japanese cultural anthropology during this period had the following characteristics: (1) there were very few anthropologists following the Western pattern of research based on long-term fieldwork in other societies; (2) the areas they were concerned with were mainly within Japan, particularly the rural areas and the Ryukyu Islands; and (3) ethnologists such as Oka Masao and Ishida Eiichirô who received their education in Austria or Germany rather than in Britain or the United States played an important leadership role. Based on these observations, Nakane concluded that Japan's most fruitful contribution to world anthropology would be made through studies comparing Japan with the neighboring societies of East and Southeast Asia.

Thirty years later, at the start of the twenty-first century, the main trends in Japanese cultural anthropology have changed considerably, reflecting changes in the real world as well as in academe. First, in parallel with Japan's economic growth since the 1960s, the importance of fieldwork outside Japan has increased, and Japanese scholars are among the most active fieldworkers throughout the world. The number of scholars carrying out long-term fieldwork has increased, and the National Museum of Ethnology, established in Osaka in 1974, has become one of the most important centers of Japanese anthropological research.

Secondly, the boundaries of the areas of interest to Japanese anthropologists have also been greatly extended during this period, and there has been a stream of work on regions outside Japan. Shimizu (1999: 161) sees in this transition the evolution of Japanese anthropology into a "global anthropology," similar to that which developed in the United States, United Kingdom, France, and Germany.[8]

Thirdly, in terms of the subject matter of research, Japanese anthropology is still comparatively traditional. According to a survey carried out by the Japanese Society of Ethnology in 1994, "religion/ritual," "history/culture change" and "social structure" were still the three main topics of interest, though the younger generation was becoming more concerned with applied anthropology and political issues.

Nan'yô and Japanese Orientalism

Throughout the history of anthropology in Japan, the areas studied by Japanese anthropologists have changed, reflecting changes in Japan's boundaries and international relations. Sekimoto Teruo has examined these changes through an analysis of the articles in *Minzokugaku-kenkyû* (*Japanese Journal of Ethnology*) published from 1934 to 1994 (Sekimoto 1995). He describes a "centrifugal trend" in which Japanese anthropologists have tended to carry out fieldwork in the most remote areas accessible to them during each period. Thus, from 1935 to 1944, during the high tide of Japanese imperialism, Japanese anthropologists tended to study areas such as Sakhalin, Korea, Taiwan, and Micronesia rather than the main Japanese islands. In this sense, Japanese anthropology followed a pattern similar to that of Western anthropologists who also studied the peoples of their colonies during the colonial period. There was a difference, however, in that Japanese anthropologists often studied peoples rather similar to themselves, especially in East Asia, while Western anthropologists focused mainly on peoples very different from themselves, especially in Asia and Africa. Accordingly, as Askew also notes in his chapter, Japanese anthropologists were likely to be more concerned with issues of similarity rather than difference. After World War II, with the collapse of the Japanese empire and colonialism, their studies shifted to peripheral areas and peoples closer to home, including Okinawa and the Ainu in Hokkaidô, from 1946 to 1966. As Japan's economy and international influence grew, Japanese anthropologists started studying Southeast Asia, Africa, and other more distant parts of the world from the 1960s.

Keeping this general trend in mind, now let us turn to the Nan'yô or "South Seas" region of the Pacific. Japanese involvement there began in the 1860s, although there had been accidental contacts between the Pacific islanders and Japanese fishermen previously. It was in 1868, the year of the Meiji Restoration, that Japanese labor emigration to Hawaii started. In 1875 Japan declared its control over the Ogasawara (Bonin) Islands, stretching in a long chain to the south of Tokyo. Because of the increasing population and limited resources in Japan, the Meiji government adopted a policy of overseas migration (Akimichi 1998).

In the 1880s and 1890s, there appeared a group of ideologues who advocated a policy of *nanshinron* or "southern advancement." Among them was Suzuki Tsunenori who went to the Marshall Islands in 1880 on the orders of the foreign minister, Inoue Kaoru, to investigate the case of the murder of a Japanese citizen by the local people. In 1892, he published a book entitled *Nan'yô tanken jikki* (Record of exploration in the South Seas) based on this journey, parts of which now appear to have been plagiarized.[9] Another important figure, Shiga Shigetaka, wrote *Nan'yô jiji* (Report on the South Seas) in 1887 based on a journey to the Pacific islands and Australia. Taguchi Ukichi wrote *Nan'yô keiryakuron* (Development in the South Seas), and established a trading company called Nantô Shôkai in 1890. Finally, Takekoshi Yosaburô popularized the image of the South Seas by publishing *Nangokuki* (Southern countries) in 1910, based on his journey to parts of East and Southeast Asia in the previous year, including Shanghai, Hong Kong, Singapore, Java, Sumatra, and French Indochina.

The political scientist, Yano Tôru, has examined southern expansionism through an analysis of the discourses of these ideologues (Yano 1975). According to him, they emphasized the economic underdevelopment and political backwardness of the South Sea regions, and the idea that developing them should be the task of Japan. Importantly, Shiga presented the Nan'yô as a "new world" that belonged neither to the civilizations of East or West. Japan's advancement into this region was, therefore, a way to establish itself as a "civilized" country compared with this underdeveloped and backward region. In this sense, these works were linked to the expansionism adopted in response to changing international circumstances after the Meiji Restoration.

As mentioned earlier, the colonial expansion to the south began with the takeover of Taiwan in 1895, and Micronesia in 1919 (Palau had been under Japanese occupation since 1914), and it reached as far as Southeast Asia in 1941. After the Japanese occupation of Micronesia in 1919 under a League of Nations' Mandate, and especially after the successful establishment of sugar plantations in Saipan and Tinian in 1920 by the Nan'yô Kôhatsu (South Seas Development Company), many Japanese, particularly people from the Okinawa region, migrated to the South Seas. The number increased every year. In 1933, Japanese accounted for 30,670 out of a total population of 80,884 in Micronesia, while in Tinian 5,538 of a total population of 7,554 were Japanese.

After 1935, as further expansion to the south started as part of the plan for a *Daitôa Kyôeiken,* or Great East Asian Co-prosperity Sphere, the Japanese population in the Pacific increased even more. In 1936, the Nan'yô Takushoku Company was established under government control. The number of Japanese residents increased to 77,000 in 1940, and 96,000 in 1942. In Palau where the Nan'yô-chô (Japanese colonial administration) was located, there were 13,000 Japanese in 1941. Big development companies opened offices, and Nan'yô Jinja, a government Shinto shrine, was established in 1940, with a ceremony to invite in Amaterasu Omikai, the Japanese sun deity. In this way, the Japanization of Micronesia proceeded apace.[10]

Through these historical processes, the popular image of the South Seas took shape in the minds of the Japanese. According to the study by Kawamura Minato, a researcher in Japanese modern literature, a particular kind of image became popular through *Bôken Dankichi,* or "The Adventurous Dankichi," a strip cartoon by Shimada Keizô serialized in *Shônen Kurabu* (Boys' Club) from 1933 to 1939 (Kawamura 1993). It relates the adventures of Dankichi, a heroic boy, who comes to an island called Banjintô ("Savage

Island") located somewhere in the southern tropics, having drifted there after falling asleep on his fishing boat. He later becomes the king of this island of cannibals with the assistance of Karikô ("clever mouse"). Dankichi is drawn with white skin, a grass skirt and a crown on his head, while his followers in the South Seas are dark skinned and referred to as *kuronbô* ("blacks"): they wear numbers on their fronts and look like stereotypical Western images of Africans.[11] Animals such as lions, elephants, and giraffes also live on Dankichi's island, even though it was modeled after Japanese Micronesia, the *Nan'yô Guntô*. Interestingly, Dankichi always wears a watch on his wrist and shoes on his feet, symbolizing that he still belongs to the civilized world.

Another example is the popular song, *Shûchô no Musume* ("The Daughter of a Village Chief"), with words and music by Ishida Ichimatsu. The song was a great hit in 1930 both on radio and on disc, though it had actually been composed in the early 1920s (Kawamura 1995: 88). The lyrics go like this:

My sweetheart is the daughter of a village chief
She's pretty dark, but in the South Seas, she's a beauty
In the Marshall Islands, below the equator
She dances slowly in the shade of the palm trees.
(Translated by Mark Peattie 1988: 216)

According to Peattie, Micronesia is thus viewed "as a distant paradise, conceived as being literally in the South Pacific, and inhabited by primitive peoples not much different from 'savages' anywhere – naked, ignorant, sensuous, and dark skinned." He adds that "after arriving in Micronesia, most colonists, who usually settled in one of the large Japanese communities in the islands, had little opportunity to change this stereotype, since they made scant effort to break out of their colonial boundaries" (ibid.: 216-217).

The Japanese image of the South, as typically portrayed in cartoons for children or in popular songs, was therefore "backward" and "primitive." In a sense, Japan needed to see its peoples in this way in order to see itself as being advanced and civilized. According to Kawamura Minato, the peculiar feature of Japan's modernity was that the "Orientalization" of Asia and the Pacific by the Japanese and the "de-Orientalization" and disassociation of Japan from Asia and the Pacific proceeded simultaneously. He writes:

The national motto of *datsua nyuô* (dissociating from Asia and joining with the West), Japan's long-cherished wish since the Meiji Era, was achieved not only by modernizing, civilizing and Westernizing herself, but also by seeing other Asian and Pacific regions as primitive and backward. Japan's civilization and enlightenment entailed regarding the regions of Asia and the Pacific, which shared the same cultural roots, as relatively primitive and savage. (Kawamura 1993: 120)

This was how the Nan'yô was represented by Japan during the process of colonization. However, this "Japanese Orientalism" is different from Western Orientalism because the Japanese stance toward the Nan'yô is actually ambiguous in terms of cultural distance: it is sometimes assumed to be "far," a remote primitive place, but sometimes "near," the presumed cradle of Japanese people and their culture. This is due to what Kawamura has described as Japan's peculiar version of modernity. The Japanese image of the South Seas has been constructed on the basis of this complicated self-consciousness.

Two Amateur Ethnographers: Matsuoka Shizuo and Hijikata Hisakatsu

This kind of consciousness toward the South can be illustrated in the work of two amateur ethnographers who were concerned with the Nan'yô. One of them, Matsuoka Shizuo (1878-1936), was actually involved in the military operation to occupy Ponape (Pohnpei) in 1914 as the second-in-command of the warship, *Tsukuba*. Though he was a navy man, he was interested in the culture of the Nan'yô, and in 1927 he published a book called *Mikuronesia minzokushi* (Ethnography of Micronesia).[12] He was also the younger brother of Yanagita Kunio, mentioned earlier.

This ethnography is unusual and unique, for it begins with his own military experience in Ponape in 1914. He writes:

> On October 17th, 1914, I landed on Ponape Island, the site of the headquarters of the Caroline Archipelago, with the military mission ... We embarked in dozens of boats in groups from the main navy vessel which was anchored off the coral reefs, and entered the bay which was like a mouth of the big river. We looked up at Mt. Nankiep and saw Sokehs Island on the right. First, I landed on the small island of Langer and summoned a German manager of the Jaluit Company to get information. (Matsuoka 1927: 1-4)

As a person who dreamed of being the ruler of a primitive tribe, Matsuoka actually occupied a South Sea island (Kawamura 1995: 152-53). Later he wrote his Micronesian ethnography in which he described the region as if he were a "stranger king" from Japan. As he described it,

> Cruising along the clear and calm coral reef was not unpleasant for me. Passing through the rocks and mangrove bushes in a native boat, we landed and found the houses of villagers which were invisible from the sea. Village children came out to see us, looking at our golden swords which attracted them. An old village chief clad in a new loin cloth welcomed us, together with his men. (Ibid.: 7)

As an ethnographer, Matsuoka was concerned with all the aspects of the people's lives: history, geography, population, language, legends, archeological sites, ethnic groups, belief system, social organization, life cycle, clothing and ornaments, housing, food and diet, and weapons.[13] He included sporadic comments on Micronesian customs from the Japanese point of view compared with that of the West. He states, for instance, "Of the islanders' customs which were unintelligible to Western eyes there are many that are quite understandable to us Japanese. Some customs categorized as superstitions are reasonable" (ibid: 94). Referring to the religious concepts, he says:

> It is difficult to explain the Micronesian spiritual culture in Western terms, because of the cultural difference in its origin. This book is an attempt at an explanation of the Micronesian people by a Japanese in Japanese. I do not follow Western theory. I have fundamental doubts about how far Western anthropologists since Bastian's days could have understood the Micronesian belief system. (Ibid: 180)
>
> In my observations, in Micronesia there were concepts of *imi* (taboo) or *tsumi* (crime, sin) similar to those which were found in ancient Japan. They are different from the Western concepts of sacred/profane as explained by Durkheim. (Ibid: 194)

As Endô Hisashi (1999: 89) has noted, one can see here an opposition between the West and Japan as well as between Japan and Micronesia. In opposition to the West, however, Japan and Micronesia are assumed to share a common cultural origin. Micronesia is, then, compared not to modern Japan but to ancient Japan. This may be a typical example of what Johannes Fabian has called the "denial of coevalness" as anthropology creates its object (Fabian 1983).

The other person I would like to discuss is Hijikata Hisakatsu (1900-1976). Born in 1900 into a wealthy middle class family, he studied art at the Tokyo University of Arts. As an ardent admirer of Paul Gauguin and with an interest in primitive culture and ancient Japan through his reading of books on ethnology and archeology, Hijikata had a strong interest in the South Seas (Hijikata 1991: 190-191).[14] He disliked cold weather and wanted to escape from "busy, civilized Tokyo" (ibid.: 180-190). Unlike most of the Japanese migrants at that time, he went to Micronesia not for economic reasons but in pursuit of something different from his life in Japan. In his old age he recollected his younger days in his "Poem of the South Seas":

> When I was there, I enjoyed myself with fishing, swimming and living naked.
> When I was there, I came to the isolated Southern island after a sudden tropical shower.

When I was there, I was young and the native girls liked me.
When I was there, I went after turtles in a native canoe.
When I was there, I chased palm crabs without sleeping on the uninhibited island ..... (ibid.: 150-151)

He left Tokyo in March 1929. Soon after arriving in Palau, he started to teach wood carving to the islanders in the public schools (*kôgakkô*) and at a handicraft school for local carpenters, as a part-time employee of the Nan'yô-chô.[15] In 1931, he moved to the isolated island of Satawal in search of a land far away from civilization, and he stayed there for the next seven-and-a-half years. He returned to Palau in 1939 to find great changes taking place there. He wrote with disappointment that it was full of Japanese people with houses, modern cafes, restaurants and company offices. He missed the old Palau that he had experienced when he first arrived there. The Nan'yô was, therefore, no longer a "paradise" for him, but the site of development which he did not want (ibid.: 243).

Hijikata was not only an artist but also an ethnographer, though he was not specially trained. During his stay in Palau, he was particularly interested in a meeting house (*abai*) with colored storyboards on which various pictures of gods, humans, birds, and animals were carved, together with plants. These were representations of Palauan myths and legends. He collected these kinds of pictures and stories and compiled them into a book called *Parao no shinwa to densetsu* (Myths and Legends in Palau), published in 1942. After World War II, he also compiled *Satewanutô minwa* (The Folk tales of Satawal Island) in 1953 with suggestions and advice from Yanagita Kunio, who rated Hijikata's work highly.

Ryûboku (Driftwood) and *Mikronesia Satewanutô minzokushi* (The ethnography of Satawal, Micronesia) are comprehensive descriptions of the culture and society of the Sawatal Islanders. The former is a sort of ethnographic diary published in 1943 in which Hijikata described the customs relating to taboo, rites of passage, social organization, forms of labor, navigation and magico-religious concepts through the events he encountered. The latter is an ethnography published posthumously in 1984 which integrated his unpublished materials with his ethnographic papers.[16] Sudoh Kenichi, a social anthropologist who visited the Satawal some fifty years later, writes of Hijikata's work:

The content of these books does not suffer at all in comparison with the research of professional cultural anthropologists or ethnologists ... In my own experience of conducting research in Satawal fifty years after Hijikata, I found a complete lack of falseness in his writing. The record of Satawalese life based on Hijikata's careful observations and direct association with the people of the island satisfies the most stringent conditions of ethnography, and I would like to affirm his qualifications as an ethnographer. (Sudoh 1991: 40)

Scientific Observers: Ethnologists and Anthropologists

Matsuoka and Hijikata were amateur ethnographers. In the Nan'yô, however, professional ethnologists and anthropologists were also involved in the colonial government. They included, among others, Sugiura Kenichi (1904-1954), Umesao Tadao (1920-) and Hasebe Kotondo (1882-1969).

Sugiura, then an assistant in the Department of Anthropology of Tokyo Imperial University, worked as a contract researcher for the Nan'yô-chô on a research project on "the Islanders' customs." He carried out field research from 1937 to 1941 in Palau, Ponape, Truk, and other Micronesian Islands, surveying land tenure systems, social organization, religion, and material culture. However, this research was interrupted by the outbreak of the Pacific War. In 1943 Sugiura began to work as a research associate at the Minzoku Kenkyûsho, the Institute of Ethnic Research. After the War he became the first professor of the Department of Cultural Anthropology at the University of Tokyo, established in 1953, though he died only a year after his appointment.

Sugiura was a cultural relativist who saw the world of the Islanders as a closed system and who used Malinowskian research methods to describe them as a functional whole. Regarding the relationship of ethnological research with the colonial governance of the Nan'yô, he wrote an article in which he emphasized the practical value of an ethnology which aimed to understand other cultures on their own terms. He concluded that the culture of the Islanders should be preserved to some extent and that change must take place gradually in accordance with their customs. Drastic reform is not only dangerous and but unfruitful (Sugiura 1941: 45). This stance towards the Islanders is clearly different from Hijikata's romantic view of them as "colonial Others." However, as the historical sociologist Tomiyama Ichirô has noted (1996), Sugiura's stance is that of the "signifying subject" who observes, describes and analyses the Islander's customs as a scientific specialist. The customs of the Islanders were given meaning by him in the name of ethnological science. In this sense, projection, though scientific, was one-way, from the colonizing Japanese to the colonized Micronesian Islanders or *tômin*. In this way he contributed to the land policy of the Nan'yô-chô colonial government.

Umesao Tadao, then a student of Kyoto Imperial University, joined the expedition to Ponape and its neighboring islands from July to October in 1941. The expedition was organized by the *Kyoto Tanken Chirigakkai* (Kyoto Society for Geographical Expeditions) and was led by Imanishi Kinji (1902-1992), then a Kyoto University lecturer. Interestingly, he and the other members of his research team had the chance to attend lectures on the ethnology of the Nan'yô by Sugiura and others who happened to be on board the same ship to Palau. After the expedition, Umesao wrote an essay on it in a book edited by Imanishi (Umesao 1944). Though he was trained in biological science, he made some perceptive socio-cultural comments on the colonial frontier of the Japanese Empire. Beginning with observations of the colors of the South Seas, he described various aspects of colonial life, including the Nan'yô Shrine, Okinawans, and the relations between the Japanese and the Islanders. Umesao, like Sugiura, adopted the stance of an exploring, observing, and describing subject. As a student of ecology, his method of observation was naturalistic: he observed people and culture as if he were observing the sea, trees, animals, and plants.[17]

On Umesao's return to Japan, the Pacific War broke out. In 1944, Umesao went to the Seihoku Kenkyûsho, the Northwestern Research Institute in Mongolia, together with his mentor, Imanishi, who was appointed Director of the Institute. After the War, Umesao published many books which includes *Mogoruzoku tankenki* (Mongolian expedition) in 1956, *Tônan Ajia kikô* (A journey to Southeast Asia) in 1964, and his most popular work, *Bunmei no seitai shikan* (An Ecological View of Civilizations), in 1967. He became the first Director-General of the National Museum of Ethnology, established in 1974.

According to Tomiyama (1996), the "signifying subject" appears more clearly in the case of biological anthropology. Hasebe Kotondo, then a biological anthropologist at Tokyo Imperial University, carried out research in Nan'yô from 1927. He classified the Islanders anthropologically and concluded that they had a biological affinity with the Japanese, because the ancestors of Japanese people for the most part came from the South Seas (Hasebe 1935: 186). This conclusion helped to justify the Japanese expansion to the Nan'yô region. Takano Rokurô, head of a bureau at the Ministry of Welfare, expressed this in the slogan, "We are the Southern Islanders":

Japanese are better suited to living in the Nan'yô in comparison with Westerners. Our skin is similar to that of the Nan'yô people and a physiologist says that our sweat glands are also similar ... biologically as well as psychologically we are *Nan'yôjin* or South Seas people. (Takano 1942: 548; Tomiyama 1996: 66-67)

It is interesting to see here that the Micronesians or the "colonial Others" were taken as anthropologically akin to the Japanese, the colonizers. Often this affinity was claimed on the grounds that they had common ancestors. In other words, as Tomiyama (ibid.: 67) has pointed out, Japanese colonization of the Nan'yô differed from European colonization in that it entailed the return of the ancestors to their homeland.

Southeast Asia as Japan's Homeland

Japan occupied in Southeast Asia in 1941. Little is known about what Japanese anthropologists did in Southeast Asia during the war period. As the war began, a huge number of publications appeared on Japan's "Greater Asia." Yano Tôru (1979: 3-4) quotes a bibliography, *Daitoa shiryô sôran* complied by Amano Keitarô, according to which, more than 2,000 books and more than 5,000 articles on Greater Asia were published in the year 1942 alone. Yano also points out that it was only after 1940 or 1941 that Southeast Asia became a national concern (ibid.: 6). Many of the books on Southeast Asia consisted of translations into Japanese from Western languages made in order to provide instant knowledge of the region.

From November 1942 to April 1943 the Minzoku Kenkyûsho organized a series of lectures in Tokyo to promote ethnological knowledge among the general public. The first lecture provided an introduction to ethnology, and the rest of the series dealt with topics such as "ethnic problems and ethnic policy," "the ethnology of China and India," "the ethnology of Europe and America," "the ethnology of Northern, Central, and Western Asia," and, finally, "the ethnology of the Southern Regions." This last lecture was concerned with Southeast Asia and Oceania, including the Philippines, the Dutch East Indies, Burma, French Indochina, Thailand, Malaya, and New Guinea (Minzokugaku Shinkôkai 1984: 21).

Some researchers, however, did carry out fieldwork in Southeast Asia during the war. One of them was Furuno Kiyoto (1899-1979), at that time a research fellow at the Minzoku Kenkyûsho. He made research trips to Singapore, Sumatra, Java, the Malay Peninsula, Thailand and French Indochina in 1944, and wrote essays based on these (Furuno 1974). Having graduated from the Department of Religious Studies at Tokyo Imperial University, Furuno was concerned with the Durkheimian sociology of religion. He conducted fieldwork among the aboriginal peoples of Taiwan in the 1930s, and wrote articles on their religious life as part of the religious tradition of the peoples of Southeast Asia. He was in charge of research into the peoples of Nan'pô or Southeast Asia at the Minzoku Kenkyûsho after his appointment in 1943.

After the war, a research project was carried out by the Japanese Society of Ethnology on Southeast Asia. The project was planned in 1954, the twentieth anniversary of the society, and under the leadership of Oka Masao it focused on the "rice culture" of the region. Supported by the Ministry of Education and Culture and the Yomiuri Newspaper Company, the field research was carried out from August 1957 to March 1958 by a team led by Matsumoto Nobuhiro (1897-1981), a historical ethnologist of Indochina who had studied with Marcel Mauss in France in the 1920s. The team consisted of researchers from various disciplines such as agricultural science, linguistics, ethnology, archeology, and history. They carried out research in the Mekong River basin, including Vietnam, Cambodia, Laos and Thailand, focusing on rice cultivation. Their main purpose, however, was an inquiry into the Southeast Asian origins of Japanese culture (Tônan Ajia Inasaku Minzoku Bunka Sôgô Chôsadan 1959: 4). This was an extension of what had been a traditional concern in Japanese ethnology since its inception, and the Southeast Asia research project reflected this by focusing on rice, the staple food for the Japanese as well as the Southeast Asians. After the research, a book was published called *Mekon kikô: Minzoku no genryû wo tazunete* (A journey to the Mekong River: Visiting the origins of Japanese culture), which describes the team's experiences exploring the culture of the Mekong River region while noting the cultural similarities between Southeast Asia and Japan. In so doing, it presented to the general public an account of the Southeast Asian origins of the Japanese culture. Iwata Keiji (1922-), one of the members of the team, later wrote a book along the same lines, entitled *Nihon bunka no furusato* (The homeland of Japanese culture), based on his own experiences during this research. In the Introduction, he confessed:

> While carrying out fieldwork among the Southeast Asian peoples, I often recalled our ancient way of life in Japan. Then I repeatedly thought over the origins of Japanese culture and asked myself whether Southeast Asia was its homeland. (Iwata 1975: 9)

The first chapter of the book is entitled "The sense of familiarity with Southeast Asia." Iwata described his invariable feelings of affinity and familiarity with the local people, whether he was visiting a Lao village in northern Laos, a Khmer village on the Thai-Cambodian border, or Yao and Lisu villages in highland Indochina. He emphasized the nonverbal communication of emotions and similarities of facial expression and gesture. In the chapters that followed, he focused on the more concrete cultural similarities between Japan and Southeast Asia, ranging from material culture including clothing, diet, housing, and agricultural technology, to life cycle and religious rituals. He mentioned not only visible similarities such as loincloths for men, waist cloths for women, tattoos, houses supported by pillars, rice, *mochi* (rice cakes) and *sushi*, but also religious concepts relating to spirits and deities. In the final chapter, "the homeland of Japanese culture," he concluded the book with these words: "there exists a fundamental affinity at a deeper level, beyond superficial forms of similarity" (ibid.: 232).

However, to the Japanese anthropologists of the younger generation who were educated after the 1970s, this kind of approach to other cultures no longer appealed. First, German historical ethnology which supported this kind of approach fell out of fashion because of its methodological inadequacies. Second, the younger generation started to show much more interest in contemporary issues than in "primitive" cultures supposed to be similar to the original culture of the Japanese. I myself began my first field research among the Toraja people of Sulawesi, Indonesia in the mid 1970s, in the hope of understanding "primitive" cultural traditions of Southeast Asia which were supposed to be related to ancient Japanese culture (cf. Torigoe and Wakabayashi 1995). But during the fieldwork, I soon realized that the Toraja were not a "primitive" people, and that Torajaland was not the homeland of Japanese culture. For me the Toraja are contemporary Others, and their "traditional" culture continues to exist only in relation to the tourism introduced by the Indonesian government as a means of regional development (Yamashita 1988).

However, it is also true that during my fieldwork I often felt that I was among people who were "similar" rather than "different." The Toraja also commented to me that we were all Asians. My Japanese friends who visited Torajaland during my stay also gave me their impressions, with comments such as "It is like the Nara Basin where ancient Japanese civilization emerged" or "It is like the countryside in my home town in Kyushu." Tourist guide-books on Indonesia published in Japan often emphasize "nostalgia," telling their readers that they can see in Indonesia "faces that remind you of old times" which have been lost in Japan (Yamashita 1999: 138). In this way, Southeast Asia is still experienced as culturally close to the contemporary Japanese.

Conclusion

Even though the Nan'yô region may not necessarily be classified geographically as the "Orient," it can be examined within the broader context of "Orientalism," as discussed by Edward Said (1978). Kasuga Naoki argues that even though Said developed this concept in the context of the relations between the West and the Middle East, it is also possible for the West to view as "Oriental" other regions as well. According to him, Oceania is such a place, though the application of the concept there is complex (Kasuga 1999: 8). To add a further complication, the subject rather than the object of Orientalism may also be Oriental as well, as in the case of Japanese Orientalism. The underlying idea is that people in one region construct images of other regions as "exotic," often using fantasy to construct their ethnographic Others. By examining the Japanese anthropology of Nan'yô within the context of the modern history of Japan, this chapter has attempted to clarify the distinctive ways in which Japanese anthropology has approached to the South Seas. Nan'yô was the place where Japanese Orientalism came to be practiced, as Japanese anthropologists projected their fantasies on to non-Japanese colonial Others. A similar approach had already been applied by Yanagita Kunio and his disciple, Orikuchi Shinobu, to Okinawa in the 1920s. They saw Okinawa as a kind of Japanese homeland where ancient Japanese culture remained alive. As Murai Osamu has discussed, by adopting this approach they concealed the history of Japan's colonial invasion of the Okinawan region (Murai 1995: 183-196). Here again one can see the logic of the "denial of coevalness" (Fabian 1983).

One can conclude, then, that Nan'yô, as a conceptual extension of Okinawa, was an area to which an anthropological version of Japanese Orientalism was routinely applied. This involved looking at the region through a Japanese lens that stressed cultural similarities with Japan rather than differences. Given this perception, Nan'yô occupied an ambiguous position for Japanese anthropologists in terms of cultural distance: it was sometimes assumed to be "far," being different from contemporary Japan, but at other times it was thought of as "near" because it appeared to have similar cultural traditions. The Japanese anthropology of the South has been constructed on the basis of this complicated self consciousness, reflecting Japan's changing position in modern world history.

There are two final remarks. First, as mentioned earlier, Japanese anthropologists of the younger generation who were educated after the 1970s have a different anthropological stance from their predecessors. They are much more oriented towards a "global anthropology" rather than "national anthropology," even though they publish mostly in Japanese.[18] As a result, the interest in the origins of the people and cultures of Japan which used to characterize the Japanese anthropological tradition has declined.

Second, the Japanese anthropological stance discussed in this paper is not opposed to Western anthropology. The issue is no longer a choice between Western or non-Western anthropology. What we need now is to cross over the cultural boundaries of the various anthropological traditions in the world and to create an interactive forum in which we can reconstruct anthropology for the twenty-first century as a discipline which discusses all aspects of the human race from a variety of viewpoints.

Notes

Sections of this paper, including the part dealing with Hijikata Hisakatsu, draw on material from an earlier paper on the Japanese encounter with the South, focusing on tourism in Palau (Yamashita 2000).

1 Southeast Asia was then called *Soto Nan'yô* ("Outer South Seas") as opposed to *Uchi Nan'yô* ("Inner South Seas"), the present-day Micronesia. Interestingly, Southeast Asia was seen in this categorization as an extension of Pacific Micronesia.

2 They reacted strongly to Morse's suggestion that cannibalism had existed in ancient Japan. Interestingly, as Shimizu (1998: 115; 1999: 126) has also

pointed out, a question posed by a Westerner led to a debate among Japanese academics and the nation as a whole concerning self definition.

3   In May 2003 the Japanese Society of Ethnology decided to change its name to the Japanese Society of Cultural Anthropology from April 2004.

4   Born in an affluent merchant family in Tokushima City, Shikoku, Torii was educated by private tutors. He never had a formal education, and did not even finish elementary school, as he did not like it. He was encouraged to study anthropology by Tsuboi Shôgorô who visited Tokushima in 1886. Torii later came to see him in Tokyo in 1889 (Suenari 1988: 48-49).

5   Rather confusingly, there are two words with similar meanings pronounced "minzokugaku" in Japanese, though they are written with different Chinese characters. One is usually translated as "ethnology," and the other as "folklore studies." However, this second usage does not refer to "folklore" in its narrow sense as a body of traditional beliefs, but rather to a wider system of folk knowledge and custom. "Folkway" may therefore be a better translation.

6   Little was known about the Minzoku Kenkyûsho, as the people concerned said little about it, perhaps because of its association with World War II. Recently, however, Katsumi Nakao (1997) has written a paper on this institute in an attempt to clarify the links between Japanese ethnology and the colonial system.

7   The term "ethnology" was still used until recently in the name of the Japanese Society of Ethnology. However, as is mentioned in note 3 above, the Society has now decided on a change of name.

8   However, interest in Asia, including Japan and the neighboring East and Southeast Asian countries, is still very strong. Asked during an interview about the orientation of anthropology at the National Museum of Ethnology, in which 46 our of 59 researchers were listed as specialists on Asia (including Japan), the Director-General of the museum, Sasaki Kômei, gave a clear and simple answer: the Museum is in Asia, and research on Asian peoples occupies a central place (Knight 1996: 18). The Museum was the base for a ten-year research project entitled "Comparative Studies of the Origins of Japanese Peoples and Cultures" from 1978 to 1987. The International Center for Japanese Studies in Kyoto organized a similar interdisciplinary study of the origins of the Japanese people and culture from 1997 to 2000.

9   Based on a critical analysis, Takayama Jun (1995) has shown that parts of the book were based on Western literature rather than Suzuki's own observations, though the book is narrated as if he himself witnessed the reality.

10 Mark Peattie notes that there was a distinct difference between the colonial landscapes of the Western residential areas and those of the Japanese. In the latter, he writes, one could not find the colonial luxuries to be

found in the Western colonies. This was partly because Japanese colonial society did not have a well-defined class structure, and partly because the Japanese did not like to display wealth and privilege to others. In other words, there was no distinct social and economic elite in Japanese colonial society (Peattie 1996: 275). In fact the Japanese migrants to the Southern Seas mostly came from the poorer classes or poorer regions of Japan such as Okinawa and Tôhoku.

11 John Russell (1991: 11) sees the black "primitives" drawn in *Bôken Dankichi* as originating in conventional Western images of black people. The cannibal image of the Pacific can be traced back to Suzuki Tsunenori's *Nan'yô tanken jikki* in which he wrote that the primitive peoples of the South Seas were very brutal and practiced cannibalism just like beasts (Suzuki 1980: 13). However, this image, too, may be of Western origin if one considers Suzuki's plagiarism from the Western literature. Or it may go back further to the reports of Japanese fishermen who drifted out to sea in the late Edo period (Akimichi 1998: 244).

12 Before the publication of *Mikuronesia minzokushi*, Matsuoka had published a book called *Taiheiyô Minzokushi* (The Ethnography of the Pacific) in 1925, based on a survey of the literature.

13 In terms of research methods, Matsuoka was an armchair anthropologist rather than a fieldworker (Shimizu 1999: 139). He sent questionnaires to the Nan'yô-chô officers, which were in turn passed on to officials on the islands concerned. They then made inquires according to the questionnaire and sent back the information collected (Matsuoka 1927: 778-781; Shimizu 1999: 139).

14 Gauguin's *Noa-Noa* gave Hijikata considerable inspiration in relation the South Seas, but Okaya Kôji, the author of Hijikata's biography, suggests an interesting difference between Gauguin and Hijikata. Gauguin could understand Tahitian beliefs and customs intellectually, because they were completely foreign to Western culture, while Hijikata could appreciate Satawal (and Micronesian) beliefs and customs emotionally because they were also found in Japan (Okaya 1990: 112).

15 In his teaching, Hijikata encouraged his pupils to learn and make "story boards." These were small rectangular wooden boards on which various motifs from the stories were carved and painted. They were called *itabori* in Japanese and were bought by Japanese residents in Palau and occasional tourists from Japan. This made Palau, as James Nason has discussed, a major exception to the general decline of the production of traditional goods in Micronesia. According to him, new motifs were introduced in a variety of other woodcarvings such as naturalistic rooster shaped bowls, and some support was provided for the making of jewelry from shell and turtle shell (Nason 1984: 434). These new handicrafts invented during the Japanese colonial period continue to play an important

role in Palau tourism today (Yamashita 2000).

16 This is included in Volume 6 of his Collected Works, under the title, "Gods and Customs in Satawal."

17 Umesao's naturalist stance can be traced back to his mentor, Imanishi Kinji, an ecologist who founded Japanese primatology after World War II. Pamela Asquith has discussed the distinctive features of Japanese primatology, noting that Japanese descriptions of primate behavior are traditionally more personal, anthropomorphic, and richly detailed in relation to individual animal's life histories than used to be common in the West (Asquith 1996: 240). Umesao is a "naturalist" in this Japanese tradition.

18 The most distinctive thing about Japanese anthropology is that it is practiced mainly in the Japanese language, a minor language in terms of international academic communication. In this respect, Japanese anthropology, unlike the Japanese economy, imports too much and exports too little. Japanese anthropology looks inward to the domestic academic market rather than contributing to the world anthropology as a whole. In order to "internationalize" Japanese anthropology, the Japanese Society of Ethnology started to publish a journal in English, the *Japanese Review of Cultural Anthropology*, to make available reviews of Japanese research in English (Yamashita 1998).

References

Akimichi, Tomoya. 1998. "Japanese views on Oceania: Modernist images of paradise," pp. 244-49 in *Image of Other Cultures*, eds. Kenji Yoshida and John Mack. Osaka: NHK Service Center.

Asquith, Pamela J. 1996. "Japanese science and Western hegemonies: Primatology and the limits set to questions," pp. 239-56 in *Naked Science: Anthropological Inquiry into Boundaries, Power, and Knowledge*, ed. Laura Nader. New York and London: Routledge.

Endô Hisashi. 1999. "Hyôshô no tatakai: Mikuronesia Parao o meguru Orientarizumu" [The battle of representations: Orientalism on Palau, Micronesia], pp. 83-103 in *Oceania Orientarizumu* (Oceania Orientalism), ed. Kasuga Naoki. Osaka: Sekaishisôsha.

Fabian, Johannes. 1983. *Time and the Other: How Anthropology Makes its Object.* New York: Columbia University Press.

Furuno Kiyoto 1974. *Furuno Kiyoto chosakushû. Bekkan* [Collected works of Kiyoto Furuno. Supplement]. Tokyo: Sanichi Shobô.

Hasebe Kotondo. 1935. "Nihonjin to Nan'yô jin" [Japanese and Southern Islanders], pp. 165-187 in *Nihon minzoku* [Japanese peoples]. Tokyo: Iwanami Shoten.

Hijikata Hisakatsu. 1974 [1943]. *Ryûboku: Mikuronesia no kotô nite* [Driftwood: On the remote islands of Micronesia]. Tokyo: Miraisha.

Hijikata Hisakatsu. 1991 *Hijikata Hisakatsu chosakushû* [Hijikata Hisakatsu collected works] Vol. 6. Tokyo: Sanichi Shobô.

Ishida Eiichirô. 1970a. *Ishida Eiichirô zenshû* [Collected works of Eiichirô Ishida], Vol. 2. Tokyo: Chikuma Shobô.

Ishida Eiichirô. 1970b. *Ishida Eiichirô zenshû* [Collected works of Eiichirô Ishida], Vol. 4. Tokyo: Chikuma Shobô.

Iwata Keiji. 1975. *Nihon bunka no furusato* [The homeland of Japanese culture]. Tokyo: Kadokawa Shoten.

Kang Sang Jung. 1996. *Orientarizumu no kanata e* [Beyond Orientalism]. Tokyo: Iwanami Shoten.

Kasuga Naoki. ed. 1999. *Oseania Orientarizumu* [Oceanian Orientalism]. Kyoto: Sekaishisôsha.

Kawamura Minato. 1993. "Taishû Orientarizumu to Ajia ninshiki" [Popular Orientalism and perceptions of Asia], pp. 107-136 in *Iwanami kôza kindai Nihon to shokuminchi* [Iwanami Series on Modern Japan and its Colonies], Vol. 7. Tokyo: Iwanami Shoten.

Kawamura Minato. 1995 *"Daitôa minzokugaku" no kyôjitsu* [The myth and reality of Great East Asian ethnology]. Tokyo: Kôdansha.

Knight, John. 1996. "Interview with Sasaki Kômei of the National Museum of Ethnology," *Anthropology Today* 12 (3): 16-20.

Kuper, Adam. 1994. "Anthropological futures," pp. 113-18 in *Assessing Cultural Anthropology*, ed. Robert Borofsky. New York: McGraw-Hill.

Matsuoka Shizuo. 1927. *Mikuronesia minzokushi* [The ethnography of Micronesia]. Tokyo: Iwanami Shoten.

Minzokugaku Shinkôkai. 1984. *Zaidanhôjin Minzokugaku Shinkôkai gojûnen no ayumi: Nihon Minzokugaku Shûdan ryakushi* [Fifty years of the Shibusawa Foundation for Ethnological Studies]. Tokyo: Minzokugaku Shinkôkai.

Murai Osamu. 1995. *Nan'tô ideorogi no hassei* [The genesis of South Sea Island ideology]. Tokyo: Ôta Shuppan.

Nakane, Chie. 1974. "Cultural anthropology in Japan," *Annual Review of Anthropology* 3: 57-72.

Nakao Katsumi. 1997. "Minzoku Kenkyûsho no soshiki to katsudô," [The organization and activities of the Institute of Ethnology], *Minzokugaku-kenkyû* [Japanese Journal of Ethnology] 62: 47-65.

Nason, James D. 1984. "Tourism, handicrafts and ethnic identity in Micronesia," *Annals of Tourism Research* 11: 421-49.

Ôbayashi Taryô. 1961. *Nihon shinwa no kigen* [The origins of Japanese mythology]. Tokyo: Kadokawa Shoten

Oguma Eiji. 1995. *Tanitsu minzoku shinwa no kigen* [The myth of the homogeneous nation]. Tokyo: Shinyôsha.

Okaya Kôji. 1990. *Nankai hyôhaku: Hijikata Hisakatsu den* [Floating on the South Seas: An Autobiography of Hisakatsu Hijikata]. Tokyo: Kawade

Shobôshinsha.

Peattie, Mark R. 1988. *Nan'yô: The Rise and Fall of the Japanese in Micronesia, 1885-1945.* Honolulu: University of Hawaii Press.

Peattie, Mark R. 1996. *Shokuminchi* [Colonies], translated by Asano Toyomi. Tokyo: Yomiuri Shinbunsha.

Russell, John. 1991. "Race and reflexivity: The Black Other in contemporary Japanese mass culture," *Cultural Anthropology* 6: 3-25.

Said, Edward. 1978. *Orientalism.* New York: Pantheon.

Shimizu Akitoshi. 1998. "Nihon no jinruigaku" [Anthropology in Japan], pp. 111-33 in *Bunkajinruigaku no susume* [Invitation to cultural anthropology], ed. Funabiki Takeo. Tokyo: Chikuma Shobô.

Shimizu, Akitoshi, 1999. "Colonialism and the development of modern anthropology in Japan," pp. 115-71 in *Anthropology and Colonialism in Asia and Oceania*, eds. Jan van Bremen and Akitoshi Shimizu. Richmond, Surrey: Curzon.

Sekimoto Teruo. 1995. "Nihon no jinruigaku to Nihon shigaku" [Anthropology in Japan and Japanese historiography], pp. 123-47 in *Iwanami kôza Nihon tsûshi. Bekkan 1* [Iwanami Complete History of Japan. Supplementary vol.1] eds. Asao Naohiro et al. Tokyo: Iwanami Shoten.

Sudoh Kenichi. 1991. "Minzokushika Hijikata Hisakatsu no Mikuronesia kenkyû" [The Micronesia research of Hijikata Hisakatsu, ethnographer], pp. 28-40 in *Hijikata Hisakatsu Ten* [Hijikata Hisakatsu Exihibition]. Tokyo: Setagaya Museum of Art.

Suenari Michio. 1988. "Torii Ryûzô: Higashi Ajia jinruigaku no senkakusha" [Torii Ryûzô: A pioneer of East Asian anthropology], in *Bunkajinruigaku gunzô* [Cultural anthropologists in Japan]. Kyoto: Akademia Shuppan.

Sugiura Kenichi. 1941. "Minzokugaku to Nan'yô guntô tôchi" [Ethnology and the colonial governance of Nan'yô], pp. 173-218 in *Dai Nan'yô* [The Greater South Seas], ed. Taiheiyô Kyôkai [The Institute of the Pacific]. Tokyo: Kawade Shobô.

Takano Rokurô. 1942. "Nan'pô hatten to jinkô mondai" [Development of the Southern Regions and the population problem], *Jinkô Mondai* [Population Problem] 4 (4): 546-554.

Takayama Jun. 1995. *Nankai no daitankenka Suzuki Tsunenori: Sono kyozô to jitsuzô* [Suzuki Tsunenori: Between truth and fiction]. Tokyo: Sanichi Shobô.

Tanaka, Stefan. 1993. *Japan's Orient: Reading Pasts into History.* Berkeley: University of California Press.

Terada Kazuo. 1981. *Nihon no jinruigaku* [Anthropology in Japan]. Tokyo: Kadokawa Shoten.

Tokyo Daigaku Tôyô Bunka Kenkyûsho [The Institute of Oriental Culture, The University of Tokyo]. 1991. *Tôyô Bunka Kenkyûsho no gojûnen* [Fiftieth Anniversary of the Institute of Oriental Culture]. Tokyo: The University of Tokyo.

Tomiyama Ichirô. 1996. "Nettaikagaku to shokuminchishugi: 'Tômin' o meguru sai no bunsekigaku" [Tropical sciences and colonialism: An anatomy of difference among the "Islanders"], in *Nashonariti no Datsukôchiku* [Deconstruction of nationality], eds. Sakai Naoki, Bret de Bary, and Iyotani Toshio. Tokyo: Kashiwashobô.

Tônan Ajia Inasaku Minzoku Bunka Sôgô Chôsadan ed. 1959. *Mekon kikô: Minzoku no genryû o tazunete* [A journey to the Mekong: In search of the origins of Japanese culture]. Tokyo: Yomiuri Shinbunsha.

Torigoe Kenzaburô and Wakabayashi Hiroko eds. 1995. *Wazoku Toraja* [The Toraja: The ancestors of the Japanese people]. Tokyo: Taishûkan.

Torii Ryûzô. 1975. *Torii Ryûzô zenshû* [The complete works of Torii Ryûzô], Vol.1. Tokyo: Asahi Shinbunsha

Umesao Tadao. 1944. *Kikô* [A Journey], in *Ponapetô* [The Island of Ponape], ed. Imanishi Kinji. Tokyo: Shôkô Shoin.

Yamashita Shinji. 1988. *Girei no seijigaku: Indonesia Toraja no dôtaiteki minzokushi* [The politics of ritual: A dynamic ethnography of the Toraja, Indonesia]. Tokyo: Kôbundô.

Yamashita, Shinji. 1998. "Viewing anthropology from Japan," *Japanese Review of Cultural Anthropology* 1: 3-6.

Yamashita Shinji. 1999 *Bali: Kankôjinruigaku no ressun* [Bali: How can we learn from the anthropology of tourism?]. Tokyo: The University of Tokyo Press (English version published as *Bali and Beyond: Explorations in the Anthropology of Tourism*, trans. J.S. Eades. Oxford and New York: Berghahn, 2003).

Yamashita, Shinji. 2000. "The Japanese encounter with the South: Japanese tourists in Palau," *Contemporary Pacific* 12 (2).

Yano Tôru. 1975. *"Nanshin" no keifu* [The history of the Japanese "Advance to the South"]. Tokyo: Chûôkôronsha.

Yano Tôru. 1979. *Nihon no Nan'yôshikan* [The history of Japanese perceptions of the South Seas]. Tokyo: Chûôkôronsha.

Chapter 5

On the Tension Between Japanese and American

Anthropological Depictions of Japan

Gordon MATHEWS

Introduction: Audiences and Power

There has been, over the past fifty years, a large gap between how Japanese and how American anthropologists – and social scientists as a whole[1] – present Japan in their writings. This seems in part an inevitable function of audience. What an American audience, professional or lay, seeks to know about Japan will likely be very different from what a Japanese audience seeks to know. As Kuwayama Takami has written,

> There are more than a few anthropologists [in Japan] who reject outright introductory books on Japan written in English, such as Reischauer's *The Japanese,* labeling them as "scholarly common sense." Such remarks and attitudes reflect the total failure on their part to understand that lecturing about Japan in a foreign language to a foreign audience whose cultural background is completely different from the Japanese, is completely different from speaking about Japan with the Japanese in Japanese. (Kuwayama 1997b: 56)

By the same token, very few American researchers pay attention to the research conducted by Japanese folklife specialists, looking for remnants of Japanese traditions; this research is for the most part completely outside American interests.[2] In both these cases, what is attractive to these scholars is alterity, difference, and otherness. However, the "Other" that American anthropologists tend to focus upon is contemporary Japanese society, a so-

114

ciety as economically developed as the United States, but that seems by many measures to have "arrived at its present position by another route, acting on different premises, and proceeding in a direction we have not taken" (Smith 1983: 138-139). The "Other" that Japanese folklife specialists focus upon is the traditional Japan now all but obliterated by the modern present, a traditional Japan that fascinates many Japanese. It is hardly surprising that these very different pursuits of alterity should have very different scholarly appeal within and beyond Japan.

One's audience does not, of course, exist in a vacuum: clearly, the nature and expectations of one's audience is linked to larger issues of power. Japan in many American anthropologists' writings – or at least in those writings as interpreted by American readers – may be seen as a society that is fascinating for its Oriental deviations from the dominant American norm. Japan in some Japanese anthropological writings is a society preserving its essence against the onslaught of modernization and Westernization; in other writings, it is portrayed as a society that Westerners in their ethnocentrism cannot fully understand. These different portrayals are underlain by history. The discipline of anthropology has been largely the prerogative of colonizers studying the colonized; anthropology has traditionally consisted of Americans and Europeans doing research in and writing about other societies, often societies they had colonized or otherwise dominated. Other than the United States and Western European societies, Japan has been the only power to have attempted to create a colonial empire,[3] an attempt eventually leading to World War II. This is linked to the development of Japanese anthropology (Shimizu 1995:157). Japanese ethnographers were out in force in the 1930s, studying peoples in Korea, Taiwan, Sakhalin, Manchuria, and other Japanese colonies (Sofue 1974: 88), just as British anthropologists studied African tribal groups in territories controlled by the United Kingdom, and American anthropologists studied American Indians on their reservations.

In the decade after World War II, Japan moved from being a colonizer to being colonized in the American military occupation. Anthropology followed suit, as Japan went from being the pursuer of anthropological knowledge in other societies to becoming once more the object of anthropological knowledge, as it had been during the Meiji period (see Askew's chapter). In recent decades, although Japan has long since shed its politically colonized status to become the second largest economy in the world, Japanese anthropology seems to continue to hold, to some extent, the stance of the colonized. To note just one obvious imbalance, Japanese anthropologists now often investigate Pacific and Asian and African societies but only rarely the United States – while Japanese anthropologists of late have studied ethnic groups such as Vietnamese-Americans and Chinese immigrants, only a very few have investigated "mainstream" American communities, institutions, and lives, as scores of American anthropologists have investigated virtually every aspect of Japanese life. There are clear institutional reasons for this imbalance.[4] The basic underlying reason, however, seems to be that of intellectual colonization. American anthropologists studying Japan still often seem to use Japan as the raw ethnographic material for their analyses using American and European theory, with Japanese writings on Japanese society often paid only scant attention.[5] Japanese anthropologists too tend to adopt this intellectually colonized stance, analyzing their ethnographic data from various societies in light of American and European theory – in this way they sometimes seem to reduce Japanese anthropology to being a matter of collecting data to confirm western theory. On occasion, Japanese social scientists raise their voices to contest this western theoretical hegemony, as in Kuwayama's chapter; but the situation remains largely unchanged today.

I have given in these initial pages a quick glimpse of the gap between Japanese and American anthropologies, a gap based in their different audiences and in the different historical trajectories of power. To understand this gap in a fuller way, let us now consider more particularly the history of Japanese and American anthropological depictions of Japan over the past fifty years. This examination will, I hope, help to illuminate not only Japanese and American anthropology of Japan, but also a little of the nature of anthropology as a discipline.

Fifty Years of Tension/Fifty Years of Gap

A major intercultural gap in Japanese/American anthropological interpretations of Japan emerged with Ruth Benedict's *The Chrysanthemum and the Sword* (1946), and the Japanese reactions to the work. At the time the book was written, social or cultural anthropology was still a relatively new discipline in Japan. Yanagita Kunio, in some ways a Japanese equivalent to Franz Boas as a founding father, had begun Japanese folklore studies in the early twentieth century, and was well schooled in the anthropology of his time, being, for example, an avid reader of Malinowski (Kawada 1993: 118). However, even though earlier associations had existed (as discussed in Chapters 1 and 3), the *Nihon Minzoku Gakkai*, the Japanese equivalent of the American Anthropological Association, was created only in 1934. Benedict's book served to alert Japanese laymen as well as anthropologists – and American laymen and anthropologists as well – to the fact that cultural patterns could be discerned in contemporary complex societies. To Japanese social scientists, "the fact that the book had been written by an *American*, a *woman*, and *one who had never visited Japan* made it an object of vast and intriguing importance" (Bennett and Nagai 1953: 404; italics in original). An early critique of the book by Japanese social scientists is quite positive, saying, in effect, that "we Japanese social scientists have to learn to use empirical data and theory as well as Benedict does." It also makes many of the same points that subsequent American critics have made: Benedict ignores historical change; she does not adequately distinguish between what people say they do and what they actually do; and she does not adequately address conflict between different groups in Japanese society (Bennett and Nagai 1953).

While this social scientific critique was relatively sober in tone, other Japanese critiques railed against what they saw as Benedict's condescension, and questioned whether a foreigner like her could ever really understand Japan. Much Japanese anger was directed at Benedict's depiction of Japan as a culture based on shame as opposed to Western cultures based on guilt (a distinction made in only a scant few pages of Benedict's book). This hit a nerve among Japanese commentators because of the implicit assumption attributed to Benedict that guilt is superior as an emotion to shame (Doi 1973: 48). As the cultural critic Aida Yuji has written, "The idea that 'shame' and 'guilt' are essentially different is nothing more than a product of that arrogance of the Europeans who consider themselves to be ... more advanced [than other peoples]" (as quoted in Dale 1986: 181). Japanese anthropologists have on the whole tended to be less prickly in their judgements about Benedict's work than have the more popular commentators on *Nihonjinron* – "discourse on the Japanese" – a genre of popular writing about Japan that really began with the translation of *The Chrysanthemum and the Sword* into Japanese in 1948.[6] A central concern of *Nihonjinron* is how Japanese are fundamentally different from other peoples, and how, more implicitly, Japanese people can only be understood by Japanese. *Nihonjinron* arose in part, I argue, because of the intellectually colonized position Japanese now found themselves in: Benedict's *The Chrysanthemum and the Sword* signified that Japan was no longer the colonizing pursuer of knowledge about others, but rather itself the other to be intellectually colonized and codified. One way to attempt to overcome this humiliation was for Japanese to intellectually take back Japan: to proclaim, "those outsiders can never really understand us! Only we can understand us!" – a central claim of *Nihonjinron*.

Immediate postwar Japan was too poverty-stricken to support anthropology, which is an intellectual luxury enjoyed by societies that can afford it. As late as 1974, Nakane could write that most Japanese anthropologists' research was conducted in rural Japan rather than abroad (1974: 59); and indeed, some Western writers today make statements such as "In Japan [unlike the U.S. and Europe]...it seems almost to be taken for granted that anthropologists will have something significant to say about ... Japanese culture" (Morris-Suzuki 1995: 771). This was apparently true thirty years ago, but is no longer the case in today's Japanese anthropological world. The large majority of articles published over the past decade in *Minzokugaku-kenkyû*, the leading Japanese journal of anthropology, bear no relation to Japan (Sekimoto 1995: 134); the recent compendium *Jinruigaku ga wakaru* [Understanding anthropology] (1995) features a number of the most prominent Japanese cultural anthropologists explaining anthropology to the Japanese public with scarcely a mention of Japan. In the 1970s and 1980s, as Japan became more affluent, anthropology became progressively more established in Japan; and this came to mean, almost by definition, that anthropologists did fieldwork outside of Japan, devoting themselves to the study of societies other than Japan. As Itô Abito has written,

> Partly because they were unable to engage in overseas fieldwork, researchers in anthropology [after World War II] ... applied anthropological methods to Japanese studies ... But since then it has become possible for researchers of the younger generation to conduct fieldwork overseas ... resulting in a rapid decline of interest in Japan. (Itô 1996: 216)

There seem to have been two very broad schools of Japanese as well as American anthropological analysis of Japan during the 1970s and 1980s, and to a degree continuing today. One of these I label objectivist; the other I label ideologist. Adherents to the former position tend to believe that anthropology is an objective science, that the cultural background of the anthropologist is only of secondary importance, at most, in shaping analysis, and that inequalities of power between the anthropologist and the people studied are also of minimal importance in shaping analysis. Adherents to the latter position tend to believe that there is no such thing as an objective science of anthropology, that the cultural background of the anthropologist is of fundamental importance in shaping what the anthropologist finds, and that power and its inequalities condition the very nature of anthropological knowledge. These labels are overly black and white, masking a wide degree of individual variation; nonetheless, they bear validity as ideal types, I think.

One noteworthy objectivist anthropological depiction of Japan – in its English version, although somewhat less so in its Japanese version – was that of Nakane Chie, in *Japanese Society* (1973 [1970]). Nakane was a specialist on the Gharo and other peoples of northern India; her study of Japanese society was a structural-functional analysis of Japan written, largely, as objective social science.[7] Many American anthropologists too wrote in an objectivist mode, in works that resulted from and contributed to cross-cultural anthropological discussion. The research that resulted in Robert J. Smith's *Ancestor Worship in Contemporary Japan* (1974), to take just one example, was discussed by the book's author with many Japanese social scientists (Smith, personal communication). The book was reviewed in Japan as addressing questions that might not have occurred to a Japanese researcher writing from within a Japanese context, but was not challenged as to its basic validity because it was the work of a foreigner.

However, even though these works were written in an objectivist mode, they could not avoid the interpretations of their audiences, interpretations that probably did not lie in their authors' intentions, but that might nonetheless have been read from their texts. Smith's *Ancestor Worship in Contemporary Japan*, for example, in its discussion of Japanese as having a spiritual orientation rooted in this world rather than any other (1974: 51), could be read as a criticism of Japanese for their lack of "true religiosity"; Lebra's *Japanese Patterns of Behavior*, in its discussion of "social relativism as the Japanese ethos" (1976: 1-21), could be read as a criticism of Japan for its lack of abstract moral principles, criticisms that I have heard made by American undergraduates. William Kelly has written that "those of us who study the most geographically Oriental of the Orient cannot always extricate ourselves from a popular and scholarly rhetoric that for over 100 years has measured Japan against an idealized West and found it deficient, deviant, or just puzzling" (1991: 396). However, even those who can extricate themselves from this rhetoric, as I think these two authors do, cannot extricate themselves from the assumptions of their largely American readers.

By the same token, Nakane's *Japanese Society*, written after Japan's economic miracle had begun to take effect, came to be read as a celebration of Japanese national achievement along different lines than that laid down by the West. Her model of Japanese society is certainly susceptible to criticism, in its assumption of group solidarity and its playing down of conflict, as anthropologists both Japanese and American have pointed out (see the essays in Sugimoto and Mouer 1989); but the careful reader will not find in her book the celebration of difference that much of the book's audience apparently read into it.

During the 1970s and 1980s, *Nihonjinron*, the popular "discourse on the Japanese," filled Japanese bookstores; if anthropologists during this period strove to be objectivists in their writings, many of the authors of *Nihonjinron* labored under no such constraints. Kumon Shunpei explained the new Japanese sense of themselves in the early 1980s as follows:

> [Japan], showing the best economic performance among the developed countries ... could at last become bluntly nationalistic for the first time since the end of World War II. The Japanese now wanted to understand fully and explain clearly why Japan was able to achieve such a miracle. They felt that this could only be done in terms of its unique "culture" because the economic success of the late 1970s was obviously unique. (Kumon 1982: 5)

Many anthropologists, particularly those educated in postwar Japan, spurned *Nihonjinron* (Aoki 1990: 173) as no more than the popular expression of hackneyed cliches about the supposed characteristics of Japanese as opposed to Western peoples, having little basis in fact. However, a number of Japanese anthropologists did engage in similar, although more scholarly reputable exercises. Anthropologists of an older generation such as Ishida Eiichiro (1974) and Umesao Tadao (1974, 1990) were concerned with explicating Japan's place in the world in the decades after World War II. Both anthropologists had done fieldwork in other societies, but returned to Japan in their later works, to offer ecological explanations for Japanese uniqueness: Japan, as a rice-based island agricultural society (Ishida), a "greenhouse" geographically protected from the violence of continental Asia (Umesao), evolved into its own particular civilization, inexplicable in terms beyond itself, argued. Some anthropologists spoke specifically about Japan's business success in terms of its earlier traditions: Sakurai Tokutaro, for example, linked the charisma of top business leaders such as Matsushita and Honda to the charismatic individualism characteristic of traditional Japanese shamanism (Kreiner 1996: 7).

These analyses, based at least implicitly on the idea of an unchanging Japanese essence, were largely ignored by American anthropologists. The audience of these analyses was largely Japanese; the purpose of these analyses was apparently to inspire in that audience a sense of pride in Japan. There was thus no need for confrontation between the different Japanese and American anthropological views of Japan. However, several Japanese anthropologists during this period, living within the same Japanese cultural climate as that which produced *Nihonjinron*, took a directly confrontational stance towards American anthropology. These anthropologists strove to create a Japanese anthropology that did not rely upon Western theory for its intellectual basis: Japanese society, these scholars argued, could not be understood through Western theory because that theory was inevitably ethnocentric. Rather, Japanese society could only be understood through Japanese theoretical underpinnings.

One such example is that of Hamaguchi, who states boldly that "the social science method that originated in Western Europe has only limited applicability to Japan" (Hamaguchi 1985: 289). Japanese and Western social scientists alike in analyzing Japan have been trapped in the Western framework of "methodological individualism," which, according to Hamaguchi, has blinded them to the reality of the Japanese self, rooted not in individual separateness but in relation to others. Hamaguchi's ideas did not receive the critical opposition that one might have expected, however, in that his ideas dovetailed with the growing American awareness that selves in different cultures indeed differ (cf. Magos's chapter on the Philippines in this volume). The American anthropologist of Japan Dorinne Kondo, for example, writes of "seemingly incorrigible Western assumptions about ... the boundedness and fixity of personal identity" (1990: 26). "Contemporary anthropologists ... myself included, are in the process of grappling with the difficulties and paradoxes of demonstrating the cultural specificity of selfhood, thereby de-essentializing the category" (1990: 37). It is highly interesting that the intellectual agendas underlying these similar sets of ideas should be so wholly dissimilar. Hamaguchi is a conservative Japanese cultural nationalist, seeking an end to the hegemony of Western theory in analyses of Japan; Kondo is a postmodernist, citing French theorists such as Derrida on the illusion of a coherent self, but never referring to Hamaguchi – she is thus riding the latest wave of Western theory. The two anthropologists make similar arguments about the Japanese self, but they never meet, for they are speaking to different anthropological audiences within different anthropological worlds.

Another Japanese challenge to American theoretical hegemony in Japan produced more sparks: Murakami Yasusuke (1984) presented a condensed version in English of his and his coauthors' monumental work in Japanese to a number of American anthropologists for their criticism, and the criticism was intense. Murakami's argument concerns the Japanese *ie* (household) organization which emerged in the twelfth century, and which, through later stages of evolution, served to shape the group-oriented Japanese society of today; Murakami argues that a distinctly different societal evolution into modernity took place in Japan, as opposed to that of Western societies, one based on "*ie* society as a pattern of civilization." To cite only one of the American responses to Murakami's argument, Thomas Rohlen wrote as follows:

> The approach taken is to define an organizational type and then trace its historical development and role in society. In anthropology, we label this kind of thinking "structural functionalism" and trace its practice back to the prewar period ...We might have been very interested in an "*ie* society" approach thirty years ago ... But ... we are seeking answers today to more complex questions. (1985: 66, 67)

This exchange is fascinating because it rests upon the nature of what anthropology is. If anthropology is an objective science, then Rohlen may be justified in his vitriol. After all, a nuclear physicist or molecular biologist basing research on theories current thirty years ago would be ignored or mocked; if anthropology is an objective science, then shouldn't the same be true for anthropology? If anthropology is not an objective science, however, but rather an endeavor conditioned by one's cultural positioning and placement within structures of power, then Rohlen's stance may represent the powerful arrogantly chastising the less powerful for their intellectual disobedience to the current academic trends set forth by the powerful. Anthropology is both these things, I argue, and probably most anthropologists today would agree. But which finally predominates? One's answer to this basic question, perhaps as much as one's reading of Murakami's complex work in itself, will determine one's reaction to Rohlen's scathing criticism.[8]

In American anthropology of Japan in the 1980s and 1990s, in keeping with anthropological trends as a whole, the ideological mode has been supplanting the objectivist mode of analysis, at least to the extent that anthropologists now explicating aspects of Japanese society tend to make their own background an explicit part of their analysis. Thus, to take just one example, a central part of Hamabata's ethnography of a Japanese business family (1990) is his own struggle over how to present himself as an American of Japanese descent: Japanese yet non-Japanese. This modal shift reflects the fact that, as Ohnuki-Tierney points out (1984), the ethnicity of the researcher is important in shaping the ethnographic data obtained in Japan – what she, as a person raised in Japan may find in her research, may substantially differ from what Kondo or Hamabata, as Americans of Japanese ancestry might find, which may substantially differ from what a European-American anthropologist might find. In her words:

> For fieldwork in Japan, foreign anthropologists initially have a tremendous advantage. All foreigners, especially Westerners, usually receive the red-carpet treatment from the Japanese, who go out of their way to accommodate their visitors ... Unfortunately, the drawback of this favorable treatment is that the host people "perform" for them; the anthropologist's presence becomes an important factor in the way the host people act and react. (Ohnuki-Tierney 1984: 585)

The standard anthropological argument for ethnographic fieldwork has been that if the fieldworker hangs around long enough, then he or she will eventually be accepted as part of the local scene, and will be able to discover the "real culture" of the people being investigated. However, if the gap between indigenous and foreign, between Japanese and *gaijin*, remains large enough within the minds of the Japanese people whose social and cultural worlds are being investigated, then that gap may never altogether be overcome. Many American ethnographies of Japan of late, such as those of Bestor (1989) and Allison (1994), make explicit the role of the foreign researcher in helping to create, at least in a small way, the ethnographic situation that their books describe, to a degree rectifying the problem that Ohnuki-Tierney describes; but the epistemological problem remains. In foreign (and particularly American and European) ethnographic research in Japan, do we fall into a social science version of quantum mechanics, whereby the presence of the observer inevitably helps to create – distort – all that is seen and heard? This surely could not be entirely true; but even if it is true only in quite subtle ways, its effect cannot be discounted in shaping foreign as opposed to Japanese depictions of Japan.

Beyond ethnicity and its effects on ethnographic research, there is the question of how much national background may affect the study of Japan. One investigation into this matter is Harumi Befu's edited volume, *Otherness of Japan: Historical and Cultural Influences on Japanese Studies in Ten Countries* (1992). As the title indicates, the assumption of the investigation is that the study of Japan can indeed be differentiated by different national approaches: the political and cultural background of the investigator matter in the study of Japan. Befu argues that "American scholarship [on Japan] ... has been characterized by much emphasis on the individual as an agent acting out in a certain structural and cultural context .... [and on] an empirical orientation which values numbers and statistics as a mode of verification" (1992: 25). However, as Plath and Smith (1992: 201-229) point out in their contribution to the book, there is such a wide variation in the ways in which American anthropologists study Japan that such generalizations make little sense. Indeed, when I consider the sixty or so American anthropologists of Japan whose work I know, work ranging from pure structural functionalism to textual analysis and cultural studies, it is hard to arrive at any coherent generalization to cover them all. Of course it also must be noted that this very insistence on individual difference among American anthropologists of Japan may confirm Befu's point concerning the individualistic orientation of American approaches to Japan. Simply put, it may be that American scholars as culturally shaped individualists refuse to acknowledge that they belong to any American cultural collectivity shaping their depictions of Japan.

There is also the question of who is Japanese or American today, and what these designations mean. Takie Sugiyama Lebra and Emiko Ohnuki-Tierney are anthropologists who were born and raised in Japan, and yet have been at the forefront of American anthropological analyses of Japan, writing largely for American audiences. John Russell, on the other hand, is an African-American anthropologist who now teaches in Japan and has written extensively in Japanese on race and what it means in a Japanese context. By upbringing, the former would be Japanese anthropologists, the latter American; but by audience, which today might serve as a more relevant criteria for the designation of anthropological national identity, the former may be considered American and the latter Japanese. It is true that in an age of frequent albeit largely one-way translation (American anthropologists writing about Japan are more likely to be translated into Japanese than Japanese anthropologists writing about Japan are to be translated in English), audiences can become blurred. Nonetheless, I maintain that today one's culture of upbringing matters less in shaping one's anthropological work than does the particular audience, Japanese or American, anthropological or lay, for whom one is writing (cf. Kuwayama 1997a: 520).

Befu's argument thus seems debatable in its emphasis on cultural background; however, it is wholly apt in its discussion of power. "The world view which Americans assume, namely that their society is the most developed and advanced economically, technologically, politically and in every other way, has had a significant impact on American scholarship on Japan, causing... American scholars to look down on [Japan]," he writes (1992: 23). American scholars of Japan, by these words, have yet to escape the Orientalist gaze of

123

which Kelly (1991) wrote, as we earlier saw: American scholars measuring "Japan against an idealized West and [finding] it deficient, deviant, or just puzzling." This seems true on two levels. First, there remains the subtle ethnocentrism of many American anthropological portrayals of Japan, an ethnocentrism no doubt unintended by writers of anthropological works but nonetheless perhaps sensed by readers. American as well as Japanese readers of Allison's ethnography of Japanese salarymen in hostess bars (1994) may read into the behavior of these men a large degree of childishness; Japanese and American readers of my own comparison of Japanese and Americans in their pursuit of lives that seem worth living (1996) have commented, to my discomfort, that the Americans seem more "mature" than the Japanese. Anthropologists of Japan are quite aware of Plath's (1980) demonstration that maturity is a culturally specific concept, with Japanese maturity having a very different meaning from American maturity; yet some readers, Japanese and American, may read into anthropologists' books on Japan the idea that America is best, with societies such as Japan being inferior to the extent that they fail to live up to American standards. I cannot speak for Allison's book; but it may be that my own book unwittingly gives readers justification for such interpretations.

This is one sense in which Befu's argument, in its assertion of American ethnocentricity, seems apt; but even more important than this is the extent to which American anthropologists of Japan assume that the United States and Western Europe form the anthropological center of the world. (It is sometimes said that the ignorance that American anthropologists often have of Japanese anthropology is mirrored in Japan, by Japanese scholars who ignore what American anthropologists of Japan are writing. However, I have consistently found that Japanese anthropologists cite far more American anthropologists in their work than vice-versa.) A number of acclaimed recent American anthropological works on Japan use fashionable American and European discourses for an American anthropological audience. The theoretical chapters of Kondo's (1990) ethnography rely on French poststructuralism as their guide, as earlier noted; Ivy's (1995) text is wholly infused with the vocabulary of cultural studies. It is the latest European and American theory which brings cachet, and these authors obtained such cachet – in terms of gaining notice from American anthropology beyond the relatively small circle of anthropologists who study Japan – by using such theory. Japanese scholars, to the extent that they are not immersed in such theory, are left out.[9]

If such theory represents intellectual advance ("science," if you will, although these authors would probably reject that label), then the fact that some Japanese scholars are not acquainted with it is simply because they haven't kept abreast of anthropological advances, advances that are globally applicable. However, if such theory represents not the development and advance of anthropology globally, but rather the latest fashion of American academic anthropology, then these writings may represent not academic advance but academic retreat: a retreat from communication with a range of scholars from Japan and elsewhere, into a world of particularly American concerns. I argue that such theory represents a combination of both these factors. There is indeed intellectual advance, in terms of new ways of thinking about anthropological data, new ways of doing anthropology that are celebrated on the American anthropological "cutting edge" at present, but are only slowly being added to the array of anthropological approaches in Japan and elsewhere. However, these new ways of doing anthropology are cloaked in distinctly local jargon – the argot of continental theory, tied to American cultural studies rhetoric – and are thus rendered all but incomprehensible to those who are not of the learned few cognoscenti: those who do not belong to the American intellectual scene. To the extent that the local and provincial thus obscure the global, the problem of Orientalism remains: Japan is no more than the source of raw materials for the refinements of the American and European theoretical mill.

In an article in *Minzokugaku-kenkyû* (The Japanese Journal of Ethnology) that aroused much attention among anthropologists of Japan, Kuwayama Takami (1997a) discusses how Japanese anthropologists are direct victims of discursive Orientalism. To quote his later English summary:

> When scientific knowledge is understood as a discourse – a socially constructed system of meaning and ideology that has emerged out of a struggle for hegemonic power among competing groups – we realize why Japanese anthropology has only had limited influence outside Japan, despite its long-standing tradition. The three "core" countries in the "world system" of anthropology – the United States, Great Britain, and France – have the power to determine the kinds of desired knowledge in the field. Japanese scholars, like those in other peripheral countries, are forced to conform to the dominant modes of discourse if they want to be recognized. (Kuwayama 1997b)[10]

Kuwayama's article, although its title is specifically addressed to Japanese and foreign anthropologists of Japan, in fact transcends that focus, to address the nature of Japanese anthropology at the periphery and its relation to American and Western European anthropology at the center. Japanese scholars must conform to the current scientific knowledge/academic fashion emanating from the center, or they will be doomed to remain ignored, Kuwayama is saying. But the fact of conforming already renders them peripheral, for to the extent that they conform, they are doomed to be followers. Japanese anthropology in a sense cannot win.[11]

Kuwayama's argument is, I think, overly monolithic. There are scores of anthropologically-related journals in the United States, and in libraries throughout "the center," that seem to advocate many different ways of doing anthropology, from conservative empiricism, to politically committed liberalism, to enlightenment humanism, to politically-correct identity politics, to cultural studies and textual analysis: the "center" has many variegated strands. Furthermore, many scholars who live in the United States are as far, professionally, from the anthropological center as any Japanese anthropologist: those who teach in community colleges, those who teach part-time, those, for that matter, who teach at any but the top universities, are in some sense far more peripheral than the Japanese anthropologist at, say, the University of Tokyo. However, Kuwayama is certainly right in his basic argument, in these ways: (a) the most prestigious anthropological journals in the West do operate within relatively narrow discursive spaces; (b) those who seek to see themselves in print in those journals must more or less conform to the rules of those narrow discursive spaces; and (c) this means that if Japanese anthropologists want to be printed in such journals, noted in such forums, they must in part discard the new and original ideas that may be emerging from the periphery, to address the center in its own terms.[12]

If, following our earlier argument, anthropology is seen as a science – an empirical, objective pursuit of knowledge undistorted by global inequalities of power – then this may be taken to mean that these anthropologists are growing up, leaving their province to engage in worldwide discourse. If, however, anthropology is taken to be an ideology – a pursuit of knowledge fundamentally shaped and constituted through global inequalities of power – then this means that these anthropologists must, if they want to be paid any attention in the center, kowtow to the center's power by following the center's forms of analysis. As I discussed earlier, anthropology partakes of both science and ideology; the discipline lies in the murky gray between the black-and-white contrast of these concepts. It is scientific in the sense that there do emerge new forms of analysis and fresh ways of thinking that add to the empirical data and theoretical sophistication of anthropology; there really is a marketplace of ideas, from which, at least ideally, the best and most fruitful ideas become the basis for anthropological research in the future. The multiple discourses in anthropology today, as discussed above, the scores of books and journals advocating different approaches to anthropology, testify to the reality of this marketplace. At the same time, however, the local concerns of American anthropologists and their audience, the fads and fashions of contemporary American anthropology, serve to slant the shelves of that marketplace, influencing what ultimately "sells" – what ideas are deemed important. The market is partially rigged, by locals in the center selling to other locals in the center, along with the occasional cosmopolitan outsider sophisticated enough to know how to play the locals' game.

Conclusion: Japanese Anthropology in a Parallel Universe

Let me now return to the underlying question of the gap and tension between Japanese and American anthropological depictions of Japan. In one sense, the tension has in large part vanished simply in that there are relatively few Japanese anthropological depictions of Japan today, and few anthropological discussions between Japanese anthropologists and American anthropologists doing research on Japan.[13] An earlier generation of Japanese anthropologists investigated Japan because postwar poverty prevented them from investigating societies elsewhere. A slightly later generation of Japanese anthropologists attacked Western methodologies, perhaps fueled in part by an inferiority complex *vis-à-vis* the West; these are scholars who remembered Japan's defeat in war and postwar occupation, and who may have been directly or indirectly shaped by such memory in seeking to assert a Japanese basis for Japanese research. Many in the younger generations of anthropologists have, however, no such memories, and no such inferiority complexes; how American anthropologists portray Japan is of no great concern of theirs, since they themselves study other societies. Thus, despite Kuwayama's article and the attention it has attracted, the major period of tension between Japanese and American anthropologists of Japan seems to have been roughly 1945-1990. A large gap in audience remains today, as discussed at the start of this paper, but the tension has to a degree dissipated.

However, as the earlier discussion of Kuwayama's article indicates, a much larger chasm is now apparent: that between Japanese and American anthropology as a whole. Japan now is the nation with the second largest number of anthropologists in the world – the Japanese Society of Cultural Anthropology now has some 2,000 members – and yet its worldwide anthropological influence remains small. A primary underlying problem seems to be one of language, and the linguistic dynamic at play in the development of Japanese anthropology. In immediate postwar Japan, when Japanese anthropologists studied Japan, at least a small audience of foreign anthropologists of Japan could read their work. But once Japan became affluent, and Japanese anthropologists began to focus on societies beyond Japan, foreign anthropologists paid less attention. A foreign anthropologist studying Japan could be expected to read Japanese, but a foreign anthropologist studying Indonesia or Madagascar could hardly be expected to read Japanese; thus the findings of Japanese anthropologists, to the extent that these were not published in English, tended to be ignored.[14] An anthropologist in Denmark or Israel or Malaysia would be likely to know English and publish in English simply because the anthropological world in these countries is so small that the anthropologist would have to reach beyond the bounds of these societies. But in Japan today, with its large number of anthropologists, there is sufficient anthropological infrastructure of journals and conferences in Japanese to make communication in English unnecessary within the boundaries of Japan.

What all of this means is that in a very curious way, Japanese anthropology exists in a parallel universe *vis-à-vis* Western anthropology. As Yamashita Shinji has said, "because [Japanese anthropologists] write in Japanese, even when they criticize European or American anthropologists, they have no impact" (Yamashita 1996: 411). The prevailing pattern of Japanese anthropology at present is one of Japanese anthropologists doing fieldwork in societies outside of Japan, and citing American and European anthropologists to provide a theoretical framework for their research. Aoki Tamotsu has written that "[in Japanese universities] the theory and methods used in studying legitimate cultural anthropology are the ones created in the U. S. and Europe" (Aoki 1990: 174). Thus, Japanese anthropologists themselves do not seem to greatly value Japanese anthropology at present; and anthropologists outside of Japan do not either, because they cannot read it.

What, then, is the future direction of Japanese anthropology? It may continue on as it has in recent decades, within its parallel universe. That position is not to be scorned, for Japanese anthropology now seems more significant for Japanese society at large than American anthropology is for the United States. My distinct impression from visiting bookstores is that there are more books by Japanese anthropologists addressing the Japanese public than there are of American anthropologists addressing the American public. Aoki Tamotsu, one of the best-known Japanese anthropologist at present, writes for the general public and is featured prominently in Japanese bookstores, in a way that one could scarcely imagine of, say, Clifford Geertz or Arjun Appadurai. Publications such as *Jinruigaku ga wakaru* [Understanding anthropology] (1995), published by a major Japanese newspaper company, feature Japan's most prominent anthropologists explaining to the public what anthropology is; it is hard to imagine an American parallel, both because most prominent American anthropologists seem little interested in writing for the public, and because, in tandem, most members of the American public seem little interested in what academic anthropologists have to say. Japanese anthropology, to repeat, seems to play a significant role in Japan today. Can it, however, play a significant role in the world beyond Japan?

Probably the greatest obstacle to its assumption of such a role remains that of language. Kuwayama (personal communication) has said to me that "It is painful to see that many brilliant Japanese anthropologists look childish, even absurd, when they speak at conferences held in America because they cannot overcome the language barrier" (I myself have winced at the same kind of unfortunate occurrence); and indeed, he is skeptical that this language barrier can ever be overcome, since one must grow up in a society to express oneself as do the native speakers of its language (1997a: 525). Certainly efforts are being made to overcome the language barrier. One hopeful sign is the inauguration of the *Japanese Review of Cultural Anthropology*, a journal started by the Japanese Society of Ethnology in 1998 that provides discussion in English of the research of Japanese anthropologists; there are other journals as well in English of Japanese anthropological research, such as *Senri Anthropological Studies*, published by the National Museum of Ethnology.

My personal hope is that this trickle of publications in English might eventually become a flood, which might just possibly sweep aside the provincialism of the American discursive center, in helping to shape a truly world anthropology. A recent Japanese book is entitled *Fifty Great Works in Anthropology* (Ayabe 1994). Forty-four of these works are authored by writers from the American and Western European center, from Morgan and Tylor to Turner, Geertz, and Sahlins; only six are Japanese, included as if an afterthought or a market ploy. Where are the Japanese Geertz and Sahlins, cited the world over? Since anthropology is a discipline that originated in the West, it is perhaps not surprising that most of the anthropologists named in the book are Westerners. But when will it be that we can see in such a book an anthropology reflecting not just the West but the world?

This leads me to a final comment as to the nature of anthropology as a discipline. Anthropology, as I earlier argued, has been progressively advancing, in that later ethnographies tend to be more complex than earlier ones because they can draw upon the findings of earlier ones; theory too, although this is perhaps more questionable, has evolved in ways that not only reflect the changing world, but also reveal the development of anthropology itself. However, this development has taken place in a very limited intellectual forum, the world of Americans and Europeans, intellectually colonizing all the world as they once physically colonized the world: because of this positioning, anthropology has also been ideological. In one sense, anthropology will inevitably be ideological, in that the ethnographer can never really escape his or her own cultural shaping, and the cultural shaping too of his or her audience; but in another sense, anthropology can perhaps escape the ideology of the colonizing center, which has characterized the discipline since its inception. The marketplace of ideas will never truly be free – one's placement within positions of power will always intrude – but by bringing in as many voices as possible, the anthropological marketplace can, perhaps, become freer; it seems at least possible that intellectual power can transcend to a degree one's inevitable placement within other forms of power in the world. This may seem a naive hope; but it is, I suspect, ultimately anthropology's only hope.

Notes

Acknowledgements: This paper has benefited greatly from suggestions for revision by Miyakawa Yoko, Joseph Bosco, and Kuwayama Takami; Yamashita

Shinji and Jerry Eades have also provided helpful comments at a later stage. The paper's flaws are, however, mine alone.

1   In this paper I deal largely with anthropologists proper, but occasionally discuss Japanese sociologists and other social scientists as well when their work seems to me to be anthropological in focus.

2   The folklore specialists do research into Japanese tradition that is not generally thought of in Japan as being anthropological. However, as noted elsewhere in the early chapters of this book, the issue is complicated by the fact that the term *minzokugaku*, written with one set of Chinese characters, means "folklore study," but with another it means "ethnology."

3   The Soviet Union and China created colonial empires too in a sense, but only within their own expanding national boundaries. That Chinese anthropology today consists largely of Han Chinese investigating "minority nationalities" seems a repetition of the global pattern of colonizers investigating the colonized.

4   One reason for the dearth of Japanese anthropological studies on the United States is that American professors of anthropology tend to encourage their Japanese Ph.D. students to go back to Japan to do research rather than do research on the United States (Morikawa Makio, personal communication), since their own research interests center on Japan. Another reason is that it is no doubt far easier for a Japanese anthropologist to gain access to all sorts of people in a poorer society, where he or she is an elite, than it might be in the United States; this is the case for research funding as well, I've been told. It is true that American anthropologists themselves study "mainstream" American life relatively infrequently; but Japanese studies are all but nonexistent – while there are many popular volumes to be found in Japanese bookstores, there is virtually no anthropological analysis. The only Japanese anthropologist that I know of who has written about the "mainstream" United States is Notoji Masako, who has published an ethnography of Disneyland (Notoji 1990), among other works on American society. Ironically, she teaches not in an anthropology department but in an American studies department in Japan.

5   This may be due in part to American anthropologists' difficulties in reading Japanese. Given the time pressures American researchers may be working under, Japanese theoretical arguments, taking far longer to read, may be given short shrift in comparison to more readily comprehensible theory written in English.

6   For discussion of *Nihonjinron* and what it signifies in Japan in recent decades, see Aoki (1990), Befu (1993; 2001), and Yoshino (1992).

7   Nakane emphasizes, in the Japanese version of her book (1967: 12–26),

that Western theoretical models must be altered in order to appropriately analyze Japanese society (although she then proceeds to use classic British social anthropology as the theoretical foundation of her analysis); but this opening chapter is absent in the English version of the book. These two faces of Nakane's work show the degree to which audiences and their expectations shape her work. Some have spoken of Nakane's work as being a form of *Nihonjinron*, seeking to justify contemporary Japanese society (Smith and Hata 1985). Her early writings do take this tone, as when she writes that the vertical nature of Japanese social relations is linked to "Japanese blood" (1964: 78), but I do not read her *Japanese Society* in that light.

8   Kuwayama has written that Rohlen's discussion of Murakami's theory "reveals his own lack of understanding more than Murakami's" (1996: 166). In any case, it is clear that the highly condensed account of Murakami's theory in English that Rohlen was commenting upon does not begin to do justice to the complexity of the six-hundred-page Japanese version.

9   There are, of course, Japanese anthropologists who are immersed in such theory. One of the most notable has been Yamaguchi Masao, who has offered symbolic interpretations of Japan based in narrative theory (see, for example, Yamaguchi 1987), and with whom Ivy notes that she had extensive consultation in conducting the research that led to her book. Among a younger generation of Japanese anthropologists, Ota Yoshinobu (1998) is notable among a group of scholars who, in parallel with their *avant-garde* American counterparts, see the future of anthropology as lying in the theoretical abstractions of cultural studies.

10 That Kuwayama, like Nakane before him, offered a different emphasis in the Japanese as opposed to the English version of his article seems to prove his point: because discourse is controlled from the English-speaking center, the Japanese anthropologist must adjust his/her message to fit the expectations of that center. In the Japanese version of his article (1997a), Kuwayama emphasized that Japanese scholars have been victimized by the West's discursive Orientalism; in the English version of his article (1997b), he emphasized more the mutual misunderstandings between Japanese and American anthropologists.

11 This is not altogether different from the situation of any assistant professor of anthropology in an American university. The difference, however, is that American assistant professors at top research institutions are expected to come up with "cutting edge" theory, whereas few American anthropologists seek any such thing from the non-American hinterlands. One reason for this particularly American expectation is that American anthropology itself is becoming ever more international, with young scholars from all over the world becoming assistant professors at American

universities. This development, however, may blend into the pernicious assumption that non-American- (or Western European-) based anthropologists have nothing really valuable to say to world anthropology.

12 It is true that a thinker such as Edward Said shook the center with ideas from the periphery, in his *Orientalism* (1978) – the periphery can in this sense still serve as a fountainhead for new ideas. However, when Said wrote this book, he had long been a professor at an ivy league university in the U.S. How many Brazilian scholars in Brazil, Indian scholars in India, or Japanese scholars in Japan really have any impact on their American colleagues? Very few indeed.

13 It is interesting that many of the American anthropologists who study Japan today make little use of Japanese anthropology but do make use of Japanese sociology. My own book (1996), to take one example, makes extensive use of the writings on Japanese lifecourse by Misawa Ken'ichi and others, industrial transition by Noda Masaaki, women's roles by Ueno Chizuko, the meanings of life in Japan by Mita Munesuke, and affluence and its meanings by Hirooka Moriho, sociologists all, but makes very few citations of any Japanese anthropologists. In this sense, communication between Japanese and American social scientists dealing with Japan does continue; but it is not a true dialogue, in that because the premises and methodologies of anthropology and sociology differ, there is little need for cross-cultural questioning. These sociologists are used by anthropologists such as myself more as sources of data and of close-to-the-ground theory than as means of questioning anthropological conceptualizations of Japanese society.

14 Jan van Bremen mentions Mabuchi Tôichi as a Japanese anthropologist of Taiwan and Southeast Asia who had considerable anthropological impact worldwide (1997: 59). These anthropologists are far fewer than one might expect, given the number of Japanese anthropologists at work today.

References

Allison, Anne. 1994. *Nightwork: Sexuality, Pleasure, and Corporate Masculinity in a Tokyo Hostess Club.* Chicago: University of Chicago Press.

Aoki Tamotsu. 1990. *"Nihon bunkaron" no henyô: Sengo Nihon no bunka to aidentitii"* [The transformations of Nihonjinron: Culture and identity in postwar Japan]. Tokyo: Chûô Kôronsha.

Ayabe Tsuneo, ed. 1994. *Bunka jinruigaku no meicho* [Fifty great works in anthropology]. Tokyo: Heibonsha.

Befu, Harumi. 1993. "Nationalism and Nihonjinron," pp. 107-35 in *Cultural Nationalism in East Asia: Representation and identity,* ed. Harumi Befu. Berkeley: University of California Institute of East Asian Studies.

Befu, Harumi, ed. 1992. *Otherness of Japan: Historical and Cultural Influences on Japanese Studies in Ten Countries*. Munich: Iudicium.

Befu, Harumi. 2001. *Hegemony of Homogeneity*. Melbourne: Trans Pacific Press.

Benedict, Ruth. 1946. *The Chrysanthemum and the Sword: Patterns of Japanese Culture*. New York: New American Library.

Bennett, J. W., and M. Nagai. 1953. "Reactions to American anthropology: Japanese critique of Benedict's 'Chrysanthemum and the Sword,'" *American Anthropologist* 55: 404-11.

Bestor, Theodore C. 1989. *Neighborhood Tokyo*. Stanford: Stanford University Press.

Bremen, Jan van. 1997. "Prompters who do not appear on the stage: Japanese anthropology and Japanese studies in American and European anthropology," *Japan Anthropology Workshop Newsletter* 26/27: 57-65.

Dale, Peter N. 1986. *The Myth of Japanese Uniqueness*. New York: St. Martin's Press.

Doi, Takeo. 1973. *The Anatomy of Dependence*. Tokyo: Kodansha International.

Hamabata, Matthews M. 1990. *Crested Kimono: Power and Love in the Japanese Business Family*. Ithaca: Cornell University Press.

Hamaguchi, Eshyun. 1985. "A contextual model of the Japanese: Toward a methodological innovation in Japan studies," *Journal of Japanese Studies* 11 (2): 298-322.

Ishida, Eiichiro. 1974. *Japanese Culture*. Tokyo: University of Tokyo Press.

Ito, Abito. 1996. "Cultural anthropology," pp. 216-39. in *An Introductory Bibliography of Japanese Studies*. Tokyo: Japan Foundation.

Ivy, Marilyn. 1995. *Discourses of the Vanishing: Modernity, Phantasm, Japan*. Chicago: University of Chicago Press.

Jinruigaku ga wakaru [Understanding anthropology] 1995. *Aera Book 8* (Asahi Shinbun Extra Report and Analysis Special Number 8). Tokyo: Asahi Shinbunsha

Kawada, Minoru. 1993. *The Origin of Ethnography in Japan: Yanagita Kunio and his Times*. London: Kegan Paul International.

Kelly, William W. 1991. "Directions in the anthropology of contemporary Japan," *Annual Review of Anthropology* 20: 395-431.

Kondo, Dorinne K. 1990. *Crafting Selves: Power, Gender, and Discourses of Identity in a Japanese Workplace*. Chicago: University of Chicago Press.

Kreiner, Josef. 1996. "Nihon minzokugaku, bunkajinruigaku no rekishi" [The history of Japanese ethnology and cultural anthropology], in *Nihon minzokugaku no genzai* [Japanese ethnology at present] J. Kreiner, ed. Tokyo: Shinyôsha.

Kumon, Shunpei. 1982. "Some principles governing the thought and behavior of Japanists (contextualists)," *Journal of Japanese Studies* 8 (1): 5-28.

Kuwayama, Takami. 1996. "The familial *(ie)* model of Japanese society." pp. 143-88 in *Japanese Culture and Society: Models of Interpretation,* eds. J. Kreiner and H.D. Ölschleger. Munich: Iudicium.

Kuwayama Takami. 1997a. "Genchi no jinruigakusha: Naigai no Nihon kenkyû o chûshin ni" [Native anthropologists: With special reference to Japanese studies inside and outside Japan], *Minzokugaku-kenkyû* [Japanese Journal of Ethnology] 61 (4): 517-42.

Kuwayama, Takami. 1997b. "Native anthropologists: With a special reference to Japanese studies inside and outside Japan," *Japan Anthropology Workshop Newsletter* 26/27: 52-56.

Lebra, Takie Sugiyama. 1976. *Japanese Patterns of Behavior.* Honolulu: University of Hawaii Press.

Mathews, Gordon. 1996. *What Makes Life Worth Living? How Japanese and Americans Make Sense of their Worlds.* Berkeley: University of California Press.

Morris-Suzuki, Tessa. 1995. "The invention and reinvention of 'Japanese culture,'" *Journal of Asian Studies* 54 (3): 759-80.

Murakami, Yasusuke. 1984. "*Ie* society as a pattern of civilization," *Journal of Japanese Studies* 10 (2): 279-364.

Nakane Chie. 1964. "*Nihonteki shakai ko no hakken*" [The discovery of a Japanese type of social structure], *Chûô Kôron* (Ma): 48-85.

Nakane Chie. 1967. *Tate shakai no ningen kankei* [Personal relations in a vertical society]. Tokyo: Kôdansha.

Nakane, Chie. 1973 [1970]. *Japanese Society.* Middlesex, England: Penguin.

Nakane, Chie. 1974. "Cultural anthropology in Japan," *Annual Review of Anthropology* 3: 57-72.

Notoji Masako. 1990. *Dizuniirando to iu seichi* [Disneyland as Holy Land]. Tokyo: Iwanami Shoten.

Ohnuki-Tierney, Emiko. 1984. "Critical commentary: 'Native' anthropologists," *American Ethnologist* 11 (3): 584-86.

Ota Yoshinobu. 1998. *Toransupojishon no shisô: Bunka jinruigaku no saisôzô* [The idea of transposition: Reimagining cultural anthropology]. Tokyo: Sekai Shisôsha.

Plath, David W. 1980. *Long Engagements: Maturity in Modern Japan.* Stanford: Stanford University Press.

Plath, David W. and Robert J. Smith. 1992. "How 'American' are studies of modern Japan done in the United States?," pp. 201-30 in *Otherness of Japan: Historical and Cultural Influences on Japanese Studies in Ten Countries,* ed. Harumi Befu. Munich: Iudicium.

Rohlen, Thomas. 1985. "When evolution isn't progressive," *Journal of Japanese Studies* 11 (1): 65-70.

Said, Edward. 1978. *Orientalism*. New York: Random House.

Sekimoto Teruo. 1995. "Nihon no jinruigaku to Nihon shigaku" [Anthropology in Japan and Japanese historiography], pp. 123-47 in *Iwanami kôza Nihon tsûshi. Bekkan 1* [Iwanami Complete History of Japan. Supplementary vol.1] eds. Asao Naohiro et al. Tokyo: Iwanami Shoten.

Shimizu Akitoshi. 1995. "Kindai Ôbei bunka jinruigakushi tenbyo." [A brief history of modern European and American cultural anthropology], pp. 154-60 in *Jinruigaku ga wakaru* [Understanding anthropology]. *Aera Book 8*, Tokyo: Asahi Shinbunsha.

Smith, Robert J. 1974. *Ancestor Worship in Contemporary Japan*. Stanford: Stanford University Press.

Smith, Robert J. 1983. *Japanese Society: Tradition, Self, and the Social Order*. Cambridge: Cambridge University Press.

Smith, Wendy, and Hata Hiroki. 1985. "Nihon tateshakairon kenkyû" [Research into the theory of Japan as a "vertical society"]. *Shisô no kagaku* [Science of thought] (September): 82-122.

Sofue, Takao. 1974. "Cultural anthropology," pp. 87-97 in *An Introductory Bibliography of Japanese Studies*. Tokyo: Japan Foundation.

Sugimoto, Yoshio and Mouer, Ross eds. 1989. *Constructs for Understanding Japan*. London: Kegan Paul International.

Umesao Tadao. 1974. *Bunmei no seitaishikan* [Civilization from the perspective of ecological history]. Tokyo: Chûô Kôronsha.

Umesao, Tadao. 1990. *The Roots of Contemporary Japan*. Tokyo: The Japan Forum.

Yamaguchi, Masao. 1987. "The dual structure of Japanese Emperorship," *Current Anthropology Supplement: An Anthropological Profile of Japan* 28 (4): S5-S11.

Yamashita, Shinji. 1996. "Comment," in "Shinpojiamu: Tenkanki ni okeru jinruigaku" [Symposium: Anthropology at the turning point], *Minzokugaku-kenkyû* [Japanese Journal of Ethnology] 60 (4): 377-435.

Yoshino, Kosaku. 1992. *Cultural Nationalism in Contemporary Japan: A Sociological Enquiry*. London: Routledge.

Chapter 6

Japanese Anthropology and Depictions of the Ainu

Sidney C. H. CHEUNG

Introduction

Japan is unusual in that it is a non-Western country whose scholars have conducted significant anthropological research both inside and outside its national boundaries. Since the differences between Japan's anthropology and that of other countries, especially the United States, have been discussed in other chapters, I will not focus on that issue. Instead, I will examine the development of anthropology in Japan as reflected in the academic journal published by the leading anthropological and ethnological society, from the establishment of the journal in the 1930s to the present. I aim to focus on the changes in Ainu studies within Japanese anthropology. Moreover, I present a few cases of difficulty and resistance in pursuing Ainu studies in Japan, including my own experience trying to publish an article with Ainu visual images in an academic journal. These cases provide insights not only into current Ainu-Japanese relations but also into the topical and theoretical development of anthropology in Japan.

Since I wrote a dissertation on Ainu-Japanese relations and received a doctoral degree from a Japanese university, my observations as an anthropologist who might consider himself both an insider (having been educated in Japan) and an outsider in Japanese society may offer an unusual perspective. I not only look at the historical development of Japanese anthropology, but also explore Ainu studies, which I perceive as a problematic area in Japanese anthropology. I argue that, though Japanese scholars realize the importance of Ainu studies, they pay surprisingly little attention to them, and I explore the reasons why this should be so.

Japanese Anthropology through *Minken*

To understand the development of anthropology as a discipline in Japan better, I looked at articles published in *Minzokugaku-kenkyû* (or *Minken*), the major Japanese quarterly journal published until 2004 by the Japanese Society of Ethnology.[1] As the leading academic journal in anthropology with more than fifty years of publication, it allows us to track the changes in Japanese scholars' views of ethnology/anthropology. Though the journal was criticized as old-fashioned, junior Japanese scholars still considered publishing their works in *Minken* to be an important rite of passage in becoming an anthropologist in Japan.

Minken was first published one year after the Society's establishment in 1934, at a time when Japanese imperialism extended to several neighboring colonies in East Asia; anthropological and ethnological studies of North China, Korea, Taiwan, Okinawa and the Ainu were the mainstream at that time. Ethnological studies in East Asia together with folklore studies in rural areas of Japan and the search for Japanese origins remained the main concerns in Japanese ethnology and anthropology until the 1970s. However, starting from the 1970s, *Minken's* articles were no longer limited simply to the same six categories (Ainu, Okinawa, Taiwan, North China, Korea, and Japan) as before, but began to show a greater diversity both in geographical area and theoretical approach (Sekimoto 1995). This could be attributed to several reasons.

One of the basic reasons for the change of geographical selection was Japan's economic take-off in the mid-1960s. Postwar poverty had made overseas field research almost impossible, but limitations on research fell away as Japan became more economically powerful, especially after the success of the Tokyo Olympics in 1964.[2] With the rapid economic growth in Japan as well as increased international exchange in terms of both culture and business, the 1970s saw an obvious increase in academic research conducted in countries outside East Asia and Japan's former colonies, and this is reflected in the articles published in *Minken*.

In addition to the geographical shift in countries chosen for anthropological field research, the theoretical approaches and interests of members of the Society, which had been relatively consistent and coherent until the early 1970s, became more diverse. Until the 1970s, the journal clearly focused on classical topics such as folklore, language, myths and legends, and material culture as relatively unchanging elements within a particular area. But then a major event in the history of anthropology in Japan occurred: the Eighth International Congress of Anthropological and Ethnological Sciences (or ICAES) was held in Japan in 1968, and was attended by scholars from around the world.

ICAES meetings have been held in different parts of the world every four or five years since 1934.[3] The ICAES was the successor of various Congresses of Anthropological Sciences (starting in 1865) brought together in the International Union of Anthropological and Ethnological Sciences (IUAES) in 1968. The IUAES has members from more than fifty countries in all parts of the world; through the Congress, discussion and dissemination of research findings are encouraged with the aim of enhancing exchange and communication among scholars of all regions of the world to promote a better understanding of human society.

After the Japanese Society of Ethnology hosted the International Congress in Japan, there were some obvious changes in theoretical approach among Japanese anthropologists. These changes are reflected in the contents of *Minken*, especially the new directions shown in volumes 33 and 34 (1968-1969). The most obvious departure from previous practice was a special issue (*Minken*, vol. 33, nos. 3 & 4), which included reports from major subfields in ethnology/cultural anthropology, such as ethnotheory and methodology; cultural history; socio-political organization, socio-cultural change, economy; religion and folklore, arts; psychological studies and education, language, and material culture. Also covered were Africa, the Ainu and the Arctic, and Japan. All of these reports were written by Japanese scholars who had participated in the Congress. One of the Congress's effects on Japanese anthropology, therefore, was that Japanese participants became very interested in a wide variety of subfields. Furthermore, in the following volume of *Minken* (vol. 34, no. 2), a review of 22 books in the form of a symposium was published under the chief editorship of Nakane Chie. She also provided a list of cultural anthropology books published in Japan from 1924 to 1969, presumably to make scholars in Japan more aware of the history of the field. By reviewing the strongest examples in terms of theory, the journal sought to promote international standards and a global perspective (Nakane 1969). In the same issue, there was also a list of ethnological and anthropological lectures held in Japanese universities.

These changes show that Japanese ethnology was moving in the direction of cultural anthropology. The Society was moving from ethnology, which puts a greater emphasis on regional studies, to cultural anthropology and multi-disciplinary approaches. Although *Minken* volumes 33 and 34 alone did not change the discipline in Japan, articles on a greater variety of geographical areas and theoretical approaches started to appear the journal from the mid-1970s on, reflecting a significant departure from the "pre-International Congress," pre-Olympics period when traditional styles of scholarship, as well as fewer contacts and resources, limited the Society's geographical and theoretical scope. In the mid-1970s, new theoretical approaches and subfields were explored, including symbolic, economic, political, and interpretive anthropology.

By 1984, the trend was clear and was noted by Japanese anthropologists. The discussion at a symposium entitled "Ethnology in Japan" held on the fiftieth anniversary of the Society's founding showed that its members were pursuing a mixture of ethnology, social and cultural anthropology and folklore, rather than focusing on a single discipline (Iwata, Obayashi, Sofue, Nakane, Yamaguchi and Kawada 1985).

Ethnology vs. Cultural Anthropology

In addition to greater geographical and theoretical diversity, another change in anthropology in Japan was the Society's debate over its own identity. An internal debate began among its members as to whether its focus should be ethnology as in the earlier period, or newer issues in cultural anthropology. In Japan, ethnology (in Japanese, *minzokugaku*) focuses on case studies and detailed description, while cultural anthropology (in Japanese, *bunka jinruigaku*) has a stronger emphasis on comparative case studies and is more concerned with global phenomena.

In 1994, it was proposed that the society should change its name from "The Japanese Society of Ethnology" to "The Japanese Association of Cultural Anthropology." The main reasons given for the change were that "cultural anthropology" would describe better the courses available in universities and research institutes; that it would promote more cross-cultural and comparative studies; and that it would give a clearer identity to the discipline within Japanese society. Two main groups emerged in the debate, which I broadly label "pro-ethnology" and "pro-cultural anthropology." Aoki Tamotsu (1998: 65), the Society's President at the time, said that ethnology sounded old-fashioned and irrelevant, and was no longer a popular major in Japanese universities since most of the teaching and research institutes in the field had already adopted the term "cultural anthropology."[4]

For a variety of reasons, however, the proposal to change the name was not supported by all members of the Society. A survey was conducted in October and November 1994 asking which name would be better, and the results were reported in the first special issue of the Society newsletter, entitled *Forum*, in early 1995 (Japanese Society of Ethnology 1995b). This debate reflected a complex situation both among individual members and in relation to institutional structures (Japanese Society of Ethnology 1995a, 1995b; 1996; 1997). Once the proposal was submitted, some members decided that they preferred to keep the old name. They argued that sixty years of history should not be ignored, that ethnology should not be downgraded to a subdiscipline of anthropology, and that the academic status of ethnologists would suffer (Japanese Society of Ethnology 1995b). It was also feared that a name change might split the society into two separate factions: ethnologists and anthropologists.[5] In the end, the vote showed that slightly more than half of the members preferred to keep the old name, and so it remained unchanged for the time being.[6]

In order to understand this decision, it is important to examine how the Japanese, including anthropologists, define themselves and the meanings of "the Other" in the Japanese context. Understanding current Japanese sensitivity towards Ainu research provides insights into other issues such as reflexivity and relations between the Self and Other in anthropology. I will argue that Japanese academics are reluctant to recognize the Ainu as their internal Other. Their reluctance to focus the anthropological lens on the Ainu suggests an unwillingness to study Japanese society analytically through anthropology, rather than descriptively through ethnology and folklore.

The Ainu in Japan: Past and Present

According to a 1993 Hokkaido local government survey, a total population of 23,830 Ainu people lived in Hokkaido where almost all the Ainu in Japan are located. This total included only those who considered themselves Ainu, though most of them did not speak the Ainu language (Kirikae 1997). As noted by Nomura (1996), the real number of Ainu is probably larger, since there are many Ainu who hide their Ainu identity. Given that ethnic homogeneity is one of the most commonly discussed traits of Japanese society, who are the Ainu, and are they regarded by the rest of Japan as Japanese?

The word "Ainu," which originally meant "human being" in the local language, is currently used by the Japanese to signify the indigenous people of the lands from northern Honshu to southern Kamchatka, including the Kurile Islands and the lower reaches of the Amur River in Manchuria (Kikuchi 1994). Historically speaking, however, the meanings of the term have varied in different periods. During the Tokugawa period, there were approximately 20,000 to 30,000 Ainu inhabitants under the suzerainty of the Matsumae feudal domain. With the formation of the Japanese state under the Tokugawa shogunate, the creation of a Japanese ethnic identity resulted in increasingly negative depictions of the Ainu. The prestige of the rulers of the Matsumae domain was therefore enhanced by their control over the "primitive" Ainu people. In other words, Ainu identity was created during the process of state boundary maintenance in a frontier zone (Howell 1994; Morris-Suzuki 1994).

After the Meiji Restoration, the northern island known as *Ezo-chi* was renamed Hokkaido, and became a major testing ground for Western technologies imported by the modern Meiji state.[7] With the 1899 Law for the Protection of Native Hokkaido Aborigines, a policy of assimilation was forced upon the Ainu people, and their social structure and living environment consequently went through a number of drastic changes as restrictions were put on their customs, language, and means of livelihood. Moreover, the expropriation law in relation to land tenure also affected the Ainu in important ways: it violated their territorial integrity by banning traditional subsistence strategies such as deer hunting and salmon fishing; it forced them to cultivate rice for the Japanese mainland; and it prohibited the use of the Ainu languages and Ainu folk customs, thus furthering the destruction of Ainu culture, given that the Ainu did not have a writing system of their own.

With the high rate of intermarriage between Ainu and Japanese, it is not surprising that traditional Ainu society had been largely destroyed by the beginning of the nineteenth century. During the last 100 years, the traditional Ainu ways of life disappeared, and their rights have been disregarded within Japanese society. Nowadays, the traditional Ainu settlement (*kotan*) can no longer be seen, and the traditional grass-thatch Ainu huts (*chise*) are almost nonexistent outside the tourist areas where dance performances or handicrafts and souvenirs are available. There remain only a few Ainu who are able to speak Ainu as their mother tongue. Nonetheless, the Ainu still remain conscious of an ethnic identity separate from that of the dominant Japanese. In 1992, the year before the International Year for the World's Indigenous People, the President of the Hokkaido Utari Kyôkai (Ainu Association of Hokkaido), Nomura Giichi, was invited to give a speech to explain the Ainu's problems and to share Ainu concerns with other indigenous groups in an international meeting organized by the United Nations. Nomura described the history of the Ainu under the Japanese government's policy of assimilation since the late nineteenth century, and requested that the United Nations set international standards to prevent discrimination and that it support the Ainu in their negotiations with the Japanese government (Nomura 1996). The Ainu New Law (Ainu Shinpô), originally proposed in 1984, was finally passed on 8 May 1997. It seems that the Japanese government has finally given formal recognition to the Ainu as an indigenous minority within Japan, or at least Hokkaido, though the general reaction from the Ainu to the law was to note that it was late in coming. Nevertheless, both the Ainu and the Japanese expected the law to lead to greater efforts to preserve language, culture, and traditions, as well as greater legal protection in land use, protection against discrimination, and an improvement in the social status of the Ainu.

As mentioned above, studies of the Ainu and their cultural traditions were popular among scholars in Japan before the 1970s, but interest has declined since then, despite continued interest among foreign scholars.[8] I believe that the decline in scholarly interest within Japan was due in part to the commodification of Ainu culture under the impact of the tourist industry. "Pure" Ainu cultural traditions could no longer be found, and the commoditized versions were not thought to be theoretically or ethnographically interesting. It can be argued that it is important for cultural anthropology to understand the underlying conflict between the Ainu and Japanese within the tourist arena. However, there has been almost no research of this kind, with the exception of works by Ohtsuka (1990) and Ota (1993).

141

Sidney C.H. Cheung

When we take a closer look at what concerns Japanese scholars undertaking Ainu research, we can see that there is sensitivity about the past conflict and hostile relations between the Ainu and the Japanese. "Studying the Ainu" is an area that Japanese researchers consider "sensitive" and about which it is difficult to be objective. In the late 1980s, the Japanese Society of Ethnology formed a committee on research ethics and in 1989 a "Statement with Respect to Ainu Research" was printed on the cover of *Minken* (volume 54, no. 1). Since then, ironically, even fewer Ainu articles have been published in the journal, even though it stated the necessity to carry out more good quality research on Ainu culture.[9] In the following section I will take a closer look at some cases where Ainu studies have been attempted within the world of Japanese anthropology, and the hindrances or dilemmas that they faced.

Ainu as Others and Ainu as Self

I would like to start with the personal experiences in Ainu studies of one of the leading Japanese anthropologists. Yamaguchi Masao is renowned for his work on semiotic theory and cultural symbolism in myths and legends. In one of his best-known books, *Chi no enkinhô* (Perspectives on knowledge), Yamaguchi (1978) tells of his shock upon meeting and talking with Ainu people in Hokkaido, where he was raised. He had decided to study the history of the Ainu, and had lived near them, but had always regarded them with exotic awe. However when he went to visit an elder in an Ainu settlement near his home town in Hokkaido, he was unprepared for the painful reality of what the Japanese had done to the Ainu people.

The elder's mother lived in the attic of the elder's home and refused to come down, and she never spoke Japanese. When Yamaguchi inquired the reason, he learned that she had given up learning Japanese as she had witnessed the period when the Ainu were driven away from their own lands by the Japanese by force and deceit, when they were forced to put their children in Japanese primary schools, and when they were weakened by liquor introduced by the Japanese.

> The elder told his story out of simple good will, but for someone as innocent as myself, his words just shocked me and prevented me from pursuing my desire to do Ainu studies ... Through the experience of hearing this history directly from Ainu people, I was totally overwhelmed due to its realistic force. Even now, I still believe that if that had been expressed in writing, I might not have felt the same impact. Later, when I started to study anthropology, Mabuchi Tôichi, my teacher, often suggested that I should study Ainu cosmology because it would be an interesting topic; however, I did not listen to his advice and left Japan for somewhere far

away like West Africa. One of the reasons may have been my wish to leave behind the shadow of this shocking experience. (Yamaguchi 1978: 141-43, translated Cheung)

Yamaguchi (1978) saw the Ainu's refusal to speak Japanese as an act of resistance against their Japanese oppressors. Despite being encouraged to study the Ainu, he preferred to "escape" far away for his fieldwork without having to face the conflict aroused by the relationship between the Ainu and Japanese that had led to his own emotional response. It seems it was easier for a Japanese anthropologist to do research in Africa than to confront the political and ethical problems presented by the Ainu.

Another similar case is that of Iizumi Seiichi, who conducted a survey of the Sakhalin Ainu in the 1950s. He was accused of exploiting the Ainu people who had been discriminated against and suppressed in the past, in order to earn academic prestige himself. Iizumi also "escaped" to the study of the Andes because of the unexpected and unpleasant experience of being treated as an aggressor just because he was Japanese (Yamaguchi 1980: 23-26; Kinase 1997).

The two scholars were politically uncomfortable with the historical legacy. They were unable to separate their identities as scholars and as Japanese, and they were unable to study the Ainu objectively as outsiders rather than as members of Japanese society. Nakane notes that Japanese society is not a good environment to train Japanese students to study Japan, since "the society is homogeneous, speaks the same language, and was socialized through a long history of political and cultural centralization" (1982: 58). In contrast to Japan, anthropologists from ethnically plural countries are more aware of the political nature of ethnic identity. For Japanese scholars researching Japan, the critical distance required for a reflexive understanding of their own culture is difficult to achieve, as is an objective analysis, especially in a case such as the Ainu where the history is both violent and painful. The decisions by Yamaguchi and Iizumi to "escape" are good examples of native Japanese scholars' unwillingness to try and understand what they see. They chose to look away. In the process, Japanese anthropology developed something of a blind spot in relation to Ainu studies.

My own experience serves as another example. When studying in Japan, I became interested in Ainu-Japanese relations, and for my M.A. I started to do research on visual images of the Ainu created by the Japanese and circulated within Japan. I took on this research because of my interest in the "hidden" meanings behind the images of the Ainu captured for posterity, and the image of their way of life which these fragmentary images presented to Japanese society (Cheung 1992). Later when studying for my Ph.D., I was encouraged to conduct further research on images of the Ainu for two reasons. First, these had been little studied, and they fitted well with contemporary interests in the media, representation, and history. Second, my status as an outsider would perhaps make it easier to be objective about Ainu-Japanese relations over the previous century.

Eventually, in my doctoral dissertation, I focused on the meaning of Ainu as a discourse among Japanese, with an emphasis on Self-Other relations as reflected in the changing depictions of the Ainu over a hundred years. I suggested that Ainu photo images could help us examine how notions such as minorities, ethnicity, tradition, modernity, and culture were conceptualized starting from the establishment of the Meiji state (Cheung 1996). Investigating the contrast between depictions of the Westernized Meiji emperor and the traditional Ainu, for example, allows us to see from a political perspective how the Japanese have shaped their Others (including Ainu, Taiwanese, Koreans, and Okinawans), and how the Japanese Self is shaped by others (Cheung 1997). I described the construction of the identities of the Japanese as powerful outsiders and colonizers, and of the Ainu as primitive, and I used my perspective as an "inside outsider" to examine aspects of Ainu-Japanese relations which Japanese scholars were unable to examine.

In writing about this in my thesis, I did not feel any constraints. A problem came up, however, when I tried to publish part of my dissertation as an article in *Minken*. The manuscript was entitled, "Shôzôshashin ni okeru kenryoku no shikakuka to shôzôka: Ainu minzoku no shashin ni kansuru jirei kenkyû" [Visualized and imaginary power in portraits: A case study of post-cards with images of Ainu].[10] It was first accepted in an Editorial Board Meeting in 1995. I was given the reviewers' comments and asked to make some small changes, and I sent the revised version back to the Editorial Board on May 2, 1995. In August 1996, after more than one year, I was informed by the editor that my paper was had been rejected.[11] A member of the editorial committee contacted me informally and said that *Minken* was worried that Ainu people might use the images to protest that their rights and sovereignty had been infringed. It seems that the journal did not want to take responsibility for publishing the article. The editor (who by this point had stepped down at the end of his term) sent a final letter saying:

> I deeply regret being unable to handle the matter promptly. After all it was once accepted and asked some revision, but finally rejected more than one year after. I apologize first of all the delay of telling you the final decision.
>
> I myself could not make up my mind should it be published or not. I hope you understand that we were afraid of jeopardize our relation to the Ainu people which had been generally good, by publishing pictures you used for your manuscript. It made arguments among the members of the board and it was main reason of the delay of making final decision. (Letter dated 25 May, 1997; original in English)

Here I would like to make two remarks on the incident. The first is that any investigation of Ainu tradition and culture has to be related to Ainu history, including conflicts that Japanese scholars may find it difficult to face up to, admit and investigate objectively. Note that it was not the Ainu people themselves, but the Japanese anthropologists who were unwilling for my paper to be published, in contrast with other cases where resistance comes from the minority. The Japanese anthropologists' own discomfort with research on the history of Japan-Ainu relations was an important factor in their decision. The journal's initial acceptance and later rejection of my manuscript reflects this unwillingness to confront unpleasant aspects of Ainu history, as opposed to the romanticized ethnological past.

The second observation is that Japanese anthropologists feel uncomfortable with the possibility of criticism that might be directed at them. Some Japanese scholars have told me that the Ainu kept an eye on academic journals for Ainu-related statements, and "attacked" authors who wrote about them, accusing them of using the Ainu people to gain academic status, irrespective of the contents of the text. However, the sensitivity towards Ainu research which I experienced was actually over the *possibility* of criticism that might have a negative impact on the journal. This was why the Japanese editorial board preferred to drop my manuscript. I firmly believe the problem had nothing to do with personal relations, or that any particular individual should be personally held responsible. Rather, because of the historical and political background of Ainu-Japanese relations, this incident seemed to reflect a problem that deserves analysis so that Japanese anthropology can be better understood and compared to that in other Asian countries.

My experience is not an exceptional one, as we can see in related cases where the method of presentation of Ainu culture has also been controversial. For example, regarding the permanent exhibit on the Ainu in the National Museum of Ethnology (*Minpaku*), in Osaka, we can see a further gap between Japanese anthropologists and non-Japanese anthropologists from "outside." Sandra Niessen, a Visiting Scholar at the Museum, has written that the representation of the Ainu was idyllic and fictitious, showing nothing about the negative social interaction between the Ainu and Japanese or anything about Ainu struggles with dominant Japanese culture (1994: 23). Niessen's paper was strongly criticized by two scholars working at the Museum, who criticized her failure to use the Japanese-language literature, her negative description of the exhibition as "a fictitious image of the past, and her use of Western standards to evaluate the exhibit without regard for the Japanese social context. Most importantly, they criticized her naivety in understanding the complicated relations between the Ainu and the Japanese since World War II, and the efforts made by the Museum staff to make the exhibition on the Ainu possible (Ohtsuka 1996; Shimizu 1996).

Ohtsuka and Shimizu did admit that the Ainu exhibition was basically nostalgic, in the same way as other exhibits at the Museum, and that this is what the Ainu also wanted. In response, Niessen restated part of her original argument, and added a further comment:

> I explain that in North America such an ahistorical emphasis on a "traditional" past time *would be* interpreted as a fundamental denial, rather than promotion of Ainu identity. *In Japan it may be argued*, however, that the roots of Ainu culture have been so eroded that icons of Ainu cultural purity and integrity have become an inspiration for cultural renewal and power. In modern Japan, this idyllic Ainu image is even politically subversive. (Niessen 1994: 24, cited with emphasis added in Niessen 1996).

> My colleagues have extrapolated from what they have read as a condemnation of their permanent Ainu installation from the extant North American discourse on ahistorical, nostalgic exhibitions, and falsely attributed to me claims which range from the irrelevant to the ridiculous ... Such pronouncements indicate that the premises upon which my article was based are not known by my Japanese colleagues and that they have interpreted observations on themes of representational politics as personal slights and criticisms. (Niessen 1996: 133)

Without an intensive study on the Ainu exhibition held at *Minpaku*, I am not able to give an opinion on this issue; however, these differences in position can be understood as consideration of the relation between Self or Other from different points of view. Niessen seems to feel uncomfortable with the Ainu constructed as a separate fictitious Other, cut off from contemporary Japan society, while Ohtsuka and Shimizu believe that representations of the Other can only be constructed on a mutually acceptable basis. In other words, the unpleasant past does not need to be mentioned explicitly, even though it did happen. Instead, we can look to a (fictitious) time before that, when Japanese and Ainu cultures operated independently and autonomously. At a time when anthropology in the rest of the world has been discovering history, imperialism, postcolonial cultures, and the global interactions of cultures, Japanese anthropology still has a tendency to revert to the descriptive ethnology of the past.

Conclusion

Anthropology has, since its beginning, set itself apart with as the study of "other" cultures in "other" societies, in contrast to other disciplines in the social sciences such as sociology, psychology, and political science which have investigated mainly issues in their "own" societies. However, with the emphasis on reflexivity and the cultural critique of power relations that developed from the "interpretive anthropology" of the 1960s (Marcus and Fischer 1986: 25), we cannot nowadays ignore the existence of Others as part of the construction of Self, nor can we imagine any apolitical investigation of the meanings of Ainu culture. The study of the Ainu in Japanese anthropology cannot be separated from previous Ainu-Japanese relations of domination and subordination that continue to affect the present situation, even though many Japanese anthropologists may prefer not to see this.

Furthermore, as Rosaldo (1989: 19) has pointed out, the "so-called natives are also positioned subjects who have a distinctive mix of insight and blindness." I would therefore ask what this blindness means. Is it something that the natives cannot "see"; or something which they can "see" but choose to ignore? And do they ignore it because it is unimportant; or because it is something which they do not want to look at carefully – for example, in the case of Japanese scholars, the hostile relations between "themselves" and the Ainu? Given the instances of Japanese scholars escaping from Ainu research, the criticism of Niessen for her own critique of an ahistorical exhibition, and the sensitivity over my own manuscript, it could be said that even in the 1990s Japanese scholars were still reluctant to investigate the construction of the Japanese Self through the depiction of the Ainu as internal Others, in an attempt to keep anthropology as "safe" as possible.

Notes

1   In Japan, there are two major anthropological societies, the Japanese Society of Ethnology/Cultural Anthropology described here (see note 6 below), and the Anthropological Society of Nippon, which publishes the journal *Anthropological Science*, and which deals mainly with physical anthropology. On the changing names of this latter association, see Askew's paper in this volume, especially note 39.

2   Karatani (1993) suggests that the "postwar" period should be considered to end with the Tokyo Olympics in 1964 because enormous social change occurred in the following decades.

3   The locations were: London (1934); Copenhagen (1938); Brussels (1948); Vienna (1952); Philadelphia (1956); Paris (1960); Moscow (1964); Tokyo (1968); Chicago (1973); Delhi (1978); Quebec and Vancouver (1983); Zagreb (1988); Mexico City (1993); Williamsburg (1998); and Florence (2003). The Congress held in Japan in 1968 was the first to be held in an Asian country.

4   Some ethnology programs remain. Keio University has a Department of Ethnology and Archaeology, and the National Museum of Ethnology has

a graduate program.

5 Personal communication, S. Yamashita, the Society's then President.

6 It was finally decided in 2003 by a large majority that the name should be changed, with effect from April 2004. From April 2004, the *Nihon Minzokugakkai* (Japanese Society of Ethnology) became known as the *Nihon Bunkajinruigakkai* (Japanese Society of Cultural Anthropology), and the journal *Minzokugaku-kenkyû* (*Japanese Journal of Ethnology*) has changed its name to *Bunkajinruigaku* (in English, *Japanese Journal of Cultural Anthropology*).

7 The establishment of dairy farms and beer factories in Hokkaido during the early Meiji era, along with salmon aquaculture and food canning showed the importance of Western technologies in the modern development of the island. These technologies, along with Hokkaido's agricultural value to mainland Japan, justified the idea of colonization, as did also the threat from Russia.

8 There were few studies of the Ainu by non-Japanese scholars after the extensive initial research by Romyn Hitchcock (1851-?), Neil Gordon Munro (1863-1942), and John Batchelor (1854-1944). Interest revived with an article published in *National Geographic* in 1967 by a Benedictine nun renowned for her work on children's education among native Americans (Hilger 1967; cf. Hilger 1971). Since then, a number of books and articles have been published on the Ainu by foreign scholars, including Peng and Geiser (1977), Hammel (1988), Howell (1994), Sjoberg (1993), Siddle 1996, and Fitzhugh and Dubreuil (1999).

9 The journal did include informative descriptive articles on the Ainu by Kinase (1997; 1998) and Irimoto (1995; 2001).

10 The paper has since been published elsewhere (Cheung 2000).

11 Needless to say, this acceptance and subsequent rejection is highly unusual. The story later circulated that the paper was poorly written, and had many grammatical mistakes. The August 1996 letter from the editor seems to try to deflect the issue away from the use of photographs to these more mundane editorial issues, but his letter began and ended by discussing the sensitivity of Ainu photographs. His letter admitted that the reason for the reevaluation of the paper was the sensitivity over the photographs. His letter of May 1997 makes this explicit. Furthermore, several persons who contacted me informally about the paper all said that the use of the photographs was the key issue.

References

Aoki Tamotsu.1998. "'Hangakumon' no susume" [Recommending semi-scholarship], pp. 64-74 in *Bunkajinruigaku no susume* [Invitation to cultural anthropology], ed. Funabiki Takeo. Tokyo: Chikuma Shobô.

Cheung, C. H. Sidney. 1992. "Datsu shashinron" [Deconstruction of photography], *Annals of Human Sciences, Faculty of Human Sciences in Osaka University* 13: 129-45.

Cheung, C. H. Sidney. 1996. "Change of Ainu images in Japan: A reflexive study of pre-war and post-war photo-images of Ainu," *Visual Anthropology* 9 (1): 1-24.

Cheung, C. H. Sidney. 1997. "Photographing the Ainu and the Emperor: Modernity in Meiji Japan," *CUHK Journal of Humanities* 1: 252-68.

Cheung, C. H. Sidney. 2000. "Men, women and 'Japanese' as outsiders: A case study of postcards with Ainu images," *Visual Anthropology* 13 (3): 227-55.

Fitzhugh, W.W. and C.O. Dubreuil, eds.1999. *Ainu: Spirit of a Northern People*. Seattle: University of Washington Press.

Hammel, E. A. 1988. "A glimpse into the demography of the Ainu," *American Anthropologist* 90: 25-41.

Hilger, M. Inez. 1967. "Japan's 'Sky People,' the vanishing Ainu," *National Geographic* 131: 268-96.

Hilger, M. Inez. 1971. *Together with the Ainu, a Vanishing People*. Norman, Okla.: University of Oklahoma Press.

Howell, L. David. 1994. "Ainu ethnicity and the boundaries of the early modern Japanese State," *Past & Present* 142: 69-93.

Irimoto Takashi. 1995. "Ainu ni shamanizumu ga aruka?" [Does shamanism exist in Ainu culture?], *Minzokugaku-kenkyû* [The Japanese Journal of Ethnology], 60 (3): 187-209.

Irimoto Takashi. 2001. "Marimo matsuri no sôjô" [Creation of the Marimo Festival: Ainu identity and ethnic symbiosis], *Minzokugaku-kenkyû* [The Japanese Journal of Ethnology], 66 (3): 320-43.

Iwata Keiji, Obayashi Taryo, Sofue Takao, Nakane Chie, Yamaguchi Masao and Kawada Junzo. 1985. "Zandankai: Nihon ni okeru minzokugaku" [Discussion: Ethnology in Japan], *Minzokugaku-kenkyû* [The Japanese Journal of Ethnology] 49 (4): 285-319.

Japanese Society of Ethnology. 1995a. *Gakkai meishô henkô teian kanren shiryô* [Material relating to the proposal for changing the name of the society.] Tokyo: Japanese Society of Ethnology.

Japanese Society of Ethnology. 1995b. *Fôramu* [Forum]. Tokyo: Japanese Society of Ethnology.

Japanese Society of Ethnology. 1996. *Fôramu* [Forum]. Tokyo: Japanese Society of Ethnology.

Japanese Society of Ethnology. 1997. *Gakkai meishô mondai nado kentô iinkai hôkoku* [A report by the investigative committee on the name change of the Society and other matters]. Tokyo: Japanese Society of Ethnology.

Karatani, Kojin. 1993. "The discursive space of Modern Japan," pp. 288-316 *in Japan in the World*, eds. M. Miyoshi and H. D. Harootunian. London: Duke University Press.

Kikuchi Isao. 1994. *Ainu minzoku to Nihonjin* [Ainu and Japanese]. Tokyo: Asahi Press (Asahi Selection No. 510).

Kinase Takashi. 1997. "Hyôshô to seijisei" [Representation and politics: A sketch of anthropological discourses surrounding the Ainu], *Minzokugaku-kenkyû* [The Japanese Journal of Ethnology] 62 (1): 1-21.

Kinase Takashi. 1998. "The heterophony of otherness: A prospect on contemporary Ainu images," *Minzokugaku-kenkyû* [The Japanese Journal of Ethnology] 63 (2): 182-191.

Kirikae, Hideo. 1997. "Social aspects of the Ainu linguistic decline," pp. 161-74 in *Northern Minority Languages: Problems of Survival*. Osaka: National Museum of Ethnology (Senri Ethnological Studies 44).

Marcus, George and Fischer, Michael. 1986. *Anthropology as Cultural Critique: An Experimental Moment in the Human Sciences*. Chicago: University of Chicago Press.

Morris-Suzuki, Tessa. 1994. "Creating the frontier: Border, identity and history in Japan's Far North," *East Asian History* 7: 1-24.

Nakane, Chie. 1969. "Texts, readings, reference books on cultural anthropology published in Japan," *Minzokugaku-kenkyû* [The Japanese Journal of Ethnology] 34 (2): 101-58. (In Japanese.)

Nakane, Chie. 1982. "The effect of cultural tradition on anthropologists," pp. 52-60 in *Indigenous Anthropology in Non-Western Countries: Proceedings of a Burg Wartenstein symposium*, ed. Hussein Fahim. Durham, N.C.: Carolina Academic Press.

Niessen, Sandra A. 1994. "The Ainu in Minpaku: A representation of Japan's indigenous people at the National Museum of Ethnology," *Museum Anthropology* 18 (3): 18-25.

Niessen, Sandra A. 1996. "Representing the Ainu reconsidered," *Museum Anthropology* 20 (3): 132-44.

Nomura Giiti. 1996. *Ainu minzoku o ikiru* [Live as an Ainu]. Tokyo: Saifukan.

Ohtsuka Kazuyoshi. 1990. "Ainu (Nihon)" [Ainu: The revival and independence], *Bunka Jinruigaku* [Cultural Anthropology] 7.

Ohtsuka, Kazuyoshi. 1996. "Exhibiting Ainu culture at Minpaku: A reply to Sandra A. Niessen," *Museum Anthropology* 20 (3): 108-19.

Ota Yoshinobu. 1993. "Bunka no kyakutaika" [Objectification of culture: The creation of cultural and identity in the tourist world], *Minzokugaku-kenkyû* [The Japanese Journal of Ethnology] 57 (4): 383-410.

Peng, Fred C. C. and Peter Geiser. 1977. *The Ainu: The Past in the Present*. Hiroshima: Bunka Hyôron Shuppan.

Rosaldo, Renato. 1989. *Culture and Truth: The Remaking of Social Analysis*. Boston: Beacon Press.

Sekimoto Teruo. 1995. "Nihon no jinruigaku to Nihon shigaku" [Anthropology in Japan and Japanese historiography], pp. 123-47 in *Iwanami kôza Nihon tsûshi. Bekkan 1* [Iwanami Complete History of Japan. Supplementary vol.1] eds. Asao Naohiro et al. Tokyo: Iwanami Shoten.

Shimizu, Akitoshi. 1996. "Cooperation, not domination: A rejoinder to Niessen on the Ainu exhibition at Minpaku," *Museum Anthropology* 20 (3): 120-31.

Siddle, Richard. 1996. *Race, Resistance and the Ainu of Japan*. London and New York: Routledge.

Sjoberg, V. Katarina. 1993. *The Return of the Ainu: Cultural Mobilization and the Practice of Ethnicity in Japan*. Switzerland: Harwood Academic Publishers.

Street, Brian. 1992. "British popular anthropology: Exhibition and photographing the Other," pp. 122-31 in *Anthropology and Photography 1860-1920*, ed. Elizabeth Edwards. New Haven and London: Yale University Press.

Van Stone, James. 1993. "The Ainu group at the Louisiana purchase exposition, 1904," *Arctic Anthropology* 30 (2): 77-91.

Yamaguchi Masao. 1978. *Shi no enkinhô* [Perspective on knowledge]. Tokyo: Iwanami Shoten.

Yamaguchi Masao. 1980. "Watashi ga hajimeta riyu, to yamenai reyu" [Reasons to start, and reasons to stop]' pp. 22-38 in *Bunkajinruigaku no susume* [Invitation to cultural anthropology], ed. Funabiki Takeo. Tokyo: Chikuma Shobô.

Chapter 7

Past and Present: Two Moments in the History of

Chinese Anthropology

Xin LIU

Bronislaw Malinowski, who claimed to be "the Conrad of anthropology," was extolled for being a fantastic teacher (Firth 1957: 6). The Malinowski seminars, so influential among British social anthropologists in the 1920s and 1930s, were more like a baptism than teaching, an initiation into the modern, scientific discipline of ethnographic research (cf. Kuper 1996: 21). Without any hesitation, Malinowski claimed himself the father in the family, i.e., the Functional School, to which he believed and insisted that he had given birth (Malinowski 1932: xxix.). The term "father" characterizes not only the charisma of the great master but also indicates the unusual bonds established between Malinowski and his students. "A Chinese student of ours once said to me: 'Malinowski is like an Oriental teacher – he is a father to his pupils. He has us to his home; he gets us to run messages for him; sometimes we even cook for him. We like to do these things for him'" (Firth 1957: 9). Theory may pass into oblivion, but one does not forget a culinary relationship with one's master. In 1995, a distinguished Chinese anthropologist, a former student of Malinowski, wrote an essay to commemorate his teacher, hoping that Malinowski's theory of culture would help rebuild anthropology as an academic discipline in today's China, a society that is seeking to say farewell to its recent past. This is Fei Xiaotong.[1]

Fei's essay, "Some Understanding of Malinowski's Theory of Culture," (Fei 1995) traces the life of Malinowski and deals largely with his theory of culture. The essay begins with the Malinowski myth, of which a few elements are crucial. Malinowski was said to have started his career as a brilliant, promising young scientist, and then he became ill, unable to go on with his original plan. Deeply impressed by Frazer's *Golden Bough*, a classic that Malinowski read in despair, he decided to convert to anthropology and went to the London School of Economics. He was in Australia when the First World War erupted. Because Malinowski was an Austrian citizen, in effect an enemy alien, he should have been interned. Fortunately he was allowed to spend his period of internment on the Trobriand Islands, continuing his ethnographic investigations. There he passed the war, participating in local life as one of the people, and he invented intensive fieldwork by participant observation in total isolation from European contacts (cf. Geertz 1983: 55-59; 1988: 73-83; Clifford 1988a; 1988b: 21-22, 29; Stocking 1992a; 1992b.) After the war he returned to England, and "in the face of pigheaded opposition of reactionary evolutionists and mad diffusionists" (Kuper 1996: 9-10), he created functionalism and gathered a group of dedicated disciples (see Fei 1995: 143). In his account Fei made almost no changes in retelling this story, except to add the sentence: "I was born in the year 1910 when Malinowski went to the LSE."

In Malinowski's own language, myth is a charter for a mode of action. What mode of action does Fei try to justify by retelling Malinowski's story in today's China? How can one understand this historic and cultural connection between Fei and Malinowski, between Chinese and Western anthropology, between the present and the past? This paper sets out to explore the significance this connection with reference to two crucial moments in the history of Chinese anthropology: the 1920-30s and 1980-90s. These two moments of this century are characterized by a similarity: the ideas and institutions of Western social sciences were translated into Chinese.[2] What are the similarities and differences between these two moments in terms of translating anthropology? My argument is that although the institutional support was rather poor in the 1920s and 1930s, anthropology as an intellectual project was full of vigor and vitality. In contrast, even though the 1980s witnessed a strenuous effort to rebuild anthropology as an academic discipline and anthropological institutions have been growing, still, however, an intellectual project for anthropology still seems to be missing.

Malinowski's Heir

Several issues that I wish to discuss were raised by Fei in his essay on Malinowski, in which Fei provided a very positive evaluation of Malinowski's contribution to anthropology, particularly his contribution to ethnographic method and the functionalist notion of culture.[3] It is amusing to notice that throughout the essay Fei addresses Malinowski as "Ma Laoshi" (i.e., "Master Ma"). "Ma" is a common Chinese surname, and this makes their relationship more accessible to the Chinese reader.[4] Fei insisted that Malinowski was the master who revolutionized British social anthropology. "As a matter of fact, he was indeed the one who first raised this revolutionary flag [functionalism] for a new generation of British anthropologists" (1995: 143, emphasis added).[5]

Fei compares Malinowski's *Argonauts of the Western Pacific* and Frazer's *Golden Bough*, and observes that Frazer did not try, or never intended, to collect firsthand materials by himself. It was Malinowski who revolutionized the concept of ethnography, bringing anthropology into the lives of real people, and forcing anthropologists to see and witness what they wanted to report. In beautifully composed lyric prose, Fei writes: "Master Ma turned around, calling upon those behind him, both his predecessors and contemporaries: 'hurry up and come out of your closed study room, please travel to the anthropological field to breathe the fresh air'" (1995: 144, emphasis added). Fei stresses the point that Malinowski for the first time placed the people – whom could be touched and talked to – at the center of anthropological investigation. One needs to note: this evaluation does not stress the isolation of the fieldworker in an exotic community but emphasizes the distinction between first and second hand sources, the discrepancy between library and field research, the difference between text and people. For Fei, in other words, Malinowski's magic is his ability to make the real enchanting.

The main part of Fei's essay consists of a positive assessment of Malinowski's notion and theory of culture. Fei tries to show that Malinowski not only placed real people at the center of his concern but that he also provided a theoretical framework for an understanding of them. Social action can only be understood in its cultural context and therefore the concept of culture is crucial for such an understanding (Fei 1995: 147; cf. Richards 1957). Fei terms Malinowski's functionalism as "a simple cultural theory" (*pusu de wenhualun*), and summarizes it as follows:

> Master Ma linked culture to the real life of people. To study the world of humanity one must start with human life. When I earlier pointed out that Master Ma and Darwin were similar in this respect, I meant that, according Master Ma, one must start to analyze human beings as biological beings if one wanted to analyze human life at all. Master Ma said that culture was created to satisfy the needs of life, and therefore culture had its function. Function is the capacity to satisfy the needs of life. To satisfy the needs of life is the function of culture. The human needs are first of all biological needs. Therefore, in a final sense, culture derives from the needs of life. (Fei 1995: 151)

Tautology at its best. However, this tautology has a historical meaning. Regardless of what Malinowski meant by the term "functional," Fei has turned it into "practical." Thus, according to Fei, culture should be viewed as a tool – only as a tool (cf. Piddington 1957), which "had no other value and was not worth preserving for other than instrumental reasons" (Arkush 1981: 53-4). A tool is a tool that can, should, and needs to be changed if necessary. This is the meaning of Fei's tautology, which reflected a moral stance rooted in the embarrassment and humiliation of Chinese intellectuals by Western powers at the turn of this century. By viewing culture as a tool, Fei (as well as other Chinese scholars) was implicitly arguing that anthropology must have a function in the transformation of society. Further, anthropologists should bear social responsibility for the society they study. It will be erroneous if one reads Fei's essay as if he were simply discussing the functionalist theory of culture. One must realize that what underlies his discussion is a moral commitment and a vision of society, historically specific to a generation of Chinese intellectuals. These feelings are still relevant, but what is problematic is that Fei made no distinction between the past and the present, the two entirely different social and political contexts in which this moral commitment is supposed to be invoked. No more and no less than Malinowski, Fei's account is a-historical. This notwithstanding, the themes of his discussion are central to our understanding of the history of Chinese anthropology: the epistemological problem brought up by the introduction of ethnographic method, i.e., the problem of the real, on the one hand and the moral question on the other.

The Argonauts of the 1920s and 1930s

It is admittedly somewhat arbitrary to choose the 1920s and 1930s to mark a significant moment of history in the "translation" of anthropology from the West to China. In fact, such a translation is a gradual process that covers several decades and goes through a series of transformations. These transformations include four important aspects: the translation of Western sociological/anthropological texts, the institutionalization of sociology/anthropology in China, the reception of Western visiting scholars, and the training of Chinese students and scholars in the Western countries.[6]

At the close of the nineteenth century nothing guaranteed the translator's status as the best interpreter of culture and society, his own included. Translation of Western texts in China started much earlier, but it had predominantly focused on religious and scientific subjects (Xiong 1994: 9; Qian 1994). The late Qing dynasty, particularly around the turn of this century, saw a tremendous growth of interest in the adoption and translation of Western literary and cultural texts into Chinese (Xiong 1994: 7-15). The persona of the translator was validated, both publicly and professionally. In the public domain, visible figures such as Yan Fu, Lin Shu, Wei Yi, and others, communicated a vision of modern life and thought as both scientifically demanding and culturally heroic (or revolutionary). The image of the translator was a sojourner, who moved from one cultural context to another, sometimes even channeling the flows of this movement.[7]

In 1892, half a century after the defeat of China by Britain in the Opium War, an anonymous translation of John Fryer's essay on the classification of mankind announced the arrival of translated anthropology.[8] In the early years of this adoption, physical anthropology, particularly primatology, was at the center of public attention. Ten years later the Chinese adoption of Aruga Nagao's *Evolution of the Family System* appeared, a piece of work based on Herbert Spencer's *Principles of Sociology* and Lewis Henry Morgan's *Ancient Society* (Chen and Wang 1981: 271). After that a kind of social or cultural anthropology began to emerge, with a clear tone of evolutionism. The term "renleixue" (anthropology) first appeared in 1916.[9] In addition, the term "minzuxue" (ethnology) was formally introduced in 1926 when Cai Yuanpei, the president of Beijing University (1916-26) and director of the Academia Sinica (1928-40), wrote an influential essay, "Shuo minzuxue" (On ethnology), to introduce the subject and scope of ethnology.[10] Two general characteristics marked this initial stage of translation.

First, evolutionism as a mode of thought was dominant, both within and outside the academic circle. "The survival of the fittest" reflected the struggle of a native spirit at the margin of colonialism after a series of defeats by the Western powers. Second, when modern social science departments began to be built across the country, the academic division of labor was relatively primitive. Sociology and anthropology or ethnology were often difficult – if not impossible – to distinguish, either institutionally or theoretically.[11]

In 1934, the Chinese Ethnological Association was founded, but its organization and activity were severely interrupted by the war beginning in 1937. Although widely taught in sociology and history departments, ethnology or anthropology had to wait for more than a decade to have a department of its own. The department of anthropology at Qinghua University, for instance, was formally established in 1947 (Chen and Wang 1981: 295-96; cf. Guldin 1994: 68). The Chinese Anthropological Association was not founded until 1981 (Ye 1991).

To examine the institutionalization of sociology or anthropology/ethnology in China, three factors need to be taken into account at once: the source of Western theoretical influence, the place where institutional support for a particular Western academic tradition was built, and the leading characters in such a cultural translation.[12] Chinese students trained in the West and Western visiting scholars to China were two crucial factors in tracing a complex process of multiple adoption and sinicization of different Western anthropological/ethnological traditions, such as German, French, British, and American.

Although Cai Yuanpei had been trained in Germany, his vision of ethnology/anthropology was evolutionist in content.[13] The German school of diffusionism was not well received during these years.[14] Some traces of the German tradition of anti-evolutionist, historicist, and geographical ethnology came to China through Franz Boas, who had moved from Germany to the United States where he was appointed to a chair at Columbia University in 1899. Boas and his theoretical assertion of "historiocultural particularism" had a considerable influence in China.[15] Sun Benwen, a leading sociologist at the time, was an enthusiastic advocate of Boasian historiocultural particularism.[16] Sun promoted a kind of theory he called "cultural sociology," based upon the Boasian idea of history and culture as spatially differentiated but not necessarily temporally connected, a view that was against evolutionism. Notwithstanding this, the Boasian influence was limited by the lack of institutional support. Apart from Sun himself, other scholars who shared a similar theoretical view were not located in any important academic institutions. A further weakness is that this group of scholars, sociologists rather than anthropologists, who tried to promote a Boasian view of history and culture, produced hardly any substantial ethnographic studies in support of their theoretical claims.

The French school of sociological thought gained a certain influence in the 1920s and 1930s. Ethnology was a more popular term than anthropology among the French scholars. Yang Kun was a central figure in introducing French sociological theory. Yang studied at Lyon and did research in Paris (see Yang 1983: 392-97). After he returned to China, Yang wrote a series of essays, systematically introducing the work of Mauss, Lévy-Bruhl, Lévi-Strauss, and Durkheim. Apart from his theoretical interest, however, Yang did not carry out any substantial ethnographic fieldwork. Among a number of scholars who were trained in France,[17] Yang Chengzhi and Ling Chunsheng were also influential. Yang Chengzhi, who worked in Yunnan among minority groups, played a significant role in building a four-field anthropology program in Zhongshan University (Guldin 1994: 50-7). Ling Chunsheng differed from Yang Kun, in that his fame was built on his detailed ethnographic research (cf. Chen and Wang 1981: 282-83). Despite a common influence, Chinese scholars who had been trained in France diverged in terms of both theory and method. This group of scholars could hardly be identified as a unified group under the influence of French sociology. Their works did not represent a whole, either in an ethnographic or a theoretical sense.

The only foreign school that gained systematic institutional support, nurtured fruitful ethnographic studies, and united a group of dedicated scholars was British functionalism. Wu Wenzao, a sociologist in training but an anthropologist in theoretical vision, played a central role in this movement. Having graduated from Qinghua University in 1923 and received his B.A. degree from Dartmouth in 1925 (Wu 1986: 79-80), Wu went to Columbia to continue his graduate studies in sociology. Besides the required sociological classes, he sat in on Boas's anthropology class, sometimes taught by Boas's student Ruth Benedict, which decidedly affected Wu's thought and future career. Wu wrote his thesis on the problem of opium and British public opinion, and received his doctorate in 1928.[18] He returned, via Europe, to teach at Yenjing (Yanjing in *pinyin*) University in 1929. A few years later he took over the chair of the Department of Sociology at Yenjing. Wu's contribution to the program at Yenjing was tremendous. His scholarly contribution was indeed significant, but he had done much more than that. He was a strategic administrator whose vision of sociology/anthropology significantly affected a generation of young scholars, among them Fei Xiaotong and Lin Yaohua, who became two of the most eminent anthropologists of China.

A long list of distinguished visiting scholars was characteristic of the 1930s. Among the most famous were C. G. Seligman, Robert E. Park, R. H. Tawney, Wilhelm Schmidt, A. R. Radcliffe-Brown, Karl Wittfogel, Leslie White, and Reo Fortune. Other prominent figures – to name only anthropologists – such as B. Malinowski, Raymond Firth and Edward Sapir had also made promises to visit, but the Sino-Japanese War prevented their planned trips (cf. Wong 1979: 20). Among this series of visits, Radcliffe-Brown's coming was significant, for he brought to his Chinese audience a powerful theoretical paradigm: British functionalism. In the summer of 1936, Wu met Malinowski at Harvard, and followed him to London. The meeting with Malinowski led to a plan for Wu to send his best students to the London School of Economics (Guldin 1994: 62-67; Wong 1979: 22; Wu 1986).

Wu, as well as his students and colleagues, wrote a series of long essays introducing British functionalism; they also translated works by Malinowski, Radcliffe-Brown, Raymond Firth and others. Besides all this, Wu's students produced ethnographic monographs in the functionalist style, known as community studies. These works resulted in Chinese anthropology being noted outside China. As a result of the efforts of Wu and his colleagues, Maurice Freedman later commented, "It could be argued that before the Second World War, outside North America and Western Europe, China was the seat of the most flourishing sociology in the world, at least in respect of its intellectual quality" (Freedman 1962: 113).

The Discursive Formation of an Intellectual Project

Due to the interruption of the war (1937-1945), the institutional establishment of anthropology in China did not materialize until the late 1940s.[19] China experienced a destructive and chaotic decade from the late 1930s. A number of important universities in the Japanese-occupied areas were closed and a significant number of scholars left for the southwestern inland areas. Despite the turmoil and disorder, anthropological research continued in the areas less affected by the Japanese invasion and often focused upon the studies of minority groups.[20] Throughout the 1920s and 1930s, anthropology/ethnology enjoyed intellectual status without much academic institutional support. A discursive space of anthropology/ethnology, which derived its condition of existence from several divergent but related sources, was firmly established.

To begin with, the distinction between sociology and anthropology was blurred (Freedman 1962: 106). Wu Wenzao's experience is a good example in point. For those who considered themselves anthropologists, this ambiguity of identity meant that anthropology as an intellectual project could take shelter in the departments of sociology. Instead of arguing about disciplinary boundaries, what was more important for Wu and his colleagues was to carry out an epistemological revolution: to leave one's desk in the library for the study of the real lives of real people.[21] The virtue of British functionalism was its explicit theorization about field study.

The idea of fieldwork became a convenient and effective means for articulating an empirical stance. A crucial transformation took place: in the hands of Chinese scholars fieldwork did not mean a lone ethnographer wandering around in an exotic community; rather, it meant an native intellectual exploring the real lives of his own people: the people of a troubled nation. In a sense, Malinowski was seen less as a hero with a dirty pair of shoes returning from the Trobriand Islands; rather, he was celebrated as a master who empowered the real. This was, in my view, the way in which British functionalism was received in the 1920s and 1930s. One should note the fact that the spirit of empiricism did not have to wait until Radcliffe-Brown's visit to Yenjing or Wu Wenzao's meeting with Malinowski in London. Even within the academic circle of sociology and anthropology, figures such as R. E. Park, S. D. Gamble, and J. S. Burgess had provided enough examples and inspirations for empirical research.[22] But the merit of British functionalism, via Radcliffe-Brown in particular, was its explicit definition of the village as the appropriate unit for field research.[23] Real people and real life have to be locatable and located. This was the function of British functionalism in this context, which helped situate the real at a cultural site – that of the village. The community studies, carried out by a group of Chinese scholars, were the result of this influence.

Although the community studies were detailed, descriptive accounts of village life in China, they were written and published in English.[24] Earlier, in an effort at sinicization, Chinese scholars had argued against the employment of Western textbooks in teaching sociology/anthropology. As Fei wrote in the preface of *Earthbound China*, "We learned from books about Chicago gangs and Russian immigrants in America, but we knew very little or nothing about the Chinese gentry in the town and the peasants in the village, because they were not in books" (Fei and Chang 1945, viii). It is nothing other than irony to write such a statement in English.[25] To whom was such a statement addressed? Given the theoretical rigor and coherence of the community studies, the language through which Chinese society and culture were being discussed was no longer Chinese.

In style, the community studies were similar to the Malinowskian type of

159

ethnographic monograph (cf. Kuper 1996: 69-71; Boon 1982: 9-21). The functionalist ethnography involved a complex enterprise, and James Clifford has sketched out some of its crucial features. First, after Malinowski's return from the Trobriand Islands, the image of the fieldworker as the scientist of culture was established. Second, the professional, new-style fieldworker was trained to use the native language efficiently, an advantage that casual travelers did not possess. Third, an increasing emphasis was placed on the power of observation. The ethnographer was trained to be an onlooker, observing rituals, ceremonies, typical behaviors of other cultures. Fourth, the fieldworker was armed with theoretical abstractions, for instance those from structural functionalism. Fifth, the ethnographer was supposed to spend one or two years in the field, and he or she should ideally focus on just one or two institutions of the "complex whole." Sixth, society or culture thus presented was doomed to be synchronic (Clifford 1988b: 30-2).

Not all these points were followed. In translating such an anthropological project, the native scholars absorbed some aspects and transformed others. They followed the functionalist conception of culture and society, focused upon particular cultural institutions such as kinship and family (Lin 1948; M. Yang 1945), ancestor worship (Hsu 1948), or economic organizations (Fei 1939; Fei and Chang 1945), and wrote synchronic studies of these communities.[26] Nevertheless, the power of the observer as an onlooker was modified. The notion of "home village" was employed by the native scholars in justifying short study trips to the field rather than extensive fieldwork. The ethnographer's immediate experience of the community was no longer central to the native's authority of representation. To be a native was sufficient good enough to bestow authority. For instance, M. C. Yang's work about a Shandong village, a well-composed, influential work on Chinese family and village life, was essentially written from memory. "The village of Taitou has been selected as the object of first study because the writer was born and reared there, and lived there until he entered high school" (Yang 1945: ix). The ethnographer was not one who came from outside and went to the field but one who used to be a member of that community. The ethnographic presence was thus transformed into "ethnographic memory." The theoretical spirit of the research remained the same but the form of constructed authenticity changed. As Yang wrote:

> to make the picture real, through the eyes of a person who actually grew up in the community and experienced most of the social life described, the study is concluded with the story of a villager's boyhood. The writer feels justified in saying that the information given in this study is reliable and that life picture thus presented is preserved in its wholeness so far as possible; he hopes that rural community of Taitou will be culturally understood by the readers. (Yang 1945: xi)

The intention was to present a "true," "real" picture, just as what Malinowski did in convincing his readers about the Trobriand Islanders. However, the technique of producing such an ethnographic authority changed: "being there" was replaced by having been "brought up there." To take another example, that of Fei's *Peasant Life in China* in which he made it clear that he chose Kaixiangong (Kaihsienkung) as his field site because he was a native of that area: "My investigation had to be limited to a period of two months. It would have been impossible in this short time to carry out any intensive study, if I had worked in an entirely unfamiliar field. Kaihsienkung is a village belonging to the district of Wukiang of which I am a native" (Fei 1939: 25).[27] More than simply being a native, this is a nativist claim. It asserts that one should be able to get closer to the truth by virtue of being a native.

Sources of influence varied. Sometimes the footsteps of Western anthropologists were followed more closely but never exactly. The influence of British functionalism was a good example of this. Chinese scholars, particularly those who engaged in community studies, employed Malinowski and Radcliffe-Brown for their own purpose, to create a methodological space for articulating a native anthropological subject. It is not important as to whether Wu Wenzao's Radcliffe-Brown or Fei's Malinowski was the same, for instance, as the one understood by Raymond Firth or E. E. Evans-Pritchard. The important thing was to employ such figures in a regional tradition of ethnographic writing for a particular purpose. Their positions were borrowed in making a methodological synthesis, in which the previous experiments of writing by Chinese scholars were to be united.

This methodological space was characterized by three critical stances. First, it was a move towards further firsthand field research. In the context of the 1920s when sociology was mainly taught in the American missionary colleges and by American teachers using American materials,[28] this call for field research was in fact one that urged sociologists/anthropologists to pay attention to the problems of their own society and culture. In this sense, British functionalism was taken by Chinese scholars to justify their position of writing about peasant communities. Second, it was a critical move away from the bookish tradition of Chinese scholarship. Sociological thinking in the traditional Chinese fashion, which was normative rather than descriptive in character, had been popular among the first generation of Chinese sociologists/anthropologists. In particular this kind of research did not touch upon the varieties of local and regional conditions. It simply reiterated the views already embedded in the historical materials, which represented the perspective of the elite. Against this tide, Fei claimed that "The real life of common people has never been fully described" (quoted in Arkush 1981: 58). Third, the method of functionalism was borrowed to articulate a critical stance against the then popular mode of sociological investigation. Influenced by J. S. Burgess, S. D. Gamble, R. E. Park, J. L. Buck and others, sociological research at that time often meant social surveys. As Fei argued, from a perspective of methodology, surveys of this kind often "produced isolated facts, schematic statistical information, and missed the complexity of social relations" (Arkush 1981: 58; cf. Fei 1945: 1-5). In contrast, the community studies would allow the researcher to know his subjects of study and the complex fields of social relations intimately.

These three critical moves cleared a methodological space, that I argue was anthropological, in which an intellectual project persisted without or with little institutional support. This marked a stance not only different from traditional Chinese scholarship but also different from the existing mode of sociological investigation of Chinese society at that time.[29] This methodological innovation was well situated in the intellectual context of the 1920s and 1930s, in which two general tendencies were evident. One is that the Chinese intellectuals were searching for a method, i.e., an epistemological revolution. The other is that they were all bound by a moral commitment: the engagement of the intellectual in the struggle of the nation.

This was the complexity of the situation in the 1920s and 1930s. There was a matrix of elements involved. Each of these elements had its own moment of dislocation, either theoretically or institutionally or both. The total field of anthropology was constituted by a chaotic order that introduced these elements at different moments in time. Invoking the metaphor of translation may be appropriate for explaining this situation. China and the West were like two languages. Anthropology as a text that needed to be translated had already had several versions in the West. Different versions of this text were attempted by different Chinese interpreters, each of them having his own theoretical taste and priority. Each started with his own expectation and understanding, with his own training in a field different from others. Each had his own starting point for translation, and some had better places for publication. This process of multiple translation took place within a political context of turmoil and a cultural context of humiliation.

The Moral Commitment of the Anthropologist

Time has changed. But not everything else. There is a link that connects the Chinese anthropologists in the 1920s and 1930s with those of the 1980s and 1990s, namely the moral commitment of the anthropologist. Fei's work, *Ren de yanjiu zai Zhongguo* (The study of man in China),[30] which is a commentary on the history of Chinese anthropology, serves as a good example to illustrate this point.[31] Fei's essay is a reply to two questions derived from his reading of Leach's book *Social Anthropology*, which is a book "about the different kinds of anthropological influence which have converged together in my own thinking" (Leach 1982).[32] In his book, Leach came to a point where he needed to explain why it was necessary for anthropologists to study an alien culture rather than their own. As an example, Leach selected the case of community studies carried out by Chinese scholars in the 1930s (Leach 1982: 122-27). In particular, he commented upon Lin Yaohua's *The Golden Wing* (1948), Martin C. Yang's *A Chinese Village* (1945), Francis L. K. Hsu's *Under the Ancestor's Shadow* (1948), and Fei's *Peasant Life in China* (1939). Apart from Fei's work, Leach claimed that the other three were total failures. They were somehow under the shadow of the author's private – rather than public —perspective. They therefore did not present a truthful account of the communities they set out to study. In general Leach believed that "initial preconceptions are liable to prejudice the research in a way that does not affect the work of the naive stranger" (1982: 126). Fei's monograph, although the earliest among the four, was the most successful according to Leach. The merit of Fei's book lies in its functionalist style.[33] Fei's reading focused upon this part of Leach's work and turned it into two questions. First, should one study one's own society? Second, in the case of China, to what extent do small-scale community studies reflect the general conditions of the society?

Fei disagrees with Leach, not so much about his criticism of other three writers, but more for his critical stance toward Chinese writing Chinese culture. Fei emphasizes that there is a difference between these two anthropologies – one represented by Leach and the other by Fei. Such a difference is not an epistemological but a moral one. As Fei argues: "I do not understand why Leach gave up his career as an engineer and chose to become an anthropologist. But I know why I wanted to choose anthropology. Different motivations may be the reason for our later differences in scholarship. I had wanted to study medicine, but I gave it up, because I later realized that to make the nation stronger was more important than to make individuals healthy. Therefore my choice came from a value judgment" (Fei 1993: 4).[34] For Fei, to study anthropology was to seek ways of understanding Chinese society, in order to find possible means to change it for the better. Fei goes on to criticize Leach's view that anthropology is a form of art rather than a branch of science. Fei insists that anthropology should and must have a teleology, and admits that his projects, from *Peasant Life in China* to *Earthbound China*, are "down to earth" projects. However, Fei argues that this "earthbound" feeling is not a personal characteristic. Instead, the "earthbound" Chinese intellectuals were products of a particular cultural tradition in a particular historical context – the crisis of the nation since the Opium War. In his whole career, Fei, a representative of many other Chinese scholars, has never been interested in the Trobriand Islands or Tikopia or the Tallensi or Nuerland; his interest, anthropological or otherwise, is solely directed at his own culture and society. He consistently hopes that anthropology will help the development of Chinese society. For Fei and his colleagues, the question is never simply to understand; rather, it is always a matter of how to improve the society by way of anthropology. This feeling, still evident, was deeply rooted in the history of the late nineteenth and early twentieth century of China.

Anthropology was "translated" to China in the early twentieth century, after a series of defeats of China by Western powers. How should Western knowledge be adopted? Earlier, Japanese reformers facing modernization had proposed combining "Eastern ethics and Western science." Similarly, the Chinese attitude toward Western knowledge can be best characterized by Zhang Zhidong's well known phrase: "Chinese learning for the substance (the essential principles or *ti*) and Western learning for function (the practical application or *yong*).[35] This attitude, that takes "Western learning as merely a set of tools" is further embedded in one of the most influential Chinese philosophical traditions:

According to Joseph Needham, Confucianism is characterized by an ambivalent attitude toward science (1956: 12-16). On the one hand, it was basically rationalistic and agnostic, thereby favoring a scientific method. But on the other hand, its interest in human life is too humanistic in that the value of knowledge was judged by whether it could benefit people and bring quick improvements to their livelihood. Thus the practical efficacy of social techniques was extolled while the value of developing a scientific logic was dismissed and the importance of theoretical investigation denied (cited in Wong 1979: 2).

This sense of social responsibility that Fei employed in attacking Leach was partly traditional, which is linked to a Confucian sense of personhood and knowledge. Another source of it seems to have come, if paradoxically, from a Western sociological influence, that of the missionary sociology. A generation of Chinese scholars were educated in missionary colleges. The Christian colleges, predominantly American, were not particularly inclined towards the social sciences but sociology seemed to be the exception. J. S. Burgess's survey in 1925 showed that ten leading Christian colleges of the China Association of Christian Higher Education all offered sociology courses, and that Yenjing University offered as many as thirty-one courses on the subject (see Wong 1979, 11-12).[36] Missionary sociology was particularly concerned with the practical functions of knowledge. This brand of sociology was not simply meant to reflect on the nature of society or frame intellectual discussions; rather, it was to encourage Chinese students to adopt Christian ideas of salvation and redemption. For such a purpose, social work was seen as equally important as sociological theory. For instance, when the President of Suzhou (Soochow) University reported to the Trustees about the teaching of sociology, he made it clear: "Our prime emphasis is not so much on social theories as on the training of social workers ... our aim is not so much to train theorists who can write essays on social problems, but practical workers who plan and direct programs of social service" (quoted in Wong 1979: 14).[37]

One may find it of interest to learn that Fei had been in Suzhou University for two years, before he transferred to Yenjing University to enroll in the department of sociology. The past and the present are not separated by decades. They are connected by a moral message that characterizes the struggle of Chinese intellectuals in the twentieth century. This moral commitment is still central to the enterprise of anthropology in today's China. However, whether fortunately or not, the methodological space and epistemological questions which Chinese anthropologists created and faced in the 1920s and 1930s no longer exist.

The Predicament of the Present

After almost thirty years absence, anthropology reappeared as an academic discipline in mainland China.[38] In 1981 the Chinese Anthropological Association was established under the auspices of the Chinese Academy of Social Sciences (CASS) and the State Education Committee. In the very same year, Zhongshan University, Guangzhou, revived its anthropology department that began to offer two majors: archaeology and ethnology. Three years later, the second anthropology department was established in Xiamen University, Fujian, where the very first major in anthropology was offered.[39] Following this tide of change, more anthropological programs and institutions have been built and a series of anthropological meetings and conferences organized (see Chen and Lin 1991; Jiejie 1995).

To compare the revival of anthropology with that of sociology is interesting. Both of these two disciplines were essentially translated ones and both had been abandoned as "bourgeois disciplines" during the years of the Maoist revolution. If affinity characterized the importation of sociology and anthropology in the early decades of this century, it is the divorce of this partnership that marks the relationship between them at the present. Embedded in either the metaphor of marriage or that of divorce, anthropology seems to be the female, dominated by her male partner, sociology. The difference seems to be that in the past anthropology took shelter in the academic abode of sociology, but that in the 1980s "she," without any property or even a surname, to pursue the analogy, was not allowed to "remarry." At least this was the view of some advocates for the revival of anthropology.

Indeed the development of sociology in the 1980s was massive. Official sociological associations were established, a large number of research institutes were founded across the country.[40] A number of major universities have founded their own departments of sociology, and sociological training programs have been reestablished; in many research centers and universities sociological libraries have been institutionalized; six national sociological periodicals are available at the present, and many sociological books published in the past fifteen years.[41] Sociology is in vogue and has attracted people into the discipline, both professionals and amateurs, which makes some scholars skeptical of it. Many are proud to be called sociologists, but few are tempted to label themselves as anthropologists (Zhou 1991: 118).

A possible confusion comes from the fact that without an agreed meaning the term anthropology was made to mean social/cultural anthropology in the 1980s. Ethnology, which used to be synonymous with anthropology in the 1920s and 1930s, had a different fate in the hands of the Maoist revolutionaries. In 1952, with the national campaign to reorganize universities and colleges, thanks mainly to Russian influence, departments of sociology and anthropology were closed. Sociologists and anthropologists had no choice but to move into other areas or disciplines, or to take up entirely new lines of work.[42] Ethnological (*minzu*) research, on the other hand, was turned into ethnic studies with an explicit communist government agenda to "help" minority groups become modern (see Fei 1981; Jiang 1981; Liang 1994: 307-09; Yang 1983: 10-45; Qiu 1993: 45-49; Lin 1985: 78-93). Despite their very different orientation and exclusive focus on minority groups, ethnological institutions and ethnic studies as a discipline survived during the years of the Maoist revolution (1949-1978).[43] Since the late 1970s, like sociology, ethnic studies have boomed, and they have mostly been carried out by the scholars affiliated with various kinds of ethnological institutions (Men 1989; Zhan 1995; Zhou and Hu 1994).

Nor did other branches of anthropology, such as physical anthropology or archaeology, disappear during the years of the Maoist revolution (see Guldin 1990). In fact, for many people in China, anthropology is often thought of as primatology or paleoanthropology, dealing only with the origin of man, studying fossils and skulls (cf. Zhou 1991: 118-19). Physical anthropology and archaeology are established disciplines, though located elsewhere in the academy. What was left out in the 1980s, after the revival of sociology, was social/cultural anthropology. Its difficulties also came from the fact that because ethnology, primatology, or paleoanthropology were established disciplines, scholars of these areas felt no need to build a unified anthropology.[44]

Unlike the situation of the 1920s and 1930s, social/cultural anthropology was in the very front line of the battle in the 1980s, fighting for its place in the academy, not for an epistemological and methodological place but for an academic and institutional seat. Unlike the 1920s and 1930s when the intellectual project of anthropology took shape with little institutional support, the advocates of anthropology in the 1980s insisted upon having their own academic niche as if academic legitimacy was the magic wand that would bring about everything they wished for anthropology. This is the context in which we the cry to rebuild institutions and departments of anthropology was heard. Liang Zhaotao, a physical anthropologist and ethnologist, one of the most enthusiastic advocates for anthropology and the first chair of the Department of Anthropology at Zhongshan University, was a good example

(Guldin 1994: 3-14. See also Liang 1994: 382-93). After convincing the university that anthropology was needed, Liang had to receive permission from the State Education Committee, the final authority in deciding whether a certain degree or major should be allowed. Traveling to Beijing and waiting for the opportunity to meet the officials in charge, Liang was determined to present his opinions. More than anything else, his passionate argument had an immediate effect on the officials who were still in doubt about anthropology. When finally Liang was able to meet with the officials of the State Education Committee, he uttered the following words:

All the other countries have this discipline; why not us? We have such a glorious culture and large population. Why not us? We Chinese must study our one billion Chinese! We must study our bountiful materials – if not us, who will? We can't leave this science only to the foreigners! Let anthropology make its contribution to the Four Modernizations (Guldin 1994: 12).

Even without having heard it, one can easily feel a loaded emotional and nationalistic tone in this argument. It must have been such an emotional plea which moved the officials of the Education Committee, because the argument itself provided nothing but the empty statement that one should study one's own society.

There are two related but different statements in this argument, which I believe represents a general sentiment of those who advocated anthropology in the 1980s. The first, which is by no means confined to anthropologists, is that China should have her own everything, anthropology included. This is the reason that "all other countries" were brought into Liang's cry. "All other countries" actually means "all Western countries." Whatever they have, we should have! This is one of the dominant themes that was deeply embedded in the debate about the scope of anthropology in the 1980s.[45] There is nothing wrong in insisting that one should study one's own society. However, this statement alone does not justify the intellectual project of anthropology.

The second message, emotionally charged, is that anthropology is – and must be – helpful to the process of modernization, a project currently occupying the very heart of the nation. A whole series of discussions in the 1980s focused upon how anthropology could be useful in a sense that is little different from Joseph Needham's characterization of the traditional Chinese spirit towards Western science. Anthropology was championed for its utility in the construction of socialism, the "four modernizations," and the "spiritual civilization" of the nation (Chen 1984: 7).[46] More specifically, research projects were developed and conferences organized in the field of applied anthropology.[47] Of the relatively limited space offered for the publication of anthropological research in the 1980s and 1990s, a large proportion was devoted to the topic of the discipline's possible applications.[48] In a review article of the development of applied anthropology in the past decade, Shi Yilong goes so far as to argue:

> Applicability is an essential character of anthropology, no matter whether it is physical anthropology or cultural anthropology. In the recent few decades, the prosperous development of anthropology abroad, is a result and evidence of anthropology's wide applications. Therefore, in rebuilding Chinese anthropology, we must emphasize its application. (Shi 1994: 59)

It seems to be dubious to argue that anthropology has flourished abroad because it has been widely applied in the improvement of human conditions. To distinguish applied anthropology from general anthropology, Eddy and Partridge pointed out four possible markers. First, applied anthropology focuses on the living culture, i.e., contemporary populations. Second, it is a branch of anthropology that is problem-oriented rather than theory-oriented. It concerns itself with food production, human migration and relocation, environmental protection, health care, aging, and so on, rather than simply being engaged in the debate about rationality or the problem of meaning. Third, applied anthropologists search for practical solutions beyond the disciplinary boundaries. In order to solve the problems they discover, applied anthropologists have to engage with other kinds of disciplines and institutions. Fourth, applied anthropologists are not always located in academic institutions. They are outsiders to the discipline in a professional sense (see Eddy and Partridge 1987: 5-7). This discussion may not reflect all the experiences of applied anthropology and anthropologists, but it suggests at least two facts. One is that applied anthropology, contrary to the expectation of Chinese scholars, is often outside the main stream of general anthropology, at least in the case of United States and Great Britain. Second, applied anthropology is a restricted discipline, which often focuses on particular problems of particular societies.

This is not to deny that in a certain particular historical context one should not argue for the centrality of applied anthropology; nor to reject the importance of developing applied anthropology in today's China. What is problematic is the tendency to essentialize anthropology as an applied science and to see it simply in terms of its utility, which is not only untrue of the discipline's experience in other parts of the world but also absurd and unhealthy. Even if we take Shi's statement as an indication that branches of the discipline have emerged in recent years such as medical anthropology, and visual anthropology which are more useful than conventional anthropological theory, it is still hardly justifiable to argue that anthropology has been turned into a discipline of social utility. Far from it: in many parts of the world, anthropology has become less practically useful than ever, a fact which some anthropologists find disturbing. What is really revealed by Shi's argument is the idea that social science must be "functional" in the sense defined by Fei in his essay which I discussed earlier. Anthropology has to be a tool. It is by no means ironic for scholars from developing countries to stress that translated disciplines should be useful in their own social and cultural environments. However, this point should not be stretched so far that a tool's function becomes the tool itself.

Discussion

To compare the situation of anthropology in the 1920s and 1930s with that in the 1980s, two observations appear to be evident. First, despite the poor academic and social conditions, the lack of institutional support and the interruptions of the war, Chinese scholars in the past managed to create and maintain anthropology as a fairly coherent intellectual project. At present, however, although a number of anthropological institutions have been built, national and regional associations established, and international conferences organized, the intellectual content of anthropology is rather empty. Three elements, as I have discussed earlier, were central to the making of anthropology as an intellectual project in the 1920s and 1930s. First, anthropology occupied a strategic location in the general intellectual movement calling for the study of the real. Second, anthropology claimed a unique methodological space. British functionalism was borrowed to articulate a stance that had not been possible before, and Chinese scholars were able to argue not only against library research inside a dark room on historical materials – which was by no means alien to the bookish tradition of Chinese scholarship – but also to challenge the newly imported mode of sociological research, the social survey. Finally, largely due to the influence of British functionalism, there was a systematic effort to produce ethnographic research based on "fieldwork" with its focus on family life in the village. The results of this were the community studies.

Gazing through a similar type of lens, one could find little intellectual coherence in the 1980s. Given the intensive debates on the scope and function of anthropology, one finds empty claims and great ambitions but little actual work being carried out within any systematic orientation, anthropological or otherwise.[49] I say that they are empty but ambitious because, instead of engaging in substantial research, most anthropological publications in the past fifteen years have focused on what anthropology should be and how it can be differentiated from other academic disciplines. This is not to argue that these debates are entirely unnecessary, but that they have reached a dead end. I argue that anthropologists in today's China should engage with scholars in other disciplines, to think about not the differences but the commonalities that anthropology shares with other subjects, such as sociology or history. The social and political context has changed. Sociology is no longer what it was. The subject of its study has been modified. The ethnographic method is not alien to Chinese sociology at the present time. Should anthropologists continue to argue for their own academic and institutional seats simply because Western countries have accommodated this kind of discipline for a long time? Obviously not. What is important, for anthropologists as well as others, is to search for a method that enables them to deal with the complexities of the contemporary situation of Chinese society. Whatever shape it takes, this method is bound to be interdisciplinary. Anthropology should, and could, play a central role in articulating such an interdisciplinary position that is still largely lacking.

My second observation is that what links the past and the present is a sentiment around which a sense of social responsibility and commitment is continually articulated. This results in a constant search for the meaning and practicality of anthropology. In both time periods, this sentiment constitutes part of a general structure of feelings among Chinese intellectuals. These feelings should not be slighted. But these feelings alone cannot justify the intellectual status of anthropology. What one must realize in today's context of cultural struggles is the fact that Chinese scholars are no longer confronting a Western subject with a monopoly of political and cultural power as the sole "author" who writes about other societies. The cultural and epistemological task seems to have become how to accommodate the native representational authority which has developed from the Maoist revolution and which has been embodied in the struggle with the West during the twentieth century.

More generally, I wish to reiterate the point that there is more than one anthropology (cf. Fardon 1990; Asad 1982). Within different regional traditions of ethnographic writing, at different times, there are complex formations of cultural "authors," asking different kinds of anthropological questions. The excitement of Chinese anthropology in the 1920s and 1930s was its connectedness with other anthropological traditions in an intellectual sense. For Chinese anthropologists, it is time to try to dissolve the dichotomy of Chinese versus Western. For Western anthropologists, it is necessary to pay closer attention to the varieties of regional anthropological traditions.

Notes

1   Although there might have been other Chinese students at the LSE in the 1930s, it is very likely that the Chinese student Firth mentioned was Fei, because Fei was close to both Malinowski and Firth. Fei referred to Firth as a friend or sometimes as a teacher. Malinowski was not only Fei's mentor at the LSE, but also wrote a powerful preface for Fei's book, *Peasant Life in China* (1939). In Fei's biography, one finds descriptions such as "with Fei he [Malinowski] developed a warm avuncular relationship, styling himself in letters 'your affectionate uncle,' and admonishing his pupil to 'be a good boy; think it out; carefully; write it down...' Fei in return

spoke of his 'filial affection' to 'my dear Master,' and asked for 'your order to your young children.'" See Arkush (1981: 43).

2   To use the metaphor of translation, I mean to indicate that anthropology was not simply shipped to China but went through a complex process of appropriation involving a matrix of authors, both Western and Chinese, situated in a specific historical setting of power and influence. For a recent account of cultural encounters between Chinese and Western literary writers and genres, an interesting exploration of the notion of translation, see Lydia Liu (1995).

3   Fei's essay was originally given as a talk at the Advanced Seminars of Anthropology, organized by the Institute of Sociology and Anthropology, Beijing University. The Institute was founded in March 1985 and initially named the Institute of Sociology. This name was changed in 1992 to the Institute of Sociology and Anthropology. Fei served as its first director. This series of Advanced Seminars, attracting scholars from all over the country, was part of the effort to revive anthropological research and theory in China. See Jiejie (1995).

4   There is a personal reason for Fei to talk about Malinowski's theory of culture. More than half a century ago, Fei translated a manuscript of Malinowski and gave it a title, "Theory of Culture" (Wenhualun). The Chinese translation, which was based on the revision of Malinowski's long article on "Culture" from the Encyclopedia of the Social Sciences, was published in 1940 in Chongqing. See Arkush (1981: 41; Fei (1995: 142).

5   Unless otherwise indicated, translations of Chinese sources in this paper are mine.

6   For an elaborate discussion of the history of Chinese anthropology, see Guldin 1994. A shorter but more comprehensive account of this history up to the late 1970s can be found in Wong (1979). David Arkush's biography (1981) of Fei Xiaotong is also a good reference book for this history. For Chinese sources, see Chen and Lin (1991); Chen and Wang (1981); Fei (1993; 1996); Yuan et al. (1991); Yang (1983; 1991); Qiu (1993); Liang (1994); Lin (1985).

7   Yan Fu is often singled out as an example of the translator's power. He received a classical education and later trained with the Royal Navy in Britain, discovering Darwin and Spencer. After his return to China, he made his reputation translating a series of Western classics, including T. H. Huxley's *Evolution and Ethics*, Adam Smith's *The Wealth of Nations*, John Stuart Mill's *On Liberty*, Montesquieu's *L'Espirit des lois* (Gernet 1996: 648-49). On his career and impact, see Gernet (1996: 648-49), Schwartz (1964); Xiong (1994: 700).

8   The Chinese title of the article is "Ren fen wulei shu" (On the five classifications of mankind). Cf. Guldin (1994: 24).

171

9 Sun Xuewu published an essay entitled "Renleixue gailun" (On anthropology) in *Kexue* (Science), 1916, vol. 2, no. 4. Cf. Chen and Wang (1981: 272).

10 Cai is today seen as the founding father of the subject. At that time, for many people the term "renleixue" (anthropology) meant a discipline describing and studying the origin and development of human species rather than its social or cultural environment. Ethnology was thought to be something similar to today's definition of social/cultural anthropology. However, in the later development of ethnological research in China, the discipline of ethnology meant almost exclusively the study of minority groups. It became essentially minority studies and thus lost its general meaning. For a discussion of Cai's significance, see Hu (1981). Cf. Yang (1983: 181-85); Qiu (1993: 45-63).

11 Sociology was more in vogue than anthropology or ethnology at that time. Tan Citong first adopted the term "shehuixue" (sociology) in 1896. Two chapters from Spencer's *The Study of Sociology* appeared in a Chinese newspaper in 1897, which may date the origin of the adoption of Western sociological thoughts in China, see Wong (1979: 4-5). However, this does not mean that sociological investigations of Chinese society had not started earlier. For instance, J.J.M. De Groot (1854-1921) began his work on Chinese religion in the later half of nineteenth century. The first department of sociology was built in 1913, at Hujiang University, Shanghai, by American Christian missionaries. Cf. Wong (1979: 11). For a detailed discussion of life in these missionary colleges at that time, see Yeh 1990. As a step towards a more coherent unification of sociological research, the first regional professional association was created in 1928, following an earlier short-lived attempt in 1922, one year after the communist party had held its first congress in Shanghai. The Chinese Sociological Society, a national sociological association, was founded in 1930. See Wong (1979: 21).

12 Chen and Wang's article, "Chinese ethnology in the early decades of the twentieth century," published in 1981, provides a concise overview of the history of Chinese anthropology. Their article was first written in 1962 for the purpose of criticizing bourgeois ethnology, and the original title of their work was "The development and influence of bourgeois ethnology in China." They view the development of Chinese ethnology/anthropology as a process of multiple adoption and sinicization, which is the theoretical vision I try to follow in this paper. For a similar but more critical view, see Qiu (1993: 49).

13 Upon his return from Germany in 1912, Cai started to lecture in Beijing University on the subject of ethnology/anthropology. Cai published a series of articles, discussing the boundaries between ethnology/anthropology and sociology. Besides writing, Cai also tried to build institutions that would help ethnological/anthropological research. He encouraged and trained students to do research among minority groups. His influence

over his students was evident, but his efforts to establish research centers and to invite foreign scholars to China was not as successful as he had planned. He managed to build an institute within the Academia Sinica, but due to the eruption of the war in 1937 he could not carry out his plans further. His initial plan of building an ethnological museum also failed. See Chen and Wang (1981: 273-74); Hu (1981).

14 Among those who had been trained in Germany, Tao Yunkui was influential. Although Tao was not interested in any particular theory, his work on Yunnan minority groups, particular his writing on "chicken bone divination" (jigubu), was praised by other Chinese linguists and ethnologists. See Chen and Wang (1981: 277).

15 Boas's book *Anthropology and Modern Society* was translated into Chinese by Yang Chengzhi in 1945. Earlier, Dai Yixuan wrote an influential article introducing Boas's theory in *The Journal of Ethnological Research*, 1943.

16 Sun's major work, *Shehuixue yuanli* (The principles of sociology), promoted the Boasian theoretical view, and was adopted as a textbook in college. This made Sun's influence spread, as did the Boasian perspective. Another pro-Boasian figure, if not more influential and important than Sun, was Huang Wenshan whose interest was also to construct an anti-evolutionist cultural theory. Cf. Chen and Wang (1981: 279-80).

17 Such as Yang Chengzhi, Ling Chunsheng, Chen Yitang, Wei Huilin, and Rui Yifu.

18 The thesis title was "The Chinese opium question in British opinion and action," cf. Arkush (1981: 30). Wu received the best foreign student award for his thesis of that year, which took him only one year to write! See Wu (1986: 81).

19 In 1947 the very first department of anthropology was established in Jinan University in Shanghai by Liu Xian, a physical anthropologist, see Guldin (1994: 68). Given its tradition and reputation, Qinghua University's Department of Anthropology was probably more often recognized as a pioneering establishment in the field, see for instance Chen and Lin (1981: 299). The year 1948 saw a few further establishments of anthropological institutions in both southern and northern China. For a discussion, see Guldin (1994: 68-70).

20 For a general discussion of anthropological/ethnological research in this period, see Guldin (1994: 57-62). During the war period Yunnan and Sichuan became centers of anthropological and sociological research: see Wang (1994) and Jiang (1981) on Yunnan and Zhao (1995) on Sichuan. For a personal account of that time, see Wu (1986: 89-90).

21 One should note that this anthropological urge to search for the real coincided with a general sentiment of Chinese intellectuals at that time: the intellectual must engage in the struggle of the people. For accounts of

this historical period in which Chinese intellectuals developed their vision of history, culture and society, see for instance Spence (1990); Yeh (1990); Chow (1960); Schwartz (1986).

22 They all engaged in what can be called "urban ethnography." The most important examples of this kind of work included, for instance, Gamble's *Peking: A Social Survey*, 1921 (with assistance by Burgess); and Burgess's *The Guilds of Peking*, 1928. For a vivid discussion of Fei's impression of these foreign teachers, see Arkush (1981: 31-36).

23 For a discussion of this definition and its justification in the context of China, see Fei (1939: 4-8). Fei later further developed his argument in relation to the idea of community studies, see Fei and Chang (1945: 13-18).

24 In a review article, Morton H. Fried lists: D. H. Kulp II's *Country Life in South China* (1925), Fei's *Peasant Life in China* (1940), Ch'en Ta's *Emigrant Communities in South China* (1939), C. P. Fitzgerald's *The Tower of Five Glories* (1941), Fei and Chang's *Earthbound China* (1945), Francis L. K. Hsu's *Under the Ancestor's Shadow* (1948), Martin Yang's *A Chinese Village* (1945), Lin Yueh-hwa's *The Golden Wing* (1948), and Morton H. Fried's *Fabric of Chinese Society* (1953). See Fried (1954: 18). My discussion in this paper is confined to those produced by Chinese scholars. For an alternative account of community studies, see Wong (1979: 28-29).

25 To note: Fei's *Lucun Nongtian*, which was later collected-together with Chang's two village studies in *Earthbound China* was first published in Chinese. But other community studies by Chinese scholars were all first published in English.

26 Ch'en Ta's work on migration, from a perspective within a local community, is the best in terms of its historical vision and breadth, see Fried (1954: 33).

27 Two months may still be an exaggeration. According to Arkush, Fei stayed in the village for only one month in July 1936, and revisited it in August for a few extra days. See Arkush (1981: 73).

28 For a discussion of missionary sociology in the 1920s, see Wong (1979: 11-18).

29 A parallel can be drawn between this methodological view and that of Mao's rural investigations. For a discussion of Mao's method, see Roger R. Thompson's Introduction in Mao Zedong's *Report from Xunwu* (Mao 1990).

30 My reference is Fei's book published in 1993. The first essay of this book, bearing the same title, was originally a talk given at the Conference of Asian Studies, July 1990, Tokyo.

31 Some basic points which Fei makes in this essay are similar to those in his earlier writings, particularly his "Toward a People's Anthropology," which was based on a talk at the 40th Annual Meeting of the Society of Applied Anthropology, held in Denver, Colorado, 1981, when Fei received the

Malinowski Memorial Award.

32 Leach is more than a casual connection. Both Leach and Fei attended Malinowski's seminars in mid 1930s. They were both born in 1910. Unfortunately, Leach passed away in 1982. A year before his death, when Fei revisited England, they met at Leach's residence in Cambridge. On several occasions, Fei used Leach as a reference point for his discussions of the place of Chinese anthropology. Fundamentally, Fei saw Leach as a groundless intellectual, searching for nothing but mind games. In contrast, Fei argued that his own anthropology was "earthbound," of which the first principle was its commitment and engagement.

33 Leach's only dissatisfaction with Fei's work is that Fei seems to have tried to provide a typical picture of peasant life in China. "Such studies do not, or should not, claim to be 'typical' of anything in particular. They are not intended to serve as illustrations of something more general. They are interesting in themselves." See Leach (1982: 127).

34 Another quotation from Fei may be even more illuminating: "As for myself, I have no interests, or perhaps my interest would be in tilling a field. But I recognize my responsibility because I know that the work I do has a function. The larger community needs this work of ours; it is directly or indirectly related to the welfare of others. For better or for worse, I have received this training and now must bear the responsibility. If one has a taste for it, fine; if not, it still must be done – that is discipline... A soldier halfway into battle cannot simply put down his arms and return home because he suddenly decides he doesn't care for fighting." Quoted in Arkush (1981: 55).

35 As Fairbank commented, this formula may not be consistent with Chinese philosophy, since traditional belief holds that each single entity should have both substance and function. "The phrase was widely used, nevertheless, since it seemed to give priority to Chinese values and decry Western learning as merely a set of tools." See Fairbank (1992: 258).

36 D. H. Kulp, J. A. Dealey, and H. S. Bucklin among others from Brown University started to teach sociology in Shanghai College in 1913, and this was the first sociology course of the kind taught in China.

37 Missionary work was aided financially from their own funding sources. Sociological research carried out in China at the time was heavily influenced by this practical missionary orientation, a Christian spirit to help the weak and the poor. Burgess's type of social investigation became popular, because it was part of social work, at least in the eyes of its conductor. See Burgess (1928: 7).

38 This paper deals with the scene of anthropology in mainland China. The stories of Taiwan and Hong Kong have been largely left out. In fact the lineage paradigm, one of the most powerful anthropological paradigms in the study of Chinese society and culture, was based upon ethnographic

materials collected in Taiwan and Hong Kong, particularly the New Territories. For a discussion of this paradigm, see Watson (1982). For a critique, see Chun (1996). For a critical review of social science research in Taiwan, see Murray and Hong (1993).

39 For a lively discussion of the revival of anthropology as an academic discipline, see Guldin (1994: 3-19; 1987; 1988; 1990).

40 Such as the Chinese Sociological Association, the Chinese Sociopsychological Association, the Chinese Association of Marriage and Family Studies, the Association of Rural Studies, the Association of Educational Studies, and so forth. Besides these national associations, twenty three provinces have established their own provincial associations of sociology. Each province has built its own sociological research institute within the academy of social sciences. Nine universities have built research institutes of sociology. There are also a number of private sociological research organizations. Cf. Han (1990).

41 According to the *Yearbook of Sociology 1979-1989* and that of 1989-1993, more than 3,200 articles and more than 500 books on sociology have been published since 1979. For a concise description of this process of revival, see Han 1996. For a slightly more thorough treatment of the reestablishment of sociology, see Cheng and So (1983); Pasternak (1983); Rossi (1985). For a translation of a discussion of sociology by Chinese scholars in the early 1980s, see Chu (1984).

42 Some found a place at the Central Academy of National Minorities, established in Beijing in 1951. It is true that those who had found their way into the Academy of National Minorities had to limit their interests and research to the minority groups, to confine their research to a certain type of ideology, and to restrict themselves to topics, techniques, and methodologies adjusted to suit the interests and direction of the government. However, this is not necessarily to suggest that all these changes and adoptions were involuntary. Many intellectuals, including those trained in the West, were very much impressed by the power and organization of the communist government in the 1950s, and were willing to offer their help to change the society. For a discussion of Fei Xiaotong's experience, see McGough (1979: 10-13).

43 This exclusive focus on the minority groups led scholars to argue in the 1980s that the study of Han (Chinese) as an ethnic group was badly needed (Yuan and Xu 1989).

44 Even Fei Xiaotong, whose reputation was closely linked to anthropology, was reluctant to help rebuild anthropology as an independent academic discipline in the beginning, for the reason that anthropology was born in connection with colonialism, see Guldin (1994: 9).

45 For a similar sentiment argued in other contexts, see Liu (1984: 17); Yang (1991: 91-95); Pei and Qiu (1984: 2); Chen (1984); Liang (1994: 307,

357-58); Qiu (1993: 118-19).

46 "Four modernizations," *sihua* in Chinese, is a government slogan, which means to realize modernization in four fields: agriculture, industry, national defense, and science and technology. The term "spiritual civilization," also promoted by the government, is based upon a dualist vision that divides civilization into both the material and spiritual.

47 In 1985, the Third Annual Meeting of the Chinese Anthropological Association (CAA) was organized around the theme of applied anthropology. The previous annual meeting could also be seen as an effort to prove the utility of anthropology. In 1983, the Second Annual Meeting (CAA) in Shanghai focused on anthropology and its relationship to the "two civilizations", material and spiritual.

48 For discussions of the significance of anthropology as an applied science, see Zhuang et al. (1995: 13-17); Zhou (1991: 126-27); Shi (1994).

49 A large amount of the anthropological work published was simply reprints of the works of the older generation of scholars. The clearest and most decisive arguments were put forward, again, by the older generation of scholars whose ideas of anthropology were formed more than half a century ago.

References

Arkush, David R. 1981. *Fei Xiaotong and Sociology in Revolutionary China.* Cambridge, Mass.: Harvard University Press.

Asad, Talal. 1982. "A comment on the idea of non-Western anthropology," pp. 284-87 in *Indigenous Anthropology in Non-Western Countries,* Hussein Fahim ed. Durham: Carolina Academic Press.

Boon, James A. 1982. *Other Tribes, Other Scribes: Symbolic Anthropology in the Comparative Study of Cultures, Histories, Religions, and Texts.* Cambridge: Cambridge University Press.

Burgess, John Stewart. 1928. *The Guilds of Peking.* New York: Columbia University Press.

Chen Guoqiang. 1984. "Woguo renmin xuyao renleixue" [Chinese people need anthropology], pp. 1-10 in *Renleixue yanjiu* [Anthropology Research], The Chinese Anthropological Association ed. Beijing: Zhongguo Shehuikexue Chubanshe.

Chen Guoqiang and Lin Jiahuang. eds. 1991. *Dangdai Zhongguo renleixue* [Contemporary Chinese anthropology]. Shanghai: Sanlian Shudian.

Ch'en, Ta. 1939. *Emigrant Communities in South China.* New York: Institute of Pacific Relations.

Chen Yongling and Wang Xiaoyi. 1981. "Ershi shiji qianqi de Zhongguo minzuxue" [Chinese ethnology in the early decades of the twentieth century], pp. 261-300 in *Minzu yanjiu,* vol. 1.

Cheng, L. and A. So. 1983. "The re-establishment of sociology in the PRC: toward the sinification of Marxian sociology," *Annual Review of Sociology* 9: 471-198.

Chiao, Chien. 1987. "Radcliffe-Brown in China," *Anthropology Today* (3): 2.

Chow, Tse-tsung. 1960. *The May Fourth Movement: Intellectual Revolution in Modern China.* Cambridge, Mass.: Harvard University Press.

Chu, David S. K. ed. 1984. *Sociology and Society in Contemporary China, 1979-1983.* Armonk, N.Y.: M.E. Sharpe.

Chun, Allen. 1996. "The lineage-village complex in southeastern China," *Current Anthropology* 37 (3): 429-50.

Clifford, James. 1988a. "On ethnographic self-fashioning: Conrad and Malinowski," pp. 92-113, in his *The Predicament of Culture: Twentieth Century Ethnography, Literature, and Art.* Cambridge, Mass.: Harvard University Press.

Clifford, James. 1988b. "On ethnographic authority," pp. 21-54 in his *The Predicament of Culture: Twentieth Century Ethnography, Literature, and Art.* Cambridge, Mass.: Harvard University Press.

Eddy, Elizabeth M. and William L. Partridge eds. 1987. *Applied Anthropology in America.* New York: Columbia University Press (2nd ed.).

Fahim, Hussein ed. 1982. *Indigenous Anthropology in Non-Western Countries.* Durham, N.C.: Carolina Academic Press.

Fairbank, John King. 1992. *China: A New History.* Cambridge, Mass.: Harvard University Press.

Fardon, Richard. ed. 1990. *Localizing Strategies: Regional Traditions of Ethnographic Writing.* Edinburgh: Scottish Academic Press.

Fei, Hsiao-tung [Fei Xiaotong]. 1939. *Peasant Life in China: A Field Study of Country Life in the Yangtze Valley.* London: Routledge and Kegan Paul.

Fei, Hsiao-tung and Chang Chih-i [Fei Xiaotong and Zhang Ziyi]. 1945. *Earthbound China: A Study of Rural Economy in Yunnan.* Chicago: University of Chicago Press.

Fei, Xiaotong. 1981. *Toward a People's Anthropology.* Beijing: New World Press.

Fei Xiaotong. 1993. *Ren de yanjiu zai Zhongguo* [The study of man in China]. Tianjin: Tianjin Renmin Chubanshe [Tianjin People's Publishers].

Fei Xiaotong. 1995. "Cong Malinnuosiji laoshi xuexi wenhualun de tihui [Some understanding of Malinowski's theory of culture], in *Beijing Daxue xuebao (shezheban)* [Peking University Journal, Social Science and Philosophy Section] (6): 53-71.

Fei Xiaotong. 1996. "Ge mei qi mei, meiren zhi mei, meimei yu gong, tianxia datong" [Each has its own beauty, each praises for other's beauty, each allows other's beauty, all beauties coexist], in *Beijing Daxue xuebao (shezheban)* [Peking University Journal, Social Science and Philosophy

Section] (1):4-6.

Firth, Raymond. 1957. "Introduction: Malinowski as scientist and as man," pp. 1-14 in his (ed.) *Man and Culture: An Evaluation of the Work of Bronislaw Malinowski.* London: Routledge and Kegan Paul.

Fitzgerald, Charles P. 1941. *The Tower of Five Glories: A Study of the Min Chia of Ta Li, Yunnan.* London: Cresset Press.

Freedman, Maurice. 1962. "A Chinese phase in social anthropology," *British Journal of Sociology* 13: 106-16.

Freedman, Maurice. 1963. "A Chinese phase in social anthropology," *British Journal of Sociology* 14: 1-19.

Fried, Morton H. 1953. *Fabric of Chinese Society: A Study of the Social Life of a Chinese County Seat.* New York: Praeger.

Fried, Morton H. 1954. "Community studies in China," *Far East Quarterly* 14 (1): 11-36.

Gamble, Sidney D. 1921. *Peking: A Social Survey.* New York: George H. Doran Company.

Geertz, Clifford. 1983. *Local Knowledge: Further Essays in Interpretive Anthropology.* New York: Basic Books.

Geertz, Clifford. 1988. *Works and Lives: The Anthropologist as Author.* Stanford: Stanford University Press.

Gellner, Ernest. 1992. *Postmodernism, Reason and Religion.* London and New York: Routledge.

Gernet, Jacques. 1996. *A History of Chinese Civilization.* Cambridge: Cambridge University Press (2nd ed.).

Guldin, Gregory E. 1987. "Anthropology in the People's Republic of China: The winds of change," *Social Research* 54 (4): 757-78.

Guldin, Gregory E. 1988. "Chinese anthropologies," *Chinese Sociology and Anthropology* 20 (4): 3-32.

Guldin, Gregory E. ed. 1990. *Anthropology in China: Defining the Discipline.* Armonk, N.Y.: M.E. Sharpe.

Guldin, Gregory E. 1994. *The Saga of Anthropology in China: From Malinowski to Moscow to Mao.* Armonk, N.Y.: M. E. Sharpe.

Han Minmo. 1990. "Shehuixue de chongjian, tansuo he tupo" [Rebuilding, exploring, and path-breaking of Chinese sociology], *Zhongguo shehuikexue* [Chinese Sociology] 1: 55-66.

Han Minmo. 1996. "Zhongguo shehuixue yibai nian" [One hundred years of Chinese sociology] in *Xinhua wengao* (4):150-153.

Harris, Marvin. 1968. *The Rise of Anthropological Theory: A History of Theories of Culture.* New York: Crowell.

Hau'ofa, Epeli. 1982. "Anthropology at home: a South Pacific Islands experience," pp. 213-22 in *Indigenous Anthropology in Non-Western Countries,* ed., Hussein Fahim. Durham, N.C.: Carolina Academic Press.

Hsu, Francis L. K. 1948. *Under the Ancestors' Shadow: Chinese Culture and*

Personality. New York: Columbia University Press.

Hu Qiwang. 1981. "Cai Yuanpei yu minzuxue" [Cai Yuanpei and ethnology], *Minzu yanjiu* 1: 251-60

Huang Xinxian. 1995. "Jiaohui daxue xuezhe dui jiu Zhongguo shehui wentide yanjiu" [Research on social problems of Old China by scholars of missionary colleges] in *Jiaoyu pinglun* (6): 45-7.

Jiang Yingliang. 1981. "Minzuxue zai Yunnan" [Ethnology in Yunnan], *Minzu yanjiu* 1: 236-50

Jiejie. 1995. "Zhongguo renleixue fazhan de xin bianzhang" [A new chapter in the development of Chinese anthropology] *Guangxi minzu xueyuan xuebao (zhexue shehui kexueban)* (4):25-27.

Keontjaraningrat. 1982. "Anthropology in developing countries," pp. 176-92 in *Indigenous Anthropology in Non-Western Countries,* Hussein Fahim ed. Durham, N.C.: Carolina Academic Press.

Kulp, Daniel H. 1925. *Country Life in South China: The Sociology of Familism,* volume I. *Phenix Village, Kwantung, China.* New York: Bureau of Publications, Teachers College, Columbia University.

Kuper, Adam. 1996. *Anthropology and Anthropologists: The Modern British School.* London and New York: Routledge (3rd ed.).

Leach, Edmund R. 1957. "The epistemological background to Malinowski's empiricism," pp. 119-38 in *Man and Culture: An Evaluation of the Work of Bronislaw Malinowski,* R. Firth, ed. London: Routledge and Kegan Paul.

Leach, Edmund R. 1982. *Social Anthropology.* London: Oxford University Press.

Liang Zhaotao. 1984. "Renleixue de yanjiu neirong yu zuoyong" [The content and function of anthropology], *Renleixue yanjiu.* Beijing: Zhongguo Sheke Chubanshe.

Liang Zhaotao. 1994. *Minzuxue, renleixue yanjiu wenji* [Collected works in ethnology and anthropology]. Beijing: Minzu Chubanshe.

Lin, Yueh-hwa [Lin, Yao-hua]. 1948. *The Golden Wing: A Sociological Study of Chinese Familism.* London: K. Paul, Trench, Trubner & Co.

Lin Yaohua. 1985. *Minzuxue yanjiu* [Ethnological research]. Beijing: Zhongguo Shehui Kexue Chubanshe.

Liu, Lydia H. 1995. *Translingual Practice: Literature, National Culture, and Translated Modernity, China, 1900-1937.* Stanford: Stanford University Press.

Liu Xiaoyu. 1984. "Lun renleixue de duixiang he zuoyong" [The object and function of anthropology], pp. 17-29 in *Renleixue yanjiu,* The Chinese Anthropological Association, ed. Beijing: Zhongguo Shehui Kexue Chubanshe.

Malinowski, Bronislaw. 1932. *The Sexual Life of Savages.* London: Routledge (3rd ed.).

Mao Zedong. 1990. *Report from Xunwu.* Stanford: Stanford University Press (trans. Roger R. Thompson).

McGough, James. P. ed. 1979. *Fei Hsiao-tung: The Dilemma of a Chinese Intellectual.* White Plains, NY: M. E. Sharpe.

Men Xianfan. 1989. "Zhongguo minzuxue shi nian fazhan shuping" [The development of Chinese ethnology in the past decade]. *Zhongguo shehui kexue* 2: 149-58.

Murray, Stephen O. and Keelong Hong. 1993. *Taiwanese Culture, Taiwanese Society: A Critical Review of Social Science Research Done on Taiwan.* Lanham, Md.: University Press of America.

Nader, Laura. 1988. "Post-interpretive anthropology," *Anthropological Quarterly* 61 (4): 149-59.

Needham, Joseph. 1956. *Science and Civilisation in China, 2: History of Scientific Thought.* Cambridge: Cambridge University Press.

Pasternak, Burton. 1983. "Sociology and anthropology in China: revitalization and its constraints," pp. 37-62 in *The Social Sciences and Fieldwork in China,* Anne F. Thurston and Burton Pasternak eds. Boulder, Colo.: Westview (AAAS Selected Symposium).

Pei Wenzhong and Qiu Pu. 1984. Daixu: wei jin yi bu fazhan woguo de renleixue er nuli [Preface: an effort to advance our anthropology], pp. 1-3 in *Renleixue yanjiu,* The Chinese Anthropological Association ed. Beijing: Zhongguo Shehuixue Chubanshe.

Piddington, Ralph. 1957. "Malinowski's theory of needs," pp. 33-52 in *Man and Culture: An Evaluation of the Work of Bronislaw Malinowski,* R. Firth ed. London: Routledge and Kegan Paul.

Qian Cunxun. 1994. "Jinshi yishu dui Zhongguo xiandaihua de yingxiang" [The influence of translated works on China's modernization], pp. 297-322 in *Zhongguo tushu lunji* [On books in China], Cheng Huanwen ed. Beijing: Shangwu Yinshuguan.

Qiu Pu. 1993. *Minzuxue zai Zhongguo* [Ethnology in China]. Beijing: Zhongguojingji Chubanshe.

Richards, Audrey I. 1957. "The concept of culture in Malinowski's work," pp. 15-32 in *Man and Culture: An Evaluation of the Work of Bronislaw Malinowski,* R. Firth ed. London: Routledge and Kegan Paul.

Roseberry, William. 1996. "The unbearable lightness of anthropology," *Radical Historical Review* 65: 5-25.

Rossi, Alice S. ed. 1985. *Sociology and Anthropology in the People's Republic of China: Report of a Delegation visit, Feburary—March 1984.* Washington D.C.: National Academy Press.

Schwarcz, Vera. 1986. *The Chinese Enlightenment: Intellectuals and the Legacy of the May Fourth Movement of 1919.* Berkeley: University of California Press.

Schwartz, Benjamin. 1964. *In Search of Wealth and Power: Yan Fu and the West.* Cambridge, Mass.: Belknap Press of Harvard University Press.

Shi Yilong. 1994. "Zhongguo yingyong renleixue de guoqu, xianzai yu weilai" [The past, present and future of Chinese applied anthropology], *Yunnan shehui kexue* 6: 57-61.

Spence, Jonathan D. 1990. *The Search for Modern China*. New York: Norton.

Srinivas, M. N. 1966. "Some thoughts on the study of one's own society," pp. 147-163 in his *Social Change in Modern India*. Berkeley: University of California Press.

Srinivas, M. N. 1989. "The insider versus the outsider in the study of cultures," pp. 172-180 in his *The Cohesive role of Sanskritization and Other Essays*. Delhi: Oxford University Press.

Stocking, George W. 1992a. "The ethnographer's magic: Fieldwork in British anthropology from Tylor to Malinowski," pp. 12-59 in his *The Ethnographer's Magic and Other Essays in the History of Anthropology*. Madison, Wisc.: The University of Wisconsin Press.

Stocking, George W. 1992b. "Maclat, Kubary, Malinowski: archetypes from the dreamtime to anthropology," pp. 212-75 in his *The Ethnographer's Magic and Other Essays in the History of Anthropology*. Madison, Wisc.: The University of Wisconsin Press.

Van Willigen, John. 1991. *Anthropology in Use: A Source Book on Anthropological Practice*. Boulder, Colo.: Westview.

Van Willigen, John. 1993. *Applied anthropology: An Introduction*. Westport, Conn.: Bergin & Garvey (rev. ed.).

Wang Shuiqiao. 1994. "Lun minguo shiqi guonei xuezhe dui Yunnan shaoshu minzu de yanjiu" [On minority studies by Chinese scholars in Yunnan during the Republican period], *Yunnan shehui kexue* 5: 72-77.

Watson, J. 1982. "Chinese kinship reconsidered: Anthropological perspectives on historical research," *China Quarterly,* 92: 589-622.

Whyte, Martin King. 1983. "On studying China at a distance," pp. 63-80 in *The Social Sciences and Fieldwork in China*, Anne F. Thurston and Burton Pasternak eds. Boulder, Colo.: Westview (AAAS Selected Symposium)..

Wong, Siu-lun. 1979. *Sociology and Socialism in Contemporary China*. London and Boston: Routledge and Kegan Paul.

Wu Wenzao. 1986. "Wu Wenzao zizhuan" [Autobiography], in *Zhongguo dangdaishehui kexuejia zhuanji congshu* [Biographies of contemporary Chinese social scientists]. Beijing: Shumu Wenxian Chubanshe.

Xiong Yuezhi. 1994. *Xixue dongjian yu wan Qing shehui* [Western knowledge eastwards and late Qing society]. Shanghai: Shanghai Renmin Chubanshe.

Yang Kun. 1983. *Minzu yu minzuxue* [Ethnicity and ethnology]. Sichuan: Sichuan Minzu Chubanshe.

Yang Kun. 1991. *Minzu yanjiu wenji* [Collected works in ethnological studies]. Beijing: Minzu Chubanshe.

Yang, Martin. 1945. *A Chinese Village: Taitou, Shantung Province*. New York: Columbia University Press.

Ye Wencheng. 1991. "Woguo renleixue de xiankuang he weilai zhanwang" [The present and the future of Chinese anthropology], pp. 46-52 in *Dangdai Zhongguo renleixue* [Contemporary Chinese anthropology], Chen Guoqiang and Lin Jiahuang, eds. Shanghai: Sanlian Shudian

Yeh, Wen-hsin. 1990. *The Alienated Academy: Culture and Politics in Republican China, 1919-1937.* Cambridge, Mass.: Harvard University Press.

Yuan Fang et al. 1991. "Qinghua, lianda shehuixi xishi" [History of the Department of Sociology at Qinghua and Lianda], *Shehuixue yu shehui diaocha* 2: 17-25.

Yuan Shaofen and Xu Jieshun. 1989. *Hanmin minzu yanjiu* [The study of the Han people]. Vol. I. Guangxi: Renmin Chubanshe.

Zhan Chengxu. 1995. "Dui wanshan Zhongguo minzuxue xueke tixi de yi dian kanfa" [Some thoughts on the completion of the system of Chinese ethnological studies], *Manhan yanjiu* 3: 3-5.

Zhao Xishun. 1995. "Kangzhan shiqi de Sichuan shehuixue" [Sichuan sociology during the Anti-Japanese War] in *Xinan minzu xueyuan xuebao (shezhe ban)* 5: 26-29.

Zhou Daming 1991. "Woguo dangdai renleixue fazhan de sikao" [On the development of contemporary anthropology in China], pp. 117-27 in *Dangdai Zhongguo renleixue* [Contemporary Chinese anthropology] Chen Guoqiang and Lin Jiahuang eds. Shanghai: Sanlian Shudian.

Zhou Xing and Hu Hongbao. 1994. "Zhongguo minzuxue de goucheng yu tezheng" [The composition and character of Chinese ethnology], *Ningxia shehui kexue* 2: 2-9.

Zhuang Kongshao et al. 1995. "Mianxiang weilai de Zhongguo minzuxue he renleixue" [Toward the future: Chinese ethnology and anthropology], in *Guangxi minzu xueyuan xuebao (zhexue shehui kexue ban)* 4: 5-17.

Chapter 8

Anthropology and the Progress of Chinese Education:

Cultural Continuity, Cultural Comparison,

and the Role of Scholars

ZHUANG Kongshao

The symbolic significance of the phrase "meeting the challenge of the twenty-first century" has become very real both because of the experience of high-speed technological and social change, and the emergence of a new aware-ness of globalization brought about by the international financial crisis of 1997-98. Educational systems in each country are also being reevaluated in the search for social development and the capacity to deal with unforeseen events. The United States, Europe, Japan, and even China, including the Hong Kong Special Administrative Region, all acknowledge the necessity of renovating their education systems, even though their different cultural back-grounds, political systems, and social policies mean that the process of re-form in each country is different.[1]

The Anthropological Vision of Ancient Education

In Ancient China, the competitive imperial examination system, which origi-nated from the Confucian respect for sages according to their different abili-ties, was highly valued. Being well versed in the Confucian literature was a prerequisite for success in the bureaucracy, and this encouraged the trans-mission of the Confucian classics. The *Han shu* (History of the Han Dynasty) records that in *Zoulu* (present-day Shandong) there was a popular saying that, "Bequeathing one's offspring a fortune in gold is not the same as teach-ing him to master one Confucian classic." Thus, from the system of "recom-mendation and selection from villages and towns" used in the pre-Han period to the imperial examination system used from the Tang period onwards, the influence of Confucius was felt throughout society, and the result was massive social education in Confucianism.

The transmission of Confucian culture was hierarchically ordered. The first line of transmission in the Eastern and Western Han dynasties was through the Imperial College in the capital and schools in the regions, which disseminated it through each grade of urban society. It was also transmitted by private teachers among the upper strata in cities, towns, and villages. Confucian culture stressed human ethics, virtue, age, and authority. The second line of transmission was from the upper to the lower levels of the cities and villages (Lu Yun 1986: 86; Zhuang Kongshao 1989). The so-called "persons of both virtue and age" – that is, prominent public figures, teachers, and local officials – acted as intermediaries in the transmission of Confucian culture. The scholar of *Li xue* (the Confucian school of idealist philosophy of the Song and Ming dynasties), Zhu Xi, not only wrote *Si shu ji zhu* (Annotations of the *Four Books*) and advocated the (feudal) code of ethics, but he also used educational institutions as a conduit for the transmission of Confucianism and *Li xue*. He also believed that knowledge should be transmitted to the lower levels of society, and that in order to educate the masses, particular attention should be paid to specific areas of life such as family ceremonies, group genealogies, village conventions of behavior, and regulations on reading (Gao Lingyin and Chen Qifang 1986; Xue Zhi 1986). We cannot judge whether ancient school education was right or wrong on the basis of current knowledge, but we can say that schools were part of the whole social education system and served very well to channel ancient politics, logic, and philosophy into both orthodox and unorthodox educational processes. One could say that planned education was the vehicle for the transmission of the Chinese cultural system (Zhuang Kongshao 1989: 186); however, it did not exclude various patterns of dissemination of numerous popular customs at the grassroots level (Zhuang Kongshao 1996: 395-417).

It is obvious that the traditional education system was imbued with political characteristics. In the early period there were slogans such as "If you excel at study, then you can become an official" ("Zi Zhang" chapter of *Lun Yu*). Later Dong Zhongshu proposed that, "Instruction is the foundation of conducting government, punishment is the final recourse of government" ("Jing Hua" section of *Chunqiu fanlu*). Zhu Xi's *Da xue* was "the model for cultivating one's moral character and governing the people" (*Yu Lei, juan* 14). All had a traditional political coloring, and politics clearly played a primary role in teaching. Once the system for selecting imperial officials from government schools had taken shape, politics became a prominent aspect of traditional Chinese education. Politics and ethics were interrelated, and both existed in educational concepts and actions. There is obvious cultural continuity between ancient and modern China, as can be seen in my discussion below of educational methods and changes in curricula.

This can be traced back to the continuity over many years of the imperial examination system and the importance of being well versed in the Confucian classics. Although the examination system stressed literary talent, there was an exaggerated worship of the past and a relatively large number of restrictions, and it ultimately inhibited the development of people's abilities and intelligence. Although we can find among the recorded utterances of a few great ancient educators sayings stressing the importance of caution and critical thinking in reading the classics,[2] in reality the Confucian customary ranking system already predetermined the unidirectional nature and inequality of the education process. As a result, we must pay close attention to the transmission of Confucian concepts over a long period of time and their use in transforming human nature (Zhuang Kongshao 1989: xi), namely their diffusion both up and down during the Confucian era, which resulted in both the ancient and modern Chinese peoples sharing more or less the same collective consciousness and unconscious cultural traits. The external manifestations of this were that, under normal conditions, the group exhibited a relatively passive acceptance of the education system, as a result of the system of group control.

Difficulties of Reforming the School System

This type of restrictive educational culture has clear continuity. In the late 1980s we surveyed fifteen children's preschools in Shanghai and examined 47 controlled children's activities conducted each day in school. Between 8 am and 4 pm there was a total of 495 minutes of activities and rest, of which only 25 minutes was directly allocated for children's free activities (Zhuang Kongshao 1989: 191). Things have improved slightly today, but even so there has been no fundamental change. This reflects the extent to which mainland teachers "manage" and control children, the ultimate example being making them all go to the lavatory at the same time, as occurs in some kindergarten schools. This restricts the development of the child's body and mind. It is a universal phenomenon that "all those involved in training children to enter society restrict the children and demand that they are obedient, [while they themselves] have control and exercise authority." (Peng Maike 1993: 16). Some teachers and instructors explicitly acknowledge that, "children should be familiar with control and order," because then "they are easy to control in the classroom" (Wu 1994).

The one-way transmission to – and passive acceptance of – knowledge by children is still common in schools today. In China, teaching materials from preschool through to senior high school are all arranged so that the teacher coaches from the books. Initially this is of some benefit in enabling the teacher to develop knowledge on the basis of the children's textbooks, but the custom of reading lifelessly from the books prevents agile thinking, since the solutions supplied by the books provide the only foundation for learning. For example, in a general knowledge class in one preschool, the teacher asked the class "what is bamboo like?" The children gave different answers, "like a rocket," like a candle," "like a pen," but the teacher was not satisfied. The reply he wanted was "like a pagoda" because this was the "correct" reply given in the teacher's reference book and teaching notes. This is undoubtedly a classic example of the restriction of the rich imaginative power of children.

Although some parents and teaching instructors recognize that an independent and enterprising child is not a bad thing, the current education system often restricts children's enthusiasm and initiative. Clearly, the style of learning and examinations that involve lifeless repetition and copying are only reiterative and imitative educational practices. Learning should be a creative activity (Zhuang Kongshao 1989: 292), and utilitarianism in education cannot imbue the students with a lasting motivation for learning. In addition, if "being ranked first" and examinations are the ultimate point of education, this involves not only the question of the learning methods inhibiting students' creativity, but also extends to a disregard for moral principles.

Since I began to teach educational anthropology in 1986, there have been no obvious changes for the better in the educational conditions in Chinese primary schools, middle schools, or universities, which is of great concern. Today, China's development is badly in need of creative thinkers and talented people of action, but the current education system does not provide students with the opportunity to take part in creative endeavors on a daily basis. Traditional Chinese government and educational culture do not encourage free development and understanding, only veneration for books, the classics, and authority. Even the composition of essays is stereotyped. For more than two thousand years, from the time of Confucius, study has involved inflexible rules and rote learning, whether in the Imperial Academy or in private schools.

One modern reflection of this educational tradition is the spoon-feeding, or lecturing style of classroom teaching. Even though for many years a number of teachers have chosen a heuristic method of teaching in some situations and achieved good results, in the majority of schools today, nonheuristic teaching or the basic exclusion of classroom discussion still prevails. Many important elements allowing a classroom atmosphere of free discussion are inhibited: for example, it is not scheduled into the curriculum, sensitive issues cannot be freely discussed, and the teacher's knowledge is sometimes inadequate to deal with the questions raised. Within such a strict educational climate, to put it bluntly, increasing the time for free educational discussion would affect students' success in the "systematized" examinations, because to a very great extent the examinations are textbook- and curriculum-based. Until the last few years, the scope of the courses and examination questions in some schools has been completely fixed. For example, several topics are chosen for an examination from 20 or 30 defined streams (for which standard answers are prepared in advance). This supports the deadening rote style of learning. This type of unsuitable examination system must be fundamentally reformed.

Applying the principles of educational anthropology, we find that the connotations of the traditional restrictive culture still continue to exist and are perpetuated in today's education process. Restrictive educational culture accounts for the partly concealed, partly revealed passive concepts and methods of modern education. They are based on China's deep-seated traditional culture, and these concepts and methods have led to the cultural stagnation that has penetrated to the deeper levels of people's consciousness and unconsciousness. Today, most of the elements of the education system are necessarily related to this. There are obvious restrictions in being constantly bombarded by this examination-based education system. Imitative testing, guessing examination topics on the basis of experience, and memorizing answers and the form of examination questions are all designed with the examination system in mind. However, the fact that examination-based education leads to the squandering of energy and reduces the vitality of young bodies and minds is already of great concern throughout society. The conservatism, repetitiveness, and imitativeness of an exam-based education means that the assimilation of people of real ability into society is very uneven, and students with cognitive flexibility or who are rich in imagination are easily excluded from the doors of academia. The trend towards quality-based education currently prevailing in Mainland China is also a move away from the present exam-based system. However, from primary to senior middle school, examination methods based on a unified system of textbooks continue today, in spite of good intentions. The question is, how can the spirit of quality education, and the principles of individual education, teaching students according to their ability, be elicited? Examinations are clearly necessary, but we should look again at the examination methods. It is a mistake to see examinations as incompatible with quality education; but the crux of the matter is to find an organic relationship between the examination system and the aims of education.

The Chinese University System and Attempts at Reform.

If one endures to university, what then? How will those students now develop after they have exhausted their energy, experienced the wear and tear on their bodies and minds, learned all the strategies for survival in the examinations, and gone through innumerable examinations in this least cost-effective method of knowledge transfer?[3] We must first look at the conditions in the school system in order to see the basic situation of the current reforms in university education. In the years since 1978, spearheaded by the rural reform of the household responsibility system linked to production, the former egalitarian socialist system has changed. It has gradually progressed to enterprise reform, for example the introduction of high-level science and technology, the study of modern management, and institutional reductions and retrenchments in accordance with the forces of market competition. However, reform in the universities has been slow, in comparison with government ministries and commissions. Since schools have an important impact on national consciousness, reforms must be very circumspect. From the perspective of the current university system, first, if the system of intellectual choices and the personnel system are not changed, it will not be possible to revitalize the education of students or scientific research. Second, the problem remains of overcoming cultural conformity in the exchange of cultural information. These are two different problems that educational reform in universities has encountered or will encounter.

Restrictions on Course Choice

The majority of students who have gone through the cruel competition of the middle school college entrance examination and entered university relax and take a breath. At least there are various departments to choose from and a limited number of textbooks to read. It is also seemingly possible to engage in debate. For example, from a general survey of American education, middle and primary school seem more "relaxed" than in China, but on entering university the system is much more strict. Chinese universities are relatively relaxed compared with Chinese schools. This "relaxation" feels like laying down a heavy burden, since university students no longer have to relive the nightmare of the school examination system. Even if they have to take the TOEFL examination, it differs from the middle school examination system in its uniformity. It is very rare to find a university student who has to repeat a year's work or who does not graduate.

However, whether or not this should be viewed as good fortune depends on the quality of the system of intellectual selection in universities. We need say nothing about universities during the Cultural Revolution, but afterwards there were obvious changes in the courses offered in the natural science faculties. Even though the changes in applied subjects may have come slowly, at least they were incorporated within the larger market economy. Knowledge at various levels was acquired in teaching and scientific research, particularly after the introduction of research studentships. The humanities, on the other hand, were only reactivated during the 1980s, and the only educational changes that occurred were partial and sporadic. Often, there were few courses, they were not of much benefit, the teaching was sloppy, and the methods were old fashioned.

If we take the anthropology department in one college in China as an example, we can consider the ways in which teaching activities remained restricted during the 1980s. For teachers that had experienced the destruction of the humanities during the Cultural Revolution, things might not have appeared too bad, thanks to the revival of anthropology and ethnology after the 1984 teaching reforms and a slight increase in the number of specialized classes. However, the limited number of courses offered still meant that the knowledge content of the curriculum was extremely low, and none of the departments could change the large number of compulsory general classes, including many on political ideology. If we do not take into account the sixteen weeks of field studies and the writing of a graduation thesis, the anthropology students at university in eight semesters over four years sat through a total of 2,934 separate classes. Of these, 316 were taken up with the Marxist theory of China's revolutionary history, philosophy, political economy, ethnic theory and nationalities policy, and another 240 with political ideology. Compulsory classes also included 802 periods of sport, foreign languages, higher mathematics, computing, administrative management, and university level Chinese. (This list does not include a total of three weeks of military training and work experience.) In addition, there were twenty-one specialized courses, covering ancient, modern, and contemporary Chinese history, selections from Chinese historical literary works, ancient and modern world history, essays on national minority subjects, basic ethnology, an introduction to linguistics, China's ethnic minorities, peoples of the world, survey methods in ethnology, ethno-archaeology, studies of the economies of national minorities, religious studies, an introduction to sociology, an introduction to folklore studies, specialist studies in ethnology, lectures on literary and historical knowledge, and lectures on ethnic cultural systems and American education, making a total of 1,576 study periods (this did not include the classes in community principles and educational anthropology introduced in the mid 1980s) (Institute Teaching Board 1991: 39-40, 303-07).

As one can see, there was a major problem with the courses on offer, even though there had been some progress since the Cultural Revolution. There were too few basic and specialized courses, and some essential courses were missing from the curriculum. Some classes were too long, and there were sixteen courses with four successive periods of instruction. The "spoon-feeding" style of teaching continued from primary and middle school and was still the main method employed in universities. Nevertheless, few university students experienced as much pressure as students in middle schools or boring classes in which they followed a book line by line. Since there were great differences between faculties and departments in each university, the final nine subjects in each specialized subject course were in theory elective, but because of difficulties in arranging the timetable, these eventually became required courses as well. This situation existed in the majority of Chinese universities, and even today many have not implemented a satisfactory elective course program or credit system. There is clearly a great disparity between this and the goals of modern education from the perspective of the operation of the university system and the flexibility of student class choices. In this type of education system, the quality of students and the organization of the curriculum remain major problems.

The Problems of the University System

There are two aspects to the conditions in universities mentioned above, particularly in terms of the development of humanities departments. One was the pressure exerted by the market economy on students' choice since the economic reforms and the open-door policy, and the other was the minimal level of communication and academic exchange with overseas universities. This is a reflection of the fact that some of those who viewed certain humanities subjects introduced from the West as "capitalist" still held important posts within the universities. They were responsible for watering-down some professional courses, and behavior which had been typical of the Cultural Revolution period continued to intrude on teaching and scientific research, with politicized language turning up in academic debate. There was still resistance to instituting modern educational reforms, because of the old system, and because the boundaries of the responsibilities of the administration were poorly defined. Some university administrators were unaware of the functions and structure of a modern university, and educational planning was very haphazard. Because the system of hiring personnel remained the same, improving the teaching and eliminating redundant personnel remained a pipedream.

The issue of university reform remained on the agenda for the administration, but the problem for many reformers is that "those who organize the reform who must also be the target of the reform" (Xu Yanling 1997: 24). This ambiguity meant that individuals looked to their own benefit at each level of the administration. As often as not, interpersonal politics interfered with streamlining the administration, reforming teaching, and rebuilding academic standards, creating new barriers to change.

Educational establishments should not simply be places for acquiring professional knowledge and skills. Experience in all disciplines suggests that one should guard against setting up university courses simply on the basis of profit or utilitarian demands. However, from the low status ethnology and anthropology had in the nation's curricula, it was clear that the education authorities still had problems in understanding the meaning of the humanities and the social sciences. The idea that a discipline in which knowledge cannot be put to immediate use has no purpose was still very common. This made it difficult to recruit students and arrange classes, and no importance was attached to teacher training or redesigning courses.

It should be pointed out that from 1977-78, when students and researchers were accepted back into universities after the Cultural Revolution, the establishment of the bachelor's, master's and doctoral academic degree system, and revision of the annual system of appraising lecturers, associate professors, and professors, were very useful in promoting the development of scientific research and education in Mainland China. This system should have remained rigorously controlled, but gradually the standards for all types of courses became ambiguous. Even greater problems arose as a result of private jockeying for power. The lack of strict control over academic degrees and the assessment of ranks and titles may benefit particular individuals, but ultimately it reduces the prestige of the nation's educational institutions.

As for the students, those in primary and middle schools throughout the country continued wearily to pursue the goal of passing the college entrance examination. However, the situation for university students was starting to change. Formally, the role of the university was the production of graduates, and the students had no doubt that they would obtain secure jobs, the so-called "iron rice bowl." Since the courses were uninteresting and there was no possibility of changing them, their approach to their studies became negative, and they spent more time going to the cinema in the evening or mixing freely with the opposite sex. But with the economic reforms, the situation changed rapidly, the state was no longer responsible for assigning jobs, and students began to express their needs in relation to their courses. For example, they might inform the director of a department that unless an incompetent teacher was replaced, they would not attend that class. Since the status of teachers and students in Chinese culture has traditionally been unequal, this type of confrontational behavior on the part of students indicated that they had reached the end of their tether. They were bored with lengthy sermon-like lessons, and increasingly unhappy at some of the more restrictive aspects of school education (Zhuang Kongshao 1989: 189-208). Since their teachers were unable to supply relevant explanations in answer to their questions about society, culture, and mankind, students began to select answers for themselves. With the gradual opening of the market economy, the mass media and the flow of information, and with schools unable to change or develop, students became an important force for educational reform.

Experiments in Course Reform

From a lecture given at the end of 1994, in which national delegates urged the reform of education in Chinese universities (Zhou Yuanxin 1994), it was clear that intelligent choices had to be made. Given the pressures from students and the needs of society, an opportune moment had arrived to effect reforms in university teaching. In 1995, compulsory classes at "C University" included courses related to political ideology, China's revolutionary history, ethnic theory and policies, the establishment of Chinese socialism, and the principles of Marxism. However, the hours devoted to such subjects had fallen by 56 percent compared with 1980, creating more space for specialization. It was estimated that the number of anthropology courses taken by students over eight semesters (four years) had increased to 58, including 26 basic courses, and 32 specialized courses, compared with the 21 specialized courses taken in 1980. The basic courses included: an introduction to anthropology, the theory of cultural anthropology, linguistic anthropology, archaeological anthropology, physical anthropology, the history of anthropology, ecological anthropology, metropolitan anthropology, applied anthropology, ethnology, survey methods, introduction to Chinese ethnology, local histories of China's northeastern national minorities, local histories of China's northwestern minorities, local histories of China's southern minority nationalities, introduction to peoples of the world, history of the Asian people, history of the European and American peoples, history of the peoples of Africa and Oceania, folklore, introduction to sociology, applied statistics, ethno-economics, the history of Chinese culture, the history of foreign cultures, the history of primitive society and history of Chinese thought. Specialized courses included political anthropology, psychological anthropology, educational anthropology, religious anthropology, literary anthropology, feminist anthropology, selected readings from well-known anthropologists, group theory, family and kinship systems, ethno-archaeology, ethno-demographics, the religious cultures of national minorities, nomadic culture, cultural comparisons between East and West, communal relationships, anthropology and applied computing science, specialization in a foreign language, the history of the development of the Chinese people, anthropological film, medical anthropology, anthropology and the law, studies of China's clan system, Buddhist culture, Islamic culture, Chinese Taoism and native culture, shamanism, the Christian religion in China, an introduction to Confucianism, China's regional cultures, Overseas Chinese organizations and their culture, and community principles and community development.

I have listed all these courses in order to show the difficulties in reforming the education system in China. From the time of the Cultural Revolution, when political sermonizing was implemented across the board, to the introduction of the first elective course system in the 1980s, a quota of courses in political education remained. Traditional basic courses were in the majority, though there were a few more specialized courses in anthropology. In the 1990s, a second group of elective courses was introduced, and the proportion of political education classes declined. Courses originating from within the discipline coexisted with courses on China. These included basic theory courses in anthropology (19 courses, or 33 percent), introductions to the subbranches of the discipline (13 courses, or 22 percent), courses on China from the perspective of anthropology (17 courses, or 30 percent), and others (9 courses, or 15 percent).

After the introduction of this second group of electives, the situation does not appear to be very different from that in some famous universities in America which still look carefully at important elements of their native cultures. However, the problems that are manifest in the teaching process clearly need to be tackled wholeheartedly by the university authorities. Above all there is a heavy need for teacher training in order to increase the number of teachers with advanced degrees. Although some courses are well developed and incorporate the best of the research from both China and abroad, the quality of teaching in other courses awaits improvement. This situation is a result of the unregulated system of teacher training which resulted from the social upheavals of the past few decades.

The second point is the question of classroom efficacy. The teachers must not only be familiar with the basic principles of anthropology, but must also practice what they preach. It would seem that anthropology teachers should be more aware than teachers in other disciplines of how to change the inequalities between students and teachers which have been passed down from ancient China. However, the "force-feeding" teaching method is still often seen in classrooms. Some teachers "initiate but do not inspire," and political sensitivity makes it difficult for others to speak out. Some teachers stubbornly continue with the teaching methods they have used for years, while others have not prepared what students should read in advance. Some students just attend class passively, and some teachers lack the knowledge necessary for the students to raise questions. In comparison, the results of class discussion in some postgraduate and undergraduate classes are relatively good, but it is difficult to overcome the inequality between teachers and students handed down from the past. However, compared to the situation in primary and middle schools, some progress has been achieved. I myself tried experiments in classroom reform for several years. However, in the Chinese environment the social and educational habits ingrained over many years are hard to break. I discovered that when there is no fundamental reform in the university system, reforming teaching is very difficult.

Today, some reforms in university anthropology courses have been achieved, but I have discovered from my own work that the modern Chinese university system faces both great inertia internally and demands for reform in the face of rapid social development from outside. University administrative officials and teachers often lack training in modern educational principles. Chinese education has undergone numerous changes over the past few decades, and educational concepts and teaching systems have not been systematized. The modernization of university administration is still managed by officials from within the administration. Educational reform in this type of environment is clearly similar to reform of government: it is extremely difficult. We can assume that if standards and rules for university reform cannot be established, or if those in charge of the reforms do not understand or enforce them, the result is likely to be disaster.

In the 26 years since the government implemented its economic reform policy, the new needs of graduate students and the market economy have given an impetus to teaching reforms in schools. Despite the entangled alliances within the university, and the passive and unstable climate of teaching, the new wave of reforms in teaching and research cannot be stopped. Some teachers have introduced new teaching methods, with the support of students, so that lively discussions between teachers and students are now quite common, even though the "force-feeding" methods of teaching still exist in other classrooms. In addition, academic exchanges between university departments and individual scholars, both domestic and international, have already become more open. This is probably the best and most efficient way of breaking down former policies. The development of new "microclimates" in the educational arena is a positive development only if they affect the entrenched systems within the university. Perhaps in the short term, Chinese anthropologists should shift their investigations to the education system itself. On the one hand, Chinese professors and scholars are themselves caught up in the hardships of university reform, and on the other, they share many of the same concerns as scholars elsewhere, about improving their teaching and carrying on with their anthropological field research.

Anthropology between Education and Society

From investigations of remote tribal societies, the subject matter of anthropology has gradually come to include the mass media and newly developing systems of communication. If this change had not occurred, anthropology would probably now be as relevant as an old photograph hanging on the wall. Education systems all over the world are striving to meet the needs of social development. However, commercial and market forces and government and administrative intervention often distort educational and academic principles. Market forces can restrict education in the humanities because of the poor prospects of talented people finding a job, which leads to the view that academics should serve the market (Agassi 1993: 92) and even to the use of common economic and commercial terminology to discuss questions of intellectual creativity (Weiler 1993: 18).[4] As for government and administrative intervention, "it appears that if academic circles do not have administrative personnel they cannot exist, but if they have no intellectuals, they can still exist in the same old way" (Agassi 1993: 92). The increasingly enfeebled status of scholars means that power of their arguments is also weakened. It is still possible to discern traditional patterns of human relationships, rituals, and customs transmitted within the political culture fixed from a child's earliest education and extending right through primary school and university, so that the schoolroom reflects society as a whole. However, as scholars and as teachers, anthropologists also play a role in social development, and our own practices and studies of the outside world should play a part in the processes of cultural transmission and intellectual advance.

The essential nature of anthropological research is to raise questions about the transformation of humankind's essential qualities, and not just to rely on blind faith and obedience. For example, how can we bring about the positive transformation of mankind within the Confucian educational tradition? Or, how can we achieve a world of open and shared learning quickly and cheaply, within the wider reform of the Chinese economic and political systems that is already underway? Anthropological learning is continuously putting forward new ideas. Modern anthropologists can bring their contemporary perspectives to bear on everything, from research in schools linked to studies of social culture, and from debates about pure scientific principles to doubts about their long-term social effects. Anthropologists encompass the concerns and meanings of different cultures, which means that, whether in Detroit, Frankfurt or Xi'an, they always carry with them the capacity for original critical thinking.

Notes

1   For a general discussion of the context of educational reforms in East Asia, see Goodman (2001). – Eds.
2   "Reading and not thinking makes one muddled, thinking and not reading makes one dangerous"; "Teaching and learning should promote each other" (*Xue ji*): and "If you are in doubt, even though certain commentaries are considered to be the words of the sages, one must examine them even more carefully" (*Zhu Wengong wenji, juan* 31).
3   The author's critique of the examination system in Chinese education is very similar to recent accounts of Japanese higher education, e.g. McVeigh (2003). – Eds.
4   The ideas expressed here have much in common with recent discussions of the spread of the audit culture in other higher education systems. See Shore and Wright (1999), and Strathern (2000). – Eds.

References

Agassi, Joseph. 1993. "Financing public knowledge," in *Knowledge across Cultures: Universities East and West,* ed. Ruth Hayhoe et al. Toronto: OISE Press; Wuhan: Hubei Education Press.

Gao Lingyin, and Chen Qifang. 1986. *Fujian Zhuzi xue* [Zhu Xi studies in

Fujian]. Fuzhou: Fujian People's Publishing House.

Institute Teaching Board 1991. *Courses Offered in 1991*. Beijing: Central College of Ethnic Minorities.

Lin Yutang. *Wu tu wu min* [My land and my people]. Taipei: Yuanjing Chubanshe.

Goodman, Roger 2001. "The state of higher education in East Asia: Higher education in East Asia and the State," *Ritsumeikan Journal of Asia Pacific Studies* 8: 1-29.

Lu Yun. 1986. "Cultural transmission and changes in cultural domains," *Fudan Academic Journal* 3.

McVeigh Brian J. 2002. *Japanese Higher Education as Myth*. Armonk N.Y.: M.E. Sharpe.

Peng Maike [Michael Harris Bond]. 1993. *Nanyi zhuomo de Zhongguoren: Zhongguoren xinlipouxi* [The Inscrutable Chinese: Psychoanalysis of the Chinese]. Hong Kong: Oxford University Press.

Shore, Cris and Susan Wright. 1999. "Audit culture and anthropology: Neo-liberalism in British higher education," *Journal of the Royal Anthropological Institute* (N.S.) 5: 557-75.

Strathern, Marilyn. ed. 2000. *Audit Cultures: Anthropological Studies in Accountability, Ethics and the Academy*. London: Routledge.

Weiler, Hans N. 1993. "Knowledge, politics, and the future of higher education: Elements of a worldwide transformation," in *Knowledge across Cultures: Universities East and West*, ed. Ruth Hayhoe et al. Toronto: OISE Press; Wuhan: Hubei Education Press.

Wu, David Y.H. 1994. "Self and collectivity: Socialization in Chinese preschools," pp. 235-50 in *Self as Person in Asian Theory and Practice*, eds. R.T. Ames, W. Dissanayake and T. P. Kasulis: Albany, N.Y.: State University of New York Press.

Xu Yanling.1997. "Zhongguo kuashiji gaige zhong de zhizhang yinsu" [Factors inhibiting China's cross-millennial reform], *Shandong Daxue Xuebao* [Journal of Shandong University], 2.

Xue Zhi. 1986. "A discussion of Zhu Xi's *Xuegui* and other issues," *Jiangxi Shifan Daxue xuebao* [Journal of Jiangxi Normal University], 3.

Zhou Yuanxin. 1994. "Guojia jiaowei guanyu putong gaoxiao kecheng tixi gaige de baogao" [A report by the State Educational Commission on curricular reforms in general higher educational institutions], Beijing: Qinghua University, December 1994.

Zhuang Kongshao. 1989. *Jiaoyu renleixue* [Educational anthropology], Harbin: Heilongjiang Education Press.

Zhuang Kongshao. 1996. *Yinchi: Zhongguo de difang shehui yu wenhua bianqian (1920-1990)* [Silver Wings: Chinese regional society and cultural change (1920-1990)]. Taibei, Taiwan: Guiguan Shuju (also published in Beijing by Sanlian Shudian, 2000).

Chapter 9

Chinese National Dance and the Discourse

of Nativization in Chinese Anthropology

David Y.H. Wu

Theoretical Considerations

This paper is an exploration of the discourses of indigenization in anthropology in China. The subject matter I draw upon to demonstrate my point is Chinese national dance (*minzu wudao*), the process of its creation, and its role in the representation of the Chinese people and culture. As a cultural form, Chinese national dance serves as an excellent if complex subject with which to approach the issue of indigenization. A fundamental question in this volume, and hence the central theme of my paper, is that of how indigenous and foreign anthropologists differ in their presentations of the same ethnographic material to a general audience and to fellow anthropologists. The first issue we have to face is the terms we use to differentiate indigenous and foreign anthropologists. We shall return to this complicated point below. For the time being, let us use the term "local" to denote Chinese anthropologists who were trained in China and pursue professional careers in China. But we also have to bear in mind that in China, until very recently, anthropologists (*renleixue zhe*) were differentiated from ethnologists (*minzuxue zhe*). Anthropologists were stigmatized for political reasons, and not many ethnologists wished to be classified as anthropologists. Chinese ethnologists confine their studies to the Chinese minority nationalities, not the majority Han Chinese. This is another important point of departure when comparing anthropology in China to foreign anthropology, especially in the United States, and a point which is also significant for the discussion later in this chapter.

The first difference between foreign and local anthropologists in relation to dance is the way they see and interpret what the dances stand for. The local scholars as dancers, dance teachers, folklorists, and ethnologists present the emergence of national dance as a triumph of scientific research, ethnological documentation, and conservation of natural cultural traditions. For these scholars, the creation of modern forms of Han Chinese or minority nationality dances and their performance serve to preserve genuine Chinese cultural forms. Foreign or non-Chinese anthropologists, on the other hand, see the national dances as newly invented or reconstructed art forms that have been developed only in recent decades as part of the socialist nation-building process. Outsiders see the creation of these dances as related to the aims of the state to construct a new hegemonic political order. Thus, the state places great emphasis on the political meaning of "the Chinese people" (*Zhonghua minzu*) and "Chinese culture" (*Zhonghua wenhua*) – a unified nation with a united people made up of fifty-six nationalities.

Also, while looking at the dances, indigenous and foreign anthropologists may also understand the representation of the Chinese Self and Chinese Others in different ways. Chinese ethnologists see *minzu wudao* as an expression of a unified China, with one identity, one ethnicity, and one unified "motherland," whereas foreign anthropologists may see it as representing both Chinese and fragmented non-Chinese identities, given that *minzu wudao* can refer to the dances of both the Han Chinese and of the fifty-five minorities. Although I may not qualify as an indigenous anthropologist (even though I have taught in Hong Kong, now part of the People's Republic of China), I may consider myself "native" according to Jones' (1970) definition. I was born, brought up, and received my undergraduate training in anthropology in China. However, I received my graduate training outside China, and have practiced anthropology as a professional in foreign countries for most of my life. While conducting fieldwork since 1985 on minority culture in China, focusing particularly on Chinese minority dances, I have found myself with a double sense of identity. I have visited the majority of the Chinese nationality autonomous regions and many smaller districts. This chapter is a reflexive account of my attempts to make sense of Chinese national dance and minority dances.

Chinese Dance Observed

Since the 1980s, Chinese minority dance has featured prominently in national holiday celebrations, local festivals, large sports events, and stage performances to entertain tourists and foreign visitors. Many times when I visited the minority nationality regions in China, I was invited to watch dance performances by members of minorities. If I had been a true native anthropologist, I would have agreed with my Chinese hosts and colleagues (including research ethnologists and nationality affairs officers) that I was watching authentic, traditional dances performed by genuine minority dancers. If I had not been a trained anthropologist, I might have interpreted the dances as the restoration of a long-lost or almost lost tradition of the "Chinese people" (*Zhonghua minzu*). Unfortunately (or fortunately), my foreign-trained professional eyes usually told me that these dances were newly invented, refined, standardized, staged, and often performed by professional dancers (including Han Chinese) trained at national or regional dance academies. I therefore became increasingly curious about the process through which Chinese dances were created. My brief field interviews yielded consistent assurances from my Chinese hosts and colleagues that these dances reflected and represented "genuine" local Chinese or minority Chinese dances, which were performed by minority artists themselves, as members of the local dance troupes.

Minzu Wudao through the Eyes of a Professional Teacher

In 1990, I invited a teacher from a national dance academy in China to work with me on my dance research and to teach for six months with the Dance Department at my university in the United States as a joint project. Professor Zhang (a pseudonym) taught Chinese *minzu wudao,* and during our weekly meetings, she explained to me the history of national dance since the 1950s. An interesting revelation of the difference between the "Chinese" and "foreign" mentalities came from the students in her classes. The students were initially upset, telling Zhang that they did not think an ethnic Han Chinese could teach them authentic minority dances. Professor Zhang protested to me that she was a reputable professional dancer, teacher, and creator of minority dances, and, of course, that she was passing on to the American students genuine dance forms from minority nationalities, on which she had carried out extensive research.

Professor Zhang's life history informs us how, at the age of eleven, she became a "literature and art worker" (*wenyi gongzuozhe* – an official name for all writers, artists, and stage performers), when she was recruited by a communist propaganda team in western China immediately after Liberation in 1949, without her parents' knowledge. She learned to dance from a famous Russian ballet dancer, and has participated since the 1960s in the work of *chuangzao*, the creation or recreation of "Chinese traditional" dances in Beijing. The "Chinese tradition" includes Han classical dance (as seen in Chinese opera), Han folk dance (as seen in peasant festivities), and dances of the minority nationalities, all under the single label of *minzu wudao*. As the classification of Chinese minority groups was officially fixed by ethnologists and the state, the minorities themselves had no say in whether the classification of dances correctly reflected reality. One minority group in Guizhou, for example, protested for years against being subsumed within the Miao nationality, believing that they belonged to a separate group called the Ge. When Professor Zhang and her field team from Beijing collected and recorded Miao dances in which the Ge villages were known to excel, the local people once more declared that they were Ge and protested about being given the wrong label. Professor Zhang found it strange that this "Miao" group wanted their dances be recognized as separate from those of the Miao. "There was nothing we could do but accept the [official] reality of the dance classification," said Zhang.

From my foreign anthropological point of view, the problems of *minzu wudao* begin with the term itself, which is so vague, ambiguous, and fluid, that it can mean different things to different people at different times and in different locales. Chinese had no "national dance" prior to the Communist revolution. As the late Premier Hu Yaobang noted, "[Han] Chinese have no dance. Only the minorities have dance" (Anonymous 1985). However, the way professional Chinese dancers and choreographers have constructed dance categories illuminates the position of the *shaoshu minzu* (minorities) as being an insignificant but necessary part of the "Chinese people" (*Zhonghua minzu*). The concept of *Zhonghua minzu* took shape at the same time that *minzu wudao* was being formed as part of the hegemonic process of building a new intellectual and political meaning for China as one people and one nation. The Chinese minorities are therefore subsumed under a higher order label, *Zhonghua minzu*, or the "Chinese race."

I was told that one major element in teaching minority dance is for the dancers to grasp the different national postures (*titai*). A clear taxonomy of kinesics for each nationality is identified on the basis of habits and pseudophysical anthropological criteria. *Shaoshu minzu* are both part of China (as members of the Chinese nation) and "non-Chinese" since their *titai* (characteristic postures) are quite different from those of the Han Chinese. The communist ideology of dialectical materialism has guided the construction and standardization of the *minzu titai*. The *minzu* dancers and choreographers worked diligently in the same way as the ethnologists (*minzuxue zhe*), following Mao's instruction to carry out fieldwork by "observing" (like ethnologists), "digging" (like archaeologists), and "learning" (like folklorists) from the *shaoshu minzu* dancers. However, they appear to have continued using preconceived assumptions about the *titai* of different minority nationalities. For instance, the stereotypes suggest that Tibetans work on hilly slops, always lean forward, and have clumsy legs, while the Mongolians, as horse riders, always hold their heads high.

Professor Zhang's personal account played down the role of the state in the invention of Chinese dance. When I looked into the official documentation of speeches and writings by state leaders, however, they showed the prominent part played by the state in the dance scene. The state authorities, party theorists, and leading dance teachers have all participated actively in the interpretation or reinterpretation of dance forms, symbolic movements, and representation of meaning. Their efforts constitute part of the process of the construction of a national Chinese "culturalism," in the sense of mobilizing identities within the context of the nation-state..

From my "native" viewpoint as an ethnic Chinese anthropologist trained in Chinese culture, I attributed Zhang's omission of the political dimension to her political sophistication and awareness of the fact that she was representing China to a Western audience. Given the reality of the political socialization of individuals in China involving endless political struggles, it is not surprising that each individual has learned to repeat the "party line" (*taohua*) in order to survive. Under the socialist system, only one correct ideology prevails: no plural interpretations are allowed. This of course raises the issue of the sensitivity of a native versus a foreign anthropologist in being able to detect or understand what is, or is not, double talk when doing research on China.

In China, I have interviewed in private other professional dancers at the national and provincial level regarding state and other official interference. Some saw me as a fellow Chinese art and literature worker and said what they really thought. They reported that the *wenyi gongzuodui* or *gongzuotuan* (troupes of literature and art workers) received constant instructions and interference from the authorities inside and outside the troupe, in the form of review, criticism, contestation, and interpretation of the dances created by the dancers. Direct orders and criticism came routinely from dance academy authorities, party authorities, officials of the Ministry of Culture, and state political leaders who happened to be in the audience. Dance workers are always playing a game, guessing which forms or which plays will be favored by the authorities and which will display national culture to the people in the politically correct way, i.e., as revolutionary, progressive (modern and scientific), patriotic, authentic, and traditional.

A national dance professor is situated at the "center" (*zhongyang*). Teachers at the center are empowered to judge and decide what local dances, folk dances, minority dances, and traditional regional dances are acceptable for public performance in terms of the guiding ideology. Local dancers cannot perform what they want to without approval from the center. (This kind of information is not usually provided to "foreign" anthropologists doing "official" fieldwork in China.) Members of ethnic minorities who are professional dancers at the provincial or county level have to go through crash training courses under the "central" dance teachers to produce acceptable programs of the dances of their nationality. Once the dances have been rearranged and standardized, the minority dancers can then take them back home and perform them publicly there.

Dances, according to the government definition of "*wenyi*" (literature and art) must serve the country and support party and state ideology. On official occasions, the highest political leaders are still reminded, and remind others in turn, that the arts must serve the people (Xinhuashe 1992). However, a leader may at different times add new interpretations to the old teachings and explain what types of current art forms satisfy the definition of "Chinese culture" as popular, revolutionary, patriotic, and progressive. At the national level, the political discourse surrounding culture in China is not contested, for a unified ideology and standardized forms have already been set up by the highest authorities of the state. Chinese dance teachers may create dances to satisfy the acceptable, correct forms or styles at given times, but they can never challenge the interpretations from on high, at the risk of being accused of undermining the foundations of the guiding ideology. The correct role of the cultural workers in China, like that of Chinese anthropologists, must remain that of enriching Chinese culture as defined by the state, by adding acceptable elements from folk and minority cultures to the canon of traditional Chinese customs and art forms.

Being a foreign anthropologist (but with a native sense of awareness), I have observed that the official discourse often leads to contestation when the authorities publicly condemn the spread of undesirable literature and art forms. Since the government launched the "four modernizations" movement in the late 1970s, and since economic development and outside art forms reached all the urban centers in the late 1980s, new dances have flooded the "performance market" (*yanchu shichang*), challenging the cultural authority of the state. In the early 1990s, for instance, the Ministry of Culture continued to issue warnings to professional musicians, singers, and dancers that had formed private companies without permission, performed for personal gain without licenses, performed unacceptably vulgar shows, and cheated audiences with unacceptable ticket prices (Ministry of Culture 1991). Until the mid-1990s, moonlighting singers and dancers trained in professional academies and still holding official positions were nicknamed *zouxue* ("touring the caves"). Moonlighting is rife in the careers of professional dancers, a triumph for a capitalist market which has commoditized new songs, music, and dances that people are willing to pay to see and hear. Cultural officials have had to compromise their ideological principles in art and music production, and lower the standard of acceptability in performance, in line with the guiding ideology of the party. Today, almost anything can be staged as long as it makes a profit for the performers and organizers.

Discussion and Conclusion: The Paradox of Being a Multi-Situational Anthropologist and the "Nativization" of Anthropology in China

I have presented the creation of Chinese national dance from an indigenous dance teacher's point of view. National dance and music specialists, like indigenous ethnologists, must carry out "fieldwork" to record (with cameras and video-recorders) and preserve the cultural forms of the "remote" (i.e. non-Han) minority peoples, as well as those of the "remote" Han. They preserve the desirable parts of the recorded art forms, on the basis of which they reconstruct, teach, and perform minority and Chinese folk dances, all under the label of national dance or *minzu wudao*.

Like the indigenous ethnologists, the folklorists or art workers serve the people and socialism. Their research produces ethnographic data, including dances that are seen as "living fossils" of supposedly long-lost forms previously hidden "in the wild." These in turn help prove the existence of the stages of social evolution according to Marxist-Leninist-Maoist theory, from promiscuous communes, via matrilineal, patrilineal, and feudal societies, to socialist paradise.

Just like the novel, drama, music, or dance, ethnography too must be produced within the collectively acceptable framework of the state's guiding ideology. Like ethnographies or linguistic reports on minority nationalities, dance forms must be standardized when presented to the public; for they represent and symbolize a single correct model of Chinese culture and society, and hence "Chineseness." The regions and issues studied by the indigenous anthropologists are also closely defined by the nineteenth-century evolutionist anthropology of the West which still prevails in China: Chinese ethnologists exclusively study the "primitive," and hence the non-Han peoples. There is no purpose in studying the majority Han Chinese people and culture because they are already at an advanced stage of civilization. Through my study of Chinese minority dances as a "foreign" anthropologist, I learned more about the field of anthropology in China. Chinese ethnologists do not study and report on dance according to the standard definitions of ethnology and ethnography. Dance is the preserve of the literature and art workers, not the ethnologists. But the Chinese ethnologists who took me to the minority dance performance took it for granted that they were authentic, and that a foreign anthropologist would want to record them as ethnographic material (I carried a video-camera). A foreign anthropologist who goes to China to do fieldwork does not need to submit to the state's guiding ideology in research and publication, and therefore does not need to share the same perspective as indigenous scholars. Until the early 1990s, when a few indigenous Chinese students who had received anthropological training outside began to return to China, it was difficult for foreign anthropologists (or native anthropologists trained in the West) to communicate with indigenous ethnologists as they had little in common in terms of professional language, purpose, audience, and academic responsibility.

Now let us return to the problem of the terms used to differentiate indigenous and foreign anthropologists raised at the start of this chapter. Can we use this simple dichotomy to understand the process of the indigenization of anthropology? This begs the more complicated question of whether indigenous means "native," "local," or "insider," in contrast to "foreign," "visitor," or "outsider." I find myself involved in all these contrasting situations when doing fieldwork in China. My various backgrounds make me an anthropologist who can claim to be native, foreign, or even indigenous when practicing professional anthropology in a university inside the People's Republic of China. I can see the contrasts between different approaches to dance, methods of academic inquiry, and methods of presenting findings. I can also see how the findings serve broader social and political ends, which is much more complicated. However, paradoxically, whatever perspective I adopt, I cannot claim that it is a complete interpretation of the ethnographic material. Furthermore, by telling the story of my research on Chinese national dance as I have above, I seem to be criticizing cultural invention and social engineering by the state in China. I do not mean to do so, even from my perspective as foreigner. From the work of Hobsbawm and Ranger (1983), we now realize that the invention of tradition and a culture industry is common in modern nation-building. Nor am I criticizing my Chinese colleagues who study nationalities. As I have explained, they come from a different political culture and live in a different academic environment. They have a different academic agenda, different theoretical priorities, and address different audiences. Nevertheless, my multi-situational position allows me to see things from the nonindigenous, nonlocal point of view as well. In this sense, I can become a nonnative, nonindigenous observer, given that I was not professionally trained in China, and am not employed there.

Anthropology in China to date means the study of Chinese minorities by indigenous Chinese. It is a field in which the center tries to understands the periphery, and the Han try to understand the non-Han. Anthropology in China, as one indigenous anthropologist has claimed (Weng 1998), never went beyond the "mountains and the wild," i.e. the minorities in remoter parts of China. Social and cultural anthropology in China has been hindered by its restriction to non-Han "Others." Weng (1998: 59) criticizes this, and advocates the inclusion of the Han nationality and Chinese social and cultural change as research subjects. Weng's article is one of dozens of papers published in the proceedings of a conference on Han nationality research and the indiginization of anthropology in China, although the English term used to translate the Chinese word *bentuhua* is "nativization" (Song and Xu 1998). As the aim of the conference was to urge the authorities to broaden the field of Chinese cultural and social anthropology to include the study of contemporary Han Chinese society, "native" logic had to be evoked to justify the plea. Some of the more radical views (i.e. departing from conventional Chinese ethnology) are expressed by younger anthropologists who have recently returned to China following years of graduate training overseas. Weng's paper contains an interesting twist. He evokes Fei Xiaotong, a politically powerful senior anthropologist (better known in China as a sociologist) to justify his plea for ethnologists to go beyond "the mountains and the wild." He argues that Fei's classic Kaixiangong (or Chiang Tsun) village research should be considered a study by a native anthropologist of the "Other," since Fei was not a native son of the area, and had a hard time understanding the local dialect, even though Fei himself made it clear that, being a native of the Wu dialect region, his study was an example of a native son carrying out research in his own homeland. Weng argues that a northerner who goes to study the local Han Chinese in Guandong or Fujian is actually studying a different culture. Thus, in his view, Chinese anthropologists should be encouraged to study these kinds of "Others" in order to revitalize the discipline in China.

If this logic is to be carried further, then, from the point of view of the younger generation, anthropology in China should include subject matter much broader than today's restricted version of Chinese ethnology. Chinese colleagues have often commented on my own work in China, including medical anthropology, child socialization, preschools, and dance, by noting that anthropology is much broader in America than "within our country." The search for a more inclusive discipline, similar to that found elsewhere, is just beginning in China, with an increasing number of students returning from abroad. However, universality may be hard to attain in China for two reasons. First, the different cultural backgrounds of anthropologists in different countries still have a great impact on the way the discipline is practiced. Second, at the level of practicality, whether the above arguments by young Chinese anthropologists will produce results depends very much on political decisions by the state authorities who control nationality studies and higher education, and not on the merits of an intellectual argument.

References

Anonymous. 1985. "Hu Yaobang dui wenyi gongzuoze jianghua zeyao" [A summary of Hu Yaobang on dance artists' work], *Minzu minjian wudao yenjiu* 2: 2.

Jones, Delmos J. 1970. "Towards a native anthropology," *Human Organization* 29 (4): 251-59 (reprinted in J.B. Cole, ed., *Anthropology for the Nineties*. New York: Free Press).

Hobsbawm, E. and T. Ranger. eds. 1983. *The Invention of Tradition.* Cambridge: Cambridge University Press.

Mao Zedong.1967. *Selected Works of Mao Tse-tung.* Beijing: Foreign Languages Press. (Chinese edition published 1953, Beijing: Renmin Chubanshe.)

Ministry of Culture. 1991. "Jiaqiang guanli yenchu chichang" [A report on reinforcing the management of the performance market], Report issued by the Ministry of Culture on Nov. 20, 1990. *Zhonghua Renmin*

Gongheguo Guowuyuan Gongbao, 5, (April 3 1991): 158-61.

Rong Shixing and Xu Jieshun, eds. 1998. *Renleixue bentuhua zai Zhongguo* [Nativization of anthropology in China]. Nanning: Guangxi Nationalities Publisher.

Weng Naiqun. 1998. "Shanyei yanji zu zouchu shanyei: Dui Zhongguo shehui wenha renleixue de fansi" [Research on social culture of minorities and the importance of going beyond it – Thoughts on social cultural anthropology in China], pp. 54-62 in *Renleixue bentuhua zai Zhongguo* [Nativization of anthropology in China], eds. Rong Shixing and Xu Jeishun. Nanning: Guangxi University for Nationalities.

Xinhuashe. 1992. "Li Reihuan taolun Wenyi fanrong" [Li Reihuan discussed prosperity for Wenyi], *Dagongbao* (Hong Kong) (August 12): 1.

Chapter 10

Local Theories and Sinicization in the

Anthropology of Taiwan[1]

Joseph BOSCO

This chapter examines the case of indigenous anthropology in Taiwan. In-digenous anthropology in Taiwan includes a movement to self-consciously sinicize anthropology, and is different from indigenous anthropology in the rest of the region. The chapter describes the nature and limitations of Taiwan's indigenous anthropology, and considers what implications the Taiwan case has for the project of anthropology generally, especially as research on one's own culture seems to be growing in the United States and elsewhere. The first task is to first describe indigenization as it appears in the Taiwan case.

Definition of Indigenous

One way to avoid the essentialized (and stereotyped) definitions of "the in-digenous anthropologist" is to focus not on the person but on the activity. I thus use the term "indigenous anthropology" to refer to the fieldwork *and writing* being done in Taiwan for a Taiwan audience. These terms do not focus on matters of authenticity, but on the relationship of anthropologists with their informants and reading publics.[2] It is naive to think that anthropologists are simply creating an objective description of culture. Writing in all the social sciences is rhetoric (McCloskey 1985); writing tries to convince the reader, and must be based on readers' assumptions. This does not mean that the writing is merely subjective, but it will be affected by the background and common understandings of the intended audience. Thus, I focus on the work of anthropologists published in Chinese and do not discuss work published by scholars based overseas who may conduct research in Taiwan but publish primarily in English. I use the term "native" anthropology to refer to the work about Taiwan by an anthropologist raised in Taiwan but based overseas and published in a foreign language like English. In terms of cultural background, persons writing native and indigenous anthropology may be identical, but the native anthropologists publish for an English-reading audience, for which they act as a kind of cultural interpreter. Furthermore, the same person can write as a native anthropologist when addressing a foreign (e.g. North American) audience, but as an indigenous anthropologists when addressing a Taiwanese audience. The boundary between "indigenous" and "native" anthropology is not sharp, and the distinction between "home" and "the field" has indeed become blurred, but the distinction is often made between indigenous and outside anthropologists. Furthermore, there is an anthropological conversation going on in Taiwan, in which the primary participants are anthropologists – and others – based in Taiwan. As we will see below, not only is this conversation taking place *in* Taiwan, but it is taking place *about* Taiwan; a high proportion of Taiwan's anthropology focuses on the island itself.

Though there is an anthropological conversation taking place in Taiwan, Taiwan's indigenous anthropological community is not isolated from anthropologists overseas. Prominent foreign anthropologists visit the island to give talks, and most anthropologists go overseas for graduate training. Eight of National Taiwan University's eleven full-time staff members in anthropology have Ph.D.'s from United States universities, and another one has an American M.A.[3] At the Institute of Ethnology, thirteen academic staff members have Ph.D.'s from the United States, while two have doctorates from the United Kingdom. All of the older staff members who do not have doctorates have studied abroad (five in the United States, two in the United Kingdom, and one in Japan). Thus, most "indigenous" scholars are foreign-trained, or at least base their specialized knowledge on overseas academic experience. In addition, there have also been dozens of Ph.D. candidates and scholars who have conducted research in Taiwan, collaborating and communicating with Taiwan host scholars. National Taiwan University's introductory courses use United States textbooks (e.g. Kottak 2003). Many Taiwan anthropologists also participate in overseas conferences and follow the English language literature. Thus, though we can in some ways see a distinctive tradition in the anthropology of Taiwan, anthropology in Taiwan also has close links with anthropology overseas, especially with the United States. The idea of indigenous does not mean autochthonous or independent. Yet, despite the growing transnationalism that has been noted by many scholars (see e.g Gupta and Ferguson 1997; Hannerz 1996), the state is still critical in funding research and hiring anthropologists in Taiwan. Transnational flows of scholarship are important, particularly the flows of students for graduate training, but once back in Taiwan these young graduates are molded under the pressure of obtaining funding, the influence of senior scholars, and the national tradition. It is the importance of this molding force that I seek to address.

The term indigenous merely means locally based, and should not imply undeveloped or primitive standards of scholarship. Despite ideals of relativism, the term indigenous can have connotations of backwardness, but this is not my meaning here, nor is it necessarily true that scholars studying their own culture will produce second-rate work. We will return to this below.

Indigenous Fieldwork in Taiwan

One of the main differences between anthropology in the United States and Taiwan is the higher proportion of Taiwan's anthropologists studying their own culture and studying in their own country. For example, of the articles published by the 23 anthropologists in the Academia Sinica Institute of Ethnology from 1984 to 1998 (as listed on the Institute web home page), 85 percent were about Taiwan or Chinese culture generally. In contrast, from 1995 through 1997, the *American Anthropologist* published just 16 percent of articles about North America.

Thus, Taiwan's indigenous anthropology tends to be done by local scholars concentrating on Taiwan society. The term "local scholars" is purposely vague, because it includes a variety of ethnic and cultural backgrounds, but emphasizes the common local (island) reference point. Many Taiwan anthropologists, though conducting research in their own country, have in fact also done research on different cultures. This further complicates the concept of indigenous anthropology, because though the work is published in Chinese, the field language is not the anthropologist's native language. There are scholars of Hokkien, Hakka, mainland, and aboriginal backgrounds, studying both their own and other groups. Their work is generally published in Chinese for local readers, both scholarly and general. It combines features of indigenous and cross-cultural anthropology. It tends to be viewed as indigenous by foreign anthropologists because of the greater linguistic, reading, and other cultural skills Taiwan anthropologists often bring to the fieldwork encounter, and because the research is published within Taiwan. Though publishing abroad is still viewed as more prestigious in the academic hierarchy, having one's work noticed in Taiwan requires publishing in Chinese.

Anthropologists the world over have turned to studying their own countries. It could be said that anthropologists have always primarily studied in their country or in their country's colonial hinterland. Thus, British anthropology concentrated on Africa, American anthropology focused on Native Americans and then the Philippines and Latin America, and anthropology was first conducted in Taiwan by Japanese ethnologists during Japan's 50 years of colonial rule. What is becoming increasingly common, however, is for the anthropologist and informants (or "natives") to share more by way of common history and language, in sum, to share a cultural system. It has long been the pattern in Third World countries for anthropologists to study within their national borders. Some of these anthropologists studied so-called "tribals" or "aborigines," though many studied peasants. But even when peasants were studied, as they were in Mexico and South America, the peasants were often still a clear "primitive Other" in contrast with the European *crillojo*, *ladino*, or *mestizo* elite. Except for a few notable exceptions (e.g Mintz 1974 [1960]), anthropologists have only studied farmers and workers viewed as ordinary citizens since the 1970s (see e.g. Bennett 1969).

The trend towards studying one's own society is also growing in Western countries because funds for foreign travel have shrunk and societies traditionally studied by anthropologists have become more sensitive about allowing outsiders to conduct fieldwork. Anthropologists are also increasingly uncomfortable with what they see as the neocolonial relationship that comes with studying other societies.[4] Yet, it is still the case that in the United States and Europe, anthropology is primarily the study of other cultures and societies. In the United States, the anthropology of American society is in many ways of lower status than "foreign" fieldwork. It is much more difficult for recent Ph.D. recipients to find an academic job if they have conducted dissertation fieldwork in the United States. Foreign fieldwork is often thought to be of key importance in making an anthropologist. Edward Bruner, for example, did his dissertation research on Native Americans using English for interviewing, but felt compelled to go overseas for additional fieldwork after receiving his Ph.D. He writes: "many of my professors at Chicago were of the belief that I would never become a 'real' anthropologist until I worked through a foreign language in a foreign land. Meyer Fortes, who had come from Cambridge as a visiting professor at Chicago, told me this explicitly and urged me to go overseas" (Bruner 1999: 464). Nigel Barley, author of the best-selling *The Innocent Anthropologist* (Barley 1983), wrote his doctoral dissertation on the medieval English, and was likewise urged to do overseas fieldwork to become a "true anthropologist." Bruner went to Sumatra, Barley to Cameroon, and though both comment on the requirement for exotic field research as outdated and something they did primarily to meet the field's expectations, their descriptions of their experiences and of what they learned seem to support the view that foreign fieldwork is important in making an anthropologist.

In Taiwan, however, it is the opposite: new faculty members are expected to have done dissertation fieldwork in their native society, even when they get Ph.D.'s from overseas. Foreign (non-Chinese) fieldwork is rare, and not encouraged. Foreign fieldwork in Malaysia and the United States is primarily on "Overseas Chinese." Recent research outside of Taiwan concentrates on mainland China rather than Southeast Asia. All of the full-time staff at National Taiwan University's Department of Anthropology do China research broadly conceived; eight out of eleven can be said to specialize on Taiwan.[5]

Similarly, judging by recent publications, 21 of 23 anthropologists in the Institute of Ethnology specialize on Taiwan. In the past, it may have been the case that lack of funds for foreign research kept students and researchers on Taiwan, but this is less true today. An equally important motivation seems to be a kind of nationalism or ideal of nation-building. On the other hand, Huang (1989: 237) has argued that the lack of research on other cultures/societies is one of the major weaknesses of anthropology in Taiwan. It leads Taiwan's anthropologists to ignore comparison, and ultimately limits the role of anthropology as a discipline. On the other hand, it also demonstrates the importance and fluidity of current cultural and political issues in Taiwan which keep Taiwanese scholars' attention focused on the island.

There are consequences for the discipline when indigenous anthropologists focus primarily and almost exclusively on their own societies. To understand this predominance of local research and its consequences, we need to look briefly at the history of the discipline in Taiwan (for fuller treatments, see Huang 1983; 1989; C.L. Chen 1989; Y.Y. Li 1995; Chuang 1995).

Historical Background

The earliest anthropological research on Taiwan was by Japanese ethnographers shortly after the island's cession to Japan in 1895.[6] This ethnographic work focused both on the majority Chinese population, and on the non-Chinese aborigines; it sought to increase knowledge of local customs to aid Japanese colonial administration (Tsu 1997: 201; Chiu 1997). Just as the American Roy Franklin Barton researched *Ifugao Law* (1969 [1919]) after the United States occupation of the Philippines, so too did the Provisional Commission for the Investigation of Taiwanese Old Customs (*Rinji Taiwan Kyûkan Chôsakai*) compile a series of studies on traditional kinship, economy, and civil law (Tsu 1997). Japanese colonial rule was more direct and penetrated deeper into society than British colonialism (Gold 1988: 104), though it did not push farmers off their land or seek to change the social organization or relations of production (Gold 1986: 38). Knowledge of the society and culture was therefore helpful for administration, and such goals are stated in the introductions to reports of the period. Japanese colonial administrators were eager to make Taiwan a model of colonial administration and development to show the international community that Japan was a worthy world power (see for example Naito 1937).

Postwar research was carried out by the anthropologists who came to Taiwan from the Mainland. Initially, anthropological research focused on the island's non-Chinese aborigines, owing to a tradition dating back to the Japanese period, as well as the specialties of the Mainland anthropologists who came in 1949 (Y.Y. Li 1995).[7] Before 1964, nearly all the anthropology published in Taiwan was about aborigines. In a sense, this was a continuation of anthropology as the study of colonized societies, with anthropologists from dominant social groups studying marginal natives. This pattern also followed the Western idea of anthropology as the study of simple societies. Anthropologists who did research in Chinese villages were not viewed as anthropologists; Martin M.C. Yang, who received his Ph.D. in anthropology from Columbia University and wrote an ethnography of a Chinese village in Shandong (see Yang 1945), taught in the Department of Agricultural Extension at National Taiwan University, not in the Department of Archaeology and Anthropology. But also important were local political considerations; Wang Sung-hsing (1991: 2) has pointed out that in the 1950s, it was considered pro-communist to want to research "peasants." Only after the mid-1960s did anthropological research expand to the Taiwanese Chinese (Li Yih-Yuan 1998: 66). Yin (1989: 320) traces this change to the arrival of Morton Fried as visiting professor in 1963-64 at National Taiwan University, and the creation in 1965 of a seminar on "The role of Taiwan studies on Chinese History" by Hsu Cho-yun and Chen Chi-lu, the chairs of the history and anthropology departments, respectively. Of the articles published from 1985 to 1997 by researchers in the Institute of Ethnology, 22 percent were about Taiwan's aborigines while 49 percent were about Taiwan Chinese. (An additional 14 percent were about "China and Chinese culture in general" and the remaining 15 percent were about other places, including Overseas Chinese).

It is also important to note that Taiwan has been the focus of intensive anthropological research. For the United States alone, a search in the UMI website for dissertations using the keyword "Taiwan" yields 189 Ph.D. dissertations (though some of these are not from anthropology departments). By 1991 alone, at least 50 dissertations on Taiwan had been completed in anthropology departments, and most of these theses were written by foreign students. Though foreign scholars have interacted with indigenous scholars, the impact on research has been minor, with few joint publications resulting (Chuang and Wolf 1995 is an exception.)

The total number of anthropologists and ethnologists in Taiwan has never been large. Today there are probably not more than 100 active anthropologists on the island, and only a few major centers. The Academia Sinica Institute of Ethnology and National Taiwan University Department of Anthropology have the longest histories, the most visible journals, and the largest number of anthropologists. National Chengchi University has an Institute of Nationality Studies with its own bulletin, but historically its focus has been on mainland minority areas to train government administrators. National Tsing Hua University has had a graduate program since the late 1980s and began offering a Ph.D. in 1996. New programs at various new universities were opened in the late 1990s; some have departments of anthropology or ethnology (such as the Institute of Ethnic Relations and Culture at National Dong

Hwa University), but most have at best a few anthropologists teaching in social science departments.

Despite these relatively small numbers, the patterns that emerge are more than the results of the idiosyncratic leadership of individuals. In particular, the move of Taiwan's anthropologists to study themselves is part of a larger movement of interest in Taiwanese culture and history. This nativism, which has exploded since the end of martial law in 1987, is not limited to anthropology but has been a major social phenomenon in Taiwan since the 1980s. New sections of bookstores have emerged for books on "Taiwan studies," and new local histories and ethnographies have been published both by private publishers and by local governments. Popular magazines regularly have articles on Taiwan history and folk culture, and a magazine *Lishi* (Historic Monthly), devoted expressly to history, began publishing in 1988. Government propaganda magazines stopped publishing articles on the Chinese Mainland and started to print articles about Taiwan. One of them, the *Free China Review*, was renamed *Taipei Review* in 2000. Beginning in the mid-1980s, Cultural Activities Centers (*wenhua huodong zhongxin*) were built in each county seat, and exhibitions on local history and culture have been presented periodically. Museums have sprung up in temples and private buildings, many of them displaying dioramas and old tools and photographs of daily life in "traditional Taiwan." In some cases, these are presented as local traditions (regional within Taiwan as well as Taiwanese in a general sense). In others, these traditions are presented as local examples of a larger Chinese tradition. An amusement park called Taiwan Folk Village has been built in Taizhong; it includes traditional homes (saved from demolition and moved to the park) and artisan demonstrations (noodle-making, pottery, etc.) in addition to amusement rides. This is not the place to go into a discussion of the origins of this "nativization" (*bentuhua*) movement, but it is worth noting that it is related to the democratization and identity crisis of the island. Though state funds are important in promoting some of the exhibits and preservation efforts, nativization is contested and is not simply orchestrated by the state for the creation of a national identity, but is part of the internal struggle over unification and independence, and the meaning of Taiwanese identity.

Effects on Anthropology of Studying Locally

Anthropology began as the study of "the Other." Where this other is sought, however, has much to do with scholars' political context. As mentioned above, scholars have found their Others most conveniently in their country's colonies. In the colony, the scholar's search for "Otherness" and the administration's need for knowledge on which to base administration combined to make anthropological research attractive and financially feasible. Asad (1973) and Said (1979) have alerted anthropologists to these colonial origins, but we have not thought enough, perhaps, about the limits that a locally focused anthropology places on the discipline as a comparative enterprise. In the United States, it is typical for departments to seek as wide a regional diversity as possible. Some departments will deliberately exclude some areas such as Africa or East Asia if they feel their library and other resources cannot support such a specialty, but the overall principle of diversity in regional specialization is very common, and is often mentioned in job advertisements. But in Taiwan, when research turned to the Chinese in the 1960s, the concern for the "Other" became less noticeable. The driving concern was understanding Chinese or Taiwanese society itself.

In contrast to the dominance of indigenous anthropology in Taiwan, the study of America is still only a small specialty in the United States. Varenne (1986: 2) has written that "There has never been much anthropology of the Unites States," and George and Louise Spindler (1986) comment that although they have had 17 studies of the United States in their famous Holt Rinehart series of ethnographies, none have sold well. Rynkiewich and Spradley (1975) even used the title "The Nacirema: A neglected culture" as the introduction to a book of readings on American culture. While many American anthropologists make implicit comparisons with American society, few actually conduct fieldwork in the United States.[8]

Exoticizing Oneself

When American anthropologists do study and write about the United States, they often exoticize it. Indeed, George and Louise Spindler (1986: ix) have argued that anthropologists writing of their own culture must exoticize by making the familiar strange. Rynkiewich and Spradley (1975: 4) note that some of the categories used by anthropologists, like "kinship and the family," "social structure" and "religion and magic," "seem strange when applied to American culture." Research on Chinese culture in Taiwan does not, however, emphasize the exotic.[9] Some topics such as religion and kinship are heavily emphasized, and others like politics are ignored, but in no article that I have seen is Taiwanese behavior presented as bizarre or exotic, even as a rhetorical device. Anthropologists are perhaps correct in essentializing and exoticizing when they seek to undermine their audience's sense that their culture is natural or better. As Arkush (1995: 146) says, "It can be argued that those who write for a Western audience are right to underline differences for they challenge our readers' sense of the naturalness of their own social institutions and values." It is therefore notable that Taiwan's indigenous anthropology does not do this. This reflects the fact that Taiwanese readers are very aware that other cultures are different, while Americans begin with the assumption that humans are basically similar and explore differences from that basis. All humans tend to assume their culture is superior, but American universalism tends to make Americans assume their culture is natural and rational, while Taiwanese tend to assume cultural differences are present and important. To choose a trivial example, many Taiwanese still ask foreign visitors if they can use chopsticks, while it rarely occurs to most Americans that foreigners might need to learn to use a knife and fork. To people who begin with the universalist assumption that everyone is similar, finding one's own culture described as exotic is especially interesting and droll, but cultural difference is already assumed by most Taiwanese. They are also aware of how cultures have changed, and are interested in understanding the fast-disappearing religious festivals and other aspects of traditional village life. Nostalgia is a major driving force in Taiwan anthropology.

Folklore

Instead of exoticism, Taiwan anthropology blends with folklore. There is no department of folklore in Taiwan; folklore-like research is conducted in Taiwan by professors of Chinese literature as well as historians, anthropologists, and others, and focuses especially on local history and popular religion, where "folk origins" are sought. Folklore is based on a search for an authentic, premodern culture (Bendix 1997). This research can be called "folklore" because as in Europe and America, it tends to be descriptive, a collection of facts. Some of the research published in anthropology journals is similarly descriptive, and tends towards the folkloric, including especially descriptions of religious rituals. Folklore emerged as a niche field of study, dealing with the customs of peasants and their remnants in industrial societies (Basham 1978: 22-23), though in most cases it failed as a discipline because its subject matter was divided between other disciplines such as ethnology and rural sociology. Some argued that "folklore" as a label referred to a type of subject matter rather than a discipline (Bendix 1997: 129).

A common criticism of indigenous anthropologies in many countries is that they are mere compendia of data, or more like folklore, not anthropology. In Europe, in fact, a separate tradition of local studies known as ethnology and ethnography has been maintained in tandem with anthropology. Ethnology and ethnography as "folk" or "national" studies have been dominant in Eastern Europe (Vermeulen and Roldán 1995: 9). Indeed, folklore was once not as distinct from anthropology as it is today. In the United States, it split with anthropology in the 1930s; Boas was among the founding members of the American Folklore Society before the split (Schippers 1995: 245 n.15). In Taiwan, there has not been such a split; folklore studies, divided among several departments including anthropology, resembles the *Volkskunde* or national folklore of Eastern Europe. Indigenous anthropologists contribute to this field, along with professors of religion, Chinese language and literature, and history. Folklore is a national literature within which local, Taiwan, and

Chinese identities are constructed. It is reminiscent of Anderson's (1983) idea of "print capital," which, he argues, was instrumental in the construction of the modern European nation-states, creating for each a language, a literature and an identity. Anthropology in many developing countries is funded specifically as part of the effort in nation-building. The exploration and construction of identity that leads to an interest in folklore moves anthropology away from the comparative emphasis it has had in the United States and United Kingdom.

It needs to be kept in mind that while in the United States and United Kingdom anthropology is thought of as a social science, in both China and Taiwan anthropology emerged from history. At National Taiwan University, anthropology was taught in the history department before the establishment of the anthropology department (Chen Chi-lu 1989: 13), and history has always been close to the nation-building enterprise. Indeed, Chen Chi-lu (1989) mentions nation-building as one of the roles of anthropology. Anthropologists in Taiwan have not had the direct ties to government that anthropologists in the United States had in the Bureau of Indian Affairs or the Agency for International Development. Instead, anthropology in Taiwan looks more like one of the trappings of modernity, a thing that every society has, a modern continuation of China's imperial histories and encyclopedias. But anthropology and anthropologists have influenced national policies and participated in the construction of national grand narratives, making anthropology part of "folk" or "national" studies.[16] Anthropologists are among the administrators of cultural and historical documentation programs, and graduates in anthropology are hired by museums and county Cultural Activities Centers. This is most visible in the creation of the Institute for Taiwan Studies within the Academia Sinica, which, though primarily staffed by historians, has many anthropologists affiliated with it who participate in its conferences. Anthropologists are also publishing local gazetteers (see e.g. Cai Zongxun 1997; Xie and Ma 1997) that are, to all intents and purposes, works of history and folklore.

The combination of folklore with anthropology is in part the result of the heavy concentration on local research. In United States anthropology, the comparative focus is predominant. Articles in *American Anthropologist* and *American Ethnologist* are not primarily about the places where the research was conducted, but about the social and cultural processes that are under study. The research could be conducted anywhere; indeed, many article titles and abstracts do not specify where the research took place. The research site may be a place where the political or historical context makes the cultural process clearer or more vivid; in some articles, it could be anywhere. But folklore is about a specific place or people. It concentrates on the timeless elements of culture that are now disappearing, and in the process it creates the "traditional" culture.

A number of critics have noted that anthropologists in Taiwan do not build on each other's work, and Huang Ying-kuei has noted that specialists on Han society do not communicate with specialists on Taiwan's aborigines (Huang 1989: 238). These problems of lack of cooperation can in part be traced to the combination of folklore with anthropology, because folklore focuses on the local rather than on an abstract general or universal theory. When research is local and descriptive, it is of interest as folklore, but it is not of interest to other nonlocal anthropologists. This is in part why so much indigenous anthropology seems, to outsiders, to be excessively descriptive, ethnography rather than ethnology.[11] The abstractions of anthropological theory need to be what Geertz has called "experience-distant" concepts (Geertz 1983: 57). "Experience-near" concepts are those used by informants, while "experience-distant" concepts are those used by "specialists," such as ethnographers, scholars, or priests. Describing a Taoist *jiao* ceremony in terms of its local symbolism and meaning and in the words of informants is useful, but it may be more anthropologically useful to view it as a purification ceremony and to see how it compares with purification ceremonies in other religions. The point of anthropology is to produce an ethnography that is "neither imprisoned within [a people's] mental horizon, an ethnography of witchcraft as written by a witch, nor systematically deaf to the distinctive tonalities of their existence, an ethnography of witchcraft as written by a geomancer" (ibid.). The issue is not one of universalism versus particularism but whether these phenomena we compare can shed light on one another (Geertz 1983: 11). Note, however, that if an American writer compares the *jiao* to a Catholic Mass, the Catholic example is understood by an American reader and it makes an exotic ceremony (the *jiao*) seem more familiar. To a Taiwanese reader unfamiliar with Catholicism, the effect is jarring; a well-known ceremony (the *jiao*) is compared to something exotic (a Mass). The comparison will be unintelligible, or may seem inappropriate, creating the impression the writer does not truly understand the ethnographic case. Much indigenous anthropology does not use experience-distant concepts and ethnographic comparisons, thereby appearing to be mere description. This is why, as Herzfeld (2001: xi) has noted, anthropology must locate itself "between the disembodied abstractions of grand theory and the ingrown self-absorption of local interests and 'national' studies."

The problem for indigenous anthropology is that universities value theory over ethnography, so that indigenous anthropology often becomes synonymous with bad anthropology. It is sometimes assumed, for example, that any good works in anthropology will be published in English, but English readers may not be interested in descriptions of traditional life. The assumption that good research will be published in English is, at least in Asia, increasingly invalid, as local funding levels surpass those of Western countries and domestic readers are interested in reading about their own society. It is increasingly the case that the most important original research on Taiwan is in Chinese, and foreign anthropologists need to be aware of what indigenous scholars are publishing.

Another feature of Taiwan's anthropology that makes it resemble folklore is its choice of research topics. Anthropological research has focused on religion and on kinship and family, but has avoided the political economy.[12] Foreign anthropologists conducted research on other issues, such as Schak (1988) on beggars and the poor, and Silin (1976) on business organization, but they have had little impact. Huang (1989: 238) argues that this concentration creates a bottleneck for research on Taiwan, because a holistic view is lacking. He also argues that utilitarianism in the study of religion – which sees all religious continuity and change as an adaptation to society – is the result of the failure to see religious phenomena as related to the political and economic system. He argues that if anthropologists cannot face these issues squarely, research on the political economy will become the monopoly of sociologists, and this has largely come to pass (see for instance the research by scholars who hived off from the Institute of Ethnology to form the Institute of Sociology). Until the mid-1990s, when Taiwan graduate students from the United States began to choose new topics, anthropologists did little research in urban anthropology (Yin 1989 is an exception), or on gender, the poor, nationalism, local politics, and economic behavior. It should be noted that the Institute of Ethnology made an effort, starting in the early 1970s, to focus on "analytical studies of current social problems" (C.L. Chen 1989: 13, citing Li Yi-yuan 1971: 2), in an attempt to move the discipline away from its origins in the humanities and towards the social sciences, but most of this research came to be conducted by sociologists and not by anthropologists. Anthropologists remained the most folkloric of Taiwan's social scientists.

I have argued that Taiwan's anthropology faces challenges much like those of folklore elsewhere, but I believe that were its empiricism to be combined with a more comparative focus, Taiwanese anthropology could instead be viewed as contributing to global anthropology. In the United States, folklore is losing its identity as an academic specialism as its subject matter vanishes, rather like anthropology, to the extent that anthropology has studied "primitive" societies. The sociologist Alan Wolfe says that the contempt for hard facts in neighboring and competing disciplines make folklore seem empiricist. "Folklore is considered undertheorized, which in today's climate is a devastating charge" (Dorfman 1997: 9). I do not seek to argue that anthropology needs to be saved simply for reasons of institutional politics. Instead, it seems worth saving as a place where cultural differences are not simply assumed away, but are carefully and systematically researched. The nativist and nostalgic impulses in folklore lead scholars to seek timeless customs and rituals rather than observe the massive sociocultural changes surrounding them. To the extent that anthropology in Taiwan follows the example of folklore, cultural issues will be covered less effectively than by other disciplines.

Informants' Critiques

Taiwan's indigenous anthropologists write in the language of their informants. This occasionally happens in the United States, and even leads to problems when informants do not like what they read (see e.g. the controversies surrounding the work of Carolyn Ellis in Allen 1997). Anthropologists in Taiwan have seldom had controversies with their informants and host communities. There have been several criticisms leveled at foreign anthropologists' work, often by "natives" who are not from the area studied, but I do not know of any criticisms by informants of Taiwan anthropologists. This is in a sense surprising, since such conflict is common, as described in *When They Read What We Write* (Brettel 1993; see also Scheper-Hughes 1981). Several authors in this book (e.g. Davis 1993) point out that informants do not necessarily object that facts are wrong, but that private information has been made public. Other authors note that informants sometimes do not like the analysis offered by the anthropologist; Handler (1993), for example, describes the way reviewers of his book on Quebec nationalism took offense at his effort to deconstruct nationalist ideology. Others were puzzled rather than indignant. Because anthropologists are ethically bound to avoid hurting their informants and the communities they study, and because anthropologists generally hope that their work might be of some interest and perhaps even of help to their host communities, they generally assume that informants should like or agree to what anthropologists write. But anthropologists are supposed to see and notice things people may not like to see and say things that people do not like to hear. As Godelier puts it, anthropologists from any country have "a certain common skill at revealing, in their own society or in some other, realities and ideas that many actors in these societies do not want to see made explicit or analyzed, or at least not in that form" (Godelier 1997: 5). Anthropologists have studied other societies to shock the comfortable assumptions of people back home. And when they study people back home, there is a common tension between pleasing and being honest. As Horwitz, an ethnographer in American Studies, puts it: "On the one hand I aim to please – print what flatters – but on the other to challenge – print what 'helps' even if it hurts" (Horwitz 1993: 137).

One reason for the lack of controversies over Taiwan's anthropologists' ethnographies may be that Taiwan anthropologists have generally tended to write articles rather than ethnographies; the reward structure of Taiwan which discourages long-term projects may be the main reason for this (Cai 1986: 16-7). Such scholarly articles are less accessible than books. Nevertheless, informants cannot be unaware that articles are being published about them. An additional reason may be that anthropologists have written such sympathetic and accurate work that no one has objected, or that they have written uncontroversial descriptive or abstract work such that no one would object. (The related argument that no one could read the books is not plausible given Taiwan's high rate of literacy, or is a variant of the argument that the work is uncontroversially descriptive.) All of this suggests that the role of anthropologists is different where they are involved or directly affected by what they write. Li Yih-Yuan (1998: 66-67) argues that the switch from the study of aborigines to Chinese villages was delayed until the mid-1960s by a feeling that social scientists should be detached and objective. Given martial law and the models of social science in the United States at the time, most research was scholarly, and little of it was aimed at the general public or public policy until the late 1980s.

Another reason for lack of controversies is that anthropologists do not use the fiction of distance between observer and observed when writing ethnographies. It seems to me, though I have not tried to measure this, that there are relatively fewer quotes, anecdotes, and examples in Taiwan's ethnographic writing. Writers seem to assume their raw data is common knowledge, unless it is something distinctly local, and their writing focuses on teasing out the structure or principles of the social phenomenon. American anthropologists, on the other hand, use the device of offering vivid details to create "an authoritative authenticity" of descriptions and to persuade the reader of the soundness of their analysis (Kuklick 1997: 60). Taiwanese anthropologists more often seem to write in a textual analysis style. In fact, it is difficult to write an ethnography for an audience that knows (or thinks it knows) the culture without appearing either naive or superficial. For example, when Metcalf and Huntington extended their analysis of death rites to the United States, they said in their final chapter that, "we risked undermining what went before if our interpretations proved unconvincing or superficial" (Metcalf and Huntington 1991: 23). They concluded (in the second edition of their book) that this had indeed happened for some readers. Speaking of America, Kuklick (1997: 63) says that "In the final analysis, then, anthropology is distinguished from the other human sciences by its methodological stance of privileging witnessing." She warns that one can slip from offering documentation to "pretensions to superior (implicitly moral) individual judgment; this is a difficult position to sustain in the academy, particularly if, as is increasingly the case, the anthropologist reports not on the remote exotic but on the nearly familiar" (Kuklick 1997: 64). Thus, in the context of indigenous anthropology, the creation of authenticity through vivid description is not as useful a tactic. Taiwan's anthropologists cannot claim privilege from witnessing or claim superior judgment from having been there. With fewer vivid descriptions, fewer people are likely to read the work, or be offended by it.

Joseph Bosco

The Distinction Between Anthropology and Sociology

One apparent effect of indigenization is that the distinction between sociology and anthropology is especially strained. Maurice Freedman (1979 [1963]) wrote that most anthropologists in the United Kingdom (and he seemed to include himself) felt comfortable with the idea that they were comparative sociologists. In the United States, the four-fields approach (in which all students studied linguistics, archaeology, physical anthropology, as well as sociocultural anthropology) made anthropology more distinct from sociology. Even now that anthropology departments have been shedding their four field requirements, the distinction between sociology and anthropology seems very strong in the United States. But in Taiwan (and Hong Kong as well), where most faculty members in anthropology are specialists on Han Chinese and teach Chinese students, the difference between anthropology and sociology is institutionally important but intellectually difficult to justify. Anthropologists and sociologists in Taiwan have regularly published books together (see the chapters in Yang and Wen 1982; Hsieh and Chuang 1985; Chen, Chuang and Huang 1994). In part, this was because until 1995, the Institute of Ethnology at Taiwan's Academia Sinica housed sociologists and anthropologists (as well as social psychologists). The sociologists in 1995 split off to form an Institute of Sociology, a rare case of sociologists dividing off from anthropology rather than vice versa. The split resulted largely from institutional competition between neighboring disciplines, as happened with splits in Departments of Human Relations in the United States. A similar split has occurred at Tsing Hua University in 1998. Many foreign anthropologists who do research on urban topics or political economy have more affinity with the sociologists in Taiwan. This is also true in the PRC, where anthropology as *renleixue* was officially relegated to the study of non-Han minorities after 1952. Sociology was the study of Han Chinese. Fei Xiaotong and Lin Yaohua began in sociology but received postgraduate degrees in anthropology; Fei ended up in sociology at Beijing University and Lin in ethnology at the Central University for Nationalities, thus straddling the two fields throughout their difficult lives.

Geopolitical factors have determined whether ethnographers/anthropologists studied their own society or foreign societies; the presence of colonies, and relative internal diversity all made a difference (Schippers 1995). Countries with colonies and overseas interests have sent anthropologists overseas, while other countries' anthropologists stayed at home, especially if they had internal minorities. If the anthropologists do not only study the minorities but also the majority population, the distinction with sociology becomes less relevant.

Indigenous anthropology, which focuses on its own society, thus differs little from sociology. Almost by definition, in Europe and the United States anthropology has been the study of other cultures, albeit with the larger goal of understanding one's own culture and all humankind. Anthropology began as the study of human physical, linguistic, and sociocultural diversity. More than simply comparative sociology, it tended to be the sociology of so-called "primitive" societies, primitives being Europeans' primary "Other." It has expanded to include peasant societies,[13] urbanism, and industrial societies, but the study of "the Other" has remained central to anthropology. One cannot help but wonder if there is not something in the cross-cultural encounter that buttresses anthropology's unique analytical stance. Many anthropologists argue that familiarity and background knowledge can inhibit the abstraction necessary in anthropology.[14] Indeed, Augé (1998: 39) points out that in doing research *chez soi* (at home), "we rediscover the validity and relevance of the old methodological prescription that ethnology must be both participatory and distanced, and, behind that, the necessity of having a consistent idea of the research object." Thus, the objectification that many anthropologists criticize and seek to avoid via experimental writing may, in fact, be at the heart of the anthropological quest for knowledge. Even an indigenous anthropologist may need to take this outsider's stance to conduct research. But just as outsiders cannot rely on their native culture to provide an analytical framework but must learn a third (anthropological) perspective, so too must indigenous anthropologists find an additional perspective.

Local Voice: Sinicization

In one sense, indigenous anthropology means taking the voice of the native instead of claiming the role of an outsider. The insider/outsider distinction is always relative, of course. There are always ways in which even the indigenous anthropologist is an outsider: gender, age, birthplace, regional and ethnic differences, class, and education all can serve to make the anthropologist different from informants. But the idea of indigenous anthropology is often used to suggest that the indigenous anthropologist has a different, local, point of view. For Taiwan and China, this process is referred to as the "sinicization"[15] of the social sciences.

The indigenization of Chinese social sciences has been discussed for decades. It was an issue for Wu Wenzao, one of China's earliest anthropologists, in the 1930s, and it has been discussed in conferences in Hong Kong and Taiwan since the 1970s (see Yang and Wen 1982; Chiao 1985, Part III "Sinicization of Social Science Researches"; Cai and Xiao 1986). By the 1990s, it was less interesting as a topic: there are only two articles on indigenization (Wen 1998; Chen 1998) in Chiao (1998) a volume originating in a conference in 1993, and none at all in the volumes edited by Xu and Huang (1999) and Xu and Lin (1999), based on a conference held in 1995. In the late

1990s, however, the topic resurfaced as a hot issue on the Mainland (see particularly Rong and Xu, eds. 1998). As mentioned in the first chapter of this volume, indigenization is not an issue in the social science of all countries. What is notable about the literature on the sinicization of the Chinese social sciences is its self-consciousness, its view of indigenization as not merely the natural result of doing research in different places, but as a goal to be pursued (exceptions are Cheung 1985, and Cai and Huang 1986: 8).

As Guldin (1994: 242) has noted, "Part of the emphasis on sinicizing disciplines is clearly bound up with fierce Chinese national pride." This is especially noticeable in articles from mainland China, where scholars, at least through the 1980s, were on the defensive for practicing what had been attacked as bourgeois pseudo-science. The Chinese Communist Party viewed Marxism as the scientific truth, making all other theories and social science disciplines superfluous. Social scientists had to justify the fields of anthropology and sociology, and especially had to justify the more open empirical approach that treated Marxism as just one of many theories. The "worship" of foreign theories is often resented; this is often a veiled criticism of returned scholars who use their foreign knowledge as a source of status.[16] Thus, Zhang (1998: 23) argues that Chinese anthropologists must learn Western theories and methods but should not accept them all, without selecting those that suit China's conditions and rejecting the bad ones. He (2000: 16) writes in his abstract that "The purpose of the indigenization (*bentuhua*) of anthropology is to give free reign to the creative energy of the Chinese people and to preserve their independent self-respect and self-confidence, as well as to create theories and methods that are suitable for researching Chinese people and all ethnic societies and cultures."

In addition, however, a number of Chinese social scientists have felt that many "Western" theories did not address Chinese conditions. Fei Xiaotong has described in lectures in Hong Kong how one of his American teachers in China in the 1930s taught about labor laws that were meaningless for China. He argued that the social sciences needed modification or adaptation before they could be useful to China. Huang (1999) makes a frequently heard argument that Chinese anthropologists do not need to adopt all Western theories but only those that aid China's development, and that they should develop their own new theories. Wen (1985) argues that because the cyclical theories of change of Ibn Khaldun, Spengler, Toynbee, Sorokin and China's traditional theory of *yin* and *yang* all have cultural values embedded in them, they cannot be used across cultures. Wen (1991: 20) argues that because the concept of "the family" is different in "the West" and China, Western theories cannot be used in China. The same is true for "class," which can be translated in Chinese as both *jieji* or *dengji*. He argues that until there is a global society, there cannot be a global sociology. Chiao (1998: 4-5) similarly argues that theories developed for small, simple, and primitive societies are not likely to be useful when applied to China because of its long history and ethnic complexity (cf. Li Yih-Yuan1998: 86). Chiao urges scholars to use the comparative method, make full use of the cultural resources offered by China, and make the particular Chinese experience available to contemporary anthropology. Most of these articles imply that new theories and methods need to be developed for China, but there are also articles that speak of "indigenization" as though it were merely a matter of doing research in China (see e.g. Weng 1998: 61), and Zhou (1998: 71) argues that anthropologists should seek cultural and historical differences between the West and China and seek to interpret the Chinese tradition.

In contrast to this is a view of anthropology as an international discipline that always uses the outsider's perspective (as recognized by Zhou 1998: 68-69). At an abstract level, it can be said that what is true in Detroit is also true in Beijing (Bernard 2002: 6), but middle-range theories often need to be regionalized (Fardon 1990). It is precisely for this reason that anthropologists studying the same region, such as East Asia or Latin American, have especially fruitful relations with other scholars who study the same region.

Chinese social scientists have often emphasized the uniqueness of Chinese society and culture, arguing that Chinese scholars are better able to understand them (see Cai 1986: 9; Chuang and Chen 1982: 292). Leaving aside the issue of uniqueness, these claims are not a form of solipsism similar to the criticism of anthropology in Ireland that claims only an insider can understand the Irish (Bretell 1993: 13). Instead, they focus on the vast historical, literary, and cultural background of Chinese society that is nearly impossible for the outsider to master. The indigenous argument is simply that, with training in Western social science, a Chinese scholar can act as a bridge linking Chinese culture and global science (Xiao 1986: 7).

The emphasis on portraying China and Chinese culture as unique, though common in Chinese social science writing in both Taiwan and the mainland, is problematic. First of all, it erases any local cultural differences. Second, all cultures are unique, but only in the trivial sense that no two societies are alike. This discourse of absolute difference has been criticized (see e.g Nathan 1993: 927, 931). When scholars make comparisons, they actually find that phenomena are more important in China than elsewhere, or that they are important in different ways, not that they are unique. Thus, sinicization cannot be justified by claiming that Chinese culture is so different that it requires its own theory. But there are other problems that sinicization seeks to address, such as the selection of research problems, the universality of theory, and the influence of national culture on the scholars' evaluations of theories (i.e. intersubjectivity).

Topics and Fashions

One important aspect of indigenization (and sinicization) is the selection of research questions. Foreign anthropologists often identify foreign problems, that is, problems that are relevant in their own home country. Kapferer (1990: 298-9) has noted, for example, that Anglo-American anthropologists focus on caste in South Asia research because it is relevant for ideologies of individualism and egalitarianism. Americans' ethnographies of Taiwan have an "implied dimension" (Rynkiewich and Spradley 1975: 4) of comparison with the United States. In fact, because most of Taiwan's indigenous anthropologists have experience in the United States, and because the United States in Taiwan's popular discourse is the modern Other or even a modern and democratic ideal, they also often write in implicit comparison with United States as well. The importance of the family, small scale economic activity, and ideas of ethnic identity are also discussed with implicit American comparisons.

Thus, advocates of sinicization have examined the degree to which the research questions posed by indigenous scholars are being driven by domestic or by foreign concerns (see e.g. Xiao 1982). If local anthropologists are merely replicating research after it has become fashionable in the United States, then they risk merely being peripheral in a world anthropology dominated by American anthropology.

It has been argued that indigenous scholars are under pressure to be practical, and to contribute to national and economic development (see the chapters by Tan and Shamsul in this volume). Indigenous anthropologists typically receive funding from their state and need to show these funds are well spent. Since developing countries typically focus on economic development and nation-building, research that can support these state efforts is more likely to be supported (Guldin 1994: 232). In China, anthropology has been called upon to help in improving national character, raising "the level of 'spiritual civilization' by helping eradicate 'backward thinking,'" or adapting "China's traditional culture to the needs of modernization" (Guldin 1994: 239).

Many societies such as Taiwan and Hong Kong may have moved beyond the developing country stage so that current research funding is less closely tied to government efforts, though it is still largely funded by government. But in both societies, recent political change has led to a sharp increase in interest in local history and folklore. As we have seen, folklore and much indigenous anthropology has long been criticized as atheoretical, or as ethnography and not ethnology. But research on important social issues such as identity and ethnicity is high on the agenda of world anthropology, and indigenous anthropologists could contribute to Western understanding of these issues. The Hong Kong and Taiwan cases offer many interesting theoretical possibilities, so indigenous scholars are in a good position to exploit these cases for the edification of a broader audience. So far, however, this has not been attempted.[17]

The commitment to contributing to the country, in the Taiwan case, conflicts with broader theoretical goals. Especially since the end of martial law, scholars have published a great deal with a mind to influence domestic policy debates. This is another way in which the social sciences are indigenized, but writing for the local politicians, policy makers, and intellectual readership competes with publishing to influence international social science theory.

The interests and assumptions that drive indigenous anthropology are themselves cultural, and not simply cumulative in the simple scientific sense. I do not mean to deny that knowledge is cumulative, but mean that our interests, definitions of problems, and approaches are also affected by the historical context. Though we must recognize the fact of theoretical fashion and the importance of social context in the generation of theory, this does not make theory weaker. For example, feminist perspectives arose alongside changes in female labor-force participation but this does not in the least reduce the contribution of feminism to anthropological theory.

It is well established that anthropologists have tended to go where the state and business ties have been. But the anthropologists who went to study simple societies in the Amazon were not following business links so much as seeking a kind of exotic. In the 1960s "in Scandinavia, Great Britain or The Netherlands many students were charmed by the 'exoticism' and social criticism of the anthropological milieu" (Schippers 1995: 242-43). Anthropologists (see e.g. S. Diamond 1981) have long noted how Western societies created the notion of the primitive other to represent themselves as civilized. This seeking of the primitive and exotic is part of what has driven anthropology in the West. Such a drive seems to be lacking in the Chinese world, though it is worth considering the degree to which the study of non-Han populations along China's borders served the same purpose, historically in defining the Han Chinese (Harrell 1995) and recently in defining anthropology.

Students in Hong Kong and Taiwan know much more about the United States than American students know about Hong Kong and Taiwan, but few Chinese students seem to be interested in conducting their fieldwork in Western societies. There are no anthropologists in the Institute of European and American Studies at Academia Sinica. This is a common pattern for students from developing countries. Money has been a primary obstacle, since developing countries have limited funds and prefer research that assists their own country. For the student from a poor country, research in industrialized countries is more expensive than fieldwork back home.

Furthermore, foreign students are being steered away from doing fieldwork in industrialized countries. Foreign students are often admitted to graduate schools in developed countries to become the assistants of, and later collaborators with, professors who specialize in the students' native cultures.

Talal Asad (1982: 287) says non-Western students are rarely encouraged to carry out studies on the West because "Western academics are not as interested in how people from non-Western societies see Western cultures as they are in studying non-Western cultures for themselves." Similarly, Hsu (1973) and Kim (1990) have also commented on how their writings about the United States are ignored by American anthropologists.

Oddly, the reverse is also notable. It is striking how often English language works are cited in Chinese publications on Taiwan, while how many fewer Chinese publications are cited in English publications. Similarly, foreign and "Chinese overseas" native scholars are accorded especially high status, being invited as external examiners for programs and for talks. It goes without saying that Taiwan scholars, when they visit the United States, are not normally accorded similarly honored treatment.

Universal vs. Local Knowledge

There is a major contradiction in the arguments for the sinicization of anthropology.[18] On the one hand, the argument is made that foreigners have made errors of fact and interpretation in the study of Chinese society which natives would not make and can correct (see e.g. Chiao 1985: 327). Chinese scholars are therefore in a position to do better research. This argument accepts a common standard for research, but says that Chinese can study Chinese culture better. This argument can be seen as simply methodological; cultural background will lead persons of different cultures to see different things. While Jones (1988 [1970]) has argued that insiders and outsiders both "distort" social reality such that multiple perspectives are valuable, most recent Chinese authors have emphasized the advantages of native fieldworkers (see especially Rong and Xu 1998). Many of the authors in the sinicization discussion have sought to hold on to what they call Western social science, but use their cultural competence and add their cultural vantage point to provide a better analysis.

At the same time, however, there is another thread in the logic of indigenization that argues that foreign theories need to be modified and changed to fit the Chinese case. There is a persistent criticism that Chinese scholars rely too much on Western theoretical frameworks and analytical methods, overlooking the cultural context or prerequisite knowledge required for studying social issues in a Chinese context, and simplifying the values of Chinese (D. Zhou 1998; F. Li 1998). This argument rests heavily on interpretivism, i.e. the idea that "the concepts used to describe and explain human activity must be drawn at least in part from the social life being studied, not from scientists' theories" (Fay 1996: 114) (in this case, Western theories). A number of authors have simply argued that sinicization stems from critical theory and from hermeneutic-historical science, in which a scholar creates a relevant interpretation rather than a causal explanation as in empirical-analytical science (Kao 1982). The hermeneutic aspect of anthropology suggests anthropology cannot be universal since part of what anthropology does is translation, in Geertz' (1983) sense. Interpretation allows one to understand how, despite surface differences between peoples separated in culture by time and space, similarities are much more profound. That means that anthropology's task is to translate, not to a universal language, but to English, French, Chinese, etc. And the audience is important; writing about a foreign culture is often done with an implied comparison with the writer's and reader's culture. For example, Anglo-American "anthropologists tend to draw comparisons with 'our' culture and thus by their very language exclude the non-Western anthropologist as reader" (Brettell 1993: 14-15, citing Chilungu 1976). Similarly, Chinese authors use the equivalent of "our country" (*woguo*) or "our ancestral country" (*women de zuguo*) in Chinese language articles (e.g. Zhao 1985: 231).

But this argument has two weaknesses. First, critical theory actually shows the illusory nature of self-understandings. "Deconstruction requires social analysts to transcend the conceptual scheme of those being analyzed" and "does not use the terms of even the ideal agent's self-understanding" (Fay 1996: 131). "This critique is necessary precisely when peoples' behavior and relations derive from the illusory nature of their self-understandings; in these cases explaining the behavior and relations is inseparable from criticizing it, and explanation centrally involves forms of evaluation" (Fay 1996: 132). The second weakness is that this line of argument implicitly rejects a universal body of theory for anthropology. But I would argue instead that universalist theory needs to be combined with interpretive particularist theory. Anthropologists cannot ignore the concepts and distinctions of their subjects, but they must also "go beyond the self-understandings of those whose lives it attempts to explain, and in this way must transcend interpretivism" (Fay 1996: 119). If an interpretive approach is taken as the only approach and each society works according to its own cultural rules, then all social science generalizations are impossible. If "all social relations and behavior must be explained on the basis of a culturally specific mentality, then social science is condemned to a purely descriptive chronicling of concrete phenomena" (Little 1991: 155). Anthropology does require interpretation, but also requires explanation; the dichotomy between interpretation and causal explanation is in fact a false dualism (Fay 1996: 225). It is correct that social science is interpretive, but it is also true – and not inconsistent – that causal and critical theories that insist on going beyond agents' self-understandings are also important (Fay 1996: 133).

Thus, whereas the first line of argument says natives can do anthropology better, the second says natives need to do it differently. The issue is not simply the contradiction between the humanistic and scientific views of anthropology,[19] because the issue of sinicization is not limited to anthropology but is common to all the social sciences in the Chinese world. Even psychologists, who see themselves as thoroughly within the scientific tradition, debate the sinicization of their field (see Yang 1982; Ruan 2000). The arguments for sinicization seek to use the prestige of universal science, but also to particularize it for local needs.

This contradiction reproduces the fundamental contradiction that is behind anthropology, that is the combination of cultural relativism with an aspiration to find universal explanations. The tension between universalism and particularism has emerged repeatedly in American anthropology, in debates on "law" and whether primitives have it, and in economic anthropology's substantivism versus formalism (Collier 1997: 121). The universalist message comes from the Enlightenment and its belief in reason, while relativism stems from Romanticism and its caution against overgeneralization and facile categorization (Koepping 1995). This dualism needs to be transcended (Fay 1996: 241-2), and a dialogue between different national traditions and anthropologists of different cultural backgrounds is one of the best ways to develop the critical intersubjectivity that allows this.

Mixed in with these two arguments is an element of national pride and frustration at the peripheralization of Chinese and Taiwan anthropology by the world system of scholarship. This is often expressed in the form of urging scholars not to adopt every new foreign theory regardless of whether it fits Chinese conditions. King (1982) argues sinicization is the natural result of the development of social science. It is notable, however, how even this sophisticated treatment of the subject mentions the importance of sinicization for the self-consciousness (*zijue*), self-examination (*fanxing*), and self-confidence (*zixin*) of Chinese scholars (see e.g. King 1982: 113). Most anthropologists in Taiwan also use the prestige of science to justify their positions. Study in "the West" has been important, even essential, to obtain academic appointment in Taiwan (Taiwan has only recently had its own Ph.D. programs in anthropology, but in political science, the degrees of students who received their Ph.D.'s in Taiwan have been referred to as *tuboshi*, literally "earth doctorates," which could imply "indigenous degrees," though the implication is that they are "bumpkins' degrees"). Yet, advocates of sinicization who themselves have foreign degrees have been critical of "Western theories." The critics are thus criticizing the basis of their prestige. In mainland China, the element of national pride is especially pronounced. The revival of the social sciences in the 1980s required emphasizing the national character of social science to make it more acceptable to conservative Marxists who were opposed to "bourgeois science" (Guldin 1994: 224). Through sinicization, the social sciences could be made useful.

Nevertheless, the premise that Western social science needs to be adapted to fit Taiwan and China is mistaken (except in the sense that all abstract theory needs to be adapted to local contexts). It implies, as discussed above, that China is unique and different (in more than the trivial sense that all societies are unique), and that theories and knowledge gained elsewhere could not fit Chinese societies. In fact, however, where received theory does not fit China, the theory must be wrong. The Chinese social scientist has an opportunity to correct unwarranted assumptions of the theory. The problem has been that "sinicization" only balkanizes the research, and does not address the origin of the problem which is an excessively universalistic, often called positivistic, view of theory. For example, to some in China, the sinicization of anthropology meant basing it on Marxism-Leninism, but as Guldin (1994: 238) notes, this does not make Chinese anthropology separate but offers an opportunity to participate in a global theoretical debate. Godelier has written: "In order to exist at all anthropology had – since its very beginnings – systematically to shift its focus away from Western categories and not only from them but from any cultural reference-worlds anthropologists may belong to by birth or education, be they Chinese, Samoan or Georgian" (Godelier 1997: 5). Though this ideal is not always achieved, this is one of the traits that distinguishes good anthropology from mere description and folklore. Interpretivism, combined with causal theories in multicultural perspective, is the most promising approach for anthropology. When scholars from different origins can agree on an analysis, we have a robust theory. From this point of view then, "national" anthropologies of the kind sometimes advocated under the name of sinicization are signs of a breakdown in intersubjectivity, and of weakness in theory.

Sinicized Research

We can examine anthropological studies of two topics as examples of sinicization. Both have been singled out as examples of the sinicization of anthropology on Taiwan (see e.g. Chuang and Chen 1982: 297; Huang Yinggui 1989). One is the study of ritual spheres, *jisiquan*. Ritual spheres can be thought of as a central temple around which a region's village temples are organized to participate in rituals and processions. In Taiwan, ritual spheres often overlap with administrative townships (*xiangzhen*). The idea of ritual sphere was first suggested by a Japanese ethnographer in 1938 (see Okada 1960). His article was translated into Chinese in 1960, but it was not widely known until the early 1970s. At that time, it was found that the relationships between villages that were expressed in the ritual sphere reflected the history of immigration. It was found that neighboring ritual spheres had been formed by competing ethnic groups. In a famous article, Hsu Chia-ming showed that a group of Hakka had become Hokloized by joining with Zhangzhou Hokkien immigrants in a ritual sphere in opposition to neighboring Quanzhou Hokkien immigrants (Xu 1973). This case showed that the location of the central temple and the identity of participating villages, along with stories about the ritual, can all help uncover the history of the community.

Several Taiwan anthropologists have commented to me that foreign anthropologists who study popular religion have overlooked or ignored the concept of ritual spheres. Sangren (1987), to pick a one example, does not use the concept, though he discusses "multi-village ritual" (ibid.: 83-86). Some Taiwanese anthropologists view ritual spheres as an indigenous concept which makes a significant contribution. Some anthropologists have, however, criticized recent efforts to expand and build on the concept. Huang (1989: 232) is critical of Lin Meirong's (1988) thesis that belief spheres (worshippers who go to temples thought to be especially efficacious to them personally) are replacing ritual spheres. He argues this contrast creates confusion because ritual spheres were intended to solve questions of social structure, not questions of religious belief or organization. Wang (1991: 8) similarly says that extending the concept only creates confusion, since its role was in reconstructing the history of settlement, not for studying religion. Because the concept of ritual spheres is merely descriptive (they reflect ethnic origins and the history of settlement, but do not answer any questions), some have argued that it is not really a theory, but at best an inductive framework for local research.

The idea of ritual spheres is often contrasted with Skinner's marketing structure (Skinner 1964; 1965a; 1965b). Skinner's geographic approach was applied by Crissman (1972; 1981) to Taiwan, where he confirmed the approach but found certain differences from the ideal pattern. Sangren (1987), in his study of Ta-ch'i, is able to describe the operation of a "ritual sphere" without using the concept or term. He argues that "Skinner is essentially correct in arguing that patterns of marketing behavior and social organization are correlated, but he may overestimate the causal priority of marketing logic in the historical process through which this correlation is achieved" (ibid.: 16). In particular, Sangren emphasizes the way ritual organizations – territorial cults and pilgrimages – established at settlement have influenced community development (ibid.). Thus, Wang (1991: 7) notes that it is cultural features that are captured by the concept of ritual spheres that disturb Skinner's purely utilitarian economic marketing model in Taiwan. Skinner's model argued for the standard marketing community as a culture-bearing unit (Skinner 1964: 32). He argued that this is the unit of endogamy, and that the major temple of the town served the same standard marketing community (ibid.: 38). He further notes that the members of the temple committee come not just from the town but from throughout the standard marketing community. He thus argued for the overlap of economic, political and religious spheres. But elsewhere, Skinner notes that local organization above the village, including the jurisdiction of particular deities and temples, was more complex and varied than he had anticipated (Skinner 1977: 721). It is important to test the model, as Sangren has done, to check how much it fits in particular cases, but it bears repeating that Sangren found the high degree of overlap in social, ritual, political and economic systems that the model would predict. Though some cultural features such as ethnic difference (as well as geographic features) can disturb the model, this does not in itself undermine the model. Indeed, the Hokloization of the Hakka in the case described by Hsu (1973) is an illustration of the model's idea that the standard marketing community is indeed the culture-bearing unit, and helps explain why the minority Hakka became Hokloized.

In teaching Skinner's theory, I have found Taiwanese and PRC students to be put off initially by its abstract nature, its formalism (as an economic model), and what they view as its functionalism. Yet, Skinner's theory has been enormously influential in anthropology (Smith 1976) as well as in sinology. Little (1989: 68-104) selected it as a case study, one of four major theories or debates in Chinese studies for his study of the philosophy of social science. On the other hand, what is striking about numerous articles on ritual spheres is the degree to which they merely describe the rituals and village temples involved in each case (but see more recently Lin Meirong 1999). The articles focus on social organization and religion; they do not consider religion's articulation with marketing networks, administration and politics. Nor is there any analysis of who organizes and participates in these processions, or the rivalries expressed and mediated through processions, and the other meanings of processions. There is no examination of their links to local politics and the capitalist transformation of the island comparable to the work of Duara (1988: 40) who builds on Skinner's work to develop his idea of a "cultural nexus." Nor, until recently, has there been any focus on the symbolism and meaning of the troupes that perform in the processions. The studies are primarily descriptive, and do not cite Skinner's work. However, Sangren did not cite work on ritual spheres either.

As noted above, the term "*jisiquan*" or ritual sphere is not a native term used by Taiwanese informants but is a Japanese term coined by Okada (1960 [1937]). The term is in fact merely descriptive, in contrast to the term "standard marketing community" that represents a model of a regional system based primarily on transport cost. One could question whether, despite its use by some indigenous scholars, it is really an indigenous concept, and whether it is really a key concept.

The second example that has been singled out as an example of sinicization is the writing on kinship by Chen Chi-nan (see especially Chen 1990; Chuang and Chen 1982). Chen's 1990 article on the lineage and its segment, the *fang*, is wide ranging, and he corrects what he feels are the errors of Western anthropologists in the study of Chinese kinship. His main argument is that father-son filiation is the kernel of Chinese kinship; it is the concept and relationship on which the system is based and from which its rules naturally flow. From this, he argues that the functionalist interpretation of Chinese lineage and kinship used by Maurice Freedman and most Western anthropologists overemphasizes property relations and makes kinship a secondary phenomenon. He compares his position to that of Meyer Fortes, who described the kinship system of the Tallensi, and argues that Freedman and other anthropologists are following Peter Worsley's critique (see e.g. Worsley 1956), which argued that kinship depended on the distribution of fertile land. Huang Ying-kuei, in his review of recent anthropology on Taiwan, notes that Chen is trying to understand local people's worldview, not the phenomenon itself; he says Chen is providing the missing the link between ancestor worship and property (Huang Yinggui 1989: 231). But Huang is also critical of Chen's article, saying it cannot offer a theory of Chinese kinship, only a critique of functionalist research. Though Huang (1989: 230) praises Chen's article as helping to make further progress in research on the Chinese lineage, he says these distinctions are much like "Firth's theoretical membership vs. operational membership, or Sahlins' ideology vs. composition [sic] of descent groups, or Scheffler's descent category (or construct) vs. descent group, which have long been common knowledge in anthropology. This not only makes one feel that they've arrived too late, but also makes one wonder whether China kinship studies have any theoretical contribution to make to general anthropology." Huang concludes that it seems it will be a long time before research on Chinese kinship can make a contribution to anthropological theory. Indeed, the father-son relationship Chen emphasizes is only the cultural ideology. Chen takes an idealist position, where ideas translate directly into action; most of his discussion is at the abstract, ideal level, not a discussion of actual people's behavior. We never see people manipulating or disputing cultural rules. Furthermore, anthropologists have emphasized functionalist factors to understand why in some places lineages are larger and more powerful than in others. An idealist theory cannot address regional variations in practices. Harrell (1976) showed that families must make offerings to any ancestors from whom they inherit property, and in some unusual cases families might have to make offerings to as many as three families if they have received property from multiple sources. This shows that in some cases, rather than being dominant, the ideology of kinship is manipulated and used to legitimize property relations.

In many ways, Chen's argument goes against the trend of views in American and British anthropology and sinology. Kuper (1982) has argued for the dissolution of lineage theory, arguing that lineage is an ideology. Instead of offering an alternative that lays bare this ideology, Chen merely systematizes the ideology. Sangren (1984) has undermined the importance of lineages by arguing that they are merely one form of a general type of Chinese association. Historian David Faure (1989) has argued that the lineage in South China is a cultural invention of the late Ming, and the authors in the volume edited by Ebrey and Watson (1986) show for various parts of China how the lineage was created by the local elite turning inward, using a new ideology by Zhu Xi at a time when state power declined. This shows that the idea that the lineage is the natural result of filiation, which is part of the kinship ideology and which Chen takes as abstract principle, does not fit the historical data on the variations in and between lineages. While we learn something about the principles and ideology of lineages from Chen's work, we cannot begin to analyze the differential presence and strength of lineages in different parts of Taiwan and China using only this viewpoint.

Thus, in the cases of the ritual spheres and the study of kinship and lineage, both prominent examples of the indigenization of anthropological theory, there are weaknesses in the indigenous theory, which prevent it from becoming influential. These are the most widely cited examples of indigenous theories being supposedly ignored. Neither theory has inspired major articles in English to publicize them. Furthermore, as I have noted, both focus heavily on cultural particulars rather than on cross-cultural patterns. These indigenous theories are thus of interest to area specialists, but do not have the explanatory or analytical leverage of major anthropological theories, useful within the discipline as a whole.

Indigenization and Globalization

One often hears discussions in Chinese of "Western anthropology" as though it was a unitary thing, but it is worth remembering that not only are there important differences between American, French, and British anthropologies, but differences within each nation can also be significant. We should expect differences in the anthropologies of other countries to be at least as great as those between the United States, France, and the United Kingdom (Colson 1982: 259). These differences in anthropologies are to be expected since humans are cultural animals and anthropology is a cultural product. But it is worth noting that within these three traditions there has been important cross-fertilization. Structural functionalism and lineage theory entered American anthropology – especially in China studies via Maurice Freedman's influence – and French structuralism and structural Marxism became American and British fashions as well. Thus, though theories arose and became predominant in separate national traditions, these theories' influences spilled over to other nations' anthropologists.

But the increasing integration of anthropology threatens to have the agenda set more tightly by the core countries. From Taiwan's point of view, Taiwan imports American theories (because Taiwan's academic as well as economic ties have been overwhelmingly with the United States) and exports very little of its indigenous anthropology. The reasons for this are many, as we have seen above, but the relative difference in resources that marked American researchers as superior disappeared in the late 1980s and is no longer a factor.

Language is an obstacle; many Taiwanese scholars, even those with American doctorates, have difficulty writing and publishing in English (much as most American anthropologists of Taiwan find it difficult to write in Chinese for publication). Furthermore, the Taiwanese face the same trade-off as discussed in other chapters in this volume: do they publish in English for an international audience of anthropologists (few of whom are interested in Taiwan) or do they write for local impact, where the audience is larger and eager for information and analysis about Taiwan? This situation is discussed as a "world-system" by Mathews and Kuwayama (this volume), but I feel it is more a prestige hierarchy. A "world system" sounds as though it is based on differential wealth or access to resources. The wealth of the United Kingdom, and later the United States, has made English the *lingua franca* of academia. In the postwar period, the prestige hierarchy developed largely because of differences in resources available for research and travel which allowed American scholars to travel more, to have better access to new books and theories, and to hire assistants in Taiwan. This was also reinforced by the flow of the most talented scholars to most prestigious jobs. This has changed, now, so that funds and jobs are also available and attractive in Taiwan, so current foreign researchers in Taiwan use more collaborative research programs.

"Indigenous" is often taken to mean autonomous or national (Cheah 1996), but it is important to remember that in the case of science, there are advantages to communication and cross-fertilization. The problem for Taiwan anthropology is that the communication is one-sided. Far more English language publications are cited in Chinese articles than vice versa. In part this is similar to the citation patterns within the United States, with scholars reading and citing the work of scholars at prestigious universities. Furthermore, it is a well-known pattern that articles in Chinese must cite English language sources on the subject, but it is not as essential for English-language articles to cite Chinese-language articles on the subject. English-language articles thus become sacred scriptures, and some Taiwan scholars feel foreign scholars get credit (via publications and citations) for pointing out the most obvious cultural phenomena – what to locals is stating the obvious.

Collaboration

Indigenous anthropology has raised the standards of research (Colson 1982: 259-61).[20] The standards for language knowledge and for knowledge of historical and political background are much higher today than in the days when anthropologists wrote for the few other Western specialists. Indigenous anthropologists have examined the works of foreign anthropologists and often offered trenchant critiques.

Some anthropologists have called for scholarly collaboration between indigenous and foreign anthropologists, some even making a political statement of it. Collaboration at first sight appears to abandon the Malinowskian ideal of participant observation. Instead of relying on personal experience to discover cultural ideas and rules, a collaborator can become a crutch, like relying on travelers and missionaries. On the other hand, it is also true that anthropology has had an artificial assumption that field assistants should be invisible, and that by working independently the anthropologist is getting at "real truth" of the culture "out there" (Gottlieb 1995: 22). Now that scholars have highlighted the degree to which ethnography is created, and created through the interaction with informants, it makes sense to work with a collaborator more fully skilled in the local culture.

But though I am all in favor of cross-cultural communication, I wonder what outside scholars bring to the research partnership. Are they the "experts" in theory who team up with the specialists in local culture? Collaboration might seem to be a way of hiding the outsider's weaknesses as a researcher. Granted that it is difficult for the foreign researcher to have command over Taiwan's historical and textural traditions, not to mention the multiple languages necessary for fieldwork, is the native scholar not just a glorified assistant? In order for this collaboration to be of interest to Taiwanese scholars now that funding is equally available in Taiwan, a project needs to be truly collaborative and of benefit to both scholars.

To some degree, the distinction between what I have called native anthropology and indigenous anthropology is decreasing in importance as globalization creates educated elites who have a common global culture. Even if a book about Taiwan or China is written in English, there are enough people around able to read English to make sure that it is discussed by the "natives," and sometimes by the subjects and informants themselves. But the fact that the book is in a foreign language makes its intended audience clear, and limits its influence in the society which it describes. And differences in language are not symmetrical: few Chinese books are reviewed or cited in English language journals, demonstrating and reinforcing the prestige hierarchy.

Conclusions

To explore the issue of indigenization, specifically the overwhelming pattern of Taiwanese anthropologists studying their own society, I have drawn too sharp a boundary between indigenous and other anthropologists. Indigenous Taiwanese anthropologists have often lived for up to a decade or more overseas, have colleagues in their departments who are Americans, meet with visiting Taiwanese anthropologists based in the United States (what I have called native anthropologists), and can watch the ABC Evening News with Peter Jennings from New York on cable television (albeit in the morning Taipei time). It can be a mistake to think of indigenous anthropologists as a clear "other." Yet, I think the preponderance of anthropologists studying their own cultures has an effect on the kind of research conducted. Just as important as the tendency of insiders and outsiders to see different things when they conduct fieldwork is that the writing style must be different when anthropologists write for an audience that includes their informants. Studying the range of human cultures is at the center of the anthropological project, and indigenous anthropologists have some advantages as well as challenges in studying their own culture. The conversation among anthropologists in Taiwan can develop in such a way that it is of interest to anthropology in general, but while it needs to be still based on ethnography, it must also be more theoretical, without simply reflecting American fashions.

The ideal of a global, universal anthropology ignores the different audiences, languages, institutional incentives, prestige hierarchies, and social contexts that affect scholarship. If American anthropologists do not read Chinese works published in Taiwan, how can a Taiwanese critique be incorporated into general theory? Whose job is it to make this Chinese-language research available "to the discipline," i.e. available to others in English and other languages? Must Taiwanese scholars publish in English, or should English-speaking scholars bring the more important work to the attention of their domestic audience? Language is an issue, but not the main factor. Many assume that Chinese authors should publish in English if they want a broader audience. Indeed, until recently it was an assumed rule of thumb that the best research from Taiwan would be published in English. The prestige of English as the language of science is also shown by recent efforts of Academia Sinica to facilitate the translation of articles into English. I would argue that it is in everyone's interest for important research to be more widely known, but that Taiwanese anthropologists must make their research on Taiwan of interest beyond Taiwan for it to be worth translating. So far, the most prominent indigenous theory has not been of sufficiently broad interest to warrant translation and publication. Most obviously, Taiwan can offer much insight on the issue of nationalism and identity, and this is an issue of tremendous importance to the public on the island. Yet research on this issue has not had much impact on anthropology.

Most national traditions of anthropology are merely local conversations, often on topics of local interest. The United States is no different, but its size, economic strength, and international interests mean that its anthropologists are more numerous and have a disproportionate influence on the discipline internationally. The Taiwan case (and more recently that of China) suggests that indigenization may operate as a form of defensive nationalism, at odds with the cosmopolitan promise of anthropology, even if not with the reality. The solution to this problem is not for foreign anthropologists to emphasize the local tradition, but to transcend that tradition, learning from multiple traditions and contributing to a global conversation. As M. Wang (1998: 115) has noted, it is important to start from the native viewpoint, but if one stops there one ends up with a "reverse Orientalism" and a xenophobic bias. Srinivas has written that one's own culture should be studied by both insiders and outsiders. "Given that anthropologists have no choice but to study other cultures through the prisms of their own, the need for anthropologists from at least two different cultures to study a single culture becomes a necessity. Anthropology has reached a state when such studies ought to be undertaken. The clash of multiple subjectivities would, to my mind, be better than a single subjectivity, whether that of insider or outsider" (Srinivas 1997: 23). Godelier (1995) has argued that anthropology must create its own culture, one that transcends individual cultures. Though I suspect this is impossible to do since scholars are shaped by national cultures, media, and funding priorities, Srinivas is right that the only way to advance the discipline is by striving for this unreachable goal.

Notes

1 This chapter is a revised version of a paper first presented at the panel on "The Indigenization of Anthropology in East and Southeast Asia" at the 14th International Congress of Ethnological and Anthropological Sciences in Williamsburg, Virginia, 30 July 1998. Parts were previously published in Bosco (1998).

2 Despite the difficulties in identifying indigenous from nonindigenous anthropologists in some interesting borderline cases (see e.g Strathern 1987; Narayan 1993: 678), it is still the case in Taiwan that there is a recognized difference between foreign born non-Chinese anthropologists and anthropologists born and raised in Taiwan and China.

3 These figures are based on staff as of the fall of 2001.

4 Anthropologists should not self-flagellate themselves on this; despite anthropology's origins as a "child of Imperialism," "anthropology in 1940 [and for several decades after-JB] was the only academic subject in which the history and sociology of non-European peoples were the primary focus of interest" (Drucker-Brown 1982: 25).

5 Oddly, even in the Institute of European and American Studies, at least half of the social scientists publish on Taiwan; see www.ea.sinica.edu.tw/index (accessed 2 February 2002).

6 There is other work by missionaries and businessmen that has anthropological qualities and is ethnographically interesting, but does not fit well under the designation of "anthropology." Some of this was carried out before the Japanese work, while some was contemporaneous with it (e.g. e.g. Campbell 1915 and Davidson 1902).

7 It is worth noting that though research on Taiwan's Chinese groups seems indigenous from our perspective today, it was probably not

viewed so at the time. It has been noted that one of the high points of social research in China came about as the result of field research projects carried out by anthropologists who moved to free areas of China during World War II (Cheng and So 1983). The anthropologists who came to Taiwan also saw themselves, at least initially, as temporarily in a remote part of China. Cultural differences (especially Minnan language and Japanese colonialism) were enough to make research in a Taiwanese village not indigenous when compared to research by Fei Xiaotong in a village near his natal home, for example. In any case, the early anthropologists chose to study aborigines.

8 This may be changing, but as Donham (2000: 179) notes, many American anthropologists write about the United States rather than do a second field project abroad, "but perhaps the 'easiest' solution is to write about, not do, ethnography or to take up theory or even history." Of course, this volume might suggest something similar is taking place in Asia as well, but I think interest in indigenization is more driven by concerns of peripheralization.

9 Chen Chi-lu (1989: 12) seems to accept the notion that anthropologists study the exotic when he suggests part of the reason for the shift in research from aborigines to Han society is that aboriginal societies have become more "open" and are therefore less "exotic." Yet, he also sees the shift towards research on one's own culture and society as universal.

10 See Chiu (1999) for a discussion of the way anthropology supported the conceptual framework for state and Han domination of aborigines in Taiwan.

11 See e.g. F.L.K. Hsu's criticism (cited in Guldin 1994: 244 n. 9) that Taiwan and PRC anthropology is just ethnography, not ethnology. A similar criticism has been directed at Dutch anthropology (Kloos 1991: 22). Note that here the term ethnology is used to mean the systematic or scientific study of culture as opposed to the mere recording of cultures in ethnographies. According to Vermeulen and Roldán (1995), mentioned above, the terms do not have this distinction in Eastern Europe.

12 For example Hu Tai-li wrote her Ph.D. thesis and first book (Hu 1984) on the political economy of development, but has written mostly on identity and visual anthropology since. There are exceptions, but most political economy is being done by others, e.g. the sociologists at Academia Sinica who split off from the Institute of Ethnology to form the Institute of Sociology.

13 One of the reasons Malinowski was enthusiastic about Fei Xiaotong's thesis *Peasant Life in China* was that it helped expand anthropology

from the study of simple societies to peasant societies. See Kearney (1996: 69) for a critique of the way the peasant was created as a category to objectivize farmers or to contain their disruptive potential.

14 I have heard stories of leading American anthropologists warning their students against spending too long in the field, suggesting "excessive familiarity" is viewed as a danger to theorizing that can afflict not just indigenous and native anthropologists.

15 In this section, I often speak of social sciences instead of anthropology generally because many of the articles published by the Institute of Ethnology or written by its members are not about anthropology alone but deal with the social sciences generally.

16 See for example the criticism of Wang Mingming's writing style in Cao Shuji (1998). Wang is criticized for citing foreigners even for common knowledge. For a Taiwan example, N. Lin (1986: 34-6) criticized sociologists for blindly borrowing Western methods.

17 Chen Chung-min, Chuang Ying-chang and Huang Shu-min (1994) is an English language exception, but two of the editors are based in North America, and only the editors' introduction has a contribution by an indigenous anthropologist. Another important exception is work by Chun (e.g. Chun 1994), but he is American, though based in Taiwan.

18 This contradiction can be found even within single articles, as in Zhou (1998) and Z.L. Wang (1998) who argue for engaging with "Western" science after arguing for creating Chinese theories and urging scholars not to blindly copy Western ideas.

19 Note also that if we define anthropology as a humanistic rather than a scientific discipline, there is less reason to seek and promote cross-cultural exchanges, as each national anthropology can engage in its own independent discussion. It is the expectation of achieving a more universalistic understanding that leads some anthropologists to seek international dialogue and exchange.

20 Colson refers to this as "standards of methodology," but I am not sure that indigenous scholars are, strictly speaking, using more sophisticated or appropriate methods.

References

Allen, Charlotte. 1997. "Spies like us: When sociologists deceive their subjects," *Lingua Franca* 7 (9): 30-39.

Anderson, Benedict R. 1983. *Imagined Communities: Reflections on the Origin and Spread of Nationalism*. London: Verso.

Arkush, David R. 1995. "Review of *Occidentalism* edited by James G. Carrier, and *Occidentalism* by Xiaomei Chen," *Journal of Asian Studies* 56 (1): 144-47.

Asad, Talal. 1982. "A comment on the idea of non-Western anthropology," pp. 284-87 in *Indigenous Anthropology in non-Western countries*, ed. Hussein. Fahim. Durham, N.C.: Carolina Academic Press.

Asad, Talal, ed. 1973. *Anthropology and the Colonial encounter*. London: Ithaca Press.

Augé, Marc. 1998. *A Sense for the Other: The Timeliness and Relevance of Anthropology*. Stanford: Stanford University Press.

Barley, Nigel. 1983. *The Innocent Anthropologist: Notes from a Mud Hut*. London: British Museum Publications.

Barton, Roy Franklin. 1969 [1919]. *Ifugao Law*. Berkeley: University of California Press.

Basham, Richard. 1978. *Urban anthropology: The Cross-Cultural Study of Complex Societies*. Palo Alto, Calif.: Mayfield Publishing.

Bendix, Reinhard. 1997. *In Search of Authenticity: The Formation of Folklore Studies*. London: University of Wisconsin Press.

Bennett, John W. 1969. *Northern Plainsman: Adaptive Strategies and Agrarian Life*. Arlington Heights, Ill.: AHM Publishing Corporation.

Bernard, H. Russell. 2002. *Research Methods in Anthropology: Qualitative and Quantitative Methods*. 3d ed. Walnut Creek, Calif.: Alta Mira Press.

Bosco, Joseph. 1998. "Anthropology among the natives: The indigenization of Chinese anthropology," pp. 22-44 in *On the South China Track: Perspectives on Anthropological Research and Teaching*, ed. Sidney C.H. Cheung. Hong Kong: Hong Kong Institute of Asia-Pacific Studies, The Chinese University of Hong Kong.

Brettel, Caroline B., ed. 1993. *When They Read What We Write: The Politics of Ethnography*. Westport, Conn.: Bergin & Garvey.

Bruner, Edward. 1999. "Return to Sumatra: 1957, 1997," *American Ethnologist* 26 (2): 461-77.

Cai Yongmei. 1986. "Xulun" [Introduction], pp. 9-27, in *Shehuixue Zhongguohua* [Sinicization of sociology], eds. Cai Yongmei and Xiao Xinhuang. Taipei: Juliu Tushu.

Cai Yongmei and Xiao Xinhuang, eds. 1986. *Shehuixue Zhongguohua* [Sinicization of sociology]. Taipei: Juliu Tushu.

Cai Zongxun. 1997. *Shuo zhuang tou* [Speaking of the Village]. Xingang, Taiwan: Xingang Wenjiao Jijinhui.

Campbell, William. 1915. *Sketches from Formosa*. London: Marshall Brothers.

Cao Shuji. 1998. "Xueshu yanjiu yu xueshu zhuzuo de pingshen — ping Wang Mingming *Cunluo shiyezhong de wenyua yu quanli—Min Tai sancun wulun*" [Academic research and academic publishing: On Wang Mingming's *Culture and power as viewed from the village: Five papers* on three villages in Fujian and Taiwan], *Wenhuibao* (Nov. 13): 8.

Cheah, Boon Kheng. 1996. "Writing indigenous history in Malaysia: A survey on approaches and problems," *Crossroads* 10 (2): 33-81.

Chen, Chi-lu. 1989. "The development of anthropology in Taiwan during the past four decades," pp. 1-14 in *Anthropological studies of the Taiwan area: Accomplishments and prospects,* eds. Chang Kwang-chih, Li Kwang-chou, Arthur P. Wolf, and Yin Chien-chung. Taipei: Department of Anthropology, National Taiwan University.

Chen, Chung-min, Chuang Ying-chang, and Huang Shu-min, eds. 1994. *Ethnicity in Taiwan: Social, Historical, and Cultural Perspectives.* Taipei, Taiwan: Institute of Ethnology, Academia Sinica.

Chen Chi-nan. 1990. "'Fang' yu chuantong zhongguo jiazu zhidu: Jianlun xifang renleixue de zhongguo jiazu yanjiu" [*Fang* and the traditional Chinese lineage system: On Western anthropology's research on Chinese lineage], pp. 129-213 in *Jiazu yu shehui* [Lineage and society], ed. Chen Chi-nan. Taipei: Lianjing,.

Chen Haiwen. 1998. "Lun shehuixue zhi chuantong yu zhongguohua: houshe shehuixue zhaji zhi san" [On sociology's tradition and sinicization: notes on metasociology, part three]," pp. 207-36 in *Shehuixue, renleixue zai zhongguo de fazhan* [Sociology and anthropology in China's development], ed. Chiao Chien. Hong Kong: New Asia College, The Chinese University of Hong Kong.

Cheng, L., and A. So. 1983. "The re-establishment of sociology in the PRC: Toward the sinification of Marxian sociology," *Annual Reviews in Sociology* 9: 471-98.

Cheung Tak-sing. 1985. "Shehuixue yanjiu chengguo de leijixing yu bentuhua" [The accumulability of research findings in sociology and its implications for indigenization], pp. 265-76 in *Xiandaihua yu zhongguo wenhua yantaohui lunwen huibian* [Proceedings of the conference on modernization and Chinese culture], eds. Chiao Chien et al. Hong Kong: Faculty of Social Science and Institute of Social Studies, The Chinese University of Hong Kong.

Chiao Chien, ed. 1998. *Shehuixue, renleixue zai zhongguo de fazhan* [Sociology and anthropology in China's development]. Hong Kong: New Asia College, The Chinese University of Hong Kong.

Chiao Chien. 1998. "Difficulty and prospects of anthropological development in China," pp. 1-7 in *Renleixue bentuhua zai Zhongguo* [Nativization of anthropology in China], eds. Rong Shixing and Xu Jieshun. Nanning: Guangxi University for Nationalities.

Chiao Chien. 1985. "Jianli zhongguoren jici xingwei moshi chiyi" [Model building in the study of Chinese strategic behavior: Some proposals], pp. 327-35 in *Xiandaihua yu zhongguo wenhua yantaohui lunwen huibian* [Proceedings of the conferences on modernization in Chinese culture], eds.

Chiao Chien et. al. Hong Kong: Faculty of Social Science and Institute of Social Studies, The Chinese University of Hong Kong.

Chilungu, Simeon W. 1976. "Issues in the ethics of research method: An interpretation of the Anglo-American perspective," *Current Anthropology* 17 (3): 457-81.

Chiu, Fred Y. 1997. "Riben zhimindi renleixue 'taiwan yenjiu' de chongdu yu zaipingjia" [Re-reading the 'Taiwan studies' of a Japanese colonial anthropology: A proposal for re-evaluation]," *Taiwan shehui yenjiu jikan* [Taiwan: A radical quarterly in social studies] 28: 145-74.

Chiu, Fred. Y. 1999. "Nationalist anthropology in Taiwan 1945-1996: A reflexive survey," pp. 93-112 in *Anthropology and Colonialism in Asia and Oceania*, eds. Jan van Bremen and A. Shimizu. Richmond, Surrey: Curzon Press.

Chuang Ying-chang and Chen Chi-nan. 1982. "Xianjieduan Zhongguo shehui jiegou yanjiu de jiantao [A Discussion of Current Research on Chinese Social Structure: Some Thoughts from Taiwan Research]," pp. 281-309 in *Shehui ji xingwei kexue yanjiu de zhongguohua* [The sinicization of social and behavioral science research in China], eds. Yang Kuo-shu and Wen Chong-I. Nankang, Taipei: Institute of Ethnology, Academia Sinica (Monograph Series B, no. 10).

Chuang, Ying-chang, and Arthur P. Wolf. 1995. "Marriage in Taiwan, 1881-1905: An example of regional diversity," *Journal of Asian Studies* 54 (3): 781-95.

Chun, Allen. 1994. "From nationalism to nationalizing: Cultural imagination and state formation in postwar Taiwan," *Australian Journal of Chinese Affairs* 31: 49-69.

Collier, Jane F. 1997. "The waxing and waning of 'subfields' in North American sociocultural anthropology," pp. 117-30 in *Anthropological Locations: Boundaries and Grounds of a Field Science*, eds. Akhil Gupta, and James Ferguson. Berkeley: University of California Press.

Colson, Elizabeth. 1982. "Anthropological dilemmas in the late twentieth century," pp. 253-262 in *Indigenous Anthropology in Non-Western Countries*, ed. Hussein Fahim. Durham, NC: Carolina Academic Press.

Crissman, Lawrence W. 1972. "Marketing on the Changhua Plain, Taiwan," pp. 215-259 in *Economic Organization in Chinese Society*, ed. W.E. Willmott. Stanford: Stanford University Press.

Crissman, Lawrence W. 1981. "The structure of local and regional systems," pp. 89-124 in *The Anthropology of Taiwanese Society*, eds. Emily. M. Ahern and Hill Gates. Stanford: Stanford University Press.

Davidson, James. W. 1902. *The Island of Formosa: Past and Present*. London: Macmillan & Co.

Davis, Dona L. 1993. "Unintended consequences: The myth of 'the return' in anthropological fieldwork," pp. 27-35 in *When They Read What We Write:*

The Politics of Ethnography, ed. Caroline B. Brettell. Westport, Conn.: Bergin & Garvey.

Diamond, Stanley. 1981. *In Search of the Primitive: A Critique of Civilization*. New Brunswick, N.J.: Transaction, Inc.

Donham, Donald. 2000. "Comments [on Mintz' "Sows' ears and silver linings"]," *Current Anthropology* 41 (2): 178-80.

Dorfman, John. 1997. "That's all, folks!" *Lingua Franca* 7 (8): 8-9.

Drucker-Brown, Susan. 1982. "Malinowski in Mexico: Introduction," pp. 3-52 in *Malinowski in Mexico: The Economics of a Mexican Market System*, Malinowski, Bronislaw and Julio de la Fuente. London: Routledge and Kegan Paul.

Duara, Prasenjit 1988. *Culture, Power, and the State: Rural North China, 1900-1942*. Stanford: Stanford University Press.

Ebrey, Patricia Buckley and James L. Watson, eds. 1986. *Kinship Organization in Late Imperial China, 1000-1940*. Berkeley: University of California Press.

Fardon, Richard. 1990. "Localizing strategies: The regionalization of ethnographic accounts," pp. 1-35 in *Localizing Strategies: Regional Traditions of Ethnographic Writing*, ed. Richard. Fardon. Edinburgh: Scottish Academic Press; Washington D.C.: Smithsonian Institution Press.

Faure, David. 1989. "The lineage as a cultural invention: The case of the Pearl River delta," *Modern China* 15 (1): 4-36.

Fay, Brian. 1996. *Contemporary Philosophy of Social Science: A Multicultural Approach*. Oxford: Blackwell.

Freedman, Maurice. 1979. "A Chinese phase in social anthropology," pp. 380-97 in *The Study of Chinese Society: Essays by Maurice Freedman*. Stanford: Stanford University Press.

Geertz, Clifford. 1983. *Local Knowledge: Further Essays in Interpretive Anthropology*. New York: Basic Books, Inc.

Godelier, Maurice. 1995. "Is social anthropology indissolubly linked to the West, its birthplace?" *International Social Science Journal* 143: 141-58.

Godelier, Maurice. 1997. "American anthropology as seen from France," *Anthropology Today* 13 (1): 3-5.

Gold, Thomas B. 1986. *State and Society in the Taiwan Miracle*. Armonk, N.Y.: M.E. Sharpe.

Gold, Thomas B. 1988. "Colonial origins of Taiwanese capitalism," pp. 101-17 in *Contending Approaches to the Political Economy of Taiwan*, eds. Edwin A. Winckler and Susan Greenhalgh. Armonk, N.Y.: M.E. Sharpe.

Gottlieb, Alma. 1995. "Beyond the lonely anthropologist: Collaboration in research and writing," *American Anthropologist* 97 (1): 21-26.

Guldin, Gregory Eliyu. 1994. *The Saga of Anthropology in China: From Malinowski to Moscow to Mao*. Armonk, N.Y.: M.E. Sharpe.

Gupta, Akhil, and James Ferguson, eds. 1997. *Anthropological Locations:*

Boundaries and Grounds of a Field Science. Berkeley: University of California Press.

Handler, Richard. 1993. "Fieldwork in Quebec, scholarly reviews, and anthropological dialogs," pp. 67-74 in *When They Read What We Write: The Politics of Ethnography,* ed. C. B. Brettell. Westport, Conn.: Bergin & Garvey.

Hannerz, Ulf. 1996. *Transnational Connections: Culture, People, Places.* London: Routledge.

Harrell, Stevan. 1976. "Ancestors in the home," in *Ancestors,* ed. William H. Newell. The Hague: Mouton.

Harrell, Stevan, ed. 1995. *Cultural Encounters on China's Ethnic Frontiers.* Seattle: University of Washington Press.

He Xingliang. 2000. "Lun renleixue de bentuhua yu guojihua" [On the nativization and internationalization of anthropology], *Guangxi Minzu Xueyuan Xuebao* [Journal of Guangxi University for Nationalities] 22 (1): 6-26.

Herzfeld, Michael. 2001. *Anthropology: Theoretical Practice in Culture and Society.* Malden, Mass: Blackwell.

Horwitz, Richard P. 1993. "Just stories of ethnographic authority" pp. 131-43 in *When They Read What We Write: The Politics of Ethnography,* Caroline B. Brettell. ed. Westport, Conn.: Bergin & Garvey.

Hsieh, Jih-chang, and Ying-chang Chuang, eds. 1985. *The Chinese Family and its Ritual Behavior.* Nankang, Taipei: Institute of Ethnology, Academia Sinica.

Hsu, Francis. L. K. 1973. "Prejudice and its intellectual effect in American anthropology: An ethnographic report," *American Anthropologist* 75 (1): 1-19.

Hu, Tai-li. 1984. *My Mother-in-Law's Village: Rural Industrialization and Change in Taiwan.* Taipei: Academia Sinica, Institute of Ethnology.

Huang Shupin. 1999. "Renleixue zhongguohua de lilun, shijian he rencai" [Anthropology in China [sic]: Theory, practice, personal talents], *Guangxi minzu xueyuan xuebao* [Journal of Guangxi University for Nationalities] 21 (4): 17-20.

Huang Yinggui [Huang Ying-kuei]. 1983. "Guangfu hou Taiwan diqu renleixue yanjiu de fazhan. " [The development of anthropological study in Taiwan, 1945-1982], in *Zhongyang yanjiu yuan minzuxue yanjiusuo jikan* [Bulletin of the Institute of Ethnology, Academia Sinica] 55: 105-146.

Huang Yinggui. 1989. "Jin liunian lai Taiwan diqu chuban renleixue lunzhuo jianjie" [Introduction to anthropological works published in the Taiwan area in the past six years], *Hanxue yanjiu tongxun* [Newsletter for research in Chinese studies] 8 (4): 227-238.

Jones, Delmos J. 1988. "Towards a native anthropology," pp. 30-41 in *Anthropology for the Nineties,* ed. Johnnetta B. Cole. New York: Free Press.

Kao Cheng-yuen. 1982. "Shehui kexue 'Zhongguohua' zhi kenengxing ji qi yiyi" [The possibility of the 'sinicization' of social science and its meaning], pp. 31-50 in *Shehui ji xingwei kexue yanjiu de zhongguohua* [The sinicization of social and behavioral science research in China], eds. Yang Kuo-shu and Wen Chong-I. Taipei: Nankang: Institute of Ethnology, Academia Sinica (Monograph Series B, no. 10.)

Kapferer, Bruce. 1990. "From the periphery to the centre: Ethnography and the critique of ethnography in Sri Lanka," pp. 280-302 in *Localizing Strategies: Regional Traditions of Ethnographic Writing*, ed., Richard Fardon. Edinburgh: Scottish Academic Press, Washington D.C.: Smithsonian Institution Press.

Kearney, Michael. 1996. *Reconceptualizing the Peasantry: Anthropology in Global Perspective.* Boulder, Colo.: Westview.

Kim, Choong-Soon. 1990. "The role of the non-Western anthropologist reconsidered: Illusion versus reality," *Current Anthropology* 31 (2): 196-201.

King, Ambrose Yeo-chi [Jin Yaoji]. 1982. "Shehuixue de zhongguohua: yige shehuxue zhishilun de wenti" [The sinicization of sociology: A problem in the epistemology of sociology], pp. 91-113 in *Shehui ji xingwei kexue yanjiu de zhongguohua* [The sinicization of social and behavioral science research in China]. eds. Yang Kuo-shu and Wen Chong-I. Taipei: Nankang: Institute of Ethnology, Academia Sinica.

Kloos, Peter. 1991. "Anthropology in the Netherlands: The 1980s and beyond," pp. 1-29 in *Contemporary Anthropology in the Netherlands: The use of anthropological ideas*, eds. Peter Kloos and Henri J.M. Claessen. Amsterdam: Free University Press.

Koepping, Klaus-Peter. 1995. "Enlightenment and romanticism in the work of Adolf Bastian: The historical roots of anthropology in the nineteenth century," pp. 75-91 in *Fieldwork and Footnotes: Studies in the History of European Anthropology*, eds. Hans F. Vermeulen and Arturo Alvarez Roldán. London: Routledge.

Kottak, Conrad Philip. 2003. *Anthropology: The Exploration of Human Diversity*, 10th ed. New York: McGraw-Hill.

Kuklick, Henrika. 1997. "After Ishmael: The fieldwork tradition and its future," pp. 47-65 in *Anthropological Locations: Boundaries and Grounds of a Field Science*, eds. Akhil Gupta and James Ferguson. Berkeley: University of California Press.

Kuper, Adam. 1982. "Lineage theory: A critical retrospect," *Annual Review of Anthropology* 11: 71-95.

Li Fuqiang. 1998. "Zouchu digu: zhanhou xifang renleixue baituo kunjing dui Zhongguo renleixue de qishi" [Stepping out of the Depression: An enlightenment on China's anthropology from Postwar Western anthropology out of trouble [sic]], pp. 82-88 in *Renleixue bentuhua zai Zhongguo*

[Nativization of anthropology in China], eds. Rong Shixing and Xu Jieshun. Nanning: Guangxi University for Nationalities.

Li Yiyuan [Li Yih-yuan]. 1971. "Shiliu nian lai de minzu yanjiusuo" [Institute of Ethnology 1955-1971, retrospect and prospect]. *Zhongyang yanjiu yuan minzuxue yanjiusuo jikan* [Bulletin of the Institute of Ethnology, Academia Sinica] 31: 1-15.

Li Yiyuan [Li Yih-yuan]. 1995. "Sishinian lai de minzuxue yanjiusuo: yige quancheng canyuzhe de huigu yu fansi," [Forty years in the Institute of Ethnology: A look back and introspection of a participant in the entire journey], *Zhongyang Yanjiu Yuan minzuxue yanjiusuo jikan* [Bulletin of the Institute of Ethnology, Academia Sinica] 80: 3-13.

Li Yiyuan [Li Yih-yuan]. 1998 "Ethnology and social anthropology: Some tendencies in Taiwan's anthropology research and development," pp. 55-80 in *Shehuixue, renleixue zai Zhongguo de fazhan* [The development of sociology and anthropology in China], ed. Chiao Chien. Hong Kong: New Asia College, The Chinese University of Hong Kong.

Lin Meirong. 1988. "You jisi quan dao xinyang quan: Taiwan minjian shehui de diyu goucheng yu fazhan" [From ritual spheres to belif spheres: The formation and development of local folk society in Taiwan], pp. 95-125 in *Zhongguo haiyang fazhan shi lunwen ji* [Reader on the developmental history of maritime China] volume 3. Taipei: Academia Sinica, Institute of Ethnology.

Lin Meirong. 1999. "Taiwan quyuxing jidian zuzhi de shehi kongjian yu wenhua yihan" [The social space and cultural meaning of Taiwan's regional sacrificial organizations], pp. 69-88 in *Renleixue zai Taiwan de fazhan: jingyan yanjiu pian* [Anthropological studies in Taiwan: Retrospect and prospect], eds. Hsu Cheng-kuang and Lin Meirong. Taipei: Academia Sinica, Institute of Ethnology.

Lin Nan 1986 "Shehuixue zhongguohua de xiayibu [The next step in the sinicization of sociology]," pp. 29-44 in Cai Yongmei, Xiao Xinhuang [Hsiao Hsin-huang], eds., *Shehuixue Zhongguohua* [The sinicization of sociology]. Taipei: Juliu tushu.

Little, Daniel. 1989. *Understanding Peasant China: Case Studies in the Philosophy of Social Science*. New Haven: Yale University Press.

Little, Daniel. 1991. *Varieties of Social Explanation: An Introduction to the Philosophy of Social Science*. Boulder, Colo.: Westview Press.

McCloskey, Deirdre. 1985. *The Rhetoric of Economics*. Madison, Wisc.: University of Wisconsin Press.

Metcalf, Peter, and Richard. Huntington. 1991. *Celebrations of Death: The Anthropology of Mortuary Ritual*. 2nd ed. Cambridge: Cambridge University Press.

Mintz, Sidney W. 1974. *Worker in the Cane: A Puerto Rican Life History*. New York: W.W. Norton & Company.

Naito, Hideo, ed. 1937. *Taiwan: A Unique Colonial Record 1937-8 edition*. Tokyo: Kokusai Nippon Kyokai.

Narayan, Kirin. 1993. "How native is a 'native' anthropologist," *American Anthropologist* 93 (4): 671-86.

Nathan, Andrew J. 1993. "Is Chinese culture distinctive? – A review article," *Journal of Asian Studies* 52 (4): 923-36.

Okada Kan. 1960 [1938]. "Taiwan beibu cunluo zhi jisi fanwei" [Ritual spheres in villages in northern Taiwan], *Taibei fengwu* 9 (4): 14-29.

Rong Shixing and Xu Jieshu, eds. 1998. *Renleixue bentuhua zai Zhongguo* [Nativization of anthropology in China]. Nanning: Guangxi Minzu Chubanshe.

Ruan Xinbang. 2000. "Cong quanshilun de jiaodu ping Yang Kuoshu de bentuhua shehui kexue guan" [An examination of Kuo-shu Yang's indigenous approach from the Hermeneutic perspective]," *Shehui Lilun Xuebao* [Journal of Social Theory] 3 (1): 1-30.

Rynkiewich, Michael A., and Spradley, James P. 1975. "The Nacirema: A neglected culture," pp. 1-5 in *The Nacirema: Readings on American culture*, eds. James P. Spradley and Michael A. Rynkiewich. Boston: Little, Brown & Co.

Said, Edward W. 1979. *Orientalism*. New York: Random House.

Sangren, P. Steven. 1987. *History and Magical Power in a Chinese Community*. Stanford: Stanford University Press.

Sangren, Steven. 1984. "Traditional Chinese corporations: Beyond kinship," *Journal of Asian Studies* 43 (3): 391-415.

Schak, David. 1988. *Begging in Chinese Society: Poverty and Mobility in an Underclass Community*. Pittsburgh: University of Pittsburgh Press.

Scheper-Hughes, Nancy. 1981. "Cui bonum – for whose good?: A dialog with Sir Raymond Firth," *Human Organization* 40 (4): 371-2.

Schippers, Thomas K. 1995. "A history of paradoxes: Anthropologies of Europe," pp. 234-46 in *Fieldwork and Footnotes: Studies in the History of European Anthropology*, eds. Hans F. Vermeulen and Arturo Alvarez Roldán. London: Routledge.

Silin, Robert H. 1976. *Leadership and Values: The Organization of Large-Scale Taiwanese Enterprises*. Cambridge, Mass.: Harvard University Press.

Skinner, G. William. 1964. "Marketing and social structure in rural China, Part I," *Journal of Asian studies* 24 (1): 3-43.

Skinner, G. William. 1965a. "Marketing and social structure in rural China, Part II," *Journal of Asian Studies* 24 (2): 195-228.

Skinner, G. William. 1965b. "Marketing and social structure in rural China, Part III," *Journal of Asian Studies* 24 (3): 363-99.

Skinner, G. William, ed. 1977. *The City in Late Imperial China*. Stanford: Stanford University Press.

Smith, Carol A. ed. 1976. *Regional Analysis (2 volumes)*. New York: Academic

Press.

Spindler, G, and L. Spindler. 1986. "Foreward," pp. v-x in *Symbolizing America*, ed. Herve Varenne. Lincoln, Nebr.: University of Nebraska Press.

Srinivas, M.N. 1997. "Practicing social anthropology in India," *Annual Review of Anthropology* 26: 1-24.

Strathern, Marilyn. 1987. "The limits of auto-anthropology," pp. 16-37 in *Anthropology at Home*, ed. A. Jackson. London: Tavistock Publications.

Tsu, Timothy Y. 1997 "Japanese Colonialism and the investigation of Taiwanese 'old customs,'" pp. 197-218 in *Anthropology and Colonialism in Asia and Oceania*, eds. J. van Bremen and A. Shimizu. Richmond, Surrey: Curzon Press.

Varenne, Herve. 1986. "Introduction," pp. 1-9 in *Symbolizing America*, ed. Herve Varenne. Lincoln, Nebr.: University of Nebraska Press.

Vermeulen, Hans F., and Arturo Alvarez Roldán. 1995. "Introduction," pp. 1-16 in *Fieldwork and Footnotes: Studies in the History of European Anthropology*, eds. Hans F. Vermeulen and Arturo Alvarez Roldán. London: Routledge.

Wang Mingming 1998 "Chaoyue wenhua juxian, jiangou Zhongguo renleixue" [Overstepping the cultural bounds, constructing the Chinese theoretical orientation in social anthropology], pp. 111-15 in *Renleixue bentuhua zai Zhongguo* [Nativization of anthropology in China], eds. Rong Shixing and Xu Jieshun. Nanning: Guangxi University for Nationalities.

Wang Shaoli. 1998. "Qiangshen yao jiankang: Zhongguo minzuxue xueke jianshe bianxi" [Good physique through physical training [sic]], pp. 108-110 in *Renleixue bentuhua zai Zhongguo* [Nativization of anthropology in China], eds. Rong Shixing and Xu Jieshun. Nanning: Guangxi University for Nationalities.

Wang Songxing [Wang Sung-hsing]. 1991. "Taiwan hanren shehui yanjiu de fansi" [Rethinking research on Han society], *Guoli Taiwan Daxue kaogu renleixuekan* [The Bulletin of the Department of Archaeology and Anthropology] 47: 1-11.

Wen Chung-i. 1985. "Shehuixue lilun de wenhua chayi: shehui kexue hongguohua de zaitantao" [Cultural differences in sociological theory: Further discussion of the sinicization of the social sciences], pp. 233-46 in *Xiandaihua yu zhongguo wenhua yantaohui lunwen huibian* [Proceedings of the conference on modernization and Chinese culture], eds. Chiao Chien et al. Hong Kong: Faculty of Social Science and Institute of Social Studies, The Chinese University of Hong Kong.

Wen Chung-i. 1991. "Zhongguo shehuixue: guojihua huo guojiahua?" [Sociology in China: Internationalization or nationalization?], *Zhongguo shehuixhue kan* [Chinese Journal of Sociology] 15: 1-28

Wen Chung-i 1998 "Zhongguo de shehuixue: guojihua huo guojiahua?" [Chinese sociology: Internationalization or nationalization], pp. 159-98 in *Shehuixue, renleixue zai zhongguo de fazhan* [Sociology and anthropology in China's Development], ed. Chiao Chien. Hong Kong: New Asia College, The Chinese University of Hong Kong.

Weng Naiqun. 1998. "Shanye yanjiu yu zouchu shanye: dui Zhongguo shehui wenhua renleixue de fansi" [Research on social culture of minorities and the importance of going beyond it: Thoughts on social cultural anthropology in China [sic]], pp. 54-62 in *Renleixue bentuhua zai Zhongguo* [Nativization of anthropology in China], eds. Rong Shixing and Xu Jieshun. Nanning: Guangxi University for Nationalities.

Worsley, Peter M. 1956. "The kinship system of the Tallensi: A reevaluation," *Journal of the Royal Anthropological Institute* 86: 37-75.

Xiao Xinhuang. 1982. "Shehuixue zhongguohua de jiegou wenti: shijie tixi zhong de fanxing fengong chutan [Structural problem in the sincization of sociology: An initial exploration of the division of labor in the world system]," pp. 69-90 in *Shehui ji xingwei kexue yanjiu de zhongguohua* [The sinicization of social and behavioral science research in China], eds. Yang Kuo-shu and Wen Chong-I. Nankang, Taipei: Institute of Ethnology, Academia Sinica (Monograph Series B, no. 10).

Xiao Xinhuang [Hsiao Hsin-hwang]. 1986. "Xiaoxu" [Preface by Hsiao], pp. 5-9 in *Shehuixue Zhongguohua* [The sinicization of sociology], eds. Cai Yongmei, Xiao Xinhuang. Taipei: Juliu Tushu.

Xie Dongzhe and Ma Chenxing. 1997. *Xizhuang baogao* [Report on Xizhuang]. Xingang, Taiwan: Xingang wen jiao jijinhui.

Xu Jiaming [Hsu Chia-ming]. 1973. "Zhanghua pingyuan fulaoke de diyu zuzhi" [Territorial organization of Hoklorized Hakka in the Changhua Plain], *Zhongyang yanjiu yuan minzuxue yanjiusuo jikan* [Bulletin of the Institute of Ethnology, Academia Sinica] 37: 165-90.

Xu Jieshun. 1998. "Zhongguo renleixue to xianzhuang yu weilai zouxiang" [The present state and future tendency of anthropology in China], pp. 4-13 in *Renleixue bentuhua zai Zhongguo* [Nativization of anthropology in China], eds. Rong Shixing and Xu Jieshun. Nanning: Guangxi University for Nationalities.

Xu Zhengguang (Hsu Cheng-kuang) and Huang Yinggui (Huang Ying-kuei), eds. 1999. *Renleixue zai Taiwan de fazhan: Huigu yu zhanwang pian* [Anthropological studies in Taiwan: Empirical research]. Taipei: Academia Sinica, Institute of Ethnology.

Xu Zhengguang (Hsu Cheng-kuang) and Lin Meirong, eds. 1999. *Renleixue zai Taiwan de fazhan: Jingyan yanjiu pian* [Anthropological studies in Taiwan: Retrospect and prospect]. Taipei: Academia Sinica, Institute of Ethnology.

Yang Guoshu. 1982. "Xinlixue yanjiu de zhongguohua: Cengci yu fangxiang" [The sinicization of psychology research: Priorities and directions], pp.

153-87 in *Shehui ji xingwei kexue yanjiu de zhongguohua* [The sinicization of social and behavioral science research in China]. eds. Yang Guoshu [Yang Kuo-shu] and Wen Chongyi [Wen Chung-i]. Nankang, Taipei: Institute of Ethnology, Academia Sinica.

Yang Guoshu [Yang Kuo-shu] and Wen Chongyi [Wen Chung-i], eds. 1982. *Shehui ji xingwei kexue yanjiu de zhongguohua* [The sinicization of social and behavioral science research in China). Nankang, Taipei: Institute of Ethnology, Academia Sinica.

Yang, Martin C. 1945. *A Chinese Village: Taitou, Shantung Province*. New York: Columbia University Press.

Yin, Alexander Chien-chung. 1989. "Urbanization and culture change in the Taiwan Area," pp. 319-50 in *Anthropological Studies of the Taiwan Area: Accomplishments and Prospects*, eds. Kuang-chih Chang, Kwang-chou Li, Arthur P. Wolf, and Chien-chung Yin. Taipei: Department of Anthropology, National Taiwan University.

Zhang Youjun. 1998. "Guanyu Zhongguo minzuxue renleixue xueke diwei wenti" [On the status of the academic disciplines of ethnology and anthropology in China], pp. 19-24 in *Renleixue bentuhua zai Zhongguo* [Nativization of anthropology in China], eds. Rong Shixing and Xu Jieshun. Nanning: Guangxi University for Nationalities.

Zhao Fusan. 1985. "Shehui kexue zhongguohua wenti guanjian" [On the sincization of the social sciences], pp. 223-32 in *Xiandaihua yu zhongguo wenhua yantaohui lunwen huibian* [Proceedings of the conference on modernization and Chinese culture], eds. Chiao Chien et al. Hong Kong: Faculty of Social Science and Institute of Social Studies, The Chinese University of Hong Kong.

Zhou Daming. 1998. "'Zhongguoshi' renleixue yu renleixue de bentuhua" [Anthropology in Chinese style and nativization of anthropology (sic)], pp. 68-74 in in *Renleixue bentuhua zai Zhongguo* [Nativization of anthropology in China], eds. Rong Shixing and Xu Jieshun. Nanning: Guangxi University for Nationalities.

Chapter 11

The Making and Indigenization of Anthropology

in Korea

Kwang-ok KIM

Introduction

The word "indigenization" is, at least in Korea, a multi-faceted conceptual term. It contains a scientific concern for the relevancy of a particular method-ology in a specific local context, but it also implies an ideological orientation related to people's primordial sentiments and ideologies of nationalism. Korea has undergone unique political and cultural processes including colonial oc-cupation and exploitation (1910-1945), national division (1945), ideological confrontation, the Korean War (1950-1953), and, most recently, the overwhelm-ing influx of foreign social and cultural elements through Westernization, modernization, and globalization. It is, therefore, a serious issue for Korean anthropologists to account for the meanings of these processes in their analy-sis of Korean culture. These anthropologists have always been, consciously or unconsciously, committed to the question of how to establish a "Korean" anthropology or, at least, an anthropology relevant to Korea.

Using the terminology of the first chapter of this book, Korean anthropol-ogy has been mainly "indigenous," with Koreans writing for Korean audi-ences about Korea. Korea never had any colonies of its own overseas nor were there any minority groups within Korea, so Koreans never felt a serious urge to study other peoples until the 1980s (Moon Ok-Pyo 1997). More than that, however, indigenous Korean anthropology originated as a response to the experience of Japanese colonial rule (1910-1945), followed by a further phase of cultural colonization by American social science and culture in the postwar period. The nature and development of indigenous anthropology are to be understood within the specific political and social conditions of Korea in the post-liberation era, following its division and devastation during the Korean War. Its more recent history is one of nation building, economic development, and the experience of political and social change against the background of the North-South confrontation

Against this background, the study of culture was marginalized in favor of the so-called "practical sciences" (i.e. law, political science, economics, and sociology). However, nationalist enthusiasm for local culture was revived during the 1960s and 1970s, first by intellectuals as a counter to the state-initiated modernization process, and then by the regime that followed as a political strategy. While scholars in the other social science fields used models and theories imported from the West to fit Korean conditions, Korean folklorists advocated the study of "authentic" national culture under the banner of *kukhak*, "national science," a term coined as part of the government's search for legitimacy. Younger intellectuals argued that folk traditions were the core of the "national" culture during the popular cultural movement of the 1980s. With the process of "democratization" in the 1990s, the new civilian government exploited popular nationalism for its own political advantage. Meanwhile, the mass media popularized the quest for authentic national culture as a commodity in the newly emerging culture market, resulting in further popularity for folklore studies. Most recently, the government has encouraged the importation of foreign popular culture under the banners of modernization and globalization, at the expense of traditional Korean culture, resulting not only in culture conflict between the generations, but also changes in the theories and research interests of anthropologists.

This paper traces the development of the discipline in Korea within this historical context. First we describe its characteristics in the colonial period, and the strong position of the folklore tradition in early research. Second we consider developments during the early postwar period, and the relations between Western anthropology and the folklore tradition which remained strong. Finally, we look at emerging trends in the discipline in recent years, under the impact of rapid economic growth and democratization, and consider the future of anthropology in Korean society. Although there have been close relations between anthropologists in Korea and abroad, the present paper deals only with indigenous anthropology, studies of Korea by Korean anthropologists.

Colonialism, Nationalism, and the Folklore Tradition

Under Japanese colonial rule (1910-1945), Japanese scholars carried out extensive research on Korean culture and misrepresented it in the name of science and modernity.[1] Korean intellectuals at the time, consciously or unconsciously, reproduced the colonial discourse on Korean culture, using such words as "primitive," "feudal," "unscientific," and "irrational" to describe it.

Very few of them attempted to collect materials representing the national folk culture.[2]

Despite this unfavorable environment, indigenous intellectuals such as Choi Nam-sun (1973), Chung In-bo (1947), and Shin Chae-ho (1977) resisted, and produced alternative accounts of Korean culture and history. Using diffusionist and culture circle theories, they attempted to prove that Japanese culture actually originated from Korea.[3] Another major concern of these scholars was the nature of Korean identity, which they described in metaphysical terms, using such concepts as "Korean spirit" (*choseon ui eol*) (Chung In-bo), or "Korean mind" (*choseonsim*) (Shin Chae-ho). They also started a "Korean studies movement" (*choseonhak undong*).[4] The term *chosunhak* was first adopted by Chung In-bo in 1931, in a series of articles in *Dong-a Ilbo* entitled *Chosun koseo haeje* [Bibliographical notes on Korean classics], and it was used widely until the early 1940s. This work also contained abundant material on subjects such as myths, shamanism, folk tales, and customs (Moon Ok-pyo 1999). One of the most active members of this movement was An Chae-hong (1891-1965), who defined Korean studies as "systematic knowledge constructed from studies of things unique to Korea, the characteristics of Korean culture, and the distinctive traditions of Korea" (Chun Kwan-woo 1974: 52).

While the nationalistic scholars concentrated on national history, another group including Son Jin-tae (1948), Song Seok-ha (1963), and Yim Seok-jae, collected material on folklore and customs based on their idea that the national culture is embedded in the lives of common people. Song Seok-ha and Son Chin-tae were members of the "Chindan Society" (*Chindanhak Hoe*), founded in 1934 by Korean scholars mostly trained at Keijô [Kyongseong] Imperial University in Korea, or in Japan. They were more concerned with methods and collecting data than with the issues of national identity and cultural superiority that preoccupied the nationalist scholars like Chung In-bo and Shin Chae-ho.[5] With increasing political repression towards the end of the colonial period, it became more difficult to research Korean cultural identity and national history, and the result was descriptive studies of folklore, without much consideration for its wider social and political context. This unfortunate trend in Korean folklore studies to a large extent survives until today.

Post-Liberation to the Mid-1970s

After the end of World War II, the study of cultural history was subsumed by history while folklore studies became a sub-genre of literature. Due to partition and the Korean War (1950-1953) that followed liberation from the Japanese, the study of Korean culture developed little during the 1950s. Some intellectuals interested in national cultural identity continued working in the folklore tradition, and these scholars came to dominate the Korean Society for Cultural Anthropology (*Han'guk Munhwa Illyuhak Hoe*) when it was first established in 1958.[6]

Until the 1970s, therefore, anthropology and folklore studies had not developed to a point where they were clearly differentiated. At this stage, scholars focused on subjects like shamanism, folk belief systems, past-time games, legends, myths, seasonal festivals, and village agricultural rituals. They defined their study as *kukhak*, "national science," and aimed to reestablish the national identity and cultural tradition that had been distorted and damaged by Japanese colonialism to the point where it was on the brink of disappearing in the face of rapid industrialization and modernization. The study of folklore was stimulated by the politics of the time, both by the nationalistic policies of the Park Chung-hee regime (1961-1979), as well as by the college students and younger intellectuals opposed to his rule. In 1965, the new regime normalized diplomatic relationships with Japan amidst angry opposition from the public. When the government announced the cultural exchange treaty and the policy of attracting Japanese capital and industry, young intellectuals criticized the government for wanting to extinguish once more the "national spirit" (*minjok jeongsin*), "national spiritual power" (*minjok jeongki*), and national culture. They questioned whether President Park and his clique had any "national consciousness" (*minjok eusik*) or any sense of national identity (*minjok jeongcheseong*). The college students became active in "excavating" folk traditions to protect Korean identity against the advance of foreign culture, especially the revival of Japanese colonial power in the guise of economic and cultural cooperation.

The government responded to the criticism by passing a law for the preservation of national cultural treasures (*munwhajae bohobeop*), and by organizing annual contests of folk customs (*minsok kyong'yeon daehoe*). Archaeological excavations were supported and cultural heritage sites were designated and renovated. Leading professional folk artists and performers were designated as intangible cultural properties (*muhyong munwhajae*) or human cultural properties (*in'gan munwhajae*), and paid monthly salaries by the government. Leading folklorists were invited to judge the annual folk customs contest, and a National Museum of Folk Culture was established. Folklorists were encouraged to mount or even invent cultural events loaded with symbols of antiquity, originality, uniqueness, and authenticity. In the face of the overwhelming power of the wave of modernization, they romanticized the past and invoked nostalgia for the culture which was disappearing or had already vanished.

Though these scholars contributed to the documentation and preservation of traditional culture and made people realize the importance of their own folk traditions in the context of national identity, they hampered, perhaps unintentionally and unconsciously, the development of scientific studies of

256

national culture. Because they were mainly concerned with typologies of "indigenous" or "authentic" Korean culture, they did not pay much attention to the political, economic, and social contexts in which folk customs were produced or reproduced, nor were they interested in theory and methodology. They failed to provide a holistic picture of a cultural community in which elite and folk traditions, or official culture and unofficial tradition, interact in a dynamic relation. The result was another distorted image of Korean culture, in which the "Little Tradition" of shamanism, folk arts, festivals, and peasant customs predominated.

Until the mid-1970s, there were only a few anthropologists properly trained in the Western tradition. They also emphasized the urgency of documenting traditional Korean culture and preventing it from disappearing in the process of modernization, but they were also concerned with introducing modern anthropological methods and perspectives for the scientific study of culture. They tried to define Korean culture systematically through the analysis of modes of thought (Kang Shin-pyo 1974) and social institutions like the family and kinship system (Lee Kwang-kyu 1975). They also argued that traditional culture was relevant to Korean modernization (Han Sang-bok 1974). However, the preference of anthropologists for portraying traditional culture as a closed system embedded in the lives of local communities was a liability in dealing with more urgent issues in a rapidly changing society like Korea. In the social and political turmoil of postwar Korea, disciplines were evaluated in terms of their relevance to the projects of nation-building, modernization, and development. During the period of rapid industrialization and economic growth since the late 1960s, increasing social inequality and political injustice became the main issues, and anthropology was regarded as of minor importance.

Much of the history of anthropology in postwar Korea is, therefore, that of the relations between the ongoing tradition of folklore studies and new anthropological approaches introduced from the West, two traditions which have not yet been completely integrated.[7] The folklorists' reconstruction of obsolete customs relied heavily upon the recollections of the elderly. These studies culminated in the *Jeon'guk minsok jonghap josa* [Nation-wide Survey of Folk Customs], carried out by the Korean Society for Cultural Anthropology.[8] But from the viewpoint of their anthropological critics, these studies de-contextualized these customs without providing an analysis or interpretation of their meanings in the lives of the people.

Among the folklorists themselves, there were two different factions. One group defined folklore as a subfield of anthropology (see Lee Du-hyun 1984; Lee Du-hyun, Chang Chu-keun, and Lee Kwang-kyu 1985 [1974]), while others claimed it as an independent discipline. The first group was mainly the older generation of folklorists. The other group, mostly younger scholars trained in Korean literature, was more nationalistic, and dismissed anthropology as the study of "alien cultures." As the number of trained anthropolo-

257

gists increased from the 1970s onwards, there was a major shift to a more anthropological type of community studies. Village ethnography depicting the lives of people and the inter-connectedness of social institutions distinguished anthropology from folklore studies. Unlike earlier folklore studies, these studies involved relatively long-term fieldwork within a particular community.[9]

From the Mid-1970s to the 1980s: Popular Nationalism versus Academism

During the early 1970s, folklore and archaeology were in favor with the government, as their nationalistic flavor fitted with some of its political aims. However, the government was ambiguous towards traditional culture. It was nationalistic in its support for the national culture but at the same time it advocated modernization.

It should be noted however that the younger intellectuals during the 1980s were interested in peasant traditions, both as part of their quest for a national cultural identity, and in the development of a political culture of resistance. After the dictatorial regime of Park Chung-hee ended with his assassination in 1979, an interim government, and a military coup led by Chun Duwhan in 1980, civil politics were outlawed, and intellectuals, college students, members of labor unions, and even religious leaders organized a variety of protest movements. Under the banner of "popular culture" (*minjung munwha*), artists and producers exploited folk culture to invent new genres in drama, music, dancing, and fine arts, and provide participants and audiences with ways of expressing resistance and alternative ideologies (Kim Kwang-ok 1994b; Song Do-young 1998). Shamanism, masked dance, solo operetta (*pansori*), and peasant music emerged as the core of this culture.

The differences between anthropology and folklore studies became increasingly clear in research topics, methodology, theoretical perspectives, and writing style. Anthropologists emphasized a holistic view, while folklorists remained primarily concerned with the forms and meanings of particular items of folk culture and their geographical distribution. In other words, anthropologists perceived culture as practice, and cultural institutions as products of processes involving power and interests, while folklorists put more emphasis on the origins of cultural forms and "authentic" national culture. The study of folklore has remained a popular subfield of Korean literature through its connection with popular nationalism.

Perhaps the most popular topics in anthropological studies during this period were kinship and the family, as many scholars assumed this was an area in which the distinctiveness of Korean traditional culture could be clearly understood. Kim Taek-kyu's study (1964) of a traditional upper class lineage village was a pioneering example. Indeed, in terms of both depth and scope, kinship is the area in which Korean anthropology has made the most substantial contribution,[10] particularly in the work of Lee Kwang-kyu (e.g. 1975; 1977; 1981; 1990; 1998a). And yet, many of these studies failed to provide a wider analytical perspective. For instance, while family structure, inheritance patterns, lineage organization, and the practice of ancestor worship were described and analyzed in great detail with regard to specific localities, few attempts were made to explain why these practices differed with region and class, and what these differences meant. Similarly, few attempts were made to interpret the role of kinship in contemporary social, political, and economic contexts. Kinship-based networks and organizations may also be important in mediating state power and private authority, as the basis for allegiance in local level politics, or a basis for identity formation, and they also operate in modern urban contexts. Their importance seems to be particularly notable in Korea where recently there has been a resurgence of lineage ideology and ancestor worship as social and cultural resources (Kim Kwang-ok 1992; 1998c; Kim Il-chul et al. 1998).

We also find various attempts to theorize the basic principles that govern Korean traditional culture. Kang Shin-pyo (1974; 1980; 1984; 1985), for instance, put forward a dyadic model for conceptualizing Korean cognitive structures. Adopting ideas from Lévi-Strauss, Kang argued that politics, economy, religion, art, and other institutions are manifestations of underlying cultural principles, a cultural grammar based on "dyadic cognitive structures" (*daedaejeok injigujo*). Others argued that reciprocity is the basic principle (Kim Juhee 1981, 1991; Chun Kyung-soo 1984). Kim Juhee, for instance, elaborated on the basic relational pattern underlying the institution of reciprocal labor exchange (*pumasi*), widely reported in traditional agricultural communities, and extended it as a general explanatory model to all types of social relationships found in Korean society.

Anthropologists of this period were distinguished from folklorists in that their works were based on long-term fieldwork and their arguments were substantiated by detailed ethnographic description. However, it was still often assumed that culture is something shared and agreed, and not much attention was given to possible subcultural differences and conflicts. This may be partly the result of a village studies approach that implied that what one finds in a particular village is representative of Korean culture as a whole (Moon Ok-pyo 1999). Many of these studies were exercises in native as opposed to indigenous anthropology, carried out as doctoral research at foreign universities (Han Sang-bok 1980), so that their audiences were mostly foreigners who were not familiar with the cultural diversity and historical complexity of Korea.

Even when heterogeneous elements were brought in, they were often presented in a simple juxtaposition without a full analysis of the dynamic interaction between them. A clear example of such an approach can be found in the oft-adopted dualistic model of Korean culture based on dichotomies of

"Great" versus "Little Traditions," Confucianism versus shamanism, hierarchical versus egalitarian principles, lineage villages versus non-lineage villages, and elite versus "peasant" traditions. Until the 1970s, anthropological studies of Korean traditional culture were often biased towards *yangban* culture based on the Confucian elite tradition, which contrasted with the shamanic tradition among non-*yangban* classes (Kim Kwang-ok 1987, 1995; Moon Ok-pyo 1999). Korean villages were classified into two categories; the lineage villages of the *yangban* class and non-lineage villages of the commoners. These two types of villages were then described as hierarchical, authoritarian, and group-oriented on the one hand, and democratic, egalitarian, and individualistic on the other (e.g. Lee Man-gap 1973; Lee Kwang-kyu 1986). Confucian and shamanic traditions were divided along similar lines as representing different sectors of the population. Shamanism has always occupied an important position in Korean studies as something that embodies the essence of the pure "indigenous" elements in Korean culture transmitted from the primitive past (Choi Kilsong 1978; Cho Heung-yoon 1983; Chang Chu-keun 1986).

Such typological approaches, however, tend to obscure the internal dynamics within the same class or same village society. They also minimize the importance of the individual by emphasizing the deterministic power of tradition. The fact that those who belonged to the elite class in the traditional estate system do not necessarily occupy an elite position in modern society further weakens the basis of cultural typologies and determinism. In other words, the dynamics of subcultures need to be observed, and analysis is needed of how individual actors select and manipulate various cultural resources for their social, economic, and political ends in modern contexts (Moon Ok-pyo 1999).

From the late 1970s, however, a new trend emerged in Korean anthropology. The emphasis shifted from the description of cultural tradition as a static entity to the analysis of social and cultural change in a modern context. A comparative study of three fishing villages by Han Sang-bok (1977), for instance, revealed how the functions of social and cultural institutions might differ with ecological conditions and the nature of economic activities. Social institutions are determined by external conditions such as economy, technology, and resources. The Departments of Anthropology at Seoul National University and Youngnam University established a research tradition which remained influential in Korean anthropology for the next decade (Kim Kwang-ok 1987). Interest shifted to the complicated processes by which village communities are connected to the wider society, the state, the market, and the world, and students started to deal with the real-world problems resulting from rapid social change.

Younger anthropologists became more interested in the lives of rural farm families, the urban poor, and the newly emerging working class. Indeed, while the government propagated an image of national prosperity under slogans such as "Korea in the World" and exploiting international sports events such as the Asian Games (1986) and Olympic Games (1988), the major interest of the postgraduates in the 1980s lay in understanding the lives of those in the agrarian or urban sectors of Korea as it industrialized.[11] They began to look at the informal sector, marginality, poor urban settlements, low-wage factory workers, impoverished and uprooted peasants, and petty commodity production. They used theories of social formations, the articulation of modes of production, dependency, and the global system, as developed by French Marxist anthropology and Anglo-American political economy. This generation of anthropologists tended to avoid the ambiguity and vagueness inherent in the concept of culture (Kim Kwang-ok 1995). Theoretically, they remained under the Western anthropological umbrella, but despite this, anthropology during the 1980s clearly moved from a discipline dominated by folklore to one that endeavored to find topics, methods, and models relevant to the study of contemporary Korean society.

Into the 1990s: In Search of "Korean" Anthropology

The 1990s was the period when Korea celebrated the achievement of democratization with the reinstatement of general elections and civilian government. The new civilian government, especially under Kim Youngsam's presidency (1993-1997), gave nationalistic support to popular culture. Popular nationalism swept the nation under the official banner of "Correcting the National History." The most important symbol was the ceremonial demolition in 1995 of a prominent colonial period building to mark the fiftieth anniversary of liberation from the Japanese. The new historical and cultural nationalism became fashionable under the slogans of "ours is the best" and "body and soil are not separate, but one" (*sin-to-bul-i*).[12]

Official nationalism was taken up by the mass media and capitalist culture industry, as they reinvented and commodified Korean culture. Documentaries were broadcast on the lost history of ancient Korea, and folklorists discussing the antiquity, originality, purity, and superiority of folk culture became popular. Journalists and scholars visited Siberia, Mongolia, Central Asia, and even Southeast Asia in search of connections with ancient Korea, symbolically reviving a cultural empire which extended beyond the present-day Korean boundaries.

The succeeding government under Kim Daejung (1998-2003), however, marked a further drastic change. Kim proclaimed his version of an open-door policy with references to "new-breed intellectuals" (*sin-jisig'in*), reminiscent of the earlier Japanese phrase, "new human beings" (*shin-jinrui*). He emphasized that Koreans desperately needed a cultural renewal to cope with globalization, and vigorously denounced the established system of education. Younger leftist liberal intellectuals enthusiastically supported this Korean Cultural Revolution. The new government criticized any trace of nationalism and officially opened the floodgates to Japanese media and pop-culture in the name of cultural exchange. Different types of popular culture were now distinguished. *Daejung munwha* (mass culture) refers to forms of mass entertainment including film, TV, video, cartoons, and pop songs; *minjung munwha* (popular culture) refers to culture that draws on the ideology of the marginalized, deprived, oppressed, and alienated; and *pap munwha* (pop culture) refers to new types of youth culture, including rock concerts, heavy metal, break dancing, rap, and hip-hop. The Kim regime was especially enthusiastic about pop culture, and high-school dropouts who were successful in pop music and sports became national idols, particularly if they had succeeded in the United States. The state seemed to be attempting to defuse political resistance and conflict between the elite and the masses through promoting popular culture in this way.

These attempts apparently appealed to the young people, especially those born after 1980 when Korea began to enjoy the fruits of economic development. With the support of the state and the media, the youth began to openly reject and criticize the established version of "Korean" culture, opening up a gulf between the generations. The new hybrid youth culture is positively associated with concepts such as modernity, globalism, creativity, adaptability, competitiveness, and the ability to meet challenges.

Wittingly or unwittingly, these policies opened Korea to foreign cultural imports, and globalization became the subject of hot debate. Government and pro-government intellectuals insisted that Koreans should abandon their emphasis on national uniqueness and actively assimilate foreign culture, while opponents stressed the need for a Korean identity. As a result, there are now widely differing definitions of Korean culture, and debates between globalization theorists and nationalists have become common, not only among academics, but also within the general public.

Against this heated background, anthropologists have become increasingly concerned with the quest to make anthropology relevant to the study of Korea (cf. Kim Kwang-ok1987). Some fear that the adoption of Western approaches may lead to yet another distorted description of Korean culture that fails to take into account historical factors such as the authoritarian state, the colonial legacy, the national consciousness, and repeated political turmoil against the background of partition. In the past, they argue, many anthropologists, both native and foreign, have produced ethnographic descriptions of an imagined Korea, because they failed to see a reality in which historical experiences, state imperatives, and the power of capital are interwoven.

A critical reassessment of Japanese colonial scholarship has also been attempted in this connection (see Park Hyun-soo 1980a; 1980b; 1981; 1993; Kim Seong-nae 1990; Choi Seok-young 1997a; 1997b; Kim Kwang-ok 1998a).

Kim Seong-nae (1990), for instance, has attempted a deconstruction of Japanese colonial scholarship and its impact upon subsequent studies, using the concrete example of studies of shamanism. Through a critical analysis of previous studies by Japanese and Korean scholars, she argues that Korean folklorists have uncritically reproduced much of the colonial discourse on Korean culture. The vast number of studies of Korean customs produced by the Japanese scholars and colonial government have hitherto been used mostly as primary data, but now they have been scrutinized more carefully with regard to their ideological implications. Cho Hyejoang's (1992-94) insistence on the use of indigenous perspectives and language in representing the Korean reality may also be understood in the same context.

State, class, and the politics of culture

Several new trends are discernible in Korean anthropology in relation to this new sensitivity towards indigenous perspectives, theories, and methods. The first concerns ways of analyzing Korean state and bureaucracy during a long history in which state power penetrated everyday life and exercised absolute authority. Korean anthropologists increasingly realize that cultural practices have to be understood within a framework of hegemonic relationships between the state and society, official power and private authority, and government policy and local social traditions. Similarly, given that people's sense of identity based on family and regional ties often overlaps with their strong attachment to an imagined national community, it is necessary to understand how people construct and manipulate concepts of community in defining their relations with the state. The politics of culture has therefore become major theme in studies the elite in local level politics (Kim Kwang-ok 1994a; 1998b) and of popular culture in anti-governmental resistance movement (Kim Kwang-ok 1989; 1994b).

These studies show how people intentionally use or invent roles and rituals to adapt to the social, political, and economic environment, These are not seen merely as a repetition of the past, but as political constructs in response to the present. The reproduction or invention of tradition at the local level is interpreted in relation to competition for cultural capital and power. For instance, prominent lineages construct their own cultural communities through reproduction of an elite culture through which they dominate local level politics, and gain advantages in dealing with political authorities at a higher level, including central government (Kim Kwang-ok 1994a). As another example, shamanic rituals became rituals of resistance within the popular culture movement launched by intellectuals in the 1980s, during conflict with the state. Interestingly, Kim Kwang-ok (1994b) showed that those who manipulated shamanic symbols most enthusiastically were not actual believers in shamanism, but were variously affiliated to Christianity, Buddhism, and Confucianism. They selected shamanism as the most effective vehicle to strengthen consciousness and provide symbols of resistance against the military regime.

A related theoretical development is the interest in class subcultures. In the 1990s, a number of younger Korean anthropologists formed a study group, "Class and Culture," that remains one of the largest and most active subsections of the Korean Society for Cultural Anthropology. Hwang Ik-joo (1997) carried out an experimental study to find out whether a working class culture is developing, despite the assumed homogeneity of Korea. Related studies include those of the newly emerging urban middle class (Moon Ok-pyo et al. 1992; Kim Eunhee 1993), the urban poor (Cho Un and Cho Oakla 1992), and youth culture (Yang Jaeyoung 1994; Cho Hyejoang 1996).[13] More recently, the research focus of this group has been the cultural implications of globalization.

Other scholars have analyzed the relationship between local, national and transnational culture. The invention of cultural specialities has been studied in relation to local food (Hwang Ik-joo 1994) and the discourses associated with particular dishes (Han Kyung-koo 1994; Kim Kwang-ok 1998d). Moon has shown how Korean "authenticity" and national identity have become commodities (Moon Ok-pyo 1997), and how foreign influences have transformed indigenous life styles (Yi Jeong-duk 1997).

History and anthropology

There has also been a growing awareness that Korea's politics, economy, and social behavior cannot be understood separately from its history. Korean anthropologists have become increasingly interested in the narratives of people who are usually silent, in relation to the historical context of memory (Kim Seong-nae 1989; Yoon Taek-lim 1992; Yoo Chul-in 1993) and local processes of transformation (Yoo Chul-in et al. 1996). Shamanism provides a space in which subordinate people can narrate an alternative history (Kim Seong-nae 1989), or express their memories of political resistance (Kim Kwang-ok 1994b). Official and private documents have been used extensively to analyze historical changes in communal ritual in relation to local and national politics (Lee Ki-tae 1997; Park Howon 1997). Anthropologists and historians have also cooperated in compiling and translating records of traditional family rites as a basis for further research (Moon Ok-pyo 1998b; Moon Ok-pyo et al 1999a, 1999b). New light has also been shed on the importance of the hereditary petty officials called *seori* or *ajeon* in the local administration during the Choseon period (Lee Hoon-sang 1990). Local politics were shaped by the power relations between the magistrate sent from the central government, the retired local-level officials and scholar-gentry (*yangban*), and the *ajeon*. The existence of the *ajeon* in the political structure had been almost totally ignored, though political processes at the local level cannot be understood without them. Despite modernization and structural transformation, local elites have maintained their power through conscious efforts to reproduce their culture and status. (Kim Kwang-ok 1994a) Recognizing the importance of the historical approach, a historical anthropology study group has been organized within the Korean Society for Cultural Anthropology, and some younger anthropologists, historians, and folklorists have established a Society for Historical Folklore (*yoksa minsokhakhoe*), using interdisciplinary approaches.

Gender studies

The emergence and development of feminist anthropology in Korea may be understood as resulting from the intersection of Western anthropology with the indigenizing efforts of Korean anthropologists. Studies of Korean culture focusing on women began to appear in the early 1980s when Cho Hyejoang, Cho Oakla and others formed a group called Alternative Culture together with other sociologists. Member of this group introduced theories and issues popular in the West to action-oriented programs in Korea, such as the dichotomy of public and private space, male dominance and female domestication, patriarchy, and gender discrimination in the family and other areas of social life. Other issues included lives of poor urban women (Cho Un and Cho Oakla 1992), discourses of reproductive practice based on feminist approaches to the body (Kim Eunshil 1993), and capitalist control of women's labor in multinational corporations (Kim Hyunmi 1996). Other studies were more concerned with issues of gender and local culture, including Confucianism, oppression, and exploitation (Kim Jinmyoung 1993), and the identity and role of urban middle class housewives in contemporary Korean society and culture (see Moon Ok-pyo 1990; 1997; 1998a; Kim Eunhee 1993; Kwon Sug-in 1998). These studies argue that the practice of gender ideology should be understood in its cultural context.

National unification, Overseas Koreans

The need for an indigenous perspective is also important in relation to the nation and cultural identity in a divided Korea. The political division and the experience of the Korean War have moulded people's ideologies, world-views, values and morals, and pattern of social and political behavior. While ideas can be borrowed from other societies that have experienced colonialism or war, there are no case studies directly comparable with the unique situation in Korea. In the post-Cold War period, Korean anthropologists are increasingly faced with the question of how to achieve cultural communication between South and North Korea in order to pave the way for eventual reunification. Some experimental research has appeared on the experiences of those who have moved to South Korea, partly to correct people's stereotyped perceptions of North Korea. The 1990s have also witnessed a growth in studies of Koreans abroad, expanding the concepts of national community beyond geographical and national boundaries, and including overseas Koreans as members of an ideologically defined transnational community, a concept which has been adopted by the government. A number of studies have been carried out on Koreans abroad, including Koreans in Japan (Lee Kwang-kyu 1983), America (Lee Kwang-kyu 1989; Yi Jeong-duk 1993a), and Russia (Lee Kwang-kyu and Chun Kyungsoo 1993; Lee Kwang-kyu 1998b), and China. Han Sang-bok and Kwon Taewhan (1993) conducted a general survey on Koreans in Yanbian Autonomous Prefecture, Northeast China, supported by the Korean National Commission for UNESCO. Kim Kwang-ok led a group studying Koreans in Jilin Province (1996), Liaoning Province (1997), and Heilongjiang Province (1998) in China. The National Unification Board invited anthropologists to conduct a series of brief surveys of Koreans abroad, and a series of detailed ethnographic reports on overseas Koreans has been planned by the National Folk Culture Museum.

Postmodernism

In the 1990s, the postmodernist perspectives on the world conception of the world as de-centered, fragmented, and refractive became popular among Korean academics, and cultural studies became popular in the major newspapers. Books with "culture" in their titles became best sellers. There is a growing perception that culture no longer exists as something that functions within a bounded locality but as something that is constructed, consciously manipulated, and politically transacted, as well as being produced, performed and consumed as a commodity in the context of the cultural industry or tourism.[14]

A considerable difference, however, can be noted between the conventional anthropological understanding of culture and its meaning in this new popular context. In the latter, culture more often means preferences, images, styles, consumer tastes, leisure, or art rather than a way of life or a way of thinking in its totality. That means that it can no longer be grasped in long-term fieldwork in a small community. It is thus approached in contemporary cultural studies as something that can only be understood through subjective and impressionistic experience, without much reference to the accumulated body of previous research within anthropology. Traditional views of culture have been openly attacked by postmodernists who concentrate on the informal, fluid, and phenomenal aspects of life instead of the more formal and permanent principles and systems. They have subjected previously established interpretations to a process of "deconstruction." By focusing largely on discourse analysis, some self-styled postmodernists unfortunately fail to describe ethnographically what the people as a whole actually do.[15] However, postmodernists have introduced an alternative view of the world through the reconsideration and critique of traditional anthropological methods.

Local and national cultures

While hostility and rivalry between regions are notorious in Korean politics, there have been few attempts to account for the historical and cultural roots of its modern manifestations. There have been some folklorists who have attempted to divide the Korean peninsula into several "culture areas" according to the distribution of yearly agricultural rites (Kim Taek-kyu 1985). Choi Hyup (1994), on the other hand, has proposed a more holistic approach to regional culture, encompassing historical background, geographical dimensions, and personality structure among other factors.

Questions of regional culture reflect not simply regional differences, but also the politics of relations with the central government. It has been argued that Seoul monopolizes political, economic, cultural, and welfare resources while other local areas are marginalized (Chung Byung-ho 1996). Song Do-young (1996) has examined how some communities develop strategies to attract external capital, and he suggests that anthropologists can contribute to the development of industries based on local culture. Other research has focused on the way local history and culture are invented and reproduced within a framework of competing local communities and the hegemony of the state (Kim Kwang-ok 1996; 1999).

In today's world, Korean culture exists more as a hybrid of alien and native elements, and it has often questioned as to what it is that all Koreans share. With the development of a culture industry supported by advanced technology and the free transfer of information, Korean teenagers have perhaps more in common with teenagers in Hong Kong, Japan, or the United States than with the parents or grandparents that they live with. A similar kind of cultural fragmentation seems to be occurring not only between generations or classes but also between urban and rural, male and female, and above all, between South and North Koreans who have now been separated from each other for half a century. This situation indicates that we can no longer assume boundaries between cultures as automatically given. Localities or nationalities no longer function as social units, and it is becoming increasingly difficult to study culture using the concepts and frameworks that are familiar to us from conventional anthropology. In other words, it does not seem possible nowadays to designate any particular cultural elements as "Korean" or to list them as representative of the lives of those who live in modern Korea. The blurring of traditional cultural boundaries, however, does not necessarily mean that they no longer exist, or that they have lost all unique characteristics. On the contrary, it means that new cultural boundaries are constantly being constructed and new identities created. Moreover, we see in this process that cultural resources, both traditional and modern, are widely selected, adopted, manipulated, and even consumed.

Conclusion: The Future of Anthropological Knowledge in Korea

The origins of the indigenization issue can be traced back to intellectuals' ideological interest in national history and cultural identity during the colonial period in the first half of the twentieth century. After the 1970s, amidst rapid modernization and the influx of Western culture, it developed into one of the most fiercely debated issues among Korean intellectuals. In anthropology the issue has been discussed since the 1980s, as a reaction to apolitical and ahistorical nature of parts of the Western anthropological tradition.

Not all anthropologists share this concern for indigenization, however, especially if they interpret it as a "nationalistic" pursuit. This skepticism and at times allergic response toward anything related to nationalism should be understood against the background of the complicated political history of Korea. Since 1945, there has been continuous tension between government and people surrounding the political manipulation of national symbols and culture. Park Chung-hee, for instance, used "nationalism" strategically in order to legitimize his power. He claimed that his authoritarian dictatorship was "Korean-style democracy" (*Han'gukjeok minjujuyi*) and that it could be properly understood only in the context of the Korean cultural system. Under the banner of "*kukhak*," folklorists utilized studies of national folk customs as a way to popularize their subject. The subsequent military regimes of Chun Duwhan and Roh Tae-woo, and the civilian government of Kim Youngsam, have also made political use of the enthusiasm for symbols of national identity.

Other intellectuals and dissident politicians have also exploited nationalism at times, but as the basis for *anti*government movements. They have attacked the state as an agent of foreign capitalism and neocolonial powers, especially the United States and Japan, and criticized its policy of supporting the large-scale influx of foreign culture in the name of modernization and globalization. Under the regimes of Park Chung-hee and Chun Duwhan, antigovernment activists organized popular cultural movements based on the peasant tradition both as a counter to the elite tradition and as a tool for popularizing their ideology.

More recently, during the Kim Daejung regime, the notion of "indigenization" has been criticized by globalization theorists and liberal intellectuals as narrow minded, chauvinistic, and outdated. But despite this skepticism, the issue of indigenization in the field of anthropology is generally interpreted as understanding something within its local context and the local meaning system. On the one hand, this has provided ideological space for opposition to colonialism, and encouraged active debates regarding the nature of anthropological knowledge relevant to the Korean reality.

Indigenization is also for many scholars a question of personal identity. Many Korean anthropologists returning from the United States with doctoral degrees describe their experience of having to change their identities several times through the stages of training, fieldwork, writing up and returning to their home country. During graduate training and applying for a research grants, they are often required to objectify their own society and approach it from the point of view of "outsider" (i.e. Americans). In the field, however, many of them experience further difficulties as natives among the natives. Often, they realize that what is meaningful to the natives is not always meaningful to Western readers. Nevertheless, in order to complete the coursework, they are forced, through suggestions or friendly criticism from other scholars, to restructure their research proposals in a way that will appeal to Western supervisors, colleagues, and funding agencies. After they return home, they generally become "native" anthropologists, studying and writing mostly for a mainly Korean readership, and therefore have to change their identity once more.[16]

These experiences clearly show that the academic community in the West exercises decisive hegemonic influence upon the choice of the title, subject, writing style, language, and theoretical orientation, as well as the nature of the knowledge thereby produced. It also affects ways in which the "natives" are imagined, presented, or even invented. To reflect critically upon these processes and to produce knowledge more relevant to Korea itself by adopting or developing new perspectives and methods is therefore an indispensable part of the process of indigenizing Korean anthropology at present.

There is, however, an ongoing tension between this process of indigenization and the universalist pretensions of anthropology as an international discipline. While the former is concerned with the relevance of anthropology for the study of culture in the local context, the latter is more concerned with the degree of acceptability of that scholarship to an international, mainly Western, readership in terms of writing style, structure of argument, and means of presentation. In Korean anthropology, this tension is particularly notable in the field of women's studies. The feminist perspective has provided a much needed alternative to hitherto predominantly male-centered interpretations of Korean culture and society, especially since the 1980s. However, issues and theoretical arguments derived from American feminist studies have tended to dominate the field of women's studies in Korea, while the gendered culture of Korea itself has not been sufficiently investigated. There are also sometimes tensions between the assumptions of feminism and nationalism. In relation to the "comfort women," who were sexually exploited by the Japanese soldiers during the colonial period, feminists see the issue as part of the history of sexual oppression by males, while nationalists insist that it should be understood within the context of colonialism. So far in gender studies, radical feminists or liberalists have been dominant because they share a vocabulary and interests with influential groups within American women's studies. "Center" and "periphery" relations are thus reconstituted within Korean women's studies in relation to their links with the Western academic community.

Another issue that has attracted the attention of indigenizing anthropologists is the persistence of seemingly irrational ideas and primordial sentiments in modern Korea that have been often neglected by scholars from the West. For instance, aspects of Korean culture like emotional or psychological affection (*jeong*), grudges (*han*), ideas of relatedness to some *a priori* spiritual elements (*yon* or *yon-jul*), socially constructed relationships (*gwan-gye*), or sentiments based on regional identity (*jiyeok gamjeong*) are all outside the framework of Western rationality but are frequently referred to as part of "typical" Korean political, economic, and social behavior (Kim Kwang-ok 1998c). In order to connect the inner world of the Koreans with more general theories, however, the specific social conditions where such behavior is found need to be accounted for, and this remains another important task for Korean anthropologists.

Finally, it should be pointed out that the gradual increase in the number of anthropologists studying other cultures adds another dimension to the discussion of indigenization in Korea. Although postwar Korean anthropology has been predominantly "native" anthropology in the sense that most scholars have studied their own cultures and interpreted them for other Koreans, the number of anthropologists doing fieldwork in other societies has grown continuously since the early 1980s, and now includes parts of Europe, Africa, South America, and South and Southeast Asia. This phenomenon has contributed toward broadening the scope of anthropological knowledge as well as helping to locate and objectify Korean culture (Moon Ok-pyo 1997). It helps native anthropologists to see their own culture as the "Other," reflect critically, and enrich their discussions of Korean society from a comparative perspective. On the other hand, it also raises the question of how to develop specifically "Korean" perspectives and methodologies in studying other cultures that are distinguishable from the dominant paradigms in the West. Many of these issues are shared with scholars in other countries outside the West where anthropology has also taken root, as is shown by many of the other chapters in this book.

Postscript

Since the present article was first drafted in 1999, a series of distinctive achievements have been made in Korean anthropology through in new fields of study and research subjects. Anthropologists have been more concerned with the practical uses of anthropology in relation to Korean studies, as well as to social issues in contemporary Korea. People have become aware that Korea is a country with a long recorded history, of which its people are deeply conscious. There is great interest in the reconstruction of the past, and in how Koreans have made their own versions of history, particularly the common people (*minjung*) rather than the elite. Social memories, together with the imagined or lived experiences of modernity, structural transformation, and institutional change, have become popular themes, along with local history, narratives, life histories, and the politics of tradition. One group of anthropologists have carried out team research in a reclamation area in order to study how the local people have invented and reinvented local legends and ritual to resist the modernity that is destroying their ecology and environment (Oh Myung-seok at al. 2000). Kim Seong-nae (2001) and Yoon Hyung-sook 2002), and Yoon Taek-lim (2003) have focused on people's memories of war and state violence in modern times in order to reinstate the histories of local people that have been silenced or buried by successive Korean regimes. Anthropological theories of narrative, autobiography, and life histories have shed new light in the fields of social and popular history. Moon Ok-pyo, Kim Kwang-ok, Park Byoung-ho, and Eun Kisoo (2004) have carried out micro-historical research which combines their fieldwork data with official and private documents from the Chosun period (*gomunseo*) to reconstruct the local lineage society. Relations between the state and society and between the official and the private have been the main frame of reference. Moon Ok-pyo's analysis of various forms of written materials on inheritance and property division (*bunjaegi*) has led to reconsideration of the conventional wisdom concerning women's status and household structure in Confucian ideology during the period between the sixteenth and nineteenth centuries. Through the analysis of lineage council documents (*waneumun*) and of letters (*tongmun*) circulating between lineage groups, Confucian academies, and families, Kim Kwang-ok has described the expanding networks of communications control of public space in precolonial Korea. The politics of cultural events, intra- and inter-class conflicts, networks based on marriage and school ties, and legal disputes are extensively analyzed in his reconstruction of the local power structure. In this way, anthropologists are playing a central role in the vigorous debates between scholars in history, social science and cultural studies in search of new methods for the study of Korea.

Postmodern theoretical orientations and waves of globalization have also stimulated a search for a new anthropology of Korean society and culture. Multi-sited, cross-boundary, and transnational studies have provided new methodological perspectives. Anthropologists are currently reexamining the social structure and cultural system of Korea from the perspectives of history and globalization.

The reproduction or invention of cultural tradition in the postmodern situation is also an important subject of study. Kim Kwang-ok (2000a) has discussed the role of traditional relationships in postmodern Korean society and Moon Ok-pyo (2000) has analyzed how local cultures are appropriated as cultural capital by tourists. Also discussed is the question of how the notions of tradition and modernity are reproduced around the issue of Korean cultural identity (Cho Oakla et al. 2003). Song Do-young (2000) has carried out research on the creation of new traditions in everyday urban life, while others have discussed the ways in which TV drama and film reflect new forms of Korean culture (see Park Christian Joon-kyu 2003, Lee Chang-ho and Chung Su-nam 2002). Yoon Hyung-sook (2000) has analyzed how local history is reflected in family history, while Yim Dawnhee and Roger Janelli (2001) have reviewed contemporary transformations of the concept of filial piety. Yoon Hyung-sook (2001) has shown how patriarchal ideology is being contested, while Kang Jeong-won (2002) has observed changes in communal ritual (*dongje*) in the process of modernization.

Discourses and definitions of Korean cultural identity are also being examined. Han Kyung-koo (2003) has reviewed anthropological discourses of Korean-ness, and Kwon Sug-in (2003) has examined popular discourses on Korean culture. Yi Jeong-duk (2003) has analyzed Korean culture critically, while Kim Young-hoon (2003) has described how Korean cultural identity is visualized in tourism postcards. Hahm Han-hee (2003) has examined how Korean culture is seen by Western eyes, and Jang Soo-hyun (2003) has investigated how it is represented in Chinese narratives. Han Gun-soo (2003) has studied how African migrant workers perceive Korean people and their culture, while Kim Joo-kwan (2003) has shown how local dialects are exploited as symbolic resources in people's economic and political lives..

At the same time, further research has been carried out on Koreans overseas. Chun Kyung-soo has led teams studying Koreans in Kazakhstan (2000), Uzebekhstan (1999), and Sakhalin (2001). A group of anthropologists under the leadership of Moon Ok-pyo has carried out ethnographic research among Koreans in Western Japan (2002) and Choi Hyup has directed team research among Koreans in Hawaii (2003). Lee Hyonjeong (2000) has carried out fieldwork in a Korean village in Northeast China, focusing on the strategic manipulation of national identity by the Korean Chinese. Seol Byung-soo (2002) has shown how Koreans in Australia use their dual ethnicity in business. Anthropologists have also paid special attention to studies of the popularity of Korean culture as a commodity (*hanlyu*) in foreign markets (see Cho Haejoang 2002; Jang Soo-hyun 2003; Kim Hyunmi 2003). Hwang Ik-joo (2002) has also been carrying out long-term research on the formation of subcultures, focussing especially on young people of the urban working class, within the contexts of industrialization, urbanization, and internal migration. In relation to the partition of Korea, anthropologists have also studied refugees from North Korea (*talbukja*) (see Park Sunyoung 2000; 2002; Jang Soo-hyun 2001), NGO activities to construct a cross-boundary national community between South and North Korea (*nambuk gongdongche*), and discourses of and transnationalism and postnationalism.

Anthropologists have become more and more conscious about issues and problems of alienation, marginalization, and inequality in contemporary Korea and are becoming increasingly committed to applied anthropology. Anthropologists of the new generation are studying women and minorities including the poor, disabled, children, the aged, and low-waged foreign migrant workers (Yoo Myung-ki 1995; 2002). These trends have been reflected in the main themes of the annual meeting of the Korean Society for Cultural Anthropology since 1999, which have included "National Division," "War, and Life History" (1999), "Revitalization of Tradition and Local Culture" (2000), "Mass Culture and the Culture Industry" (2002), and "Identity in the Transnational Era" (2003). In 2003, the Korean Society of Cultural Anthropology launched long-term projects on the life histories of the common people (*minjung saengwhalsa*) under Park Hyun-soo, and on the history of household and family life (*jip-gwa gajok-eu saengwhalsa*) under Moon Ok-pyo, involving the collection of narratives, oral traditions, micro history, and material culture. In the context of globalization, anthropologists now play active roles in the study of the practical issues that Korean society faces in its transformation. Power, the state, the nation, history, globalization, and trans-nationalism are the keywords that characterize the general trends in the anthropology both in and of Korea at the present day.

Notes

1   The most prominent colonial scholars were Murayama Chijun, Akiba Takashi, and Akamatsu Chijo in the field of folk cultures, i.e. shamanism, folk belief systems, rituals and rites, and social institutions.

2   On Japanese colonial distortions of Koreans and their culture, see Park Hyun-soo (1998).

3   Choi Nam-sun's theory was appropriated by the colonialists as an indigenous intellectual's support for colonial assimilation policy and the eradication of Korean culture on the grounds that Japanese and Korean cultures are from the same origin.

4   For the native intellectuals' studies of "national culture" under colonial rule, see Kim Kwang-ok (1998a).

5   On the ideological implications of so-called "scientism" during this period, see Kim Kyeong-il (1998).

6   Before this, there was a short-lived anthropological association in Korea called the Chosun Anthropological Society (*Joseon Illyuhak Hoe*) whose members were in fact mostly folklorists. After Liberation, the society was renamed *Daehan Illyuhak Hoe* in 1946, after the new name of the independent republic of Korea. It existed until 1949 (Han Sang-bok 1974).

7 For a comprehensive review of anthropology in contemporary Korea, see Kim Kwang-ok (1987; 1995.)

8 Subsidized by the Korean Ministry of Culture and Information, the survey began in 1968 in South Cholla Province and was completed in 1981 with the publication of the South and North Hamgyong Province editions.

9 The first Korean to obtain a doctorate in the field of anthropology was Han Chungnim who obtained her degree from the University of Michigan in 1949 with a dissertation on a lineage village.

10 See Choi Jae-seok (1966; 1979; 1983); Yeo Jung-chul (1980); Yoo Myung-ki (1977); Lee Kwang-kyu (1977; 1986; 1990); Song Sunhee (1982); and Kim Yongwhan (1989). The works listed here and later are not meant to be exhaustive but include only those that we regard as typically representing the trends of the period discussed. Additionally, it should be noted that the studies by foreign anthropologists of Korean society are not covered here.

11 For a comprehensive list of M.A. and Ph.D. dissertation topics submitted to the anthropology departments of Korean universities, see Kim Kwang-ok (1987: 81-87).

12 This is taken to mean that, for Koreans, those foods and medicines produced on Korean soil using Korean methods are the best because one's physiological state is affected by the environment.

13 For the unpublished theses with similar theoretical focus, see Chae Suhong (1991); Choi Horim (1993); Chin Pil-soo (1994); Chang Chung-a (1995); Chang Hojun (1995).

14 The subjects of M.A. theses submitted in Korean departments of anthropology clearly demonstrate these shifts in interests reflecting the redefinition of the concept of culture. There are two universities in Korea, Seoul National University and Youngnam University, that offer doctorates, but the number of dissertations completed is yet too small to be used as an indicator of the general trend of the direction of research.

15 For a structuralist criticism of postmodernism, see Yi Jeong-duk (1993b).

16 For a very vivid depiction of the series of changes of identity, see Yoon Hyung-sook (1996).

References

Chae Suhong. 1991. "Nodongja gyegeup inyeom hyeongseong gwajeong-e gwanhan yeon'gu" [A study of the process of formation of working class ideology], Unpublished M.A. Thesis: Seoul National University.

Chang Chung-a.1995. "Gieop inyeom yupo-wa suyong yangsang-e gwanhan yeon'gu" [A study of dissemination and accommodation of ideological orientation in a business company], Unpublished M.A. Thesis: Seoul National University.

Chang Chu-keun. 1986. *Han'guk minsok non'go* [Essays on Korean folklore]. Seoul: Kyemongsa.

Chang Hojun. 1995. "Gongdongchejeok gieop munhwa damron-eu hwalyong-gwa gwageo-eu jaeguseong" [Manipulation of organizational culture in a company as a community and as a reconstruction of the past], Unpublished M.A. Thesis, Seoul National University.

Chin Pil-soo. 1994. "Bongje gieop jageopjang munwha-e gwanhan yeon'gu" [A study of the shop floor culture of a clothing factory], Unpublished M.A. Thesis, Seoul National University.

Cho Heung-yoon. 1983. *Han'guk-eu mu* [Korean shamanism]. Seoul: Jeong'eumsa.

Cho Hyejoang. 1992-1994. *Tal-sikminji sidae jisik'in-eu geul'ilgi-wa sam'ilgi* [Reading the writings and lives of intellectuals in the post-colonial age]. Seoul: Tohana-eu Munwha.

Cho Hyejoang. 1996. *Hakgyoreul geobuhaneun a-i, a-i-reul geobuhaneun sahoe* [Children who refuse school, the society that refuses children]. Seoul: Tohanaeu Munhwa.

Cho Hyejoang. 2002. "Dong/seoyang jeongcheseong-eu haechewa jaeguseong: Global jigak byeondong-eu jinghuro ikneun hanlyuyeolpung" [Modernity, popular culture and East-West identity formation: A discourse analysis of the Korean wave in Asia], *Han'guk munwha illyuhak* 35 (1): 3-40.

Cho Oakla, Choi Bong-young, and Shin Kyung-a. 2003. "Han'guk'ineu munwhajeok jeongcheseong-e naejaedoin jeontong-gwa geundae-eu munje" [Issues of tradition and modernity in Korean cultural identity], *Han'guk munwja illyuhak* 36 (1): 3-42.

Cho Un and Cho Oakla. 1992. *Doshibinmin-eu samgwa gonggan: Sadangdong jaegaebal jiyeok-eu hyeonjang yeon'gu* [Life and living space of the urban poor: Field research in the Sadangdong redevelopment area]. Seoul: Seoul National University Press.

Choi Horim. 1993. "Saengsanjik gwanrija-eu jiwiwa yeokhal-eu byeonwha-e gwanhan yeon'gu" [A study of changes in the status and role of work team leaders in the production unit], Unpublished M.A. Thesis: Seoul National University.

Choi Hyup. 1994. "Honam munhwaron i mosaek" [On the character of *Honam* culture], *Han'guk munwha illyuha*k [Korean Cultural Anthropology] 25: 29-45.

Choi Hyup et al. 2003. *Miguk Hawaijiyeok Hanin donpoeu saengwhalmunwha* [The life and culture of Koreans in Hawaii]. Seoul: National Folk Culture Museum.

Choi Jae-seok. 1966. *Han'guk gajok yeon'gu* [A study of the Korean family]. Seoul: Iljisa.

Choi Jae-seok. 1979. *Chejudo-eu chinjok jojik* [Kinship organization in Cheju Island]. Seoul: Iljisa.

Choi Jae-seok. 1983. *Han'guk gajok jedosa yeon'gu* [A history of the Korean family system]. Seoul: Iljisa.

Choi Kilsong. 1978. *Han'guk musok-eu yeon'gu* [A study of Korean shamanism]. Taegu: Hyeongseol Chulpansa.

Choi Nam-sun 1973 *Yukdang Choi Namsun jeonjip* [A compilation of Choi Nam-sun's writings]. Seoul: Hyunamsa.

Choi Seok-young. 1997a. *Ilje-eu donghwa ideology-eu changchul* [The Japanese colonial invention of assimilation ideology]. Seoul: Seokyoung Munhwasa.

Choi Seok-young. 1997b. Ilje-eu gugwanjosawa sikminjeongchaeko [The imperial Japanese investigation of old customs and colonial policy in Korea], *Bigyo minsokhak* [Comparative Study of Folklore] 14 (1): 337-76.

Chun Kwan-woo. 1974. *Han'guksa-eu Jaeinsik* [A reconsideration of Korean history]. Seoul: Ilchogak.

Chun, Kyung-soo. 1984. *Reciprocity and Korean Society: An Ethnography of Hasami*. Seoul: Seoul National University Press.

Chun Kyung-soo. 1999. *Uzbekstan Hanin dongpoeu saengwhalmunwha* [The life and culture of Koreans in Uzbekistan]. Seoul: National Folk Culture Museum.

Chun Kyung-soo et al. 2000. *Kazakstan Hanin dongpoeu saengwhalmunwha* [The life and culture of Koreans in Kazakhstan]. Seoul: National Folk Culture Museum.

Chun Kyung-soo et al. 2001. *Russia Sahalin Yeonhaeju Hanin dongpoeu saengwhalmunwha* [The life and culture of Koreans in Sakhalin, Russia]. Seoul: National Folk Culture Museum.

Chung Byung-ho. 1996. "Han'guk jisiksahoewa jung'ang jungsimseong-eu geukbok'" [How to overcome the intellectuals' center-orientation in Korea], *Han'guk munhwa lllyuhak* 29 (1): 37-62.

Chung In-bo. 1947. *Chosunsa yeon'gu: Och'onnyeon Chosun-eu eol* [A study of Korean history: The spirit of Korea over five thousand years]. Seoul: Seoul Daily Press.

Hahm, Han-hee. 2003. "Korean culture seen through westerner's eyes," *Korea Journal* 43 (1): 106-28.

Han Gun-soo. 2003. "African migrant workers' views of Korean people and culture," *Korea Journal* 43 (1): 154-73.

Han Kyung-koo. 1994. "Otton eumsikeun saengkak hagie jota: Kimchiwa han'guk minjokseong eu jeongsu" [Some food is good to think with: Kimchi and the essence of Korean national identity], *Han'guk munwha illyuhak* 26: 51-68

Han Kyung-koo. 2003. "The anthropology of the discourse on the Koreanness of Koreans," *Korea Journal* 43 (1): 5-31.

Han Sang-bok. 1974. "Han'guk munwha illyuhak-eu banseong-gwa jihyang" [Reflection and prospects of cultural anthropology in Korea] in *Han'guk munwha illyuha*k [Korean Cultural Anthropology] 6: 213-217.

Han, Sang-bok. 1977. *Korean Fishermen: Ecological Adaptation in Three Communities*. Seoul: Seoul National University Press.

Han Sang-bok. 1980. *"Illyuhak"* [Anthropology], pp. 198-215 in *Mun'yeyeon'gam* [Yearbook of Literature and Art]. Seoul: Munye Jinheungwon.

Han Sang-bok and Kwon Taewhan. 1993. *Jung-guk Yeonbyeoneu Joseonjok* [Koreans in Yanbian, China]. Seoul: Seoul National University Press.

Hwang Ik-joo. 1994. "Hyangto eumsik sobi-eu sahoe munwhajeok eumi" [The socio-cultural meaning of the consumption of a special local dish], *Han'guk munwha illyuhak* 26: 69-93

Hwang Ik-joo. 1997. "Gongjang nodongjadeul eu yeoga saenghwal" [Leisure of factory workers], *Han'guk'ineu zobiwa yeoga saenghwal* [Consumption and leisure life of Koreans], ed. Moon Ok-pyo. Seongnam: Academy of Korean Studies.

Hwang Ik-joo. 2002. "Han'guk dosieseo-eu 'hyanwuhoe'-eu jojik pattern" [Organizational pattern of 'hometown association' in urban Korea], *Jiyeok sahoehak* 4 (1): 107-42.

Janelli, Roger L. and Dawnhee Yim Janelli. 1982. *Ancestor Worship and Korean Society*. Stanford: Stanford University Press.

Jang Soo-hyun. 2001. "Jung'guknae bukhan nanmineu sahoejeok gotong: Han'gyejeok sangwhang-gwa ojeom mandeulgi" [Social suffering among the North Korean refugees in China: Marginal status and stigmatization], *Han'guk munwha illyuhak* 34 (2): 211-36.

Jang, Soo-hyun. 2003. "Contemporary Chinese narratives on Korean culture," *Korea Journal* 43 (1): 129-53.

Kang Jeong-won. 2002. "Geundaewhawa dongjeeu byeonwha" [Modernization and change in a village ritual], *Han'guk munwha illyuhak* 35 (1): 41-72.

Kang Shin-pyo. 1974. "Dong'asia-eseoi han'guk munwha" [Korean culture in East Asia], *Han'guk munwha illyuhak* 6: 191-94.

Kang Shin-pyo. 1980. "Han'guk-ineu jeontongjeok saengwhal yangsik-eu gujo-e gwanhan siron" [A preliminary study of the Korean traditional way of life], *Han'guk-eu sahoe-wa munwha* [Korean Society and Culture] 3: 231-316.

Kang Shin-pyo. 1984. "Jeontongjeok saengwhal yangsik-eu gujo" [Structure of traditional way of life], in *Dongwon Kim Hungbae baksa gohi ginyeom nonmunjip* [Festschrifts for the Seventieth Birthday of Dr. Dongwon Kim Hungbae]. Seoul: Hankuk University of Foreign Studies Press.

Kang Shin-pyo ed. 1985. *Han'guk munwha yeon'gu* [Studies of Korean culture]. Seoul: Hyonamsa.

Kim, Eunhee. 1993. "From Gentry to the Middle Class: The Transformation of Family, Community, and Gender in Korea," Ph.D. Thesis: University of Chicago.

Kim, Eunshil. 1993. "The Making of the Modern Female Gender: The Politics of Gender in Reproductive Practices in Korea," Ph.D. Thesis, University of California, Berkeley.

Kim Hyunmi. 1996. "Nodongtongje-eu kijeroseo-eu seong" [Gender/sexuality as a mechanism for labor control], *Han'guk munhwa illyuhak* 29 (2): 167-194.

Kim Hyunmi. 2003. "Ilbon daejungmunwha-eu sobiwa fandom-eu hyeonsang" [The inflow of Japanese pop culture and the historical construction of fandoms in South Korea], *Han'guk munwha illyuhak* 36 (1): 14-186.

Kim Il-chul, Moon Ok-pyo, Kim Pildong, Han Dohyun, Song Jungki. 1998. *Jongjok maeul-eu jeontong-gwa byeonwha* [Tradition and change in a lineage village]. Seoul: Baeksan.

Kim Jinmyoung. 1993. *Gulle sok-eu Han'guk yeoseong* [Korean Women in Bondage]. Seoul: Jipmundag.

Kim, Juhee. 1981. "*Pumasi*: Patterns of Interpersonal Relationships in a Korean Village," Ph.D. Thesis: Northwestern University.

Kim Juhee. 1991. *Pumasiwa jeong-eu In'gan gwan'gye* [Interpersonal relationships of reciprocal exchanges and human feelings]. Seoul: Jipmundang.

Kim Joo-kwan. 2003. "Eoneo jawoneu jabonwha gwajeong-gwa sangjingjabon-eu hyeongseong" [Capitlaization of linguistic resources and formation of symbolic capital], *Han'guk munwha illyuhak* 36 (1): 247-268.

Kim, Kyeong-il. 1998. "Intellectual context of Korean studies in colonial Korea," *Review of Korean Studies* (Songnam: The Academy of Korean Studies) 1 (1): 53-75.

Kim Kwang-ok. 1987. "*Han'guk illyuhak-eu Pyeong'gawa Jeonmang*" [Appraisal and prospect of Korean anthropology], in *Hyeonsang-gwa insik*. 11 (1): 53-89.

Kim Kwang-ok. 1989. Jeongchijeok damnon kijeroseo-eu minjung munhwa undong: sahoeguk-uroseo-eu madang'geuk" [People's cultural movements as a mechanism for political discourse: *Madang'guk* as a social drama], *Han'guk munhwa illyuhak* 21: 53-77.

Kim Kwang-ok. 1991. "Jeohangmunwha wa musok eurye" [Shamanism and culture of resistance], *Hankuk munwha illyuhak* 23: 131-72

Kim, Kwang-ok. 1992. "Socio-political implications of the resurgence of ancestor worship in contemporary Korea," pp. 179-203 in *Home Bound: Studies in East Asian Society*, eds. Chie Nakane and Chien Chiao. Tokyo: Center for East Asian Cultural Studies.

Kim Kwang-ok. 1994a. "Munwha gongdongche-wa Jibangjeongchi" [Cultural community and local level politics], *Han'guk munwha illyuhak* 25: 116-82

Kim, Kwang-ok. 1994b. "Rituals of resistance: The manipulation of shamanism in contemporary Korea," pp. 195-219 in *Asian Visions of Authority*, eds. C. Keyes, L. Kendall, and H. Hardacre. Honolulu: University of Hawaii Press.

Kim Kwang-ok. 1995. "Han'guk illyuhak-eu banseong-gwa gwaje" [Retrospect and prospect of Korean anthropology: Personal and reflexive appraisal], *Hyunsang gwa Insik* 19 (2): 75-102.

Kim Kwang-ok. 1996. "Jibang-eu saengsan-gwa geu jeongchijeok eyong" [Production of the "local" and its politics], *Han'guk munhwa illyuhak* 29 (1): 3-35.

Kim Kwang-ok. 1998a. "Iljesigi tochakjisik'in-eu minjokmunwha insik-eu teul" [Concept of national culture among the native intellectuals under Japanese colonialism], *Bigyo munwha yeon'gu* [Cross-cultural Studies] 4: 79-120.

Kim, Kwang-ok. 1998b. "The Confucian construction of a cultural community in contemporary South Korea," pp. 65-94 in *Anthropology of Korea*, eds. M. Shima and R. Janelli. Osaka: National Museum of Ethnology.

Kim Kwang-ok. 1998c. "The communal ideology and its reality," *Korea Journal* 38 (3): 5-44.

Kim Kwang-ok. 1998d. "Sansang-I gyeongjaenghaneun gong'gan: Han'gukeseo-eu Jung'guk eumsik" [A contested space of imaginations: Chinese food in Korea], pp. 285-315 *in Han'guk illyuhak'eu seong'gwawa jeonmang* [Achievements and prospects of Korean anthropology]. Seoul: Jipmundang. .

Kim Kwang-ok. 2000a. "Jibang yeon'gu bangbeopnon gaebaleul wihan siron" [In search of a new methodology for the study of local society and culture], *Jibang sahoewa jibang munhwa* [Local society and local culture] 2: 9-41.

Kim Kwang-ok. 2000b. "Jeontongjeok gwan'gye-eu hyeondaejeok silcheon" [Private relations in postmodern Korean society], *Han'guk munwha illyuhak* 33 (2): 7-48.

Kim Kwang-ok. ed. 1998. *Munwha-eu dahakmunjeok jeopgeun* [Multi-disciplinary approaches to culture]. Seoul: Seoul National University Press.

Kim Kwang-ok et al. 1996. *Jung'guk Gilimseong Hanin dongpoeu saengwhalmunwha* [The life and culture of Koreans in Jilin Province, China]. Seoul: National Folk Culture Museum.

Kim Kwang-ok et al. 1997. *Jung'guk Yoneongseong Hanin dongpoeu saengwhalmuwha* [The life and culture of Koreans in Liaoning Province, China]. Seoul: National Folk Culture Museum.

Kim Kwang-ok et al. 1998. *Jung'guk Heuklyong'gangseong Hanin donpoeu saengwhalmunwha* [The life and culture of Koreans in Heilungjiang Province, China]. Seoul: National Folk Culture Museum.

Kim, Seong-nae. 1989. "Chronicles of Violence, Rituals of Mourning: Cheju Shamanism in Korea," Ph.D. Thesis: University of Michigan.

Kim, Seong-nae. 1989. "Lamentations of the dead: The historical imagery of violence on Cheju Island, South Korea," *Journal of Ritual Studies* 3: 251-86.

Kim Seong-nae. 1990. "Musok jeont'ong-eu damron bunseok" [Discourse analysis of shamanic traditions], in *Han'guk munwha illyuhak* [Korean Cultural Anthropology] 22: 211-44.

Kim Seong-nae et al. 2001. "Jeju 4.3eu gyeongheomgwa maeul gongdongche-eu byeonwha" [A changing village community in the living history of the April Third Jeju Uprising]. *Han'guk munwha illyuhak* 34 (1): 89-137.

Kim Taek-kyu. 1964. *Dongjok burak-eu saengwhal gujo yeon'gu* [A study of the structure of life in a lineage village]. Daegu: Cheong'gu University Press.

Kim Taek-kyu. 1985. *Han'guk nonggyeong sesi-eu yeon'gu* [A study of yearly agricultural rites in Korea]. Kyongsan: Youngnam University Press.

Kim, Yong-whan. 1989. "A Study of Korean Lineage Organization from a Regional Perspective: A Comparison with the Chinese System," Ph.D Thesis, Rutgers University.

Kim, Young-hoon. 2003. "Self-representation: The visualization of Koreanness in tourism posters during the 1970s and 1980s," *Korea Journal* 43 (1): 83-106.

Kwon Sug-in. 1998. "Cha hanjanae-eu chodae" [Invitation to a cup of tea: fieldwork, identity of the ethnographer, and Japanese studies by a Korean scholar], *Han'guk munwha illyuhak* 31 (1): 49-73.

Kwon Sug-in. 2003. "Popular discourses on Korean culture," *Korea Journal* 43 (1): 32-57.

Lee Chang-ho and Chung Su-nam. 2002. "Television documentary-e natanan geundaejeok siseon-gwa jaehyuneu jeongchi" [The politics of modern views and representation in TV documentary], *Han'guk munwha illyuhak* 35 (2): 223-74.

Lee Du-hyun. 1984. *Han'guk minsokhak non'go* [Essays on Korean folklore]. Seoul: Hakyeonsa.

Lee Du-hyun, Chang Chu-keun, and Lee Kwang-kyu. 1985[1974]. *Han'guk minsokhak gaeseol* [Introduction to Korean folklore]. Seoul: Hakyeonsa.

Lee Hoon-sang. 1990. *Chosun hugi-eu hyangli* [Local officers in the Late Chosun]. Seoul: Ilchogak.

Lee Hyonjeong. 2000. "Han'guk chui-eop-gwa jung'guk joseonjok-eu sahoemunhwajeok byeonhwa" [The "Korean dream" and socio-cultural changes among the Koreans in China], M.A. thesis, Seoul National University.

Lee Ki-tae. 1997. *Eupchi seonghwangje juchejipdaneu byeonhwawa jeeujeontong-eu changchul* [Changes of masters in city god worship and the invention of ritual tradition]. Seoul: Minsokwon.

Lee Kwang-kyu. 1975. *Han'guk gajok-eu gujo bunseok* [An analysis of Korean family structure]. Seoul: Iljisa.

Lee Kwang-kyu. 1977. *Han'guk gajok-eu sajeok yeon'gu* [An historical study of the Korean family]. Seoul: Iljisa.

Lee Kwang-kyu. 1981. *Han'guk gajok-eu simli munje* [The psychological problems of the Korean Family]. Seoul: Iljisa.

Lee Kwang-kyu. 1983. *Jaeil Hanguk-in* [Koreans in Japan]. Seoul: Ilchogak.

Lee Kwang-kyu. 1986. "Burak saengwhal-eu daerip-gwa jowhareul tonghan jilseo eusik" [The idea of order through conflict and harmony in village life], *Han'guk-eu sahoewa munwha* [Korean society and culture] (Seongnam: Academy of Korean Studies) 6: 181-212.

Lee Kwang-kyu. 1989. *Jaemi Han'guk-in* [Koreans in America]. Ilchogak.

Lee Kwang-kyu. 1990. *Han'guk-eu gajok-gwa jongjok* [Korean family and lineage]. Seoul: Mineumsa.

Lee Kwang-kyu. 1998a. *Han'guk gajok-eu sahoe illyuhak* [The social anthropology of the Korean Family]. Seoul: Jipmundang.

Lee Kwang-kyu. 1998b. *Russia Yeonhaejueu Hanin sahoe* [Korean society in Sakhalin]. Seoul: Jipmoondang.

Lee Kwang-kyu and Chun Kyungsoo. 1993. *Jaeso Hanin* [Koreans in Russia]. Seoul: Jipmundang

Lee Man-gap. 1973. *Han'guk nongchon sahoe-eu gujowa byeonwha* [Structure and change in Korean rural society]. Seoul: Seoul National University Press.

Moon, Ok-pyo. 1990. "Urban middle class wives in contemporary Korea: their roles, responsibilities and dilemma", *Korea Journal* 30 (11): 30-43.

Moon, Ok-pyo. 1998a. "Ancestors becoming children of God: Ritual clashes between Confucian tradition and Christianity in contemporary Korea," *Korea Journal* 38 (3): 148-77.

Moon Ok-pyo. 1998b. "Yeseo-e natanan yugyosik gwanhonsangjerye-eu eumibunseok" [Interpretations of Confucian rites of innitiation, marriage, funeral, and ancestor worship in the Text of Rites], pp. 181-210 in *Han'guk illyuhak-eu seonggwa-wa jeonmang* [Achievements and prospects of Korean Anthropology], ed. Professor Lee Kwang-kyu Festchrift Committee. Seoul: Jipmundang.

Moon, Ok-pyo. 1999. "Korean anthropology: A search for new paradigms," *Review of Korean Studies* 2 (September): 113-37.

Moon Ok-pyo 2000. "Gwan'gwang-eul tonghan munwhaeu saengsan-gwa sobi: Hahoe maeul-eu saryereul jungsimeuro" [Hahoe village appropriated: Production of tourist culture in Korea, 1970s-1990s], *Han'guk munwha illyuhak* 33 (2): 79-110.

Moon Ok-pyo ed. 1997. *Han'guk'ineu sobi-wa yeoga saengwhal* [Consumption and leisure among Koreans]. Seongnam: Academy of Korean Studies (Monograph Series 97-9).

Moon Ok-pyo, Chung Yang-wan, and Lee Chung-koo. 1999a. *Chosun sidae gwanhonsangje* [Rites of passage during the Chosun Period] (I). Seongnam: Academy of Korean Studies.

Moon Ok-pyo, Chung Yang-wan, and Lee Chung-koo. 1999b. *Chosun Sidae Gwanhonsangje* [Rites of passage during the Chosun Period] (II). Seongnam: Academy of Korean Studies.

Moon Ok-pyo, Kim Kwang-ok, Chun Kyungsoo, Yim Bong-kil, and Kim Busoung. 1992. *Dosi Jungsancheung-eu Saengwhal Munwha* [Lifeways of the Urban Middle Class]. Seongnam: Academy of Korean Studies (Monograph Series 92-10).

Moon Ok-pyo et al. 2002. *Ilbon Gwanseojiyeok Hanin donpoeu saengwhalmunwha* [The life and culture of Koreans in the Kansai region of Japan]. Seoul: National Folk Culture Museum.

Moon Ok-pyo, Kim Kwang-ok, Park Byoung-ho, and Eun Kisoo. 2004. *Chosun yangbaneu saengwhal segye* [Yangban: The life-world of the Korean scholar-gentry]. Seoul: Baiksan.

Oh Myung-seok et al. 2000. *Seosan gancheokji josabogo* [A report on research on the reclamation area in Seosan] (Report paper)

Osgood, Cornelius. 1951. *The Koreans and Their Culture*. New York: Ronald Press.

Park, Christian J. 2003. "Television drama 'Gyeoul Yeon'ga'wa diaspora-jeok jeongcheseong'" [Television drama 'Winter Love Song' and diasporic identity], *Han'guk munwha illyuhak* 36 (1): 219-44.

Park Howon 1997. "Han'guk gongdongche sinang-eu yeoksajeok yeon'gu" [A historical study of communal ritual in Korea]. Ph.D. Thesis, Academy of Korean Studies.

Park Hyun-soo. 1980a. "Ilje-eu chimryakeul wihan sahoemunwha josawhaldong" [Japanese investigation of social and cultural institutions for their colonial invasion], *Han'guksa yeon'gu* 30: 131-140

Park Hyun-soo 1980b. "Chosun chongdokbu jungchuwoneu sahoemunhwa josa" [Investigations of Korean society and culture by the Central Council of the Japanese Colonial Government General], *Han'guk munhwa illyuhak* 12 (1): 70-92.

Park Hyun-soo. 1998. "Han'guk munwha-e daehan ilje-eu sigak" [The Japanese colonial view of Korean culture], *Bikyomunwha yeon'gu* 4: 35-77

Park Hyun-soo. 1993. "Ilje-eu Chosun josa-e gwanhan yeon'gu" [Surveys of Korea by Imperial Japan], Unpulished Ph.D. Thesis: Seoul National University.

Park Sunyoung. 2000. "Bukhan siklyang wigieu jangijeok pyeong'ga: Incheeu seongjangbalyukgwa geongang-e michineun yeonghyang-gwa geu sahoejeok hameu"[An assesment of the long term effects of food crisis on children's growth and development in North Korea], *Han'guk munwha illyuhak* 33 (1): 207-40.

Park Sunyoung. 2002. "Talbukja inchecheukjeongjaryoreul yiyonghan bukhaneu saengmulhakjeok bokjisujune daehan yeon'gu" [A study of North Korean biological standards of living using anthropometric data from North Korean escapees], *Han'guk munwha illyuhak* 35 (1): 101-28.

Seol Byung-soo. 2002. "Hojunae hanindeuleu sogyumo saeopgwa jongjok jawoneu du eolgul" [Small business activities of Koreans in Australia and the duality of their ethnic resources], *Han'guk munwha illyuhak* 35 (2): 275-301.

Shin Chae-ho. 1977. *Danjae Shin Chae-ho jeonjip* [Collected works of Danjae Shin Chae-ho]. Seoul: Eulyoo Munhwasa.

Son Jin-tae. 1948. *Chosun minjok munhwa-eu yeon'gu* [A study of Korean national culture]. Seoul: Eulyoo Munhwasa.

Song Do-young. 1996. "Jibang munhwa haengjeong hwaldong chamyeo-eu illyuhak" [The anthropology of participation in the local administration of culture], *Han'guk munhwa illyuhak* 29 (1): 63-101.

Song Do-young. 1998. "1980 nyeondae Han'guk munhwa undong-gwa minjok minjungjeok munhwa yangsik-eu tamsa" [The Korean cultural movement in the 1980s and the search for national popular cultural modes], *Bigyo munhwa yeon'gu* [Cross-cultural Studies] 4: 153-180.

Song Do-young. 2000. "Munwhasaneup-eu sokdoseong-gwa disijeok ilsangmunwha seong'gyeok-eu hyeongseong," [The making of the culture of everyday urban life in Korea," *Han'guk munwha illyuhak* 33 (2): 49-78.

Song Seok-ha. 1963. *Han'guk minsokgo* [Essays on Korean folklore]. Seoul: Ilsinsa.

Song, Sunhee. 1982. "Kinship and Lineage in Korean Village Society," Ph.D. Thesis: Indiana University.

Yang Jaeyoung. 1994. "Cheongsonyeon jipdan-eu daejung munwha suyong gwajeog-e gwanhan yeon'gu" [A study of popular youth culture], M. A. Thesis: Seoul National University.

Yi, Jeong-duk. 1993a. "Social Order and Contest in Meanings and Power: Black Boycotts against Korean Shopkeepers in Poor New York City Neighbourhoods," Ph.D. Thesis, City University of New York.

Yi Jeong-duk. 1993b. "Illyuhakjeok postmodernism-e daehan bipanjeok geomto" [A critical review of postmodernism in anthropology], *Bigyo munwha yeon'gu* 1: 113-38.

Yi Jeong-duk. 1997. "Oiguk munwhayoso-eu suyong-gwa sobi-eu munwha jeongchihak: cheongbaji-eu sarye" [Accommodation of foreign cultural elements and the cultural politics of consumption: The case of American blue jeans], in *Han'guk'ineu sobi-wa yeoga saengwhal* [Consumption and leisure among Koreans], ed. Moon Ok-pyo. Seongnam: Academy of Korean Studies. pp. 75-123.

Yi ,Jeong-duk. 2003. "What is Korean culture anyway?: A critical review," *Korea Journal* 43 (1): 58-82.

Yim Dawnhee and Roger Janelli. 2001. "Han'guk hyo munwha-eu byeonyong" [Transformations of filial piety in South Korea], *Han'guk munwha illyuhak* 34 (2): 31-60.

Yeo Jung-chul. 1980. "Chuirak gujowa sinbun gujo" [Village structure and status structure], *Han'guk-eu sahoewa munwha* [Korean society and culture] (Seongnam: The Academy of Korean Studies) 2: 97-154.

Yoo, Chul-in. 1993. "Life Histories of Two Korean Women who Married American GIs," Ph.D. Thesis: University of Illinois.

Yoo Chul-in et al. 1996. "Haebang ihu Chungnam Seosan jiyok-eu jibangsa: yoksajeok damlonae daehan illyuhakjeok jeopgeun" [A local history of the Seosan area, Chunnam since the Liberation of Korea: Ethnographic representations of historical discourse], *Han'guk munwha illyuhak* 29 (1): 245-311.

Yoo Myung-ki. 1977. "Munjung-eu hyeongseong gwajeong-e gwanhan gochal" [An investigation on the process of lineage formation], *Han'guk munwha illyuhak* 9: 123-26.

Yoo Myung-ki. 1995. "Jaehan woegugin nodongjaeu munhwajeok jeogeung-e gwanhan yeon'gu" [A study of cultural adaptation among the foreign workers in Korea], *Han'guk munhwa illyuhak* 27 (1): 145-181.

Yoo Myung-ki. 2002. "minjok-gwa gungmin sa-i-e-seo: han'guk cheryu Chosunjokdeuleu jeoncheseong insik-e gwanhayeo" [Between ethncitiy and nationality: on the ideology of Chosunjok working in South Korea], *Han'guk munhwa illyuhak* 35 (1): 73-45.

Yoon Hyung-sook. 1996. "Geudelgwa woorisa-i-e-seo: Illyuhak yon'guhagi, illyuhakja doegi" [In limbo between "they" and "we": Doing fieldwork and becoming an anthropologist], *Han'guk munwha illyuhak* 29 (1): 103-29.

Yoon Hyung-sook. 2000. "Gajoksareul tonghaebon jibangsa" [Local history seen through family hstory], *Han'guk munwha illyuhak* 33 (2): 173-200.

Yoon Hyung-sook. 2001. "Tanjindaem sumoljiyeok jumineu gajokgaldeung-e natanan gajok ideology" [Family conflicts and reproduction of patriarchal ideology among residents in the Tajin multi-purpose dam construction area], *Han'guk munwha illyuhak* 34 (2): 31-60.

Yoon Hyung-sook 2002. "Han'guk jeonjaeng-gwa jiyeokmineu daeung" [The Korean War and local responses], *Han'guk munwha illyuhak* 35 (2): 3-30.

Yoon, Taek-lim. 1992. "Koreans' Stories about Themselves: An Ethnographic History of Hermit Pond Village in South Korea," Ph.D. Thesis: University of Minnesota.

Yoon Taek-lim 2003. *Illyuhakjaeu gwageogihaeng: Han balgaeng-I maeul-eu yeoksareul chajaseo* [An Anthropologist's journey into the past: The history of a Red Communist village]. Seoul: Yeoksa Bipyeongsa.

Chapter 12

Anthropology, Identity, and Nation Formation

in Malaysia

A.B. SHAMSUL

Anthropology at its best is analytic, comparative, integrative, and critical, all at the same time. It is a mode of knowledge like no other. (Wolf 1999: 132-133)

Introduction

The teaching of anthropology as an academic discipline within the universities of Southeast Asia is relatively new. Even though it was taught as early as 1911 in the Philippines, it was formally introduced in other parts of Southeast Asia only after the Second World War. In fact, the newest national anthropology program, established in 1995 within the Academy of Brunei Studies of the Universiti Brunei Darussalam, is less than ten years old.

However, we all know that anthropology made its entry into Southeast Asia much earlier than 1911, mainly through European colonialism, and that a corpus of anthropological knowledge regarding the peoples and societies within the region was already available before the Europeans appeared. Even though we are all aware of the political and ideological role of anthropology under colonial rule, be it in Africa, Asia or Latin America, I think that we also need to take a closer look at its influence on the politics of identity and nation formation in these regions, particularly Southeast Asia with special reference to Malaysia.

I would say that many of the internal markers of national identity in the newly-formed nation-states of Southeast Asia arose out of a combination of social science research and analysis, especially anthropology, and the needs of colonial administration. What is less well understood in this context is the

role of the anthropologists in laying down some of the intellectual foundations of the postcolonial nation-states in the region, often unwittingly. In fact,
the internal markers of identity that arose under colonialism were adapted and
adopted by the nationalists in the individual Southeast Asian nation-states
for their own purposes.

What is also not really discussed and understood is the role of anthropology in assisting the United States of America in establishing its political dominance in Southeast Asia, particularly after World War II. Of course, we have
heard of the Thailand-based "Camelot Project" during the Vietnam War, but
little else regarding the culpability of anthropologists as willing if ineffectual
servants of imperialism (Wakin 1992: 2-5; Wolf 1999; Shamsul 2001: 195-98).

However, it is not my intention in this essay either to praise or condemn
anthropology. I am basically interested in highlighting some of the issues
that have been the concerns of the community of Southeast Asian anthropologists, both those involved in academic planning and others who have
been actively involved in public life. I would also like to mention that we
have been encouraged by the unexpected popularity of anthropology among
our undergraduates. We are still struggling to find a satisfactory explanation
as to why this has been so. Perhaps it is owing to the plural nature of our
societies in Southeast Asia, in which "living anthropologically" is an everyday thing and being able to cope with different cultures is an economic and
political virtue. The economic crisis of 1997-98 did nothing to diminish undergraduates' interest in anthropology in favor of more practical subjects
(Shamsul 2001: 190-92).

It is for these reasons, among others, that I think it is useful to reexamine
the role of anthropology beyond its academic boundaries; we need to examine its influence, whether visible or invisible, especially in the political realm
and particularly in the process of identity and nation-state formation in Southeast Asia, both during and after the colonial period. I wish to argue and reiterate that anthropology's political role in Southeast Asia has always been
understated, or even covered up, for a variety of reasons, even though anthropology and its practice in the region or elsewhere has never been really
apolitical (Shamsul 1993: 2).

I shall begin this brief essay, by looking, in a general manner, at the
relationship between the nation-state and social scientific disciplines, especially anthropology, all of which are modern inventions. I am specifically
interested in its role in the formation of the "colonial knowledge" that subsequently came to be accepted as the basis of the history and the territorial and
social organization of the postcolonial state. I am also interested in the role of
anthropologically-based "cross-cultural knowledge" – an intellectual construct which is specifically American but which, methodologically, is not unlike "colonial knowledge" in nature – and its impact on the politics of identity
and nation-formation in the decolonized states I shall then proceed to examine

287

anthropology's direct and indirect contribution, in the redefined political situation, to the process of identity and nation formation in postcolonial Southeast Asia, with an emphasis on the Malaysian experience. The focus will be on the "formal" relationship between the state and anthropology, both in academe and in state policy formulation and its impact on the society at large, which I hope will shed some light on the continuing popularity of anthropology among our undergraduates.

From "Colonial Knowledge" to "Cross-Cultural Knowledge"

We generally recognize that both the nation-state and the social sciences are modern inventions. An acknowledged feature of modernity is the crucial role of knowledge for the expression, maintenance and reproduction of power. While knowledge represents a form of power, certain modes of power under conditions of modernity, such as policing, crowd control and policy implementation, can only be expressed through their relationship with knowledge, such as the activity of intelligence gathering, continuous surveillance and feedback reporting. Even as social science requires the resources of the modern nation-states for its teaching and research needs, it is equally dependent on a vigorous civil culture distinct from the state, lest the state conflates its own national interests with those of civil society at large. In other words, knowledge is not only a relationship of power, but rather power requires new forms of knowledge, such as social science, to be effective in modern society.

The close links between social science and the modern state were forged at a time when European nation-states were engaged in establishing a new global order (Chakrabarty 2000). Imperialism and colonialism required that the main European powers reach an understanding for the efficient exploitation of resources. The global economy, then, required the increasing coordination of transnational regions of production, exchange, and consumption. This required a basis of consensus beyond the nation-state, which was provided by the transnational community of scholars, namely, the social scientists, who provided the much-needed ideal of a universal and empirical social science. Systematic regional surveys of cultures and societies developed in this context throughout the colonial world. These forms of knowledge have acted as powerful but often subtle political tools that came to shape the ways in which people imagined and represented reality, which in turn became seen as natural and taken for granted as given.

It is widely recognized that, within the social sciences, anthropological knowledge played a crucial role in the politics of identity and nation-state formation, both during and after the colonial period. It still does, even in the present so-called era of globalization, and particularly in the former colonies.

During the colonial period anthropologists were always directly or indirectly involved in the colonial project. In fact, the origins of anthropology as a distinctive form of knowledge lay in the internal and external colonies of the Europeans (Asad 1973; Giddens 1995). They played a crucial, if ambivalent, role mediating between the colonial subjects and the rulers. They helped to construct "official ethnography" for the colonial government and developed practices that sought to erase the colonial influence by claiming that what they recorded was genuine indigenous culture. Nonetheless, their epistemological universe remained part and parcel of European social theories and classification systems shaped by the projects of the colonizing state that were meant to reshape the lives of the colonized subjects. Anthropological knowledge became an integral part of what is now known as "colonial knowledge", which, in turn, became the accepted basis of the postcolonial state (Cohn 1996).

However, besides contributing to "colonial knowledge," anthropology also contributed to the construction of "cross-cultural knowledge" and "national character studies" introduced and developed extensively in the United States for overt and covert political use globally, before and after the Cold War. Initially, however, it all started in America. Since the 1930s, anthropology and anthropologists in the United States were heavily involved with Native American affairs, from writing histories and accounts of social organization, to planning economic development programs for Indian Reservations, with the overall long-term political objective of bringing the Native Americans into the mainstream economy and culture, thereby hastening the process of assimilation. Besides interests in Native Americans, anthropology and anthropologists in the United States were actively developing a new subbranch within anthropology called "applied anthropology," one that focused on the study of socio-cultural implications and impacts of so-called "development projects" (Embree 1945; Suzuki 1980; D'Andrade 1975).

During the Second World War, in pursuit of its goal to consolidate itself as a world imperialist superpower, the United States was dependent on social scientific knowledge, social analysis and research (Wolf 1999). The setting up of a multi-disciplinary social science research center called the Institute of Human Relations at Yale University demonstrated this. The Institute brought together sociologists, anthropologists, psychoanalysts and psychologists, and the dominant intellectual mode was positivism. The Institute had several research projects but the most significant was anthropological, the creation of the now famous Human Relations Area Files (HRAF). These were, and continue to be, the most elaborate and sophisticated compilation available of anthropology-based "cross-cultural knowledge"; they incorporate a vast and ethnographically rich descriptive literature into a precise and accessible comparative analytical framework. Like colonial knowledge, cross-cultural knowledge defined, quantified, classified, and categorized anything and everything perceived as cultural. But it went beyond colonial knowledge to create a global cross-cultural map (Embree 1945; 1946).

To complement this already impressive anthropological effort, the cross-cultural knowledge made available through HRAF greatly assisted the psychoanalytical studies on "national culture" and "national character," which were conducted by well-known American anthropologists such as Ruth Benedict and Margaret Mead (Suzuki 1980; Barclay 1999). Both the cross-cultural knowledge and national culture studies became directly involved with the war effort of the United States, especially in the Asia Pacific region, because of their great strategic value. For instance, when the United States Navy was getting ready to liberate Micronesia and Melanesia from Japanese control, it had to take charge of the civilian government and their native populations in these territories. The HRAF staff stepped in to assist the naval officers and policy makers to learn quickly about the "customs and practices" of the local natives (Bremen and Shimizu 1999). At the macro political level, the national culture studies helped the United States shape its military and foreign policy towards Japan and other countries in Pacific Asia (Shimizu and Bremen 2003; Minnear 1980). In other words, the practical knowledge provided by the HRAF was deployed beyond the boundaries of academe, not only in the business of international relations but also in the local *realpolitik.*

After the war, the incredibly rich pool of accumulated cross-cultural knowledge became important, in at least two significant forms, for the United States' global political project that directly affected the process of nation-state formation in the decolonized territories in Asia and Africa. First, the "war scholars" founded the "area studies" programs as we know them in the American academic world. In fact, the term "Southeast Asia" developed as a result of the war, hence "Southeast Asian studies" (Shamsul forthcoming). More importantly, anthropological knowledge, together with knowledge derived from economics and political science, helped to create the famous "evolutionary modernization model" to apply to the newly independent states. The model, framed and funded within the Bretton Woods Agreement of 1944, became the cornerstone of American postwar foreign policy towards these states. Contributions from anthropologists such as Julian Steward and economists such as W.W. Rostow were integral components in the formulation of this policy (Embree 1946; Dormael 1978).

It is in this context that cross-cultural research was critical in evaluating the success and the "problems of modernization" in the "new nations," as Clifford Geertz called them, namely through a monitoring of the trajectory of social change in those territories perceived as moving from the "traditional" to the "modern" stage (Geertz 2000). The Vietnam War was seen as an unfortunate political hiccup in this modernization drive. Both anthropology and the anthropologists played a critical role in that war through the support they gave to the United States military ground forces' efforts in trying to win the "hearts and minds" of the Vietnamese but with negative and tragic results (Summers 1995).

If anthropology during the colonial era was involved in the exercise to construct and constitute group and national identities that became the basis of postcolonial nation-state formation through "colonial knowledge," the anthropologically-based American "cross-cultural knowledge" further reinforced and consolidated these identities through the implementation of the grand "modernization project" initiated by the United States in the newly decolonized Third World territories, largely funded by the two important Bretton Woods institutions, the International Monetary Fund (IMF) and the World Bank (Bandow and Vasquez 1994; Shamsul 2002).

Indeed, the new nation-states began to implement their own specific programs of nation-building within the framework of this modernization model, with social scientific knowledge providing the intellectual basis. Anthropology has a special role in this new relationship, namely that between the new nation-states and the social sciences, because the latter were inevitably grounded largely in "colonial" and "cross-cultural" knowledge. The relationship was often dominated and characterized by the new nation-states continuous attempts to "indigenize" the social sciences (Atal 1974; Alatas 1993).

Anthropology in the New Nation-States of Southeast Asia

The process of the "indigenization" of social science in Southeast Asia has taken place in the context of decolonization. Political independence and the growing cultural awareness demand that the social sciences be harnessed to the new enterprise of nation-building. The notion of political sovereignty assumed by the nation-state presupposes control over the production of knowledge and self-identity. The social sciences become a resource to be developed for the "national interest." This view of social science as a weapon in the neo-colonial struggle or as a vehicle for discovering a national spirit and identity has been advocated by the new nation-states in Southeast Asia (Shamsul 1999; 2001).

The first stimulus was provided by academe, but not without the support of the government of the day. For instance, it came mainly from the Faculty of Arts at the University of Malaya in Malaysia; from the Institute of Sciences in Indonesia; from the Ateneo de Manila University as well as the Xavier University in Mindanao in the Philippines; and from Chulalongkorn University in Thailand. From the 1950s to 1970s, these institutions conducted wide ranging studies of the societies and cultures within their respective nation-states, which established a new basis for a national social science. By the 1980s, the local scholars and administrators in the region were in control of the local practice of social science and had started to explore the possibilities of indigenizing its theoretical and methodological practices (Firth 1948; Leach 1950; Koentjaraningrat 1987; Chitakasem and Turton 1991; Perteirra 1996; Shamsul 2001).

As a result of the organization of social life around the principle of the "nation-state" or "nationality," the nature of social enquiry came to be dominated by what could be called "methodological nationalism." For instance, the occurrence or absence of "modernization" in a country came to be accounted for in terms of "internal circumstances," with little if any attention to the ways in which the resident population was integrated into social relations on a global scale. Hence, it seems as though preoccupations with nationality as a basis of identity and community in contemporary history infiltrated academe, where they have distracted researchers from the global social conditions within which all nations, including those in Southeast Asia, have developed.

Anthropology became important in elaborating and constituting the nationality principle and its related sub-concepts such as "national identity" and "national culture." Using anthropology, the new nation-states in Southeast Asia, since the 1950s, have carried out a major exercise in "butterfly collection" involving the different customs, subcultures, traditions and so on of ethnic and sub-ethnic groups. This was for archival and recording purposes, as well as for use in the construction of new social categories for policy purposes, other than those already provided by the colonial census reports (British, Dutch, or French) or the cross-cultural and "national character" reports made available by American researchers (Wolf 1999; Suzuki 1980).

The Malaysian nation-state, for instance, is forever indebted to Edmund Leach for his excellent efforts in bringing some kind of classificatory order into what seemed to be a disconcerting chaos of cultures, languages and societies in British Borneo. In his report entitled *Social Science Research in Sarawak* (1950), Leach recommended that a total of seven major anthropological research projects should be carried out in Sarawak for academic and policy purposes by researchers trained in social anthropology. This research resulted in a series of reports later published as monographs: on the Iban by Derek Freeman, the Bidayuh by William Geddes, the Melanau by H.S. Morris, the Chinese by J.K. T'ien, the Kenyah-Kayan by Jerome Rousseau and the Sarawak Malay fishermen by Lim Jock Seng. They also provided each of these groups with an official account of their "modern history" and sociology (Firth 1948; Leach 1950; Appell 1976; Ishikawa 1998). Similar efforts in group identity construction by foreign and local anthropologists in Indonesia, Thailand, Myanmar, Vietnam, Laos, and the Philippines became significant contributions to national politics and the formation of nationally-sponsored identities because of their constituting power. To construct is, in varying degrees, to constitute.

In other words, there is a dialectical interplay between the two types of representation, namely, the nominal and the political. To name or label people or an entire community (e.g. Iban, Malays, Toraja, Karo, and so on) as belonging to a certain type and then to elaborate a theory of the essential elements of their social identity is to create a symbolic representation of the people or the community. If this representation then becomes naturalized, that is, accepted as the "obvious" depiction of its referent (which has been the case, for instance, in the Sarawak context), it becomes a mould that shapes the second type of representation – the political. Put simply, for a community to be labeled "Iban," for instance, and to accept the label as valid, implies that its members will adopt political goals and strategies that are consistent with this "Ibanness"; similarly, non-Iban who also assume that a community is "Iban" will treat it as such.

Modern electoral politics, based on ethnicity, especially in Malaysia and Singapore, has survived and thrived on these constructed ethnic identities which are often dependent on anthropology or anthropological knowledge for their ideological sustainability. Anthropology does have a role in such nation-states in providing a nationalist and instrumental social science orientation to counterbalance what has been perceived as overly colonial or Western cultural influence. It is also perceived as useful in the exercise of creating national solidarity or national unity. Anthropology departments, along with psychology and political science departments, were established in Malaysia in the early 1970s, soon after the ethnic riot of 1969, to serve that specific purpose. The setting up of a "Department of National Unity" within the national administrative structure, with the active participation of anthropologists and sociologists, is another example.

But despite the nation-state's official attempts to redirect the orientation of social science, including that of anthropology, through its absorption into the structure of government, other factors prevented its total incorporation as an arm of the state. For instance, in the Philippines, the Marcos regime's period of martial law (1972-81) stimulated much independent and critical social science, indicating how its practice is also a product of a vigorous civil society. An example was the establishment of the Third World Studies Center (1971) at the University of Philippines at the height of martial law. In Malaysia, in the late 1970s, the Institute for Social Analysis (INSAN) was established after the 1974 student riot and the introduction of the University College and Colleges Act that prohibited academics and students from participating in partisan politics, rendering them almost second class citizens (Ramasamy 1983; Shamsul 1993; 1995a; 1995b; Perteirra 1996).

In other words, even though the nation-state has been a major agent of modernity, it is by no means the only player in this process. Society, through the market mechanism, has been an equally important agent of modernity. The market needs and consumes social scientific knowledge as much as the nation-state does, but for a different purpose, most evidently for profit-making.

In this so-called private sector context, anthropology in Malaysia, for example, has found its own niche. Anthropology graduates seem to be sought after by both small and medium size firms (e.g. soya sauce factories and computer companies) as well as large ones (e.g. banks and locally-based multinationals), apparently for their breadth and depth of knowledge regarding the complex and sensitive local poly-cultural configurations, particularly those which are political in nature. They have been found to be more competent than graduates in economics, business administration, or political science in dealing with the everyday demands of government rules, regulations, policies, and strategies, as well as the specific cultural values and norms of their clients who belong to various ethnic groups. As a result, in the last decade or so, the anthropology graduates from my own department have seldom had to wait more than six months for employment, whether during periods of economic growth or recession. Our only problem is that, as a public university, we can only enroll a limited number of new students per year (between 150 and 200 students) according to the quota set by the government. We wish we could go private!

A large proportion of research funding for anthropological research in Southeast Asia comes from outside the region. As such, funding bodies based in the United States, Europe and Japan have a critical impact on the state of Southeast Asian social science in general, and anthropology in particular. Admittedly, many of these foreign-funded studies investigate better ways for Southeast Asian nation-states to achieve desirable goals such as functional democracy or an efficient economy. The Ford and Asia Foundations have supported anthropological and other social scientific research which is heavily biased towards developing "appropriate" state institutions or improving the official apparatus for community development. Other institutions, such as the Volkswagen Foundation, have looked at auxiliary functions such as population control or the sources of insurgency in order to suggest mechanisms for strengthening the state's capacities (Shamsul 1995a).

But other projects, often funded by the same agencies, have realized the importance of civil society or the informal sector in shaping Southeast Asian society and the economy. Support for NGOs and much bilateral research aid in the Philippines, Indonesia and Thailand, for instance, is often directed at understanding and, at times, encouraging non-formal institutions to act in place of the state. Increasingly, these studies are recognizing the importance of civil society. Factors such as locality, class, religion, gender, and overseas labor are now accepted as shaping significantly the broad features of the nation-state.

As such, the funding of anthropological research in Southeast Asia, both by the state and non-state actors (the latter mostly from outside the region) is not divorced, in most cases, from the interests of the nation-state, which are mainly political and economic. Most local NGOs, in which many local and foreign anthropologists are involved and which are usually funded by foreign bodies, are also political in nature, especially those dealing with human rights issues and eco-politics (Perteirra 1996). Viewed in terms of the political economy of research funding, one could argue that the power of the Southeast Asian nation-states to inform and manipulate constructed identities is slowly diminishing. However, the strict state control of research permits, especially for "academic" anthropologists, such as in Brunei, Indonesia, and Malaysia, indicates that the state is not willing to surrender its political dominance that easily (Ramasamy 1983; Koentjaraningrat 1987; Perteirra 1996; Shamsul 1993).

Anthropology in Postcolonial Malaysia

The introduction of anthropology within the Department of Anthropology and Sociology in the University of Malaya in 1970 was not only related to the interest of the postcolonial state, then struggling with some urgency to restore the ruptured social order as a consequence of a bloody ethnic riot in 1969, but also to the global and regional interests of the United States, which was then deeply involved in the Vietnam War. Clutching at straws, the Malaysian state immediately adopted the recommendations of the report mentioned above on *Social Science Research for National Unity* (29 April 1970). This was authored by four prominent American social scientists, whose brief "research" for the report was funded by the Ford Foundation. Anthropology and sociology and other disciplines within the social sciences were introduced and taught at the local universities within this context. From the Malaysian state's point-of-view, social science disciplines, such as anthropology, are functional in terms of their perceived roles as "agents" of national unity or at least in fostering "national integration." Seen in this "nationalist" context, the state's interest in homogenizing national narratives through anthropology is obvious.

However, anthropology remained combined with sociology, as it had been in the Department of Malay Studies. In fact, in the 1970s, many of the founding academic teaching staff of the Departments of Anthropology and Sociology in the local universities in Malaysia were graduates or academics recruited from the Department of Malay Studies. They were joined by anthropology and sociology graduates from universities in the Commonwealth and the United States. A few expatriates and established anthropologists were also recruited, such as Kirk Endicott (later at Dartmouth College, in the United States), Terry Rambo (later at Kyoto University) and Suichi and Judith Nagata (also anthropology teachers in Canada).

The new departments also embarked on aggressive training programs, fully sponsored by the state. Each department sent graduates or prospective academic staff to universities in the Commonwealth or the United States for graduate studies, or recruited those who were already abroad completing their studies. Others were trained locally for their master's degrees and subsequently went abroad for their doctorates. Almost all of them came back to Malaysia to conduct field research. Hence the project to train local staff resulted in a sudden increase in the number of in-depth anthropological studies, mostly in the form of unpublished M.A. and Ph.D. theses, not only on the Malays but also on other ethnic groups in Peninsular Malaysia, Sabah and Sarawak. These covered a number of themes, ranging from the burial rites of the Sarawak Iban to the career pattern of members of the Malaysian scientific community, and they employed a variety of theoretical approaches which were in vogue in the 1970s and 1980s in the United States, the Commonwealth, Latin America, and Continental Europe. A number of these theses, and I have listed them elsewhere (Shamsul 1998), have been published and became classics of the genre.

These works, and the contributions of foreign researchers from that period, enriched anthropological studies about Malaysia and kept alive an interest in Malaysian social studies abroad (Lent 1979). One interesting feature of anthropological studies in Malaysia, which reflects the unresolved majority-minority discourse in this multiethnic society, is that they show a tendency to become ethnicized: anthropology is used as an instrument to support the cause of one or other ethnic group or to launch a purportedly "objective and scientific" critique of ethnic relations. Some anthropologists seemed to adopt a "prophet of doom" approach in their analyses of social life in Malaysia, giving the impression that another outbreak of ethnic rioting is imminent. In this sense, anthropological and sociological studies of Malaysia have become rather politicized (Shamsul 1998).

However, the most encouraging development in the last decade has been the increased popularity of anthropology amongst Malaysian undergraduates. Being very sensitive to the demands of the job market, they have enrolled in their hundreds in the various departments of anthropology in the local universities. For instance, taking the Department of Anthropology and Sociology at the National University of Malaysia alone, there has been an average annual enrollment of nearly a thousand students during the last decade. This would make many anthropology departments abroad envious, especially those struggling to survive. This situation has arisen because both the public and private sectors in Malaysia prefer to employ anthropology graduates. They have the perception that anthropology graduates are excellent generalists, good at coping with multicultural situations, and are thus best suited to Malaysia's multiethnic conditions, either in the public or market sectors, for employment as civil servants, business executives, or development workers at the grassroots level.

Perhaps it is useful to examine the so-called "Malaysianization" process that anthropology in Malaysia has undergone in the last twenty-five years. I have chosen to call that process "Malaysianization" instead of "indigenization" because of the fact that the latter is historically and politically a problematic term, indeed a highly contentious one. This is particularly true in Malaysia for it has its specific domestic implications. In fact the English term "indigenous" has a local Malay equivalent in the word *bumiputera*, literally meaning "son of the soil."

Anthropology Domesticated

I would argue that the "Malaysianization" process began in the early 1970s with the setting up, for the first time ever, of three full-fledged teaching departments of anthropology and sociology at Universiti Sains Malaysia (USM), Universiti Malaya (UM) and Universiti Kebangsaan Malaysia (UKM). There are at least four main reasons why I call it a "Malaysianization" process and I have elaborated them elsewhere (Shamsul 1993).

First, the establishment of the departments of anthropology signaled a critical departure in the development path of anthropological studies in Malaysia. Previously, anthropology was part and parcel of a discipline called "Malay studies" introduced during the colonial era by colonial administrator-scholars and informed by various forms of Orientalism, perhaps to serve some aspects of the colonial state's needs (Shamsul 2004). But in the early 1970s, it began to map out and embark on a new course rather consciously as a result of the academic-cum-bureaucratic demands imposed by its new form of existence as a "teaching department." It was inevitable then that careful and detailed planning of courses to be taught in these new anthropology departments had to be done, and in such circumstances there was a conscious effort to ensure that a certain percentage of the courses contained a "Malaysian content."

Second, following on from the above, an equally important reason was the need for trained academic staff in anthropology to teach in the new departments. Funded by the government, these departments went on an aggressive training program, sending their newly-recruited staff to the United States, United Kingdom, Australia, New Zealand and even continental Europe. This itself enriched the content of anthropology in Malaysia, feeding into it numerous different traditions which, when combined, formed a unique "Malaysianized version" of the growing discipline.

Third, the ethnic riot in 1969 was a critical watershed for Malaysians, not only in terms of its collective impact on the history of postcolonial Malaysia as a whole, but also in terms of its individual, personal impact on all Malaysians from various ethnic groups and classes. One could argue that after that tragic event ethnic consciousness and centrifugal tendencies were heightened. The Malaysian government of the day, and the "friendly" Western powers led by the United States, realized this, and they worked together successfully to "solve the problem" while fulfilling their own different interests. The setting up of the Department of National Unity, for instance, was one of the many strategies devised to bring together and unite all Malaysians after the tragic May 13 ethnic riot incident. There was then a conscious, planned effort to create a united Malaysian nation, with an emphasis on "Malaysian."

As a consequence, if "Malay studies" had previously influenced the construction of anthropological knowledge in Malaysia, now the "non-Malay studies" component, as it were, has to be seriously considered. This conscious effort to combine the Malay and non-Malay components, both within the public and private sectors, gave rise, for the first time since the war, to a genuine attempt to see Malaysia not only as a "plural entity" in socio-political terms but also in analytical terms. This led to the sudden increase, for instance, in the studies of inter-ethnic relations, as opposed to the studies of single ethnic groups and intra-ethnic relations. This pattern of change has been critical in shaping what we see as Malaysian studies today.

The fourth reason, following on from the second, is perhaps the most critical in the process of Malaysianization in anthropology. The role of both the public and private sectors is important here, especially in their attitude towards graduates from the new anthropology departments. We must also recognize the role, and the enthusiasm, of the "new graduates" in anthropology in the early 1970s, and particularly their tireless collective efforts to impress upon the "senior managers" in both the public and private sectors that they could become capable civil servants or company executives.

On the management side, there was a general awareness that as a result of the conscious efforts by the government to foster "national unity" amongst the ethnically-mixed population, managers also had to reposition themselves to fit this new socio-political environment. In the public sector, there was, for instance, an obvious need for "community development" officers to attend to the interests of each of the ethnic groups at the grass roots. Anthropology graduates were then perceived as the most suitable for this role, and they began to be recruited into the civil service. The fact that they dominated the top twenty positions among the civil service entrants in the early 1970s enhanced the relevance of "anthropology" in the eyes of the senior civil servants; previously, anthropology graduates had been employed only in the department of museums and prehistory or in the Department of Aboriginal Affairs. But after 1970, these graduates came to be accepted by the government as "useful" in a variety of fields and departments, including the psychological war unit, the drug rehabilitation centers, the social welfare departments, the national art gallery, the immigration department, the labor department, and even in the customs and police departments.

Anthropology Consumed

The positive reaction that the anthropology graduates received from the private sector was a total surprise to many. Sensitive as usual to market demands, senior company executives from companies both large and small began to realize that in a society with a high level of ethnic awareness, especially after the May 13 1969 incident, ethnic stereotypes had become more important in everyday discourse, as well in shaping the perceptions of people at the grassroots. This led to a process by which ethnic identities, such as "Malayness," "Chineseness," "Indianness," and so forth, became "essentialized," both in the media and in political campaigns. From the market surveys conducted in the early 1970s, senior company executives knew that there was a need to recruit marketing officers with some "cultural knowledge," as they put it. It was no coincidence that a large number of anthropology graduates began to apply for jobs in the private sector around the same period. The combination of these two circumstances worked well for anthropology in Malaysia, as well as making it more Malaysian-oriented.

As a result, potential university students, who are always sensitive to job opportunities available in the public sphere and who decide on what they want to specialize in at university according to job market demand, started to get interested in anthropology, and they enrolled in their hundreds in the three departments of anthropology in Malaysia. Realizing this positive trend, these departments began to increase the Malaysian content in their courses during the routine exercise of up-dating them. Here I wish to narrate the experience of my own department at Universiti Kebangsaan Malaysia (UKM).

I shall focus specifically on the result of a pilot survey I conducted in mid-1993 amongst ex-students of my department at UKM and their employers, both in the public and private sector, with a small sample of 150 students and 50 employers. The intention of the survey was to find out, or more specifically, to give me some ideas about two inter-related issues. Firstly, I was interested in the "intellectual impact" of our courses upon our students: whether they were finding them intellectually enlightening or interesting, and whether or not the courses were equipping them sufficiently, both to comprehend the general and specific contexts of their social environments, and to have a certain measure of confidence in dealing with the immediate demands of their workplaces. Secondly, I was interested in finding out about the general job market situation for our graduates: the range of jobs they were holding, how they coped with the job market or found a niche, and what other knowledge they needed to make them more competent to handle their jobs, in addition to information about opportunities for promotion and salaries.

The research was very exciting because I did not use any research assistants. I was intent on gathering the information personally and, at the same, meeting my former students and the employers face-to-face. In between teaching, meetings and commitments abroad, it took me about 10 months to complete the whole task. About 10 percent of the former students had been interested in pursuing academic careers before they joined the university but they decided otherwise when they learnt of the good job prospects with an undergraduate degree in anthropology. About 85 percent had known exactly which department they wanted to enroll in based on their perceptions of job prospects after graduating and the relatively short period waiting to find employment. All had prior knowledge about the department from ex-graduates and also from their own research. They also knew about the department through the contributions by the department's lecturers to local newspapers and magazines. Many of these lecturers had previously come to their schools to give talks on all kinds of issues during "speech day" celebrations or on other special occasions.

Of the 150 ex-students, 50 worked in the public sector (in government departments and other semi-government bodies) and the rest in the private sector. Those who joined the public sector did not expect to get their jobs based on their special interest in anthropology because they needed only a good degree (first and second class honors). But, according to government officials and executives of the semi-government bodies in charge of recruiting new officers and executives, they found that anthropology graduates performed very well in the entrance exam and interviews compared with graduates in history, geography, or Malay studies. The anthropology graduates seemed to have a good all-round knowledge about important government policies, the internal dynamics of Malaysian society, global issues besetting the countries of the South, and Malaysia's position relative to other countries in the world; and they were able to conceptualize and discuss national issues competently, such as "national unity," "ethnic politics," "federal-state relations," "absolute and relative poverty," and "development planning and social change." The employers' conclusion was that the anthropology graduates were excellent "generalists" and well-suited to become good civil servants and executives in semi-government bodies dealing with the implementation of government policies.

Those who joined the private sector, all began as "marketing officers" in companies involved in a wide-range of business activities, from Coca-Cola to computers, banks to bakeries, soya sauce to sporting goods, detergents to dental equipment, and recreational clubs to real estate. The attraction, from the ex-students' perspective, was that these jobs provided good starting salaries and perks, involved a lot of travel locally and abroad, and gave opportunities for quick promotion based on performance evaluation. They could also change their jobs or companies relatively easy should an opportunity to increase their income arise. Often, they were allowed to use company cars or company credit cards to cover expenses. It seemed that their dream of living a middle-class lifestyle had become a reality in this type of employment.

However, the employers seemed to have other reasons for employing them, which are interesting for us to take note of. Ignoring personality differences, they were of the opinion that our anthropology graduates, compared with the economic or business school graduates they had employed, could understand their clients' habits, cultures, and behavior patterns much quicker, and were thus able to clinch deals faster, whether small or large. They were able to learn basic accounting quickly because they had a good grounding in statistics and were computer literate. They were able to understand the market better and willing to conduct market research on their own initiative. They were also good at entertaining their clients (in karaoke bars, perhaps); they were able to talk about all sorts of matters relating to Malaysia, together with other general issues; and they were very aware of government policies affecting the businesses of their employers. Most importantly, they seemed to know each of the ethnic communities in Malaysia, their subcultures and stereotypes, much better than other graduates, and were able to understand and mix with prospective buyers and government officials with little difficulty. This increased their employers' opportunities for expanding their business networks, while at the same time remaining in the good books of the relevant local government officials.

At the beginning of the research, I wondered why private financial institution, such as banks, found anthropology students useful as executives. The explanation given by personnel officers from two banks which employed a number of anthropology graduates was that, from their experience, they found that they made excellent credit officers, especially in the rural areas, where the sizes of the Malay, Chinese, and Indian communities are almost equal. They seemed to understand the borrowing habits of each of the communities better and quickly understood the cultural preferences of each community as to the type of collateral offered when borrowing. For instance, the Malays prefer to use land, the Chinese real estate property (mainly houses or apartments), and the Indians gold. A good understanding and empathy regarding cultural issues such as these allowed smoother negotiations for the amount to be loaned to the client, the choice of collateral, the method of payment, and smoother completion of the paperwork itself. Often, problems related to loan defaulters could be resolved amicably by the anthropology graduates. One must also be reminded that banks, as lending institutions, are relatively new in Malaysian rural society, where most people prefer private money lenders or the pawnshop as sources of credit or loans for reasons of expedience (there is no paper work) and privacy (going to the banks to borrow money is perceived as a public activity).

I do not wish to paint too rosy a picture about the "marketability" of our graduates but nonetheless they seemed to be in demand for their supposed "anthropological talent." One must also take into account the generally favorable economic conditions during the period between 1986 and 1997. For instance, in recent years, Malaysia has posted a phenomenal annual economic growth of over 8 percent, one of the highest in the world. The economy, technically speaking, is experiencing full employment. The jobless are jobless because of their own choice, not because of the lack of employment. Previously, "walk-in" interviews were the method of labor recruitment utilized by plantation companies to get part-time contract workers. But now the same method is being used by most companies, both local and foreign, in Malaysia to recruit employees, be they engineers, computer programmers, nurses, lawyers, or production workers in semi-conductor factories. With such an excellent economic situation it became generally easier for graduates to obtain employment quite quickly after successfully completing their studies.

It might have seemed that the privileges the anthropology graduates enjoyed until mid-1997 in terms of job-placement would simply disappear if the economy were to take a turn for the worse, as happened as a result of the Asian economic crisis of 1997-98; but the crisis affected all graduates, and not only those in anthropology. The bottom line is that every employer only chooses the best graduates to work for them, whether the economy is buoyant or not. In fact, they need the best even when the economy is in recession. The reality at present is that the "hot" choice still seems to be anthropology graduates. They seem to be very good at dealing with different cultures, which is all-important in a multi-ethnic Malaysia. Whether this would work in other multi-ethnic societies of the world, I am not quite sure. Even if it does work, anthropology departments may not exist there, or, if they exist, they might be seen as producing too many radicals and critics of the state.

Anthropology not only teaches its students to have in-depth knowledge about many things, and to acquire a good range of analytical tools and apply them well. It also trains its students in "critical thinking," directly and indirectly, so as to seek alternative explanations of all kinds of social phenomena continuously, without fear or favor, as best summed up by the late Eric Wolf in the quotation at the beginning of this essay. This may not go down well with authoritarian or fascist states.

Conclusion: The "Anthropological Pendulum"

We have witnessed worldwide how, first, anthropological knowledge and later anthropology became part and parcel of the investigative program of the colonial state which produced "colonial knowledge." In Southeast Asia, colonial knowledge not only elaborated and explained the concept of the plural society, but also sustained and justified it through the construction of the essentialized ethnic categories which became the key to the success of the divide-and-rule policy. It is not surprising therefore that when the "colonial states" became "new nation-states" after independence, these categories became the natural way of thinking about their history, society and territory. Thus the establishment of the postcolonial nation-state depended upon determining, codifying, controlling and representing the past as well as the present by using again techniques for the construction of "facts" and "knowledge" already set in place by the colonial state.

The "cross-cultural knowledge" generated by the United States since World War II became critical to the new nation-states of Southeast Asia, not only in reinforcing further colonial knowledge, but also in their efforts at modernization which were mainly funded by the United States within the Bretton Woods framework. It was within this context of decolonization that the quest for nation-building took place in earnest, within which the main agenda was that of seeking homogeneity expressed in idioms such as "national culture," "national unity," "national security," "national identity," and other authority-defined national narratives, informed by anthropological knowledge. But later, local and ethnic interests found space to express both their differences and the pluralism of society, also with the support of anthropology and anthropological knowledge – indeed this corresponded to the need of civil society to establish its independence.

In the Malaysian case, for instance, we have witnessed how the anthropology-based departments of Malay studies have been critical of the construction of "Malay" and "Malayness" by the Malay-dominated government, along with its subsequent efforts to create a homogenized "national culture" with Malay culture as the core. The pro-Malay affirmative action policy implemented by the government (1971-1990) was also informed by such a "Malay anthropological understanding." However, we also have observed how anthropology, taught as "anthropology" and not under the guise of Malay studies, has played an equally "unifying" if utilitarian role, in a rather different political period and scenario, due to the demands of consumers and the market. But at the same time it has created significant space for the heterogeneous elements in society to be expressed openly. The high level of demand for anthropology graduates in the both the public and private sectors has demonstrated this healthy trend.

In the former case, what we have observed is that, in the quest for homogeneity, authority-defined national narratives informed by anthropological knowledge often erase differences. But in the latter case, local and ethnic interests have found space to air their differences, as well as encouraging "difference" to flourish in activities allowing the emancipation of civil society. Such being the case, it could be argued that anthropology in Malaysia occupies an interesting, indeed unique, position. It is consumed both by the state and civil society for almost opposite reasons, one for the pursuit of homogeneity and the other to maintain and enrich heterogeneity.

This is the anthropological pendulum in Southeast Asia, including Malaysia, framed within the politics of identity and nation-state formation in the region. The direction of its swing in the future depends very much on the state of relations between the state and civil society in the region. But one thing is, however, certain: anthropology has proven to be part of the staple diet of both state and society, as indicated clearly by well-known Malaysian anthropologist, J.K. Wazir (1994; 1996). It thus occupies an important niche in the region. Perhaps what is interesting to observe is how it is reinvented or reconstituted over time in response to the speed and nature of the swing of the state-civil society pendulum.

References

Alatas, Syed Farid. 1993. "On the indigenization of academic discourse," *Alternatives* 18 (3): 307-38.

Appell, George N. 1976. *Studies in Borneo Societies: Social Process and Anthropological Explanations.* Dekalb, Ill.: Center for Southeast Asian Studies, Northern Illinois University.

Asad, Talal, ed. 1973. *Anthropology and the Colonial Encounter*, London: Ithaca Press.

Atal, Yogesh, ed. 1974. *Social Science in Asia.* New Delhi: Abhinav Publications.

Bandouw, Doug and Ian Vasquez, eds. 1994, *Perpetuating Poverty: The World Bank, the IMF, and the Developing World.* New York: National Book Network.

Barclay, Paul David. 1999. "Japanese and American Colonial Projects," Unpublished Ph.D. Thesis, University of Minnesota.

Bremen, Jan van and Shimizu. Akitoshi. 1999. *Anthropology & Colonialism in Asia and Oceania.* London: Curzon.

Chakrabarty, Dipesh. 2000. *Provincializing Europe: Postcolonial Thought and Historical Difference*, Princeton: Princeton University Press.

Chitakasem, M. and Andrew Turton. 1991. *Thai Constructions of Knowledge.* London: SOAS, University of London.

Cohn, Bernard. 1996. *Colonialism and its Forms of Knowledge: The British in India.* Princeton: Princeton University Press.

D'Andrade, R.G. et al. 1975. "Academic opportunity in Anthropology 1974-9," *American Anthropologist* 77 (4): 753-73.

Dormael, Armand van. 1978. *Bretton Woods: Birth of a Monetary System.* New York: Macmillan.

Embree, John. 1945, "Applied Anthropology and its relationship to Anthropology," *American Anthropologist* 47: 635-37.

Embree, John. 1946. "Anthropology and the War," *Bulletin of the American Association of University Professors* 32: 485-95.

Firth, Raymond. 1948. *Report on Social Science Research in Malaya.* Singapore: Government Printer.

Geertz, Clifford. 2000. *Available Light: Anthropological Reflections on Philosophical Topics,* Princeton: Princeton University Press.

Giddens, Anthony. 1995. "Epilogue: Notes on the future of anthropology," pp. 272-277 in *The Future of Anthropology and its Relevance to the Contemporary World,* eds. Akbar Ahmed and Cris Shore. London: Athlone.

Glazer, Nathan, Samuel Huntington, Manning Nash, and Myron Weiner. 1970. "Social Science Research for National Unity: A Confidential Report to the Government of Malaysia." New York: Ford Foundation.

Hirschman, Charles. 1986. "The making of race in colonial Malaya: Political economy and racial category," *Sociological Forum* (Spring): 330-61.

Ishikawa, Noboro. 1998. "Between Frontiers: The Formation and Marginalization of a Boderland Malay Community in Southwestern Sarawak, Malaysia, 1870s-1990," Ph.D. Thesis, City University of New York.

Koentjaraningrat. 1987. "Anthropology in Indonesia," *Journal of Southeast Asian Studies* 27: 1-35.

Leach, Edmund. 1950. *Social Science Research in Sarawak,* London: HMSO.

Lent, John, ed. 1979. "Malaysian Studies: Present Knowledge and Research Trends," Occasional Paper No. 7. Dekalb, Ill.: Center for Southeast Asian Studies, Northern Illinois University.

Minnear, Richard H. 1980. "Cross-cultural perception and World War II: American Japanists of the 1940s and their images of Japan," *International Studies Quarterly* 24 (4): 555-80.

Perteirra, Raul. 1996. *Explorations in Social Theory and the Philippines Ethnography.* Quezon City: University of the Philippines Press.

Ramasamy, P. 1983. "The state of social science in Malaysia: A brief historical overview," *Ilmu Masyarakat* 4: 67-69.

Shamsul A.B. 1993. *Antropologi dan Modenisasi: Mengungkapkan Pengalaman Malaysia,* [Anthropology and Modernization: Narrating the Malaysian Experience]. Syarahan Perdana (Professorial Inaugural Lecture). Bangi: Universiti Kebangsaan Malaysia Press.

Shamsul A.B. 1995a. "Malaysia: The Kratonization of social science," pp. 87-109 in *Social Science in Southeast Asia: From Particularism to Universalism,* eds. Nico S. Nordholt and Leontine Visser. Amsterdam: VU University Press.

Shamsul A.B. 1995b. "The state of Anthropology and Anthropology and the state in Malaysia," *Minpaku Anthropological Newsletter* (Osaka) 1 (1): 5-6.

Shamsul A.B. 1998. "Ethnicity, class, culture or identity? Competing paradigms in Malaysian Studies," *Akademika*, 53 (July): 33-60.

Shamsul A.B. 1999. "Anthropology and the politics of identity and nation-state formation in Southeast Asia," *Paideuma* 45: 103-14.

Shamsul A.B. 2001. "Social science in Southeast Asia observed: A Malaysian viewpoint," *Inter-Asia Cultural Studies*, 2 (2): 177-98.

Shamsul A.B. 2002, "The European-American-Asian knowledge complex: A critical commentary," pp. 139-155, in *The European Union, United States and ASEAN: Challenges and Prospects for Cooperative Engagement in the 21ˢᵗ Century*, ed. K.S. Nathan. London: ASEAN Academic Press.

Shamsul A.B. 2004, "Malay, Malayness and Malay Studies: An organizational response," paper presented at the International Symposium on Thinking Malayness, organized by Research Institute for Languages and Cultures of Asia and Africa, Tokyo, June 19-21.

Shamsul A.B. forthcoming, "South East Asia as a form of knowledge," in *Southeast Asian Studies Reconsidered,* ed. Amitav Acharya, Singapore: Singapore University Press.

Shimizu, Akitoshi and Jan van Bremen, eds. 2003. *Wartime Japanese Anthropology in Asia and the Pacific*, Osaka: National Museum of Ethnology (Senri Ethnological Studies No.65).

Summers, Harry G., Jr. 1995. *On Strategy: A Critical Analysis of the Vietnam War* (Reissue Edition). New York: Presidio Press.

Suzuki, Peter. 1980. "A retrospective analysis of a wartime 'national character' study," *Dialectical Anthropology* 6 (1): 33-46.

Wakin, Eric. 1992. *Anthropology goes to War: Professional Ethics and Counter-insurgence in Thailand*. Madison, Wisc.: University of Wisconsin, Center for Southeast Asian Studies.

Wazir, Jahan Karim 1994. "'Do not forget us': The intellectual in indigenous anthropology," Public Lecture, Universiti Sains Malaysia, 22 January.

Wazir, Jahan Karim 1996. "Anthropology without tears: How a 'local' sees the 'local' and the 'global,'" pp. 115-38, in *The Future of Anthropological Knowledge,* ed. Henrietta Moore. London: Routledge.

Wolf, Eric. 1999. "Anthropology among the Powers," *Social Anthropology* 7 (2): 121-34.

Chapter 13

Anthropology and Indigenization in a

Southeast Asian State: Malaysia

TAN Chee-Beng

Introduction

Anthropology as a discipline was established in the West but from the beginning it was associated with studying the "primitive" in the rest of the world.
In this enterprise, early anthropologists benefited from colonialism, which at
least facilitated access to the peoples of colonized societies. Anthropology in
post-independent countries continued to be dominated by anthropologists
from the West or, to use another equally imprecise term, the "North." It was
generally in the post-World War II period that there were more anthropologists from the non-West studying their own societies, although in the case of
China, for instance, indigenous anthropology in the form of community studies started as early as the 1930s. In Malaysia, it was from the 1960s that one
can speak of local Malaysian anthropologists.

As anthropology has been practiced by more people from non-Western
societies, and as the discipline has become more established in the local universities, an interest has grown in examining the indigenization of anthropology and the situation of anthropologists studying their own "societies"
(Jones 1970; Fahim 1982; Ohnuki-Tierney 1984; Kim 1990; Narayan 1993). The
indigenization of anthropology involves the participation of local
anthropologists in the study of their own societies. Such anthropologists have
become known as "native anthropologists." The term "native" is broad in
meaning, however, and in some nations it can involve peoples of different
ethnic origin. The term "indigenous anthropology" is also used, but it is equally
broad and vague, and in some societies it too has political implications. In

Malaysia, for instance, "indigenous" refers to people of Southeast Asian origin and excludes the Chinese and Indian citizens. However, when a Malay from Peninsular Malaysia conducts a study among the Kenyah indigenous minority in interior Sarawak, East Malaysia, is he "native" or "indigenous"? In fact, an American scholar who carries out research among the Kenyah may not necessarily be seen by the people as more foreign than a Malay researcher from Peninsular Malaysia. However, it is convenient and justifiable to use the term "indigenous" to refer to all people who belong to a particular unit such as a state; hence the term "indigenous anthropologists" and the "indigenization" of anthropology.

I have used the term "local anthropologists" to refer to anthropologists who conduct research in their own national societies. I further distinguish "local in-group investigators" from "local out-group investigators." The former refers to local anthropologists who study people belonging to the same ethnic category as themselves. The latter refers to local anthropologists who study people of another ethnic category in their own country (Tan 1988: 17-19). To go deeper, there is also a difference between local in-group investigators who study their own home communities and those who study communities away from home.

We shall not be concerned with making a distinction between native anthropology and indigenous anthropology, as discussed by Bosco (1998, and in chapters 1 and 10 of this book). I prefer to use the term "local anthropology" when the context of "local" is clear. In this chapter, I am concerned with the development of anthropology in a national society. Using Malaysia as an example, I will consider whether anthropology in a national society has a particular orientation or a set of local features. I define local anthropologists as anthropologists who participate continuously in a national society, such as by living in that society permanently and following local events. Thus an anthropologist of Malaysian origin who has migrated permanently to another country and who does not participate in Malaysian academic circles regularly cannot be considered as a Malaysian local anthropologist.

Development of Anthropology in Malaysia

It may be said that the first modern anthropological research in Malaysia was carried out by Raymond Firth who in 1939-40 carried out fieldwork among a community of Malay fishermen in Kelantan. His book *Malay Fishermen: Their Peasant Economy* (1946) is an important contribution to economic anthropology and it is still referred to by anthropologists and students in Malaysia. In 1947 Firth was invited by the Colonial Social Science Research Council (CSSRC) to report on the "research needs and priorities in Malaya." He recommended research on Malay and Chinese communities as well as on the Portuguese and the aboriginal people (Firth 1948). While the colonial government might have found it relevant to promote anthropological research, the research conducted by the anthropologists was professional even though the anthropological knowledge produced was for the benefit of the anthropologists and the government rather than for the people studied.

Before delving into the discussion of indigenization (or lack of it) in Malaysia, it is necessary to know a bit about the development of anthropology in the country. Malaysia was administered as a plural society by the British colonial government, with "different sections of the community living side by side, but separately, within the same political unit" (Furnivall 1948: 304). This "plural society" discourse justified colonial rule, which colonial scholars such as J.S. Furnivall assumed to be necessary to bring the society together. This administration along ethnic lines left a legacy for post-independent Malaysian society, which became ethnically stratified. This makes the development of anthropology somewhat different from that in, say mainland China or Taiwan, where there is a core of anthropologists or ethnologists from the Han Chinese (the majority people) conducting research on both Han and non-Han peoples. In Malaysia the development of anthropology has paralleled ethnic divisions, with Malay anthropologists generally studying Malay and aboriginal communities only, while the anthropology of the Chinese and Indian communities is poorly developed as there are few anthropologists of Chinese or Indian origins.

According to the 2000 Census, 65 percent of the 21.9 million citizens in Malaysia were Malays and aborigines (Orang Asli), followed by the Chinese (26 percent), Indians (7.6 percent), Iban, Kadazan and many other ethnic groups (Dept. of Statistics 2001). Malaysia is made up of Peninsular Malaysia (also called West Malaysia) and East Malaysia comprising Sarawak and Sabah. Peninsular Malaysia was known as Malaya before the formation of the Federation of Malaysia in 1963. East Malaysia has a rather separate history and demographic structure. Unlike Peninsular Malaysia, which is predominantly Malay, the largest ethnic groups are the Iban in Sarawak, and the Kadazan in Sabah. The ethnically stratified nature of Malaysian society developed from the colonial period when the different categories of peoples were administered rather separately. It is thus reasonable and convenient to consider the development of anthropology by examining the study of each major ethnic category. Here our purpose is merely to show the general trends in the development of the subject, rather than provide a comprehensive survey of the work done.

Malay communities

Before Raymond Firth's anthropological research, there were numerous writings on Malays and the aborigines in Peninsular Malaysia. Some of the writings are very informative. An early subject of interest was magic in Malay society, as shown in W.W. Skeat's famous *Malay Magic* (1900), and in more recent times Kirk Endicott (1970) has provided an anthropological analysis of this subject. Of the colonial "officer-scholars," R. J. Wilkinson (1906) and R.O. Winstedt (1950) contributed tremendously to the early study of Malaya's history and cultural heritage, and Khoo (1968) has provided a critique of this colonial historical work.

Firth's recommendations for further research were very specific. Among other things, he recommended doing research on the Malay communities in Jelebu in Negri Sembilan, where the Malays observe matrilineal descent. The research was eventually carried out by M. G. Swift (1965) who became influential as an anthropologist of Malay society; and a number of Malaysians studied under him at Monash University in Australia. Firth had already noted the emergence of the Malay as an ethnic group, and he recommended studying Indonesian immigrants becoming Malays. Through the work of Judith Nagata (1974) and others, anthropologists are now familiar with Malays of different origins stressing their identities situationally. Nevertheless we have yet to see more substantial ethnographic work on Malay ethnogenesis.

By the 1960s and 1970s, there were a number of Western anthropologists, mainly from the United Kingdom and the United States, who studied the Malay communities. Most of their works were published in the 1970s. Interestingly most of the anthropologists still chose Malay villages in the overwhelmingly Malay state of Kelantan, as their research sites. The book *Kelantan: Religion, Society and Politics* (1974) edited by the well-known historian of Malay nationalism, William R. Roff, contains contributions by Clive S. Kessler (1974), Robert L. Winzeler (1974), Manning Nash (1974), Douglas A. Raybeck (1974), and Raymond Firth (1974). There were a few anthropologists who conducted their research in other parts of Peninsular Malaysia. For example, David J. Banks (1972) studied Malay kinship in Sik, Kedah, while Narifumi Maeda (1975) used his study of a village in Melaka to compare the "individualism" of Malay social life with the familism and group orientation of Japanese life. A refreshing change was Ronald Provencher's (1971) study of Malays in both rural and urban settings. All these studies, except those of Provencher and Nagata (1974) are of villages. Nevertheless Clive Kessler (1978) successfully relates his research to the wider issues of religion and politics in Kelantan.

It was in the 1960s and 1970s that local Malay anthropologists emerged, the most influential being Syed Husin Ali (1964; 1975) who received his doctoral degree from the London School of Economic and Political Science, University of London. He became a well-known anthropologist and teacher as well as a social activist in support of the poor. Many younger Malaysian anthropologists and sociologists were his students, including A.B. Shamsul who later did his doctoral work under M. G. Swift, and who is noted for his study of local-level Malay politics (Shamsul 1986). Since the 1980s we have a small group of Malaysian anthropologists who have studied Malay society. They are largely ethnic Malays, such as A.M. Shamsul and Zawawi Ibrahim (1998), although there are also some non-Malay scholars like Diana Wong (1987) and Ng Choon Sim (1985).

Foreign anthropologists have conducted research on many aspects of Malay cultural life, especially religion, kinship and ethnicity. The local scholars have shown more interest on issues of poverty, development and politics. Malaysia (formerly Malaya) became an independent country in 1957, and local scholars became concerned with nation-building. For example, Ungku Abdul Aziz (1958; 1964), an economist who later became Vice-Chancellor of the University of Malaya, and Syed Husin Ali (1964; 1972) both studied Malay poverty. There was also concern with the perpetuation of Malay feudalism, as discussed by Syed Hussein Alatas, a Malay sociologist who is also known for his critique of colonial discourse (Alatas 1977). It is significant that Syed Husin Ali has not only been concerned with poverty but also with stratification and local politics, and he has set a fine example as a concerned and committed anthropologist. He was even detained without trial by the government because of unwavering defense of the interests of poor peasants (Husin Ali 1997). Many of his students continue to relate anthropology to socio-economic issues, and in this sense there has been some indigenization of anthropology, but we shall say more about this later.

Orang Asli studies

As noted, the aborigines of Peninsular Malaysia – now known as Orang Asli, literally meaning "Original People" – also attracted the early interest of some Western writers. For those in search of "noble savages," the aborigines, then known derogatorily as *Sakai* (connoting slave status) provided good case material. Nevertheless the early works such as that of the Italian adventurer, Cerruti (1908), provided useful information and photographs of these people at a time when little was known about them. Others such as W.W. Skeat wrote more comprehensive accounts, such as *Pagan Races of Malaya* (1906) coauthored with C.O. Bladgen. By the 1920s and 1930s, there were a few important works on specific categories of aborigines, such as Paul Schebesta (1973 [1928]) and I.H.N. Evans (1937) on Negritos, and H.D. Noone (1936), a trained anthropologist, on Temiar Senoi.

After World War II, and especially in the 1950s when the communists retreated into the jungles, the aborigines were caught in between the communist insurgents and the government. The government established a department of aboriginal affairs. In 1952, the colonial officer P.D.R. Williams-Hunt published *An Introduction to the Malayan Aborigines*. This was the first comprehensive general introduction to the aboriginal peoples in Malaysia, a more modern one being that of Carey (1976). Like H.D. Noone before him who was married to a Temiar, Williams-Hunt married a Semai wife, and he was knowledgeable about the Senoi. The works of this period were associated with the colonial administration of the Orang Asli. Williams-Hunt's book, for instance, was "for use by British bureaucrats and soldiers" (Dentan et. al. 1997:64).

The modern anthropological works on the Orang Asli may be traced to the 1960s. In 1962-1963, Robert Knox Dentan, an American, carried out his field-work among the Semai in Perak and in Pahang. His book *The Semai: A Non-violent People of Malaya* (1968) became popular with anthropology students. Geoffrey Benjamin did his research on the Temiar, the other major group of Senoi (e.g. Benjamin 1966). Since then various foreign anthropologists have worked on specific groups of the Orang Asli. For example, Kirk Endicott (1979), Shuichi Nagata (e.g. 1997) and Terry A. Rambo (1985) are noted for their works on the Negritos. Other scholars include Rosemary Gianno (1990), Signe Howell (1984), and Marina Roseman (1991). There has been continuing interest in the study of the Orang Asli, mostly the Austroasiatic-speaking groups (Negrito and Senoi) and much less in the Austronesian-speaking Jakun groups (but see Siti Nor 1996 for a recent work). Perhaps the Austroasiatic-speaking groups stand out as unique in the Austronesian-speaking world, and the fact that many of them still live in remote regions made them appealing to foreign students who wanted to experience the lives of modern-day "primitive" peoples. Furthermore, the Semai and Temiar (both classified as Senoi) are the largest groups of Orang Asli, and hence they have attracted greater attention.

Only in the 1970s did local scholars become involved in the study of the Orang Asli. In fact most local anthropologists from Peninsular Malaysia have had some experience of working with one or more Orang Asli communities. Hood Salleh (Hood 1978) of the Universiti Kebangsaan Malaysia (Malaysian National University) and Wazir Jahan Karim (Wazir 1981) of Universiti Sains Malaysia (Science University of Malaysia), for example, are professional an-thropologists working on the Orang Asli. They, together with other local anthropologists as well as foreign anthropologists such as Shuichi Nagata, Anthony R. Walker and Terry A. Rambo, have supervised many undergradu-ate and post-graduate students working on these peoples. A local anthro-pologist who now teaches in Australia is Alberto G. Gomes. He has done a large amount of work on the economic life and marginalization of the Semai (e.g. Gomes 1986). Another local anthropologist, Baharon Azhar (1973), served as Director of the Department of Orang Asli Affairs. Of the younger scholars, Colin Nicholas (e.g. 1994; 2000) deserves special mention for his role as an activist articulating Orang Asli interests. He has been instrumental in the formation and organization of the Centre of Orang Asli Concerns, a vocal Orang Asli NGO.

Of particular interest is the emergence of an Orang Asli intelligentsia since the 1980s. Anthony Williams-Hunt (e.g. 1995), the son of P.D.R. Williams-Hunt, and Juli Edo (e.g. 1995), have also been active in articulating Orang Asli interests. In fact Juli Edo (1998) was the first Orang Asli to receive a Ph.D. degree in anthropology. As more Orang Asli receive higher education, not only are more of them able to articulate these issues more effectively, but they are also able to examine and participate in the discourse on anthropological knowledge about their own peoples, as shown in the work of Akim Buntat (1993).

The Chinese and other communities

Raymond Firth's proposal recommended studies of the Chinese: the Chinese family in relation to economic and social changes in Malaya, Chinese associations, and the newly-formed agricultural communities. The first recommendation was taken up by Maurice Freedman who studied the Chinese in Singapore and whose book *Chinese Family and Marriage in Singapore* was published in 1957. A pioneering study of Chinese social organization was carried out by T'ien Ju-K'ang, whose report on the Chinese of Sarawak, submitted to the Sarawak government, was published in 1953. These together with Allan Elliott's *Chinese Spirit-Medium Cults in Singapore* (1955) are the pioneering anthropological studies of the Chinese communities in what was then Malaya. Since then there have been a few other studies by foreign anthropologists, and those based on long-term fieldwork include William H. Newell (1962), David Harry Fortier (1964), Li Yih-yuan (1970), Richard C. Fidler (1973), Judith Strauch (1981), Sharon Carstens (1980), and Donald M. Nonini (1983). By the 1970s, there were more local scholars of various disciplines writing on Chinese communities, but local anthropologists included only Cheu Hock Tong (1988), Tan (1988) and Lawrence Siaw (1983).

There are only two major anthropological studies of the Indians, by Ravindra K. Jain (1970), a foreign Indian anthropologist, who studied the life of Indian laborers on a rubber estate in Malaysia, and David Mearns (1982), who studied the Chitty, a "Malay-speaking" Indian community in Melaka. Nevertheless, local scholars from the Department of Indian Studies, University of Malaya, such as R. Rajoo (1993), R. Rajahkrishnan (1993) and K. S. Susan Oorjitham (1993), although not anthropologists by training, have produced works that are of anthropological interest, in particular about caste and ethnicity and the life of estate-workers.

The Portuguese of Melaka are a unique community and Raymond Firth had a paragraph on them, even though he did not devote one to the Indians. A few linguists, historians, and even geographers have done some work on the Portuguese, but there has been no intensive anthropological study, though E. Allard (1964) did publish a paper on their social organization. On the other hand, the other minority group in Malaysia, the Thai, has attracted considerable attention. Louis Golomb (1978), Robert L. Winzeler (1985) and Mohamed Yusoff Ismail (1993) all studied Malaysians of Thai origin in Kelantan. Mohamed Yusoff Ismail is unusual as a Malay anthropologist who has studied a community that is neither Malay nor Orang Asli. The unique patterns of interaction between the Thai, the Chinese, and the Malays in Kelantan have also led these scholars to report on local ethnic relations. Robert Winzeler has also contributed to the study of the acculturated Chinese in Kelantan, as have Roger Kershaw (1981), Tan (1982) and more recently Teo Kok Seong (2003). Although not trained as an anthropologists, Roger Kershaw and Teo Kok Seong have contributed to the ethnography of the region.

Anthropological studies in East Malaysia

Borneo has a different history with a much more complex composition of ethnic groups. Western scholars have long been interested in the headhunters of this part of the world. Some early works such as those of Henry Ling Roth (1896) and Owen Rutter (1929) are still useful sources of information on the history and cultural life of the peoples in the early part of the twentieth century. Indeed the Rajahs and their officers also wrote informative works on the diverse groups of people in Sarawak. For example, Charles Hose and William McDougall's two-volume *The Pagan Tribes of Borneo* (1912) and Odoardo Beccari's *Wanderings in the Great Forests of Borneo: Travels and Researches of a Naturalist in Sarawak* (1904) are still referred to by present-day scholars. Since the early period of colonial rule, there have also been writers writing about their travels and experiences in Sarawak and Sabah. A more recent example of such writing is Tom Harrisson's account (1984 [1959]) of the Kelabit during World War II.

Research by professional anthropologists in Sarawak and Sabah began only after the Second World War. In 1947 Edmund Leach was sent by the colonial government to undertake a four-and-a-half month tour of Sarawak with the purpose of suggesting projects for sociological research. In his report, he recommended the study of Iban, Land Dayak (Bidayuh), and Melanau (Leach 1950: 39-41). The results of this recommendation were the pioneering works by Derek Freeman (1955) on the Baleh Iban, W. R. Geddes (1954) on the "Land Dayak," and H. S. Morris (1953) on the Melanau, published under the auspices of the British Colonial Social Science Research Council and the Government of Sarawak. There was also Rodney Needham's study of the Penan (1953). Since then there have been a number of works on various groups of peoples by foreign anthropologists, mainly from the United Kingdom, Australia, United States, and Canada. Some of the recent ones include: Vinson H. Sutlive, Jr. (1978) and Motomitsu Uchibori (1984) on the Iban; Jerome Rousseau (1990) on the Kayan; Peter Metcalf on the Berawan (1982); William M.

Schneider (1978) on the Selako; Roger D. Peranio (1970) on the Bisaya; and J.L Deegan (1973) on the Lun Bawang. There are, of course, other foreign anthropologists, among whom Victor King (e.g. 1993) has been quite prolific. The Sarawak Museum has been instrumental in encouraging and even sponsoring foreign anthropologists to do research in Sarawak. As a result, there are now quite a number of studies on the various peoples in the Belaga District alone. Perhaps the numbers of studies sponsored or encouraged are linked to the plan to build the Bakun Dam there. Some of the studies from this district include Shanthi Thambiah (1995), Peter Brosius (1992) on the Penan, Rita Armstrong (1991) on the Badeng (Kenyah), Jennifer Alexander (1989) on the Lahanan, Ida Nicolaisen (1986) on the Kajang, and Antonio J. Guerreiro (1988) on the Kayan and the Lahanan.

There are now a number of local researchers, even though trained anthropologists are still few in numbers. They include the late Benedict Sandin who was a well-known ethnologist on the Iban, and Lucas Chin who served as curator of the Sarawak Museum. There are two Iban anthropologists who are prominent figures in Sarawak. Peter M. Kedit (1980) is a former museum director, while James Masing (1981) is a prominent politician. The prolific local researcher Jayl Langub (1975; 1987), although trained as a rural sociologist, may be regarded as an anthropologist as he has written many papers which contribute to our understanding of Sarawak ethnography, especially those on his own people, the Lun Bawang, and on the Penan. As a government administrator, he has the opportunity and the interest to visit many ethnic communities throughout Sarawak. There is also the archaeologist Ipoi Datan (1993). Another archaeologist who has studied the prehistory and archaeology of Sarawak is Zuraina Majid (1982), who teaches at the Science University of Malaysia in Penang. Kahti Galis (1990) and Julayhi Tani (1991) both study their own people, namely the Bisaya and Kadayan respectively. None of the local anthropologists in Sarawak are academics and so they are not in a position to train other anthropologists. A few anthropologists from Peninsular Malaysia have conducted serious research in Sarawak, such as Evelyne Hong (1987), who has become a vocal social activist against logging and an advocate of the indigenous peoples, and Tan (1994; 1997).

There has been altogether less anthropological research in Sabah. Although there were a number of studies by foreign anthropologists in the 1960s, the state governments since the 1970s have not encouraged research by foreigners. The best-known anthropologist to carry out research in Sabah is George N. Appell (1965) who studied the Rungus. There has been more work on the Kadazan/Dusun, as in fact the CSSRC sponsored Monica Glyn-Jones (1953) to study the "Dusun" of Penampang. Two later studies of these peoples are those of Thomas Rhys Williams (1965) and Robert Harrison (1971). The Lun Dayeh (similar to the people in Sarawak known as the Lun Bawang) were the focus of a doctoral study by Jay Bouton Crain (1970). The Bajau Laut or

Sea Bajau of the Semporna region have been studied comprehensively by Clifford Sather (1971; 1997), who has since also study the Iban of Sarawak. But there is still a lack of in-depth anthropological studies of other ethnic groups, including the Malays, and there is still room for further study of the Kadazan, the largest ethnic category. Even the anthropological study of the Chinese awaits interested researchers. Compared to Sarawak, there are even fewer professional native anthropologists from Sabah, although there are students who have written anthropological theses. In addition, Yap Beng Liang (1994) from Peninsular Malaysia, has studied the Bajau while other scholars have also carried out research on aspects of Sabah ethnography.

Institutions and Journals

In examining the development of anthropology in Malaysia, it is also necessary to consider the roles of institutions and publications that promote research. An early journal on Malaysia was published by the local branch of the Royal Asiatic Society, known as the Straits Branch from 1878 to 1922, and as the Malayan Branch since 1923. Today this journal is called the *Malaysian Branch of the Royal Asiatic Society*. Papers of ethnological interest were also published in *The Journal of the Federated Malay States Museums*, which began publication in 1905. In Sarawak, the *Sarawak Gazette*, established in 1870, was the crucial source of information for researchers on the history and society during the Brooke regime, and today it continues to publish aspects of history and culture of Sarawak. *The Sarawak Museum Journal* has been the most important local publication on the people and their cultural life in Sarawak. To be sure, these journals are not professional anthropological journals but many articles are either contributed by anthropologists or are of anthropological interest.

Modern anthropological studies began with the interest of the CSSRC in encouraging sociological research in Malaysia. It was significant that the two consultants they hired were both well-known anthropologists, namely Raymond Firth and Edmund Leach. Their proposals and the auspices of the CSSRC led to a number of pioneering modern anthropological studies.

The emergence of a pool of local anthropologists was brought about by the return of Malaysians who had studied overseas, mainly in the United Kingdom, the United States, and Australia. The establishment of local universities was important to the local training of anthropologists. The first university to be established in Malaysia was the University of Malaya, which was originally established in Singapore in 1949. A division was established in Kuala Lumpur in 1959, and this finally became a separate university in 1962. This resulted in the establishment of the University of Malaya in Kuala Lumpur and the University of Singapore (now the National University of Singapore) in Singapore. In 1953 the Department of Malay Studies was established at the University of Malaya and this was important for the promotion of studies of Malay communities. In the 1959/60 session, the first local scholar, Mohd. Taib Osman, was recruited to join the Department of Malay Studies (Zainal Kling 1995). Initially interested in language and literature, Mohd. Taib Osman later took up the study of Malay folklore and cultural life (see Mohd. Taib Osman 1989). Both he and Syed Husin Ali, who was initially also from the Department of Malay Studies, contributed much to research and the training of local scholars, many of whom are now lecturers in various universities in Malaysia. In fact the Department of Anthropology and Sociology at the University of Malaya branched off from the Department of Malay Studies. At first administered under the Dean's office as the "Social Science Programme," the Department of Anthropology and Sociology was finally established in 1971 with Syed Husin Ali as Acting Head (Zainal Kling 1995). Since then, the department has contributed much to promoting local anthropological and sociological research as well as training anthropologists and sociologists.

With the establishment of the National University of Malaysia in Bangi, Selangor, and the Science University of Malaysia in Penang, there are now more local anthropologists and sociologists. Right now there are Departments of Anthropology and Sociology at the University of Malaya and the National University of Malaysia, while in Penang there are a few anthropologists in the School of Social Sciences. Both departments at the first two universities are dominated by Malay scholars, a result of racial recruitment in favor of Malays, a practice which is now taken for granted by most Malay nationalists, including academics. Indeed the mainstream anthropology in Peninsular Malaysia is the anthropology of the Malays and to some extent the Orang Asli. The latter are officially classified as Malays even though the majority of them are not ethnic Malays. Those who study the Chinese and Indians are really rather marginal. In fact it is difficult for Malaysian anthropologists of Chinese or Indian origins to get a job in academic institutions in Malaysia, and this does not encourage non-Malay Malaysians to become professional anthropologists in the country.

The most significant contribution of universities to the local development of anthropology is that they provide some facilities and encouragement for local scholars to do research in the country. More significantly, the tradition of the anthropology and sociology departments in the two universities in requiring major students to do fieldwork and write an academic exercise (basically a B.A. thesis) has produced a number of informative studies. (For a list of Ph.D. and M.A. theses as well as Academic Exercises at the department in the University of Malaya, see Tan, 1995). Many of the students study their own ethnic communities, and in some cases their own villages. When I was a lecturer at the University of Malaya, I encouraged students to do research on the communities most familiar to them, often their own communities. With adequate supervision, including supervision in the field, the students generally wrote very informative theses (see Tan 1996). In general, students who worked on other ethnic groups faced initial problems of acceptance as well as the problems of living in a remote settlement, if such a site was chosen. The visit of the supervisor usually helped in gaining local acceptance and cooperation. In the case of students who worked on their own settlements, the usual problem was "where to start," since everything seems to be so familiar and so much is taken for granted. Supervision in the field helped to direct students to explore relevant issues. In one case a student was not sure where to start, but when I found that his father was very knowledgeable, I recommended that he started with him. This might seem a simple matter, but the student had never thought of treating his own father as an informant. He did not realize that his father knew so much until my own talk with him.

With the establishment of the University of Sarawak Malaysia in Sarawak and the Sabah University Malaysia in Sabah, more local students can be trained to do research, and more lecturers can be encouraged to do research on the peoples and their cultural life in East Malaysia. It is necessary to have lecturers from Sarawak and Sabah, not just lecturers from Peninsular Malaysia. In fact, so far few anthropologists in Peninsular Malaysia have shown serious interest in doing research in East Malaysia, while, as noted, the anthropologists and anthropologically-inclined researchers in Sarawak and Sabah are not academics. The establishments of the two universities in East Malaysia will help to bridge the gap in interests and encourage cooperation between anthropologists in Peninsular and East Malaysia. Indeed the presence of universities is crucial to the promotion of anthropological research.

Overall, local anthropology in Malaysia is still rather weak. This weakness is reflected in the local journals. Both the departments of anthropology and sociology at the University of Malaya and the National University of Malaysia have their respective journals of anthropology and sociology. The one at the University of Malaya has become more irregular than the one at the National University of Malaysia. The Malaysian Social Science Association publishes a journal called *Ilmu Masyarakat* [Societal Knowledge] but there are very few anthropological articles in that. All three journals are bilingual, in Malay (mainly) and English. There is really a need for the anthropologists to cooperate in running a refereed journal in order to promote anthropological knowledge. The anthropologists themselves need to communicate more with one another, improve communications between Peninsular and East Malaysia, and to show more interest in each other's work. In fact, the only journal that may be said to be anthropological and playing the role of promoting anthropological knowledge is the *Sarawak Museum Journal*. This journal and its monograph series publish works by professional anthropologists and amateur researchers as well as by observers of the archaeology and socio-cultural life of peoples in Sarawak. Both the Sarawak Museum (which is the best ethnological museum in Malaysia) and the journal have been playing a crucial role in promoting research and publishing original work.

Obviously, universities and research centers are important for the development of indigenous anthropology. In Taiwan, the Department of Anthropology at the Taiwan National University and the Institute of Ethnology of the Academia Sinica have played an important role in promoting anthropological research. More recently similar departments in other universities, Tsing Hua University in particular, are also promoting anthropological research and the teaching of anthropology. This has helped bring about a substantial volume of anthropological studies, which have in turn assisted the indigenization of the discipline. In Malaysia, there is a lack of a central institution or organization that can bring together a pool of anthropologists who can share and examine anthropological knowledge critically, as well as transcending the boundaries of ethnicity.

Discussion

There have been a growing number of significant anthropological studies in Malaysia by both foreign and local anthropologists. However there are less than thirty professional anthropologists in the country and these largely study their own ethnic communities. Many students who have graduated from the departments of anthropology and sociology now work in a variety of other occupations (cf. Shamsul 1995, and in this volume). As for undergraduates, one of the benefits of studying anthropology is that both private and public sectors are still willing to employ anthropology and sociology graduates. Some employers think that the broad training the students have received in the study of human societies and culture is relevant to the analysis of social issues, doing research, or dealing with public relations in their firms or institutions.

Given the small number of scholars and their diverse interests, there is still no clearly defined local tradition of anthropology to speak of. The development of anthropology was influenced by the British tradition through anthropologists such as Raymond Firth, Edmund Leach and Maurice Freedman. Indeed the well-known local anthropologist Syed Husin Ali studied under Raymond Firth and Maurice Freedman. Except for a few archaeologists, anthropologists in Malaysia are generally social/cultural anthropologists. Furthermore, there is no separate anthropology department in Malaysia: the discipline coexists with sociology or with other social science disciplines. In China for example, there was no clear distinction between anthropology and sociology when the disciplines were introduced, and the prominent anthropologist Fei Xiaotong, who studied under Malinowski, is today regarded as both an anthropologist and a sociologist. In Singapore, anthropology is taught within the Department of Sociology. In non-Western societies, anthropologists generally study the peoples and cultures in their own country, so that when anthropology and sociology were introduced it did not seem necessary to draw a clear boundary between them. Also the limited number of anthropologists and sociologists makes it practical to teach the disciplines in one department. Thus in Malaysia, it is often not easy to distinguish between anthropologists and sociologists except according to research methods, although even this is not always clear-cut. For example, the scholars who have studied under Professor Syed Husin Ali may be regarded as either anthropologists or sociologists depending on the theme of their research. For the scholars themselves, the distinction may not be very relevant in the context of Malaysia.

On the whole anthropology and sociology in Malaysia do have some common concerns, including ethnic relations, ethnic identities, and development. There is an interest in studying these issues, which are seen as relevant to the scholars' concerns about the development of the multi-ethnic Malaysian nation. These areas of interest were reflected in the book *Ethnicity, Class and Development: Malaysia,* edited by Syed Husin Ali and published by the Malaysian Social Science Society (1984). Malaysian scholars have been interested in the issue of class, ethnicity, and development, and more recently gender issues as well. The concern with major social issues in the country characterizes indigenous anthropology. This explains why local scholars who were trained overseas in different countries and universities have generally chosen the main themes mentioned above. There is, for example, no interest in structural and symbolic anthropology, which is seen as not relevant to Malaysia in the present stage of development. In fact two of the earlier prominent anthropologists who did their fieldwork in Malaysia were anthropologists of the structural and symbolic school, namely Rodney Needham and P.E. de Josselin de Jong (1951), and Needham's student Signe Howell has also published a book in that tradition (Howell 1984). However, their works have not inspired the interest of Malaysian scholars in that direction. In fact, even though foreign anthropologists have contributed so much to the study of social organization (including the general work of Clifford Sather and David J. Banks, and the work of Derek Freeman and George Appell on cognatic descent), local anthropologists have not shown much interest in this topic.

Some "indigenization" is reflected in teaching. Students and teachers generally share an interest in criticizing colonial practices and discussing Western (United States) dominance in the region and the world. There is an interest in studying ethnic relations and development, as reflected in students' academic exercises. A local sociological contribution to the discourse on colonial practices is that of Syed Hussein Alatas, in his book *The Myth of the Lazy Native* (1977). It is significant that students are taught about Ibn Khaldun (1332-1406) when discussing the rise of anthropology and sociology to counter-balance the overwhelming emphasis on sources from Western civilization. But this is as far as "indigenization" in teaching goes.

The local anthropologists are not homogeneous. They belong to different ethnic groups, and they are interested in writing about their own groups. Of these anthropologists, those from indigenous minorities are fewest, but more researchers from these peoples can be expected with the provision of greater opportunities for them to receive higher education. While some local scholars may criticize foreign anthropologists as not really understanding local issues, scholars from indigenous minorities can also complain of scholars from larger ethnic groups within the country misrepresenting them or failing to represent local concerns. This comparison shows the superficiality of the issue of "foreign" versus "indigenous" researchers. There are two issues here. First, there is the issue of the people themselves being able to read and comment on what has been written about them. With education becoming more common, even members of the indigenous minorities are able to read and form opinions about what has been written. From their perspective, work by scholars from other parts of the country is not necessarily more accurate or better than those of foreigners. The whole issue of the indigenization of anthropology has to do with the "Others" being able to know how they have been represented. Good ethnography – for this is what the local people look for – requires good research and understanding of local issues. Whether an anthropologist is a foreigner or local person matters little, even though the latter may have certain advantages in terms of language and the knowledge of national or local issues. A local researcher who does superficial research cannot produce good work, and in fact local scholars may be judged more severely for misrepresentation. On this matter, Shamsul (1982) points out that Malay anthropologists and sociologists do not necessarily possess "superior knowledge" about the Malay communities they study.

This leads us to the issue of concerned anthropology and advocacy. For anthropologists in developing countries the major issues of concern are poverty, development, and human rights. In theory, local anthropologists are able to be more involved in local issues, but this is not always true. Many foreign researchers, perhaps because they are politically neutral or are concerned about their future research opportunities, are generally not vocal about local issues that impinge on the livelihoods of the people studied. Nevertheless there are some foreign anthropologists who have highlighted the plight of the people they are familiar with. For example, Kirk Endicott and especially Robert K. Dentan have been quite vocal about the plight of the Orang Asli in Peninsular Malaysia. They and a few others have also lent support to local NGOs. In fact Harries-Jones (1996: 169) goes to the extent of arguing that, since all knowledge is "interested knowledge," anthropology departments should have reciprocal relationships with NGOs as well as helping global NGO activity.

Local researchers and students in Malaysia who have worked among the Orang Asli have generally been critical of government policy and the administration of the aborigines. However, it would be wrong to assume that local scholars are all more concerned with local issues than foreign scholars. Indeed, a local anthropologist who becomes a politician on the government side, for instance, may defend a government plan to resettle indigenous minorities in order to make way for the building of dams or roads, while ignoring the injustice imposed on these people. The issue is really the commitment of anthropologists to the local, irrespective of whether they are local or foreign scholars. In fact in Malaysia, there are many local scholars who have contributed to the construction of Malay-dominated nationalist ideology. To be sure, advocacy in anthropology, is a complex issue (cf. Paine 1985; Hastrup and Elsass 1990), but surely it is not too much to expect anthropologists who are aware of injustice and oppression at the local level to at least expose them. They have a moral commitment to do so, even if they do not wish to be social activists.

Conclusion

I began the paper by defining indigenous anthropology narrowly to refer to the anthropology of a local society as practiced by local anthropologists. This is fine for discussing the situation in Malaysia as well as countries in the South. However, it is necessary to make it clear that indigenous anthropology can and should have a broader reference, a reference to the rooting and development of anthropology in a particular society, irrespective of whether the research is conducted locally or not. Japan is a good example. Japanese anthropologists have done research in both Japan and in foreign countries, especially in the Asia-Pacific region and in Africa. The twin causes of a lack of research funds and an emphasis on relevance to local societies has led to anthropologists in countries in the South generally doing research in their own countries. When I began my Ph.D. program at Cornell University, I wanted to do my doctoral research among the Yao in North Thailand, but had to turn homeward because of the fear of not getting a job in my own country if my research was not in Malaysia. This is different from anthropology in the West where it is generally more prestigious to conduct research in other countries. In countries in the South, especially in the so-called new states, the production of anthropological knowledge is expected to be part of a national project, to contribute to nation building or to the understanding of the national society – in other words, to write about the local for the local. Anyway, the very idea of the indigenization of anthropology suggests that the discipline is imported from the West, so that therefore it becomes interesting to examine to what extent it has become rooted and indigenized in non-Western countries.

In our discussion, we have not contrasted colonial discourse with indigenous discourse. In the study of history this is a very important issue, for the colonial interpretation of history ignores local perspectives. It is necessary to write indigenous history. Cheah gives a good discussion of writing indigenous history in Malaysia, but as he points out very significantly (1996: 55), indigenous history can be written not only by local scholars (such as Khoo Kay Kim) but also by foreign scholars (such as W.R. Roff). While it is important to write indigenous history, the Malaysian case highlights the danger of communal nationalism in scholarship: since the 1970s, with the resurgence of Malay communalism, nationalist scholars have promoted Malay-centric history as "indigenous" history.

In anthropology, anthropological and ethnological works produced by foreigners during the colonial era may still shed light on the "local," given the nature of ethnology. They may not convey local voices, but this is not only a problem of the anthropology of the colonial era. Views of the natives as "savage" and "primitive," or even as "noble savage," have already been sufficiently criticized. What is still worth examining is whether there is an underlying colonial discourse in this work which justifies colonial rule or racism, as Buck (1991) has shown in the case of European discourses on cargo cults which justified and mystified the labor relations between Europeans and Papuan New Guineans. In relation to Southeast Asia, I have already mentioned Hussein Alatas' analysis of "lazy native" discourse by European writers. But overall in the context of Malaysia, even though British anthropologists like Raymond Firth and Edmund Leach did not question the role of British rule, it is better to look for what is valuable in their ethnographic work rather than to simply dismiss it as "colonial" writing. They did strive for excellence in ethnography according to the standards of the time, and their writings are still important.

Local scholars who write about indigenous anthropology generally stress that Western anthropologists do not produce knowledge that is beneficial to the local people and that their works are not representative enough (e.g. Wazir 1996). I choose not to emphasize this rhetoric. Instead I find it more relevant to relate the practice of anthropology to the concern of anthropologists with local social issues. Furthermore anthropological work should not be judged purely from the perspective of whether it is beneficial to the local people or not. Indeed it is possible to treat anthropological research and highlighting social issues as separate enterprises, although it is also possible to combine the two. Furthermore, as we have seen, research on indigenous perspectives is not the monopoly of local scholars, nor are all works of local scholars necessarily beneficial to the local people, however the notion of "benefit" may be defined.

We have discussed indigenous anthropology as anthropology developed by anthropologists in a national society. This allows one to examine whether this development leads to a distinctive local approach. However, this should not lead one, as some nationalistic scholars would claim, to see indigenous anthropology as "better" and as separate from the overall anthropological production of knowledge. We have seen that the indigenous anthropology of Malaysia is still limited in terms of the number of local anthropologists and in the quantity of the research output. Nevertheless, this limitation makes it obvious that it is more useful to speak of the anthropology of a country or a region as being produced by both local and foreign scholars. Even if local anthropologists have a distinct approach and local orientation, their production of anthropological knowledge cannot be separated from that produced by foreign anthropologists. The advancement of anthropology can only be built upon mutual sharing and mutual influence. For example, in the study of women and gender in Malaysia, it makes no sense to separate the work done by foreigners (e.g. Rosemary Firth 1943; Rudie 1994) from that done by local scholars (e.g. Ng 1985: Karim 1992).

The debate on local versus foreign anthropology can be meaningless. Ultimately good anthropology requires good ethnography, which has little to do with ethnicity or nationality. In fact a fair number of good anthropological works on Malaysia are by foreign anthropologists. Local anthropological works tend to be less theoretical. This is also the case in Mainland China, Taiwan, and other Asian countries. One reason for this is that local scholars have to be concerned with local readers who are interested in accurate description and who will be quick to criticize if the description is not accurate. Generally anthropologists in Asia have the vision to describe their own cultural tradition, and some even think that they have a mission to describe their own cultural heritage better than foreigners. They are interested in using ethnographical methods to compile an account of the cultural heritage of their own country. Some younger Western-trained scholars, armed with post-modernist theory, are reacting to this descriptive approach, but their writings are more for Western than local consumption. Nevertheless, with regards to the issues of poverty and development, many Malaysian scholars actually analyze in the framework of political domination and exploitation, dependency theory and the hegemony of the world capitalist system, even though they may not explicitly relate to these relevant theories. It is also said that a concern with detailed description makes it difficult to theorize. However, it is important to make generalizations based on details. The concern of non-Western local anthropologists with good description has to do with their audience who are other local scholars and the local public. They do not have to theorize for the Western anthropological market. The local market expects accurate description and good analysis, not local knowledge repackaged according to contemporary Western theories, which often are not convincing to those who are very knowledgeable about the local.

Too much emphasis on detailed local ethnography results in a lack of comparison with other societies and restricts the ability to theorize. Some local scholars have failed to follow major international publications including journals and this limits their scholarship. In Malaysia, part of the problem is that some younger local scholars, who are products of Malay nationalism, are weak in English, and this does not encourage them to read international publications. The implementation of nationalist policies has also eroded professional standards based on merit, and this has affected the quality of scholarship too.

Indigenous anthropology is concerned with the local production of knowledge. It is indigenous in that it is practiced by local scholars. Anthropology today as practiced in any society is increasingly indigenous in one way or another, as more and more anthropologists study the cultural life of people within their own national societies. Both local and foreign anthropologists can contribute to the production of anthropological knowledge. Foreign anthropologists can and should play a part in the development of a scientific tradition of research in the societies in which they work. Increasingly, many anthropologists have begun to publish their findings in journals and other publications in the country or region of research. It is important that academic institutions outside the United States and Europe should not discriminate against publications in established local and regional journals by rating publication in journals in the West more highly. An approach to evaluating academic achievement centered on Britain or America, as practiced in Hong Kong, will not encourage local academic publication, and will in fact hinder its development. Back in the 1940s, Raymond Firth (1948: 43) already stated that in anthropology, "the day has passed for the equivalent of big game hunting – for a visit to an unknown tribe from which the anthropologist returns with a collection of new customs as his trophies: he has a duty not only to himself but also to further science in the territory in which he works." Both local and foreign anthropologists should contribute to the development of anthropology in a particular society, and both should be concerned with social issues that impinge upon the lives of the people who have been their teachers and friends. Ultimately anthropology is concerned with the human condition: equality, justice, and freedom.

References

Abdul Aziz, Ungku. 1958. "Land disintegration and land policy in Malaya," *Malayan Economic Review* 3 (1): 22-29.

Abdul Aziz, Ungku. 1964. "Poverty and rural development in Malaya," *Kajian Ekonomi Malaysia* [Malaysian Economic Studies] 1 (1): 70-105.

Akim B. Buntat. 1993. "Close historical relationships of indigenous societies: Some case studies." Paper presented at the International seminar on indigenous people (1993), 29 November – 1 December 1993, Kuala Lumpur, Malaysia.

Alatas, Syed Hussein. 1977. *The Myth of the Lazy Native.* London: Frank Cass.

Alexander, Jennifer. 1989. "Culture and ethnic identity: The case of the Lahanan of Ulu Belaga," *Sarawak Museum Journal* 40: 51-59.

Allard, E. 1964. "Social organization of Eurasians in the Malayan Federation," *Current Anthropology* 5 (5): 422.

Appell, G. N. 1965. "The Nature of Social Groupings among the Rungus of Sabah, Malaysia," Ph.D. Thesis: The Australian National University.

Armstrong, Rita. 1991. "People of the Same Heart: The Social World of the Kenyah Badeng," Ph.D. Thesis: University of Sydney.

Baharon Azhar bin Raffie'i. 1973. "Parit Gong: An Orang Asli Community in Transition," Ph.D. Thesis: University of Cambridge.

Banks, David J. 1972. "Changing kinship in North Malaya," *American Anthropologist* 74 (5): 1254-75.

Beccari, Odoardo. 1904. *Wanderings in the Great Forests of Borneo: Travels and Researches of a Naturalist in Sarawak.* London: Archibald Constable & Co. Ltd.

Benjamin, Geoffrey. 1966. "Temiar social groups," *Federation Museums Journal* 11: 1-25.

Bosco, Joseph. 1998. "Anthropology among natives: The indigenization of Chinese anthropology," pp. 23-44 in *On the South China Track,* ed. Sidney C. H. Cheung. Hong Kong: Institute of Asia-Pacific Studies.

Brosius, J. Peter. 1992. "The Axiological Presence of Death: Penan Gang Death-Names" (2 vols), Ph.D. Thesis: University of Michigan.

Buck, Pem Davidson. 1991. "Colonized anthropology: Cargo-cult discourse," pp. 24-41 in *Decolonizing Anthropology: Moving toward an Anthropology for Liberation,* ed. Faye V. Harrison. Washington, DC: American Anthropological Association.

Carey, Iskandar. 1976. *Orang Asli: The Aboriginal Tribes of Peninsular Malaysia.* Kuala Lumpur: Oxford University Press.

Carstens, Sharon A. 1980. "Images C community in a Chinese Malaysian Settlement," Ph. D. Thesis: Cornell University.

Cerruti, G. B. (Captain). 1908. *My Friends the Savages.* Como, Italy: Tipografia Cooperativa Comense.

Cheah, Boon Kheng. 1996. "Writing indigenous history in Malaysia: A survey on approaches and problems," *Crossroads* 10 (2): 33-81.

Cheu, Hock Tong. 1988. *The Nine Emperor Gods: A Study of Chinese Spirit-Medium Cults.* Singapore: Times Books International.

Crain, Jay Bouton. 1970. "The Lun Dayeh of Sabah, East Malaysia: Aspects of Marriage and Social Exchange," Ph.D. Thesis: Cornell University.

Deegan, J. L. 1973. "Change among the Lun Bawang: A Borneo People," Ph.D.

Thesis: University of Washington.

Dentan, Robert Knox. 1968. *The Semai: A Nonviolent People of Malaysia.* New York: Holt, Rinehart & Winston.

Dentan, Robert Knox et. al. 1997. *Malaysia and the Original People: A Case Study of the Impact of Development on Indigenous peoples.* Boston: Allyn & Bacon.

Department of Statistics. 2001. *Population Distribution and Basic Demographic Characteristics.* Kuala Lumpur: Dept. of Statistics Malaysia.

Elliott, Allan A. 1955. *Chinese Spirit-Medium Cults in Singapore.* London: Royal Anthropological Institute.

Endicott, Kirk Michael. 1970. *An Analysis of Malay Magic.* Oxford: Oxford University Press.

Endicott, Kirk Michael. 1979. *Batek Negrito Religion: The World-View and Rituals of a Hunting and Gathering People of Peninsular Malaysia.* Oxford: Clarendon Press.

Evans, I.H.N. 1937. *The Negritos of Malaya.* Cambridge: Cambridge University Press.

Fahim, Hussein, ed. 1984. *Indigenous Anthropology in Non-Western Countries.* Durham, N.C.: Carolina Academic Press.

Fidler, Richard C. Kanowit. "An Overseas Chinese community in Borneo," Ph.D. Thesis: University of Pennsylvania.

Firth, Raymond. 1946. *Malay Fishermen: Their Peasant Economy.* London: Kegan Paul, Trench, Trubner & Co. Ltd.

Firth, Raymond. 1948. *Report on Social Science Research in Malaya.* Singapore: Government Printing Office.

Firth, Raymond. 1974. "Faith and scepticism in Kelantan village magic," pp. 190-224 in *Kelantan: Religion, Society and Politics in a Malay State,* ed. William R. Roff. Kuala Lumpur: Oxford University Press.

Firth, R. M. 1943. *Housekeeping among Malay Peasants.* London: Lund Humpries. (LSE Monographs on Social Anthropology, 12 No. 7; Second edition published by Athlone Press, London, 1966.)

Fortier, David Harry. 1964. "Culture and Change among Chinese Agricultural Settlers in British North Borneo," Ph.D. Thesis: Columbia University.

Freeman, J.D. (Derek). 1955. *Iban Agriculture: A Report on the Shifting Cultivation of Hill Rice by the Iban of Sarawak.* London: HMSO.

Freedman, Maurice. 1957. *Chinese Family and Marriage in Singapore.* London: HMSO.

Furnivall, J. S. 1948. *Colonial Policy and Practice.* Cambridge: Cambridge University Press.

Geddes, W.R. 1954. *The Land Dayaks of Sarawak.* London: HMSO.

Gianno, Rosemary. 1990. *Semelai Culture and Resin Technology.* New Haven, Conn.: Connecticut Academy of Arts and Sciences.

Glyn-Jones, Monica. 1953. *The Dusun of Penampang Plains in North Borneo.*

London: Colonial Social Science Research Council. (Mimeo.)

Golomb, Louis. 1978. *Brokers of Morality: Thai Ethnic Adaptation in a Rural Malaysian Setting*. Honolulu: Hawaii University Press.

Gomes, Alberto G. 1986. "Looking-for-Money: Simple Commodity Production in the Economy of the Tapeh Semai of Malaysia," Ph.D. Thesis: The Australian National University.

Guerreiro, Antonio J. 1988. "Cash crops and subsistence: Towards a comparison of Kayan and Lahanan economics," *Sarawak Museum Journal* 39 (60): 15-52.

Harries-Jones, Peter. 1996. "Afterword: Affirmative theory: Voice and counter-voice at the Oxford decennial," pp. 156-72 in *The Future of Anthropological Knowledge*, ed. Henrietta L. Moore. London and New York: Routledge.

Harrison, Robert. 1971. "An Analysis of the Variation among Ranau Dusun Communities of Sabah Malaysia," Ph.D. Thesis: Columbia University.

Harrisson, Tom. 1984 [1959]. *World Within: A Borneo Story*. Singapore: Oxford University Press.

Hastrup, Kristen and Peter Elsass. 1990. "Anthropological advocacy: A contradiction in terms?" *Current Anthropology* 31 (3): 301-11.

Hood, Mohamad Salleh. 1978. "Semelai Rituals of Curing," D. Phil. Thesis: Oxford University.

Hong, Evelyne. 1987. *Natives of Sarawak: Survival in Borneo's Vanishing Forests*. Penang: Institut Masyarakat.

Hose, Charles and William McDougall. 1912. *The Pagan Tribes of Borneo* (2 volumes). London: Macmillan.

Howell, Signe. 1984. *Society and Cosmos: Chewong of Peninsular Malaysia*. Singapore: Oxford University Press.

Husin Ali, Syed. 1964. *Social Stratification in Kampung Bagan*. Singapore: Malaysian Branch of the Royal Asiatic Society.

Husin Ali, Syed. 1972. "Land concentration and poverty among rural Malays," *Nusantara* 1: 100-13.

Husin Ali, Syed. 1975. *Malay Peasant Society and Leadership*. Kuala Lumpur: Oxford University Press.

Husin Ali, Syed. 1997. *Two Faces: Detention without Trial*. Kuala Lumpur: Insan.

Husin Ali, Syed, ed. 1984. *Ethnicity, Class and Development: Malaysia*. Kuala Lumpur: Malaysian Social Science Association.

Ipoi Datan. 1992. "Archaeological excavations at Gua Sireh (Serian) and Lubang Angin (Gunung Mulu National Park), Sarawak, Malaysia," *Sarawak Museum Journal* 45 (Special Monograph no. 6).

Jain, Ravindra K. 1970. *South Indians on the Plantation Frontier in Malaya*. New Haven: Yale University Press.

Jones, Delmos J. 1970. "Towards a native anthropology," *Human Organization* 29 (4): 251-59.

Josselin de Jong, P.E. de. 1951. *Minangkabau and Negri Sembilan: Socio-Political Structure in Indonesia*. Leiden: E. Ydo.

Julayhi Tani. 1991. *Sosioekonomi Komuniti Kadayan: Satu Kajian Kes* [Kadayan socioeconomic studies: A case study]. Kuala Lumpur: Dewan Bahasa dan Pustaka.

Juli Edo. 1995. "The economic activities of Orang Asli living on the periphery: A case study of Kampung Pengkalan Daun, Cenderong Balai, Perak," pp. 259-84 in *Dimensions of Tradition and Development in Malaysia*, eds. Rokiah Talib and Chee-Beng Tan. Petaling Jaya (Malaysia): Pelanduk Publications.

Juli Edo. 1998. "Claiming our Ancestors' Land: An Ethnohistorical Study of Seng-Oi Land Rights in Perak, Malaysia," Ph.D. Thesis: Australian National University.

Kahti Galis. 1990. *Adat Perkahwinan Masyarakat Bisaya Sarawak* [Sarawak Bisaya marriage custom]. Kuala Lumpur: Dewan Bahasa dan Pustaka.

Karim, W. J. 1981. *Ma'Betise'Concepts of Living Things*. New Jersey: Athlone Press.

Kedit, Peter M. 1980. *Modernization among the Iban of Sarawak*. Kuala Lumpur: DBP.

Kershaw, Roger. 1981. "Towards a theory of Peranakan Chinese identity in an outpost of Thai Buddhism," pts.1 and 2, *Journal of the Siam Society* 69: 74-106.

Kessler, Clive S. 1974. "Muslim identity and political behavior in Kelantan," pp. 272-313 in *Kelantan: Religion, Society and Politics in a Malay state*, ed. William R. Roff. Kuala Lumpur: Oxford University Press.

Kessler, Clive S. 1978. *Islam and Politics in a Malay state: Kelantan 1938-1969*. Ithaca, N.Y.: Cornell University Press.

Khoo Kay Kim. 1968. "Recent advances in the study and writing of Malaysian history," *Peninjau Sejarah* 3 (1): 1-12.

Kim, Choong Soon. 1990. "The role of the non-Western anthropologist reconsidered: Illusion versus reality," *Current Anthropology* 31 (2): 196-201.

King, Victor T. 1993. *The Peoples of Borneo*. Oxford: Blackwell.

Langub, Jayl. 1975. "Distribution of Penan and Punan in the Belaga district," *Borneo Research Bulletin* 7 (2): 45-48.

Langub, Jayl. 1987. "Ethnic self-labelling of the Murut or Lun Bawang of Sarawak," *Sojourn* 2 (2): 289-99.

Leach, E.R. 1950. *Social Science Research in Sarawak*. London: HMSO.

Li, Yih-Yuan. 1970. *Yi ge yizhi de shizhen: Malaiya Huaren shizhen shenghuo de diaocha yanjiu* [Immigrant town: life in an overseas Chinese community in southern Malaya]. Taibei: Zhongyang yanjiuyuan minzuxue yanjiusuo [Academia Sinica, Institute of Ethnology] (Institute of Ethnology Series B, No. 1).

Maeda, Narifumi. 1975. "Family cycle, community, and nation in Malaysia," *Current Anthropology* 16 (1): 163-66.

Masing, James Jemut. 1981. "The Coming of the Gods: A Study of Invocatory Chant of the Iban of the Baleh River Region of Sarawak," Ph.D. Thesis: The Australian National University.

Mearns, D. J. 1982. "Religious Practice and Social Identity: The Social and Ritual Organisation of South Indians in Melaka," Ph.D. Thesis: University of Adelaide.

Metcalf, Peter. 1982. *A Borneo Journey into Death: Berawan Eschatology from its Rituals*. Philadelphia: University of Pennsylvania Press.

Mohd. Taib Osman. 1989. *Malay Folk Beliefs: An Integration of Disparate Elements*. Kuala Lumpur: Dewan Bahasa dan Pustaka.

Mohamed Yusoff Ismail. 1993. *Buddhism and Ethnicity: Social Organization of a Buddhist Temple in Kelantan*. Singapore: Institute of Southeast Asian Studies.

Morris, H.S. 1953. *Report on a Melanau Sago Producing Community in Sarawak*. London: HMSO.

Nagata, Judith A. 1974. "What is a Malay? Situational selection of ethnic identity in a plural society," *American Ethnologist* 1 (2): 331-50.

Nagata, Shuichi. 1997. "Working for money among the Orang Asli in Kedah, Malaysia," pp. 13-31 in *Sociocultural Change, Development and Indigenous Peoples*, ed. Chee-Beng Tan. Suva, Fiji: Suva Fiji: University of Pacific, Institute of Pacific Studies (*Contributions to Southeast Asian Ethnography*, No. 11).

Narayan, Kirin. 1993. "How native is a 'native' anthropologist?" *American Anthropologist* 95 (3): 671-86.

Nash, Manning. 1974. "Ethnicity, centrality and education in Pasir Mas," pp. 242-56 in *Kelantan: Religion, Society and Politics in a Malay State*, ed. William R. Roff. Kuala Lumpur: Oxford University Press.

Newell, William H. 1962. *Treacherous River: A Study of Rural Chinese in North Malaya*. Kuala Lumpur: University of Malaya Press.

Needham, R. 1953. "The Social Organization of the Penan," D. Phil. Thesis: Oxford University.

Ng, Choon Sim. 1985. "The Organization of Gender Relations in Rural Malay Community with Special Reference to Semanggol and Pulau Tawar," Ph.D. Thesis: University of Malaya.

Nicholas, Colin 1994. "Pathway to dependence: Commodity relations and the dissolution of Semai society," in *Monash Papers on Southeast Asia*, 33. Clayton, Victoria, Australia: Centre of Southeast Asian Studies, Monash University.

Nicholas, Colin 2000. *The Orang Asli and the Contest for Resources: Indigenous Politics, Development and Identity in Peninsular Malaysia*. Copenhagen: International Work Group for Indigenous Affairs.

Nicolaisen, Ida.1986. "Pride and progress: Kajang Response to economic change," *SarawaknMuseum Journal* 36 (57): 75-116.

Nonini, Donald M. 1983. "The Chinese Community of a West Malaysian Market Town: A Study in Political Economy," Ph. D. Thesis: Stanford University.

Noone, H.D. 1936. "Report on the settlements and welfare of the Ple-Temiar Senoi of the Perak-Kelantan watershed," *Journal of the Federated Malay States Museums* 1 (1).

Ohnuki-Tierney, Emiko. 1984. "'Native' anthropologists," *American Anthropologist* 11: 584-86.

Oorjitham, K.S. Susan. 1993. "Urban working class Indians in Malaysia," pp. 504-12 in *Indian Communities in Southeast Asia,* eds. K.S. Sandhu and A. Mani. Singapore: Institute of Southeast Asian Studies and Times Academic Press.

Paine, Robert, ed. 1985. *Advocacy and Anthropology: First Encounters.* St. John's: Institute of Social and Economic Research, Memorial University of Newfoundland.

Peranio, Roger. 1970. "The Structure of Bisaya society: A Ranked Ambilineal Social System," Ph. D. Thesis: Columbia University.

Provencher, Ronald. 1971. *Two Malay worlds: Interaction in Urban and Rural Settings.* Berkeley: Center for South and Southeast Asian studies, University of California.

Rajakrishnan, R. 1993. "Social change and group identity among the Sri Lankan Tamils," pp. 541-57 in *Indian Communities in Southeast Asia*, eds. K.S. Sandhu and A. Mani. Singapore: Institute of Southeast Asian Studies and Times Academic Press.

Rajoo, R. 1993. "Indian squatter settlers: Indian rural-urban migration in West Malaysia," pp. 484-503 in *Indian Communities in Southeast Asia,* eds. K.S. Sandhu and A. Mani eds. Singapore: Institute of Southeast Asian Studies and Times Academic Press.

Rambo, A. Terry. 1985. *Primitive Polluters: Semang Impact on Malaysian Tropical Rain Forest Ecosystem.* Ann Arbor: Museum of Anthropology, University of Michigan.

Raybeck, Douglas A. 1974. "Social stress and social structure in Kelantan Village Life," pp. 225-42 in *Kelantan: Religion, Society and Politics in a Malay State,* ed. William R. Roff. Kuala Lumpur: Oxford University Press.

Roseman, Marina. 1991. *Healing Sounds from the Malaysian forest: Temiar Music and Medicine.* Berkeley: University of California Press.

Roff, William R. ed. 1974. *Kelantan: Religion, Society and Politics in a Malay State.* Kuala Lumpur: Oxford University Press.

Roth, Henry Ling. 1896. *The Natives of Sarawak and British North Borneo* (2 vols). London: Truslove & Hanson.

Rousseau, Jerome. 1990. *Central Borneo: Ethnic Identity and Social Life in a Stratified Society*. Oxford: Clarendon Press.

Rudie, Ingrid. 1994. *Visible Women in East Coast Malay Society: On the Reproduction of Gender in Ceremonial, School and Market*. Oslo: Scandinavian University Press.

Rutter, Owen. 1929. *The Pagans of North Borneo*. London: Hutchinson.

Sandin, Benedict. 1967. *The Sea Dayaks of Borneo before White Rajah Rule*. London: Macmillan.

Sather, Clifford. 1971. "Kinship and Domestic Relations among the Bajau Laut of Northern Borneo," Ph.D. Thesis: Harvard University.

Sather, Clifford. 1997. *The Bajau Laut: Adaptation, History, and Fate in a Maritime Fishing Society of South-Eastern Sabah*. Kuala Lumpur: Oxford University Press.

Sather, Clifford. 2001. *Seeds of Play, Words of Power: An Ethnographic Study of Iban Shamanic Chants*. Kuching, Sarawak (Malaysia): Tun Jugah Foundation in cooperation with the Borneo Research Council.

Schebesta, P. 1973 [1928]. *Among the Forest Dwarfs of Malaya*. Kuala Lumpur: Oxford University Press.

Schneider, William M. 1978. "The Selako Dayak," pp. 59-77 in *Essays on Borneo Societies*, ed. Victor T. King. Oxford: Oxford University Press.

Shamsul, A. B. 1982. "The superiority of indigenous scholars? Some facts and fallacies with special reference to Malay sociologists and anthropologists in fieldwork," *Man and Society* 3 (N.S.): 24-33.

Shamsul, A. B. 1986. *From British to Bumiputera Rule: Local Politics and Rural Development in Peninsular Malaysia*. Singapore: Institute of Southeast Asian Studies.

Shamsul, A. B. 1995. "Peddling culture: Reconstituting and consuming anthropology in Malaysia," Panel Discussion Text, "Cultural Anthropology in Asia: Past Present and Future", 29th Annual Meeting, Japanese Society of Ethnology, Osaka, 2 June 1995.

Siaw, Lawrence K. L.1983. *Chinese Society in Rural Malaysia: A Local History of the Chinese in Titi, Jelebu*. Kuala Lumpur: Oxford University Press.

Skeat, W. W. 1900. *Malay Magic*. London: Macmillan.

Skeat, W. W. and C. O. Blagden. 1906. *Pagan Races of the Malay Peninsula* (2 vols). London.

Siti Nor binti Awang. 1996. "Pembangunan dan perubahan sosial: Kajian kes di Kalangan komuniti Jakun di Kampung Langkap dan Kampung Batu Tiga, Rompin, Pahang" [Development and social change: A case study of Jakun in Kampung Langkap and Kampung Batu Tiga, Rompin, Pahang], M. T. Thesis: University of Malaya.

Strauch, Judith. 1981. *Chinese Village Politics in the Malaysian State*. Cambridge, Mass.: Harvard University Press.

Sutlive, Vinson H., Jr. 1978. *The Iban of Sarawak*. Arlington Heights, Ill.: AHM

Publishing Corporation.

Swift, M.G. 1965. *Malay Peasant Society in Jelebu*. London: The Athlone Press.

Tan, Chee-Beng. 1982. "Peranakan Chinese in northeast Kelantan with special reference to Chinese religion," *Journal of the Malaysian branch of the Royal Asiatic Society* 55 (1): 26-52.

Tan, Chee-Beng. 1988. *The Baba of Melaka: Culture and Identity of a Chinese Peranakan Community in Malaysia*. Petaling Jaya: Pelanduk Publications.

Tan, Chee-Beng. 1994. *Communal Associations of the Indigenous Communities of Sarawak: A Study of Ethnicity and National Integration*. Kuala Lumpur: Institute of Advanced Studies, University of Malaya.

Tan, Chee-Beng. 1995. "Theses of the Department of Anthropology and Sociology, University of Malaya, 1972 – 1992," pp. 491-553 in *Dimensions of Tradition and Development in Malaysia*, eds. Rokiah Talib and Chee-Beng Tan. Petaling Jaya: Pelanduk Publications.

Tan, Chee-Beng. 1996. "Theses on Sarawak and Sabah presented to the department of anthropology and sociology, University of Malaya, with some general remarks," *Borneo Research Bulletin* 27: 90–97.

Tan, Chee-Beng. 1997. "Indigenous people, the State and ethnogenesis: A study of the communal associations of the 'Dayak' communities in Sarawak, Malaysia," *Journal of Southeast Asian Studies* 28 (2): 263-84.

Teo, Kok Seong. 2003. *The Peranakan Chinese of Kelantan: A Study of the Culture, Language and Communication of an Assimilated Group in Malaysia*. London: ASEAN Academic Press.

Thambiah, Shanti, 1995. "Culture as Adaptation: Change among the Bhuket of Sarawak, Malaysia," Ph.D. Thesis: University of Hull.

T'ien, Ju-K'ang. 1953. *The Chinese of Sarawak: A Study of Social Structure*. London: Department of Anthropology, London School of Economics (Monographs on Social Anthropology, no. 14).

Uchibori, Motomitsu. 1984. "Transformation of Iban consciousness," *Senri Ethnological Studies* 13: 211-34.

Wazir, Jahan Karim. 1992. *Women and Culture: Between Malay Adat and Islam*. Boulder, Colo.: Westview.

Wazir, Jahan Karim. 1996. "Anthropology without tears: How a 'local' sees the 'local' and the 'global,'" pp. 115-38 in *The Future of Anthropological Knowledge*, ed. Henrietta L. Moore. London and New York: Routledge.

Wilkinson, R.J. 1906. *Malay Beliefs*. London: Luzac & Co.

Williams, Thomas Rhys.1965. *The Dusun: A North Borneo Society*. New York: Holt, Reinhart & Winston.

Williams-Hunt, Anthony. 1995. "Land conflicts: Orang Asli ancestral laws and state policies," in *Indigenous Minorities of Peninsular Malaysia: Selected Issues and Ethnographies*, ed. Razha Rashid. Kuala Lumpur:

Intersocietal and Scientific.

Williams-Hunt, P.D.R. 1952. *An Introduction to the Malayan Aborigines*. Kuala Lumpur: Government Press.

Winstedt, R.O. 1950. *The Malays: A Cultural History*. London.

Winzeler, Robert L. 1974. "The social organization of Islam in Kelantan," pp. 259-71 in *Kelantan: Religion, Society and Politics in a Malay State*, ed. William R. Roff. Kuala Lumpur: Oxford University Press.

Winzeler, Robert L. 1985. *Ethnic Relations in Kelantan: A Study of the Chinese and Thai as Ethnic Minorities in a Malay state*. Singapore: Oxford University Press.

Wong, Diana. 1987. *Peasants in the Making: Malaysia's Green Revolution*. Singapore: Institute of Southeast Asian Studies.

Yap, Beng Liang. 1994. *Orang Bajau laut Omadal: Aspek-aspek budaya* [Omadal Sea Bajau: Cultural aspects]. Kuala Lumpur: DBP.

Zainal Kling. 1995. "Foreword," pp. vi-xv in *Dimensions of Tradition and Development in Malaysia*, eds. Rokiah Talib and Chee-Beng Tan. Petaling Jaya, Malaysia: Pelanduk Publications.

Zuraina Majid. 1984. "The West Mouth, Niah, in the prehistory of Southeast Asia," *Sarawak Museum Journal* 31 (Special Monograph No. 3).

Zawawi Ibrahim. 1998. *The Malay Labourer: By the Window of Capitalism*. Singapore: Institute of Southeast Asian Studies.

Chapter 14

Towards Indigenization: Responses, Challenges and

Experiences in the Philippines

Alicia P. Magos

Introduction

The vast Asia-Pacific region was a rich field once monopolized by European travelers, missionaries, and scholars employed by colonial governments. Their material, which consisted mainly of firsthand impressions and highly personalized accounts, served as notes for systematization by armchair anthropologists.[1] Today, the region is no longer the domain of Western ethnographers or expatriate scholars. Asian ethnographers have also found new excitement in researching or reexamining works written about their peoples (Aunger 1995: 97). Many of these scholars received anthropological training in the West, but opted to do fieldwork in their own countries. As such, the unfamiliarity which outside observers traditionally experienced was lost, though the Western orientation they used in their studies made them view their own culture through a foreign lens. They unwittingly saw their own people as "the Other," with themselves as "the foreigners." Considering that sociocultural anthropology aims to understand a society's culture in its own (emic) context, this raises some question. How can foreign ethnographers accurately depict the inner world of a culture foreign to them, and how can native anthropologists describe their own culture without bias? For the Filipino scholars, the solution is the indigenization of the social sciences.

It has long been realized that Western concepts, theories, and methods are inappropriate for research in the Asian setting, as evidenced by a growing literature. In a symposium held in Burg Warteinstein, Austria, in 1978 to discuss indigenous anthropology in the non-Western world (Fahim 1979), an underlying assumption was that a "change in the anthropologist's role and perspective might require a set of theories based on non-Western precepts and assumptions" (Jones 1970; cf. Fahim and Helmer 1980). In Asian countries, there have also been attempts to Asianize anthropology, as is evident from various surveys published in 1976 and 1977 on the status of the social sciences and funded by UNESCO (1976; 1977a; 1977b). In 1979, social science representatives from Asia also met in Manila and a substantial part of the discussion dealt with the indigenization of the social sciences and the inappropriateness of Western methods and theories (Third AASSREC Conference 1979: 175-95). In the Philippines, the Department of Anthropology of the state-supported University of the Philippines spearheaded a drive in 1977 to create a more appropriate anthropology attuned to the conditions, needs, and visions of the nation (Bennagen 1978; 1980). Scholars from the College of Arts and Sciences of the University of the Philippines, Diliman, also developed indigenous perspectives from the early 1970s.[2] The concepts and perspectives they proposed challenged outsiders' views of Philippine culture and history. The felt need for the decolonization of academe drew Filipino scholars to look at the historical and cultural roots of their own country.

The Problem

Knowledge, whether prescientific or scientific, can be viewed as advancing from a preparadigmatic to a paradigmatic stage. As it evolves and develops, it passes through certain stages, from an assumption to an inquiry followed by investigation and testing for reliability. It reaches a point where it becomes valid and acceptable (cf. Kuhn 1970: 23). So does the growth of indigenous knowledge, including both concepts and theories. It can also grow, given time. Furthermore, it should come from among and within the people and be a part of their consciousness. In the case of the Philippines, the production of knowledge was largely in the hands of scholars academically trained in the West. This is not surprising given the 334 years of Spanish colonial rule in the Philippines (1565-1898) followed by nearly 50 years of American rule (1900-1946). Colonial education imposed on society alien concepts, ideas, beliefs, and practices. The government of the Philippines was not able to provide the right educational direction because its political institutions were borrowed from outside. The question raised then and now is that of the appropriateness of Western concepts in the Philippine setting. To understand the Philippine response to the widespread movement for indigenization, the following questions have to be addressed: how did indigenization evolve in the Philippines; how do Filipino scholars and academicians view the concept of indigenization; what is the government response to the movement for indigenization; and what problems, issues, and challenges confront the native Filipino anthropologist working "at home"? This chapter describes the struggles of the country for indigenization, from its colonial roots to a period of self-consciousness in which it is finding its identity. I begin with the background to indigenization, followed by a discussion of leading scholars' reactions to the concept. In a third section, I discuss government support for indigenization to protect the institutions and customary law of Filipino indigenous groups. Lastly, I discuss my own experiences in meeting the challenge of indigenization during the course of my fieldwork.

The word "indigenization" simply understood in this paper means the process of deciding which native ideas, concepts, or institutions are valid or appropriate in the present state of research in a given country. As a concept, it can serve as an analytical tool to explain a phenomenon occurring or taking place in a country. The word "indigenous" in this chapter therefore, means "native to a place" while "indigenize" means "to make something originate from a place" (Bennagen 1998). Indigenization in this paper will be considered from four viewpoints: first, as a *historical process* which shows the efforts and the long struggle of a people to escape from their colonial roots; second, as a *problem* concerning education (the curriculum) and research since colonial or neocolonial education is not supportive of indigenization; third as a *perspective* which espouses the revalidation of native concepts, ideas, methods, and existing native political structures; and fourth, as a *reaction* and *solution* to the problems created by colonial education, as evidenced by the reexamination by scholars of their concepts and by government support for indigenization. Viewed as a *strategy*, the process of indigenization has to evolve from the *individual* (i.e., emancipation or liberation of the individual mind from cognitive captivity or bias) to the *professional* (i.e., the critical reexamination of concepts and methods by scholars in academe) and the *institutional* (i.e. reaffirming and strengthening existing native social and political structures) (cf. Third AASSREC Conference 1979: 20). These perspectives and strategies will be discussed during the course of this chapter.

The Struggle for Indigenization

Beginning and growth

First, we need to consider the early studies of indigenous culture, which spurred the development of an interest in indigenization. This section provides a brief survey of the main phases of Philippine history, including Spanish colonial rule (1560-1898), American colonial rule (1898-1941), the postwar period (1946-1968), the revolutionary period (1970-1986) and the period of heightened cultural consciousness (post-1986), drawing on material from the work of Bennagen (1983; 1985; Panopio and Bennagen 1985). Indigenization in the Philippines, which is now having an impact on academe, government, and nongovernment cultural associations, is a product of a long historical process. Following its colonial experience, the country passed through a process of self-examination during the early 1970s, a period of political and social unrest. Since the 1980s, indigenization has made some gains in academe, particularly at the University of the Philippines, Diliman, and has achieved some government support. Here is the story as it relates to the discipline of anthropology.

The Spanish colonial period (1560 – 1898)

Sociocultural anthropology in the Philippines can be traced back to the ethnographic descriptions by Spanish missionaries and chroniclers and by other European travelers. Their notes, which dealt with the customs and animistic practices of the Filipinos in the sixteenth, seventeenth, and eighteenth centuries, the period of Spanish rule in the Philippines, are used today for comparing Prehispanic Filipino culture and society with that of the present. A few written accounts of early inhabitants in the Philippines once existed, but due to the ravages of time, these notes written on materials of an ephemeral quality (i.e. tree bark) did not survive. Manuscripts were also burned by the early missionaries in their desire to do away with what they considered to be pagan practices.[3] The colonizers gave preference to the regime's written words over the oral culture and literature of the natives. Colonization undermined oral culture.

The American colonial period (1898-1941)

Towards the end of the nineteenth century, some efforts were made by Filipinos, notably Jose Rizal and Dr. Trinidad Pardo de Tavera, to write about the Filipino people. But it was during the second period of colonization by the United States that anthropological writing was pioneered by American educators and anthropologists who took a special interest in minority groups. H. Otley Beyer worked among the Ifugaos, Fay Cooper-Cole among the Tingguians, and Roy Franklin Barton among the Kalingas and Ifugaos. The published ethnographies of these anthropologists provided the United States colonial government with information useful in understanding their native institutions. Their scholarly undertakings were in line with President McKinley's instruction to the colonial officials in the Philippines, "to take careful account of the customs and traditions" to help with the pacification and integration of tribal elements into the mainstream of Philippine society (Bennagen 1985). Unlike the previous regime, "ethnological knowledge rather than theological orthodoxy was the basis for administering society" (Pertierra 1997: 26).

In 1914, during the second decade of American rule, anthropology became part of the curriculum of the University of the Phillipines and was taught by H.

Otley Beyer. Three years later, a separate anthropology department was established, which merged with the sociology department in 1921. In 1922, graduate courses in physical and cultural anthropology were offered, based on American models, and the works of the early American anthropologists became the standard reading. Anthropology in the Philippines was also influenced by Filipino scholars who studied in America.[4] The impact of scholars such as Fred Eggan could be seen in the dominance of structural functionalism in the Philippines, especially from the 1950s to the 1960s, but diffusionist theory also became popular. Later on, the Ateneo de Manila University in Quezon City, Silliman University, the University of San Carlos in the Visayas, and Xavier University in Mindanao also came to offer courses in anthropology and sociology in a single department.

The postwar period (1946-1968)

In the 1950s and 1960s, graduate training was given a boost as Filipino scholars studied for master's and doctoral degrees in the United States on Ford, Rockefeller, and Fulbright grants. Several of them became teachers in Philippine universities. Theoretical and practical concerns related to development problems made it necessary and fashionable to study ethnicity, culture change, and values. The anthropologists were few in number, but since they were prolific writers, the discipline flourished. Anthropology attracted the interest of several students at the premier state university.

The late 1960s also foreshadowed the coming of political turmoil. Simmering student activism led to the founding of a radical left movement in the campuses, led by the Kabataang Makabayan (KM), the youth arm of the Marxist movement. Political developments consequently affected the academic climate in Metro Manila's schools and universities. As will be seen later, the University of the Philippines was at the forefront of the activism, which contributed to the process of decolonization through preaching national pride and identity. As could be seen later, more students and researchers were encouraged to pursue studies or research in Philippine culture and history, whether funded or not.

The revolutionary period: Social and political consciousness (1970-1986)

At the onset of the 1970s, there was a growing political ferment and Marxist ideology was popular. Frustrated with the oppressive and corrupt social structure, students demanded a social science that could address the pressing problems of poverty, corruption, and unemployment. Their radical ideas made this a revolutionary period. Students raised fundamental questions about the social and political structure, and favored drastic change. At the height of the activism in the early 1970s, mainstream Philippine education was branded by the activists as either "colonial" or "neocolonial." This charge reflected a growing discontent with the curriculum, as expressed in the slogans of the demonstrators in campuses in Metro Manila. After the declaration of Martial Law in September 1972, "constitutional authoritarianism," a form of dictatorship based on a democratic constitution, was established as the politico-economic framework for pushing forward national economic development. Economics, political science, and sociology were disciplines that were favored because of their direct relevance to policy making and development planning. The authoritarian regime made use of sociology as knowledge to legitimize itself, as in the studies of population and poverty carried out during the regime of President Ferdinand Marcos. Anthropological studies, though not highly favored, were still funded due to the presence of no less than 100 ethno-linguistic groups in the country. Historical studies of national development were also funded due to a perceived crisis of national identity. As long as social scientists were willing to do research to serve the ends of the state, there was plenty of research funding available.

Within the climate of political restraint, however, the more vocal nationalist anthropologists and writers risked harassment and investigation. Those interested in developmental anthropology were often branded as communists or Marxists. Tension arose in symposia and conferences if a developmental anthropologist in the audience criticized the political establishment, especially the military. Vocal anthropologists were perceived as politically dangerous, and some simply chose to hide because of the threat of imprisonment.

In the early 1970s, Filipino scholars abroad watched and monitored current developments in the country through constant communication with friends and colleagues. While there were scholars or academicians who worked for the political establishment through research projects which helped promote government policies, there were a few who managed to keep their academic independence from a government perceived to be oppressive. It was difficult for scholars who had to earn a living to escape unscathed.

By the latter half of the 1970s, however, there was a general feeling, even among conservative social scientists, that their social analyses and interpretations should relate as closely as possible to the economic and socio-cultural realities of the country in order to be relevant. Thus, they abandoned the outmoded structural functionalism of the 1950s and 1960s, and adopted conflict models, including Marxism, which were seen as more suitable for a country in crisis.

The turmoil of the early 1970s triggered a bout of soul-searching among social scientists who had spent years of training abroad, and also among academics in the non-social science disciplines. In the social sciences, a new impetus came from anthropology, history, and psychology to look at the Filipino soul and psyche in order to discover what was really Filipino. The reexamination led to calls for the "indigenization" of these disciplines, as in other countries which had experienced colonialism (cf. Kim's chapter on Korea in this volume).

At the University of the Philippines, responses to indigenization took three forms: *Pambansang Samahan ng Sikolohiya* pioneered by Virgilio Enriquez to develop indigenous psychology; *Pantayong Pananaw* established by Zeus Salazar and his associates in the history department to promote the "New History" (*Bagong Kasaysayan*); and *Pilipinohiya* established by Prospero Covar in the Graduate School of the Arts and Sciences. These were all established in the 1970s and made more gains in the 1980s and 1990s. The common denominator for all three was the search for the indigenous cultural and historical roots of the country. A similar trend was seen in other disciplines such as literature. The Philippine Folklore Society was also founded in the latter part of the 1970s. Although there were folklore studies before this, the growth of folklore research was also related to the development of indigenization. The Philippine Anthropological Society, or *Ugnayan ng Agham Tao* (UGAT), founded in 1977, was also an important development because it made anthropology relevant to the issues confronting the country. Overall, the bulk of these studies in anthropology and allied disciplines such as history originated from the University of the Philippines in the 1970s and 1980s. Resource centers in other parts of the country, such as the Center for Cordillera Studies in Baguio City, the Center for West Visayan Studies at the University of the Philippines, Visaya, Iloilo City, and the Cebuano Studies Center in Cebu City, also started in the 1970s. These resource centers showed an interest in indigenous or cultural studies, and some began their programs by collecting folklore materials. Other scholars and researchers responded to the needs of the time by asserting Filipino national or historical identity, or by continuing with the politico-cultural struggles of their own peoples, as in the case of the Muslims in the south and the Cordillera peoples in the north.

The period of heightened cultural consciousness (after 1986)

The presidency of Corazon Aquino, which began in 1986, gave a new impetus to the promotion of culture and the arts through the creation of the National Commission for Culture and the Arts (NCCA), directly under the Office of the President. There are twenty-two National Committees assigned to different areas of culture and history. One focus was to assist the indigenous cultures of ethno-linguistic groups throughout the country. The National Museum, which had been active in work on Philippine prehistory in the 1960s and 1970s, helped with the establishment or improvement of museums in places outside Metro Manila. Individual scholars and researchers who came under the influence of mentors at the University of the Philippines, Diliman, also pursued cultural research, either on their own or attached to government and private research institutions. There were missionaries and private individuals who had been working with ethnic groups such as the Mangyans, Kalingas, Ifugaos, T'boli's, Bataks, and Isnegs, even before the 1970s. In addition to their missionary work, their research helped document the indigenous cultures of these peoples and promote ethnic pride.[5]

A noteworthy development in the 1980s was the existence of many NGOs, some of which were not only sympathetic to the cause of the indigenous peoples (IPs) but also gave assistance to their legal rights. They formed a group, the National Coalition for Indigenous Peoples (NCIP), and were instrumental in the passage of the Indigenous People's Rights Act (IPRA) which took effect on November 29, 1997. This act recognized the ancestral rights of the IPs and was considered a landmark in legislation.

Overall, the research carried out from 1600 to the postwar period all showed an interest in the indigenous culture, though conscious efforts towards indigenization only began in the 1970s. These efforts did not only come from anthropologists but from other scholars as well – from historians, psychologists, literati, and political scientists.

Reactions and Criticisms from Scholars

In the Philippines, where tertiary education was patterned after the United States, the concept of indigenization elicited varied reactions from scholars. Most of them were trained abroad and they reflected on and analyzed Philippine culture and society in relation to their work as scholars. Felipe Landa Jocano, the first Filipino anthropologist, emphasized the need for a local framework, though he was not too particular about the medium of writing:

> Indigenization is recording culture in a factual manner irrespective of the language or media. Even if one uses a native language, if his feelings are foreign to his country, it is still of no use. What is needed is for the anthropologists to go back to the field and see how people look at their own world and what their adaptive responses are to the environment. What we need today is a local framework ... I use the English language for a wider audience ... although language [referring to the national languages] is important.[6]

Virgilio Enriquez, a pioneer in the indigenization of social science and an exponent of indigenous Filipino psychology (see Enriquez 1979; 1994a; 1994b; Pe-Pua et al. 1998) commented on the use of indigenous methodology:

> It is not enough for the *katutubong pamamaraan* [indigenous method] to respond to the concerns of science. The actual development and implementation of the method should also be sensitive to the situation and needs of the Philippines as a Third World country. The methods should

by all means be objective, but the approach cannot be otherwise but total ... Filipino psychologists have long known that methods can be objective but they should always be appropriate. A *katutubong pamamaraan* or indigenous method in the Philippine context is not just culturally sensitive and appropriate. It is people-oriented, above all considerations. (Enriquez 1994a, 1994b)

The historian and anthropologist, Zeus Salazar, criticized the notion of indigenization for its Western bias. Referring to the adoption or adaptation of concepts, theories, and knowledge, he said:

Implicit [in indigenization] is the idea that there is no systematic body of knowledge in the indigenous or native knowledge, which could be compared to that of the West like America [the United States]. Inherent also is the idea that there is only one medium for scientific discourse which is the Western language like English, French, German and others which should be learned by all. The result is that the Philippines becomes only a receiver of Western knowledge and we do not have the capacity to have our own scientific discourse; which means also that other nations (less developed ones) would remain to be native (the "Other") and the "Our" becomes the Western ... briefly, the Filipino becomes the "Other " in himself. [7]

Prospero Covar, the pioneer of *Pilipinohiya*, underscored the importance of the native language in indigenization:

Native knowledge must be encoded in a native language. The use of another language would require translation. In translation, something is either lost or added. Cultural equivalence in translation is usually a cultural approximation. Knowledge from outside a culture may be adopted or adapted by another. Strictly speaking, the process is not indigenization, even if it becomes a part of a new whole ... Indigenization is imposition.[8]

Ponciano Bennagen adopted a nationalist perspective and exhorted Filipino colleagues to look at Philippine society as a structural reality over time. He also criticized the old imported paradigms as counter-productive to the growth of the discipline and to development. Commenting on indigenization, he wrote:

Indigenization, as doing social science reflective of and responsive to local circumstances, needs and aspirations, must take into account the kind of social analysis outside the dominant paradigm. Failure to do so will result in a severely limited national perspective in social science development. It will impair the concomitant proposal for theory building and for development action. (Bennagen 1985)

Actually, questions about the unsuitability of Western concepts and methods had already been raised by the University of the Philippines Community Development Research Council in the 1960s and by some professors at the University, as can be seen from the articles by Feliciano (1965), Santos-Cuyugan (1967), and Espiritu (1968). Espiritu suggested that "the social sciences prevailing in Asia might reflect too much of the value systems of their sponsoring societies." On the other hand, Feliciano concluded in her empirical research on 80 communities in the northern Philippines that "in diagnostic studies, Western defined concepts need to be stated in more refined and precise terms and that an adaptation is needed to avoid getting inaccurate data." In addition to questions about indigenization, the language issue, which had long been the concern of the University of the Philippines Filipino Department in particular, became increasingly important as the indigenization movement in academe gathered speed.

Overall, the views of these scholars reflected a variety of opinions on the needs and situation of the country within the context of the social and political ferment of the 1970s and 1980s. Along with this intellectual ferment came the need to examine the legal basis of government (the Marcos Constitution of 1972) especially as it addressed the sociopolitical structures of the indigenous groups in the southern Muslim and northern Cordillera regions of the Philippines.

Recent Government Support for Indigenization

Throughout the 1970s and 1980s, there was political and social ferment in many developing countries. The 1970s were anti-establishment years and the 1980s were characterized by disillusionment with development efforts led by the state. In the Philippines in the 1970s when he was at the height of his power, Ferdinand Marcos made pronouncements about making the country great again, using words such as *malakas* (strong) and *maganda* (beautiful) to glorify himself and his wife, as well as prop up his regime. After Marcos was ousted in 1986, Corazon Aquino was catapulted into the presidency through people power, a rare example of a dictator being toppled through bloodless means.

As soon as Aquino took over, representatives of various sectors were convened to write the new Constitution. An academic anthropologist, Ponciano Bennagen, represented the concerns of the indigenous groups of the country. The elitist concept of culture and the arts propagated by the political establishment under Marcos was reversed by the Aquino regime, which viewed culture and arts from an indigenous viewpoint. However, funding support was still inadequate because the government had to give priority to national reconciliation and the urgent economic needs of the country.

The struggle for indigenization among the Filipino Muslims and the Cordillera peoples is actually a form of cultural reassertion, a move towards the revalidation of existing viable native political institutions. This was given due recognition by the Philippine government through an initiative of President Corazon Aquino (1986-1991), continued by President Fidel Ramos (1992-1997). This was a matter of urgent national concern, as failure to attend to existing ethnic problems could undermine national unity and internal security. The Muslims in the south and the Cordillera peoples in the north were demanding autonomy to protect their indigenous institutions. It is for this reason that indigenization is also a political issue and a continuing struggle in the Philippines.

The need for autonomy found its way in the 1987 Philippine Constitution. This paved the way for the creation of the Cordillera Autonomous Region (CAR) which was proposed in Republic Act 6766 on October 23, 1989.[9] Autonomy was envisioned by the Cordillerans to protect their ancestral lands and to persuade the government to recognize communal and indigenous property rights which coexisted with the Western political structure in the Cordillera villages. The Local Government Code of 1991 does not have any provision for institutions among indigenous groups that differ from those of mainstream society, such as the system of tribal courts or laws of property and persons.[10]

Indigenous institutions in these communities like the *bodong* or *pudong* (peace-pact) have been known for centuries to allow these peoples to be self-reliant and autonomous in their local government. The institutions are closely interwoven with the economic, political, and socio-cultural fabric of their society and are linked to the preservation of social order in the community.[11] They have evolved through time and once dominated political life in the Cordillera region.

Another special form of local government which potentially supported the move to indigenization was the Autonomous Region for Muslim Mindanao (ARMM), created by Republic Act 6734 on August 1, 1989,[12] and covering the four provinces of Sulu, Maguindanao, Lanao del Sur, and Tawi-Tawi. There were powers, structures, and functions peculiar to the ARMM that were not included in the Philippines Local Government Code, including the preservation of the Islamic way of life. These were: (1) Shariah courts using Islamic customary law in adjudication; (2) measures for the protection and preservation of ancestral lands; (3) *madrasah* or Koranic education for Muslims; and (4) compulsory teaching of Arabic for Muslims.

Customary laws and the protection or preservation of ancestral lands are common concerns among the IPs because the prevailing practices of the mainstream are different from theirs. Thus, they view the standard methods of the national government as an encroachment on their institutions and ancestral domains. Aside from the Muslims and the Cordillerans, there are other cultural communities in the country, like the Aetas in Pinatubo, the Mangyans in Mindoro, and the Lumads in Mindanao (e.g. Yakans, Tirurays, Manobo and Bila-an) who would also like to preserve their cultural distinctiveness, although little is known about them and their customs and traditions. Their arts and literature do not find their way into the textbooks and the school curriculum, which has contributed to their marginalization. In this context, indigenization is not only an anthropological and political issue, but also an educational one.

The passage of the Indigenous People's Rights Act on November 22, 1999 was a landmark piece of legislation. It is the only existing law in Asia which recognizes the IPs' ancestral domains. (The Muslims of the southern Philippines are not included in it because they have their own law.) The enabling act is the Philippine Constitution of 1987 which provides in Sec. 22, Art. II that "The State recognizes and promotes the rights of indigenous cultural communities within the framework of national unity and development." In addition, Sec. 17, Art. XIV provides that "The State shall recognize, respect and protect the rights of indigenous cultural communities to preserve and develop their cultures, traditions and institutions." If these concerns are given enough weight, the process of indigenization (i.e. reaffirming or revalidating indigenous institutions) in the Philippines can be strengthened and hastened. There is the fear, however, that the trend towards indigenization and the establishment of autonomous regions could pave the way to complete separation due to the intrusion of outside elements threatening the sovereignty of the country.[13] The big irony is that, even if greater autonomy were granted to the autonomous region of Muslim Mindanao, there would be no guarantee of peace. The political reality is that there are several factions each with their own political interests, even among the Muslims.

As of now, the newly created law needs to be fully functional and operational. While the state tried to respond to the needs of the ethnic communities by providing them with special forms of governance through the creation of seven commissions within the National Commission for Indigenous People, as provided by Indigenous People's Rights Act for the administration of the seven ethnographic regions of the Philippines, the central government remained hesitant to release the full budget for this purpose.[14] The Office of the President took the view that here was a need to further enhance capacity building in the newly reorganized structure (the Commission) as provided by law. Thus, the Indigenous People's Rights Act is not yet in full operation.

The development of indigenization cannot be really successful over time without institutional support through government policies. A dissonance exists between trends towards indigenization and other government policies because the government sees these problems and issues from a different perspective. There are at least three levels of analyzing the issues raised by indigenization: first, from that of the primary stake holders (the natives) whose daily lives are affected; second, from that of the social scientists and academics whose theories or analyses of the problem are used as inputs for government policy decisions; and third, from that of the government which evaluates the inputs to determine what may be an appropriate response or decision. Therefore, government policies do not always fit the ways in which the indigenous people view them.

Indigenization is a continuing political struggle today. As the Cordillera and Muslim peoples of the Philippines continue to assert their own aspirations, it is likely that other indigenous groups will be encouraged to follow their lead in future, given the right political climate. Native concepts of indigenization are likely to be challenged by other sectors of Philippine society, both public and private.

With the trend towards the globalization of communications and the economy, there are scholars who have expressed the need for Third World countries to retain tight control of their local cultures, for when markets are globalized and homogenized, the next step is the globalization of culture or lifestyle. This is because, when two or more cultures meet, the one backed by superior technology tends to prevail. This is where there is a danger of the loss of cultural identity. This was reflected in a speech commemorating the fiftieth anniversary of the United Nations given by Secretary General Boutros Boutros Ghali to the UN General Assembly on October 22, 1995, when he said:

> The world of the twenty-first century will confront two great opposing forces – globalization and fragmentation ... the impersonal forces of globalization will cause people to seek refuge in smaller groups which can result to fanaticism, isolation, separatism, and civil war ... Within states, issues of identity and ethnic separation will be decided by the ballot box and the parliament, not by the gun and ethnic cleansing.

As can be seen in the earlier sections of this paper, indigenization has passed through several phases: the colonial period (1560-1946), the postwar period (1946-1968), the revolutionary period (1970-1986) and a period of heightened cultural consciousness (after 1986). The last two were periods of gains and breakthroughs in which scholars and academics became involved, given that they had already accumulated or published a body of research on the cultural and historical roots of the country. The last phase has also seen the political struggle of the Muslims and the Cordillera peoples for indigenization and autonomy during the administrations of Aquino, Ramos, Estrada, and Arroyo. In recent years there have been a number of further developments along these lines in the Philippines. A new breed of younger professors are now teaching *Sikolo Pilipino* started by Virgilio Enriquez forty years ago, and a new generation of history teachers are pursuing the *Pantayong Pananaw* (New History) of Zeus Salazar and his associates.[15] The National Commission for Culture and Arts, which funds projects on culture, began to fund "Schools for Living Traditions" from the mid-1990s, with varying degrees of success, in order to revitalize indigenous cultures.[16] In addition, a third national conference of indigenous educators has already been convened by SIKAT, in a move to establish directions for the indigenization of school curricula.[17]

In summary, the key issues in indigenization can be viewed as a historical process in which students and scholars became critical of the colonial or neocolonial system of education, leading to its reexamination. From there, a new social consciousness evolved among academic social scientists. As a viewpoint or perspective, indigenization is also a response to the social realities of a country in ferment. As a problem in education, it is also faced with the challenge of making its social science curriculum relevant amidst the forces of globalization which threaten the loss of cultural and ethnic identity.

The Making of a Native Anthropologist

This section illustrates the process of indigenization at the individual level, the way in which I integrated native theorizing or concept building into my own research and teaching. Social science has gone through an evolution in which indigenous folk culture is now being given due consideration as an alternative source of knowledge. In sharing this experience, I highlight the lessons and experiences which motivated and challenged me to pursue the investigation of indigenous concepts. Educated in a Western-based curriculum followed by study abroad, I discovered that I had to examine carefully the applicability of concepts, theories and methods learned outside once I was back home. It is a difficult process for one has to unlearn many things to be able to see from a native perspective. But just as a country struggles and undergoes a learning process, so does the native anthropologist whose perspective moves from the observation of the external world to internal self-reflection.

Way back in 1975, I did fieldwork for my graduate research on the *babaylan,* people with shamanistic beliefs and practices on Panay Island in the Central Philippines, in order to understand a cultural phenomenon which I had previously been unable to comprehend. I grew up believing that practices in folk medicine were inferior and irrelevant to modern society. My research was timely because folk medicine was still a new area of study for anthropologists in the Philippines in the early 1970s. One of my mentors was from Panay Island and had done fieldwork there, although on another topic. Anthropology, therefore, allowed me to do research on indigenous knowledge. Fieldwork in the Philippines was inexpensive, which was important for a self-supporting student. From my professor's work among the mountain dwellers of Central Panay, I learned that people who spoke the same language as myself (Kinaray-a) were quite different, especially in their worldview. I discovered more about this after retrieving, transcribing, and translating their epics which were chanted in an archaic Panay language.

In 1985, while I was defending my thesis on the *babaylan* at the University of the Philippines, a professor in my panel refused to accept at face value my assertion that the experiences of the *babaylan* in Mari-it village, Southern Panay, were similar those of shamans in other societies. I came to this conclusion after exhaustive reading of the shamanism literature. To me, the psychology of shamans and their experiences in different societies are broadly similar, except that their forms vary due to local cultural differences. This professor denied that they were similar, and insisted that I should first study and define what a *babaylan* is in the Philippines context, and specifically on Panay Island (which I thought I had already done in a previous study). This forced me to look for criteria for defining shamanism cross-culturally, as in the work of Peters and Price-Williams (1980: 397-413). Fortunately, I had substantial ethnographic notes on the *babaylan* and their experiences to back me up, and these validated my assumption. I realized that the other professor and I were looking at the same phenomenon from opposite directions. While I began from a universalist perspective, before zeroing in on a particular phenomenon, he started from a particularist perspective, the uniqueness of the Philippine *babaylan*, before arriving at generalizations. From this encounter, I saw the importance of native explanations of phenomena.

I later worked on the Bisayan concept of *dungan* ("soul" or "double"), a word usually used by the *babaylan* when they talked about illness and curing rituals. I wondered if this could be related to the natives' explanation of illness, and I carried out more interviews of key informants to get a holistic view of *dungan*. I also discovered that, from the *babaylan* point of view, the condition of one's body and health is determined by the state of the *dungan*, giving rise to a series of other questions. Is the *dungan* weak and in need of nurturing? Does it need to be emboldened so as not to be overpowered by stronger *dungan*? Has it been lured out of the body and harmed by malevolent spirits? It became clear that *babaylan* ideas about illness cluster around the concept of *dungan* and have nothing to do with the germ theory of the West. The natives have various types of illnesses categorized under the concept of *dungan*. When I first presented this idea in a medical anthropology class at a university in America in 1984, my American professor did not believe it as he had not encountered the concept during the course of his own fieldwork on a nearby Bisayan Island. He got hold of a Bisayan dictionary authored by a foreign missionary, and found only one meaning for *dungan* ("together" or "to be together"), but no mention of a use related to illness. Given the same fieldwork site and the same phenomenon, there is a considerable difference between what a foreigner and a native researcher can see and grasp, and their interpretations of the data gathered are also likely to be different, as shown in this instance. Native and foreign researchers may also differ in their choices of research issues: another professor writing a research proposal at the same university suggested that I use a gender perspective on *babaylan*, given that she was interested in gender. Taking on board the gender perspective that was new to me that time (1983) meant giving up the direction of my own research on which I had already gathered substantial data, but I had no other choice. Research problems therefore vary as a result of academic fashions and the concerns of a given country. The issue, therefore, is that of research for whom?

I have learned, therefore, that the priorities of anthropologists can affect their choice of a problem as well as their approach to it, as can their beliefs and values when interpreting data. This is stated clearly in an interview with Ofelia Pacete, a professor and researcher at the University of the Philippines in the Visayas, Iloilo City. "Our own beliefs and values will guide us in interpretation. Our value system conditions our value judgment. Our value judgment conditions our decisions and interpretations. Data can be neutral, but we as social scientists are guided by our belief system way back home."[18] The same dilemma may be encountered by the researcher carrying out commissioned research, especially if the commissioning agency is a foreign one. The interpretation of data may be dictated by the objectives of the study. As one leading Filipino anthropologist said, "There is the danger that one's commitment or loyalty to citizenship could impinge on his commitment to social science where the interest of social science, in the universal sense, is incongruent with the needs of a developing country."[19]

How then are the Filipino native anthropologists different in training and experience from foreign anthropologists? Filipino anthropologists' first introduction to extended fieldwork usually happens when they collect data in the Philippines for their theses after finishing their M.A. or Ph.D. coursework in a university at home or abroad. They may have already been exposed to fieldwork for a term paper during their undergraduate training. At home, the native anthropologists have some psychological advantages over outsiders in terms of adjustment. They have little or no problem in settling down and getting used to the food, the climate, and the inconveniences. They also have little or no problem in learning the language, as Philippine languages are closely related. But they often have constraints in securing funds for fieldwork. In the 1970s and 1980s, it was difficult for anthropology neophytes in the Philippines to get funding unless they were connected with an institution that supported their studies with a fellowship or scholarship, and these were also very limited.

The native Filipino anthropologists can also experience being caught between two camps. Given the restrictive political climate of the Philippines in the 1970s under the Marcos regime, anthropologists had little option but to accept participation in developmental research projects endorsed by the government. Inevitably, they were also drawn to politically sensitive field sites where they became involved in ideological conflicts or were suspected of favoring the government. I experienced this in my own fieldwork in the Cordillera, Central Panay, and to a limited degree in a Muslim area in Mindanao. In contrast, foreign anthropologists are less likely to become involved with politically sensitive issues, and they may be advised not to visit politically sensitive areas for their own safety.

Graduate students of anthropology in a Philippine university have a training similar to that of American students in the sense that, before they go out to do fieldwork for their thesis, they are made to prepare a research proposal which has to be approved by a panel. The problem has to be well defined, with specific questions raised. A hypothesis may also be suggested, and concepts and theories are chosen together with an appropriate data gathering method. After their fieldwork is over and their research reports are drafted, their advisers and critics go over their work and, if it is ready for presentation, the students defend it before the panel members. In many instances, it takes time for graduate students to finish their theses because they are looking for jobs to support themselves after completing their coursework. Sometimes, they get absorbed in their jobs, or encounter academic problems which discourage them from completing their theses. However, if they are lucky, they are able to pursue their career, which may be in teaching or research or in a museum-related job.

After finishing their degrees, Filipino anthropologists may join or initiate development-oriented projects organized by a funding agency which may be the government or an NGO. Funding priorities are, therefore, determined by what the funding agency (e.g. the government) perceives as its most urgent concerns and not what anthropologists consider as beneficial to their country. Their choice of research topics is thus dictated by the needs of the funding agency. In the West, where governments are financially and politically more stable, the issues and problems for anthropological research are more concerned with the advancement of theory or knowledge which can be tested or validated by undertaking fieldwork. Consequently, their interpretations of the data are also determined by the theoretical frameworks approved by their panel members. However, there are also native anthropologists who are not beholden to a funding agency who come to the field without a preconceived ideas. They are able to build a theory or concept out of the empirically gathered data, which, of course, bears the imprint of their own native value system and judgements. This has been the basis of theory and concept building for a number of native anthropologists committed to the revalidation, preservation, and strengthening of their native culture. They may also find that the concepts they draw from their data are entirely different from the concepts or theories derived from Western books.

In summary, there are a number of differences between native and foreign anthropologists, owing to differences such as location, field exposure, access

351

to funding, adjustment, interests, training, values and sentiments. A combination of these factors may account for differences in perspectives and interpretations between the two groups.

Conclusion

How then do we bridge the gap between the approaches of the native and the foreign anthropologists? We all study the same human phenomena, but adopt different positions from which to view them. Like a cameraman, anthropologists choose their preferred angle, and this results in differences between what they see. However, the growth of anthropology in the Philippines, especially in the 1970s and 1980s, was dictated by the practical concerns of the government. As shown by the criticisms and comments of leading scholars involved in Filipino indigenization, there was a strong call for education to be relevant to the country from the early 1970s. Indigenization, therefore, can also be viewed as a response to the call to make social science relevant to, or reflective of, the realities of a country undergoing political and social ferment. This means that we have to review seriously the questions of what anthropology is for, for whom it is intended, and whom it serves. As one Filipino anthropologist, Eufracio Abaya, aptly stated:

> The indigenization movement cannot be separated from the politics that inhere in the practice of the social science. In particular, anthropologists have to invariably confront the issue of knowledge production which implicates issues of what constitutes truthful representations of designs of life. In effect, these issues call attention to the social positionality of the observer and the power and authority he/she claims as legitimate producers of knowledge relative to the producers. In a sense, the indigenization movements should be understood in terms of the ideological loads that animate it. It is symptomatic of a larger issue of cultural politics that calls attention to the myth or fallacy of a value-free social science.[20]

Seen from my experience as a native anthropologist involved in development projects, the production of knowledge and the reality it is supposed to represent is to a large extent affected or determined by the funding agency and its ideology. This is in turn determined by the politics of the society, controlled by powerful actors with their own strongly defined cultures. The whole debate on indigenization boils down to the politics of representation and the question of who has ethnographic authority.

How then do we prepare for the challenge posed by globalization? At present, globalization is viewed by some as an obstacle in the struggle towards indigenization, and as a new wave of imperialism. Like a *tsunami* or tidal wave, globalization is a reality that can sweep away the hard-earned gains of efforts to indigenize. Because globalization is intimately connected to the growth of information technology and economic integration, no society can entirely close its doors to it or prevent it from happening. What then is the future of the struggle towards indigenization? How will this be affected by the integration of the country into the global community? It is imperative that a developing country like the Philippines, which recognizes some of globalization's adverse consequences, should prepare itself by strengthening the more empowering, participatory, ecologically sustainable, and gender-responsive aspects of its native cultures which have served its various communities well over time. In the light of this, the gains of indigenization should be vigorously protected, pursued, and consolidated.

Acknowledgement

I would like thank the following colleagues from the University of the Philippines in the Visayas at Iloilo for their comments on earlier versions of this paper. Prof. Ofelia Pacete of the College of Management, Prof. Teodoro Ledesma, Prof. Henry Funtecha, Prof. Tomasito Talledo, Prof. Tita Torio and Prof. Pepito Fernandez, Jr., of the Social Sciences Division, College of Arts and Sciences. I would also like to thank Dr. Raoul Cola, Dr. Carmen Abubakar, Dr. Adel Beringuela, and Prof. Akira Goto for their useful comments, and Prof. Maria Joji Tan for her editing of an earlier draft.

Notes

1 For more in this discussion, see Yogesh (1985: 1-2).
2 Efforts towards producing a distinctly Filipino social science in the 1980s received some of their impetus from three schools of thought dating from the early 1970s, namely: *Sikolohiyang Pilipino, Pilipinohiya*, and *Pantayong Pananaw*, which started in the early 1970s. *Sikolohiyang Pilipino* carried out research on values and the definition of Filipino personality. *Pilipinohiya* began as an offshoot of the Ph.D. degree program in Philippine Studies at the University of the Philippines in 1974, and aimed to produce students able to articulate the nature of their society and culture. *Pantayong Pananaw* aimed to write Philippines history from a Filipino viewpoint for Filipinos, as opposed to explaining it to foreigners.
3 Hundreds of manuscripts in ancient Tagalog scripts were willfully destroyed by a Jesuit priest, Chrino, in Batangas, but the ancient manner of writing had survived the burning of manuscripts. See Enriquez (1994: 17).
4 These students were Moises Bello, Alfredo Evangelista, F. Landa Jocano, E. Arsenio Manuel, and Frank Lynch. Fred Eggan, sometimes called the American heir of Radcliffe-Brown's functionalism, was also associated with this group, and Robert Fox, who did anthropological work in the

Philippines until he died in the 1970s, also came under that influence. See Bennagen (1985).

5 This assertion was also confirmed through communication, observation, and informal talks with colleagues at the University.

6 From an interview conducted by the author with Dr. Jocano at the University of the Philippines, Diliman Campus, Quezon City, in August 1998. Dr. F. Landa Jocano graduated from the University of Chicago, Illinois, and was formerly Chairman of the Department of Anthropology at the University of the Philippines, Diliman. In the late 1960, he wrote an article criticizing Otley Beyer's theory of prehistoric migration to the Philippines.

7 From an interview conducted by the author at Dr. Salazar's residence in the University of the Philippines, Diliman Campus in August 1998. Dr. Zeus Salazar, formerly Dean of the University of the Philippines, Diliman College of Arts and Sciences, gained his Ph.D. from the Sorbonne and has lectured abroad, particularly in Germany. He uses the Filipino language as a medium of instruction in his classes at the University of the Philippines. The quotation from Zeus Salazar here was originally in Filipino.

8 Personal communication from Dr. Prospero Covar, December 1998. Dr. Covar was formerly Dean of the Graduate School of the University of the Philippines College of Arts and Sciences, Diliman. His *Pilipinohiya* perspective also influenced many mature students at the University of the Philippines Diliman Graduate School to write their theses on Philippine culture using indigenous concepts. For more on Professor Covar's indigenous perspectives, see Covar (1998).

9 At the time, the Cordillera Autonomous Region was still considered an Administrative Region because only the province of Ifugao had voted "yes" in the plebiscite. The other provinces withheld their votes because of some issues to be resolved concerning minoritization.

10 The demands were: (i) Creation of a system of tribal courts; (ii) provisions for personal family, tribal and property relations, (iii) protection and preservation of ancestral domain and lands, and (iv) development of a common regional language. The third demand is similar to that of the ARMM (the Autonomous Region of Muslim Mindanao).

11 Brillantes and Garming (1998) stated that "What makes these institutions a 'blueprint' in the experience of autonomy is the extensive practice of democracy at all levels of decision-making in community affairs."

12 In these four provinces, Muslims comprise 65 percent of the people. Cotabato province, Marawi City, Lanao del Norte and parts of Sultan Kudarat, Saranggani, Zamboanga and Palawan have Muslim populations of 35 percent.

13 Some Filipino scholars assert that Islam is not indigenous to Filipino culture and that the move towards indigenization is equivalent to Arabization or separatism, with support from the Middle East. On Muslim Mindanao,

see Tangol (1998: 631-662).

14 For example, the Comprehensive Agrarian Reform Act was passed without considering the indigenous people's rights to their ancestral land. In fact, protecting their homeland has been the major factor in the Cordillera people's struggle for self-determination since it substantially shapes the indigenous institutions of the region. Another delay in the operation of NCIP is that former Supreme Court judges, Isagani Cruz and Cesar Uropa, questioned the constitutionality of the IPRA (Indigenous People's Rights Act, or Republic Act No. 8371) and appealed to the Supreme Court, arguing that it should be declared unconstitutional because it is contrary to the Regalian Doctrine which states that all land should belong to the King or the State.

15 On developments in indigenous psychology in the Philippines, see Church and Katigbak (2002). For a discussion of the meaning and recent developments in *pantayong pananaw*, see Guillermo (2003).

16 "A School of Living Traditions (SLT) is one where a living master/culture bearer or culture specialist teaches skills and techniques of doing a traditional art or craft. The mode of teaching is usually non-formal, oral and with practical demonstrations. The site maybe the house of the living master, a community social hall, or a center constructed for the purpose" (http://www.ncca.gov.ph/organization/ncca_schooltradition.htm, downloaded 2 July, 2004).

17 SIKAT is an abbreviation for Sentro para sa Ikauunlad ng Katutubong Agham at Teknolohiya. Its activities include national assemblies of indigenous educators from the Philippines, and visits to educational programs for indigenous peoples elsewhere in the Asia Pacific. "The SIKAT school is born from our belief that education is a strong pillar for empowerment. It transmits knowledge crucial to the survival of our tribes. The school encourages students to learn in our own languages, maintain our strong positive values, sustain community life cycles and events and protect our identity and rights as Indigenous people. In establishing community-owned culturally responsive schools, we create linking pathways for the promotion of indigenous education among various tribes across the country" (http://www.acpc.ph/philosophy/framework.htm, downloaded July 2, 2004).

18 Personal conversation with Professor Ofelia Pacete at her residence, March 5, 2000. Professor Pacete studied for a Ph.D. degree in Philippine Studies at the Asian Center of the University of the Philippines, Diliman.

19 I would interpret Dr. Jocano's statement as follows: When data is gathered in social science research, it undergoes analysis or interpretation. The choice of model, concept, or theory to take determines the interpretation the researcher makes. Is it favorable for the people studied, or does it follow the views of outsiders, or that of the funding agency or the country conducting the research? There is often sensitive information which na-

tive researchers may feel that they have to keep from the agency or company hiring them, such as names of people involved in politically sensitive issues, names of unpatented medicinal plants, and the location of mining reserves.

20 From an interview with Professor Eufracio Abaya, Professor of Anthropology and Curator of the Vargas Museum at the University of the Philippines, Diliman, conducted at his office on October 1998, cf. Abaya et al. (1999). For an interesting article touching on the difficulty, if not the impossibility of a value free social science, see Stavenhagen (1971). To quote Stavenhagen, "The applied social scientist cannot by definition be neutral to the larger political and ideological issues which determine the framework of his professional practice ... it must be recognized that social scientist themselves are a product of the way social science in general has developed."

References

Abaya, Eufracio et al. 1999. "Shifting terms of engagement: A review of the history of anthropology in the Philippines," pp. 1-9 in *The Philippine Social Sciences in the Life of the Nation*, vol. 1, ed. V.A. Miralao. Quezon City: Philippine Social Science Council.

Aunger, Robert. 1995 "On ethnography: Story telling or science," *Current Anthropology*, 36 (1): 97-130.

Bennagen, Ponciano L. 1978. "Opening Remarks," First National Conference of UGAT (*Ugnayan ng Agham* Tao/Anthropological Association of the Philippines), April 14-16, 1978.

Bennagen, Ponciano L. 1980. "The Asianization of anthropology," *Asian Studies*, 18: 1-26.

Bennagen, Ponciano L. 1983. "Philippines: Background to swidden cultivation research," pp.229-269 in *Swidden Cultivation in Asia: A Content Analysis of Existing Literature*, vol. 1. Bangkok: UNESCO, Office of the Regional Adviser for Social Sciences in Asia and the Pacific.

Bennagen, Ponciano L. 1985. "Social sciences development in the Philippines," in *Asian Perspectives in Social Science*, ed. W.R. Geddes. Seoul: Seoul University Press.

Bennagen, Ponciano L. 1998. "Localization and indigenization of the public school curriculum," Paper read at Tagaytay City, Seminar-Workshop for Training High School Teachers, March 1998.

Brillantes, Alex B. and Maximo B. Garming. 1998. "The continuing quest for nation building: Prospects in the Philippines," pp. 729-746 in *Local Government in the Philippines: A Book of Readings (Current Issues in Governance)*, vol. 2, eds. P.D. Tapales et al. Diliman, Q.C.: Center for Local and Regional Governance, National College of Public Administration and Governance and the University of the Philippines.

Church, A. Timothy and Marcia S. Katigbak. 2002. "Indigenization of psychology in the Philippines," *International Journal of Psychology* 37 (3): 129-48.

Covar, Prospero R. 1998. *Larangan: Seminal Essays on Philippine Culture.* Intramuros, Manila: The National Commission for Culture and the Arts.

Enriquez, Virgilio. 1979. "Towards cultural knowledge through cross-indigenous methods and perspectives," *Philippine Journal of Psychology*, 12 (1): 9-15.

Enriquez, Virgilio. 1994a. *From Colonial to Liberation Psychology: The Philippine Experience.* Manila: De La Salle Press.

Enriquez, Virgilio. 1994b. "Pagbabagong Dangal: Indigenous psychology and cultural empowerment. Theme: Bridging Filipino consciousness through generations," Second Annual Sikolohiyang Pilipino-Northern California Conference, San Francisco State University. May 14, 1994.

Espiritu, Augusto Cesar. 1968. "The limits of the applicability of Western concepts, values and methods in the social sciences to the concrete realities of Asian societies," pp. 35-44 in *The Relevance of Social Sciences in Contemporary Asia.* Tokyo: World Student Christian Federation.

Fahim, Hussein, ed. 1979. *Indigenous Anthropology in Non-Western countries.* Durham, N.C.: Carolina Academic Press.

Fahim, Hussein and Katherine Helmer. 1980. "Indigenous anthropology in non-western countries: A further elaboration," *Current Anthropology.* 21: 644-62.

Feliciano, Gloria D. 1965. "Limits of Western social research methods in rural Philippines: The need for innovation," *Lipunan* 1: 114-28.

Guillermo, Ramon. 2003. "Exposition, critique and new directions for *pantayong pananaw*," review article, Center for Southeast Asian Studies, University of Kyoto, available at http://kyotoreview.cseas.kyoto-u.ac.jp/issue/issue2/article_247.html, downloaded 2 July, 2004.

Jones, Delmos J. 1970. "Towards a native anthropology," *Human Organization,* 29 (4): 251-259.

Kuhn, Thomas S. 1970. *The Structure of Scientific Revolutions.* Chicago: University of Chicago Press.

Panopio, Isabel and Ponciano Bennagen. 1985. "Philippines," in *Sociology and Social Anthropology in Asia and the Pacific.* New Delhi: Eastern Ltd.

Pe-Pua, Rogelio and Elizabeth P. Marcelino. 1998. "Sikolohiyang Pilipino (Filipino psychology): A Legacy of Virgilio G. Enriquez," IACCP Conference on "Forty years of cross-cultural and indigenous research in the Philippines," Bellingham, Washington State, August 3-8. 1998.

Pertierra, Raul. 1997. *Explorations in Social Theory and Philippine Ethnography.* Quezon City: University of the Philippines Press.

Peters, Larry G. and Douglass Price-Williams. (1980). "Towards an experiential analysis of shamanism," *American Ethnologist* 7(3): 397-413.

Santos-Cuyugan, Ruben. 1967. "Man and his works: A new challenge to the Filipino intellectual," Paper read during the 1967 University of the Philippines Faculty Conference, Baguio City, Philippines, June 26, 1967.

Stavenhagen, Rodolfo. 1971. "Decolonizing applied social sciences," *Human Organization* 30 (4): 333-44.

Tangol, Sukarno D. 1998. "Managing the Muslim problem for Philippine 2000: issues and prospects," pp. 729-746 in *Local Government in the Philippines: A Book of Readings (Current Issues in Governance)*, vol. II, eds. P.D. Tapales et al. Diliman, Quezon City: Center for Local and Regional Governance, National College of Public Administration and Governance and the University of the Philippines.

Third AASSREC Conference (Final Report). UNESCO National Commission of the Philippines, Manila, September 12-17, 1979.

UNESCO. 1976. *Social Sciences in Asia I: Bangladesh, Iran, Malaysia, Pakistan, Thailand.* Paris: UNESCO.

UNESCO. 1977a. *Social Sciences in Asia II: Afghanistan, Indonesia.* 1977. Paris: UNESCO.

UNESCO. 1977b. *Social Sciences in Asia III: Burma, Mongolia, New Zealand, Philippines, Singapore.* 1977. Paris: UNESCO.

Yogesh, Otal. 1985. "Growth points in Asian and Pacific sociology and social anthropology," in *Sociology and Social Anthropology in Asia and the Pacific.* Paris: UNESCO.

Index

Abaya, E. 352, 356
aborigines 9, 211, 212, 240, 311; in Malaysia 20, 309, 311; in Taiwan 10, 15, 210, 212-13, 221
Academia Sinica 10, 26, 156, 173, 210, 213, 217, 222, 227, 238, 240, 319
Aeta 346
Africa 6, 15, 98, 115, 210
Age of the Gods 65
Agency for International Development 217
Ahern, E. 11
Ainu 5, 6, 9, 17, 57-60, 62-63, 65, 67-72, 74, 77, 78, 80-82, 91, 96, 136-47, 148; Association of Hokkaido 141; New Law 141
ajeon 264
Akamatsu Chijo 273
Akiba Takashi 273
Akim Buntat 313
Alexander, J. 315
Alexander the Great 73
Allison, A. 122, 124
Amano, K. 104
Amaterasu Omikai 97
America 7, 8, 12, 16, 45, 47, 114, 115, 123, 125, 129, 161, 215, 266, 336-37; see also United States
American Anthropological Association 116
American Anthropologist 91, 210, 217
American Ethnologist 217
American Folklore Society 216
American Indians 115
Amur River 140
An Chae-hong 255
ancestor worship 259
Ancestor Worship in Contemporary Japan 118
Ancient Society 156
Anderson, B. 217

Anthropological Science 82
Anthropological Society of Nippon 77, 91, 147
anthropology, colonial 90-107; global 23-24; in China 10-13, 152-170, 184-96, 197-206; in Japan 2-10, 57-78, 91-95, 114-129, 136-47; in Korea 256-73; in Malaysia 286-304, 307-325; in the Philippines 335-356 in Taiwan 208-39; indigenous 13-23; world-system of 35-50
Aoki, T. 128, 139
Appadurai, A. 128, 202
Appell, G. 315, 320
applied anthropology 168, 273, 289
Aquino, C. 341, 345, 347
Arabic 345
Arai H. 65
Arai, H. 80
archaeology 166, 258
area studies 22, 290
Argonauts of the Western Pacific 49, 154
Armstrong, R. 315
Arroyo, G. 347
Asad, T. 75, 214, 228
Asia Foundation 294
Asia-Pacific Sociological Association 52
Askew, D. 2, 3, *57-89*
Asquith, P. 40, 50, 51, 110
assimilation 9, 140, 289
Association of Educational Studies 176
Association of Rural Studies 176
Assyria 73
Ateneo de Manila University 291, 339
audience 2, 8-10, 16, 17, 20,-22, 115, 208, 238
audit culture 196
Australia 13, 23, 96, 153, 297; Koreans in 272
Austria 95, 153
Austroasiatic-speaking groups 312